AF893881

Legislative Drafting for the EU

Legislative Drafting for the EU

Transposition Techniques as a Roadmap for Better Legislation and a Sustainable EU

Helen Xanthaki

Professor, University College London, UK; Dean, Postgraduate Laws Programmes, University of London (Worldwide); President, International Association for Legislation; Member, Committee for the Scrutiny of the Quality of the Law-Making Process, Presidency of the Government, Hellenic Republic

Edward Elgar PUBLISHING

Cheltenham, UK • Northampton, MA, USA

© Helen Xanthaki 2024

All rights reserved. No part of this publication may be reproduced, stored in a retrieval system or transmitted in any form or by any means, electronic, mechanical or photocopying, recording, or otherwise without the prior permission of the publisher.

Published by
Edward Elgar Publishing Limited
The Lypiatts
15 Lansdown Road
Cheltenham
Glos GL50 2JA
UK

Edward Elgar Publishing, Inc.
William Pratt House
9 Dewey Court
Northampton
Massachusetts 01060
USA

A catalogue record for this book
is available from the British Library

Library of Congress Control Number: 2024930503

This book is available electronically in the **Elgar**online
Law subject collection
http://dx.doi.org/10.4337/9781788114349

ISBN 978 1 78811 433 2 (cased)
ISBN 978 1 78811 434 9 (eBook)

EEP Bo

Contents

1. Transposition techniques for EU legislative reform: serving EU longevity and sustainability

A. A BASIS FOR LEGISLATIVE REFORM: LEGISLATING FOR SUSTAINABILITY AND LONGEVITY OF THE EU

In the history of polity and policy of the EU and its predecessors, the friction has traditionally been between those who sought wider versus deeper integration. The choice seems to have been whether the EU would benefit from widening the net of its policy coverage versus whether it should stop expanding and start performing vertically within the areas of policy covered already. In a beautifully diverse EU, the answer was never clear. The dilemma continues to be replicated.[1]

However, the choice between wide versus deep EU integration seems to be unnecessarily narrow. There can be a third option that simply transfers the strategic tools for the future of the EU to a different basis. So, instead of focusing on the microcosm of the strategic means by which flourishing of the EU can be achieved (wide versus deep integration), perhaps it is time to take a step back, and look at the goal itself, by agreeing what exactly this flourishing future can be. The EU, as a union of States and peoples, and of course as an organisation, can only aim to achieve its longevity and its sustainability. In other words, the EU's measure of future success can only really be whether it survives the constant change of international and national environments within which it is placed, and whether it sustains its political, social, and economic following. And here lies the answer to the eternal question of wide versus deep integration: it does not matter! What matters is whether the strategic means selected will actually bring success with sustainability and longevity.[2] Whether

---

[1] See F B Jacobs, *The EU after Brexit* (2018, Palgrave Studies in European Union Politics, London), 9.

[2] See K Nicolaïdis, 'EU 2.0? Towards Sustainable Integration', 2010, Open Democracy, at: https://www.opendemocracy.net/en/can-europe-make-it/project-europe-2030-towards-sustainable-integration/; also see K Nicolaïdis, 'Sustainable Integration:

this can be achieved via actions that widen the EU's regulatory coverage or deepen its regulatory grasp is really neither here nor there. In fact, there is no reason to promote, or indeed to exclude, either of the two. Functional regulation uses the most appropriate means to achieve the regulatory super goal: and for the EU, as indeed every union and organisation, the super goal is survival and prosperity for the ideal that it represents, for the States and peoples that are its members, and for the organisation that administers the ideal and serves the membership.

The EU remains a union of nations and States, who choose to come together in order to promote their common goals. The Treaty of Lisbon clearly sets the aim of the Union: to promote peace, its values, and the well-being of its peoples. The EU's legitimacy, and power, come ultimately from its citizens, for the benefit of whom the EU was created and continues to function. So, there is little doubt that the constituting Treaties envisage a benevolent organisation servicing the union and its peoples.

The pursuit of these benevolent policy super-goals is undertaken by means of regulatory choices. The EU identifies areas, within its competences, where common regulatory results are best achieved via common action. Once agreement on the policy aim is offered by the Member States, the regulatory analysis of the current regulatory status in the Member States is explored, and common trends are identified. On the basis of the juxtaposition of this survey and analysis against the aim to be achieved, policy options are put forward and consensus is gauged amongst Member States. If consensus is present, the EU proceeds with its regulatory process.[3] The most appropriate regulatory tool is selected, with legislation being, at least in theory, a solution of last resort. If necessity and subsidiarity allow, legislation is put forward as a tool for regulation. This starts the ball of law-making rolling.

So, also in the EU, legislation is simply a tool for regulation. It is a mere mechanism that EU regulators use to achieve the desired regulatory results. For the purposes of achieving the desired regulatory results, thus reaching efficacy of regulation, EU law-makers communicate the regulatory message to all of the nations and peoples of the EU. They express what rights and obligations EU citizens acquire by virtue of the legislative text, and they state

---

Towards EU 2.0? – The JCMS Annual Review Lecture' (2010) 48 *Journal of Common Market Studies* (Annual Review), 21; K Nicolaïdis, 'Project Europe 2030: Reflection and Revival', 2010, Open Democracy, https://www.opendemocracy.net/kalypso-nicola%C3%AFdis/project-europe-2030-reflection-and-revival-part-one both accessed 13 December 2023.

[3] On the EU as a regulator, see G Majone, 'From the Positive to the Regulatory State: Causes and Consequences of Changes in the Mode of Governance' (1997) 17 *Journal of Public Policy* 139.

what modification of action or behaviour is sought by the EU for the purposes of achieving efficacy of regulation. This communication is crucial. It is only through legislation as a channel of communication between the EU and its legislative users that reform requirements are expressed. If they are conveyed in an accessible manner, the users may understand them, and, in turn, may decide to actually put them to effect. Implementing the regulatory reforms en masse leads to the successful execution of the selected regulatory mechanisms. This allows the latter to perform as envisaged by the EU regulators. And so, if their regulatory strategy was correct, they will reap the desired regulatory results. So, accessible communication of the new requirements to the users of EU legislation is absolutely crucial for the EU's regulatory success. As the latter constitutes the main means of EU governance, it is absolutely crucial for the long-term sustainability of the EU as a union of States and peoples.

Traditionally, this crucial communication is entrusted to Member States, which, via the transposition of EU measures, communicate the EU regulatory message and its implementation in the Member State to their own nationals. However, the conceptual basis of this traditional EU set-up is no longer current. EU law is often still viewed as *droit diplomatique*, namely an expression of diplomatic success in achieving consensus via compromise. For a long time, this is indeed what it was. But this is no longer the case. EU law has evolved. First, the principle of direct applicability now renders EU legislative texts binding as they stand: there is no intermediary and no interpreter of the regulatory message. This is the law for Member States and EU citizens, and it communicates the regulatory message via the legislative expression that it, rather than national implementing measures, contain. Second, the principle of direct effect has empowered EU citizens to invoke EU legislation before the national courts, thus pushing out national implementing legislation as an intermediary. So, on the basis of direct applicability and direct effect, EU law is not diplomatic law at all. It is now not just a source of national legislation but, more importantly for the purposes of this book, the legislative expression of the EU's regulatory message to EU citizens directly. Third, and irrespective of direct applicability and direct effect, a pragmatic assessment of transposition shows that the EU legislative expression is replicated verbatim in most transposition instruments. Leaving the grave concerns attached to copying out as a transposition technique,[4] Member States tend to simply copy the EU text,[5]

---

[4] See D Greenberg, 'The "Copy-Out" Debate in the Implementation of European Union Law in the United Kingdom' (2012) *Legisprudence*, 243, 256.

[5] See W Voermans, 'Transposition of EU Legislation into Domestic Law: Challenges faced by National Parliaments', EP Policy Department for Citizens' Rights and Constitutional Affairs Directorate-General for Internal Policies, PE 608.845, November 2018.

thus eliminating themselves from the envisaged role of intermediary in the communication process between the EU and its citizens.

It is realism in the necessities and needs for a sustainable EU (rather than a response to a crisis) that calls for a reform of EU law-making as an initiative and as a policy, to reflect the current usage of EU legislative texts as the final legislative text for EU regulation both at the EU and the national levels. In other words, the demand for corrective, strategic, reformative action in the EU's law-making strategies and procedures derives directly from the now blindingly marked change in the usage of EU legislative texts. They are no longer just a generic expression of EU regulatory goals that national law-makers and drafters nationalise and express for the purposes of their concrete national regulatory needs. Instead, EU legislative texts are expected to serve as the often unique EU/national legislative expression of the EU's regulatory effort at EU and national levels. This is schizophrenic. A single legislative text is now, in theory and practice, called to express and serve both the generic EU regulatory results and the diverse national regulatory sub-results of 28 Member States. From a legislative drafting perspective, this is an impossible task, especially since the real pursuit is the actual achievement of regulatory results rather than the passing of a legislative text. And this impossible task becomes even more unrealistic if EU law-making continues to be bound by processes and traditions of law-making and legislative drafting that are no longer fit for purpose: the aim to be achieved has changed and the environment within which the legislative text is to function has also changed dramatically from a supra-state union to a supra-state union plus 28 Member States.

There is little doubt, therefore, that in order to support and incite sustainability, the EU must proceed to a reform of its law-making approaches and tactics in order to respond to the now changed usage of its legislative texts. How this can be done is analysed in Chapter 10.

However, apart from the functional necessities exposed above, there is a second, equally important, argument for EU legislative reform. It is again one directly linked with sustainability, and it relates to the communication of the EU's regulatory messages as carriers of information on the rationale and rationality of its regulatory decisions. Let us explore that further. Legislative texts aim to contribute to the regulators' desired regulatory results. They do so in two main ways. First, by detailing how the users' behaviour must be changed in order to participate in the selected behavioural change, how this change contributes to the selected regulatory mechanisms, and how this feeds to the desired regulatory results. And second, perhaps even more importantly, in narrating the above regulatory story, they offer the user an understanding of the regulatory aim and entice them to undertake often burdensome action in order to achieve a longer term positive result. In other words, the expression of a beneficial ultimate regulatory aim cajoles the execution of the demands of the legislation, thus not only promoting regulatory success but, even more importantly, rendering users as participants to the regulatory effort. This sense of participation instils a sense of ownership of the regulatory effort, and creates a sense of trust to the regulators and loyalty to the regulating organisation.[6]

If this structure is applied to the EU, then there is a second imperative for legislative reform. Reformed EU legislative texts can detail not just the demands of EU regulators but also the rationale behind them. They can offer EU citizens and Member States, as the collective demos of the EU, an understanding of the benevolent reasoning behind legislative measures. They can tell the EU's regulatory story without possible distortion from national texts[7]: namely why legislate, how this contributes to regulatory results, and what is the added value for citizens and States.[8] Unfortunately, communication remans the Achilles heel of the EU.[9] A detailed application of this concept is in Chapter 9.

Until recently, this latter message was not being received from EU citizens. Only 34 per cent of citizens saw a benefit in EU membership, against 71 per cent amongst the European elites.[10] The EU's popular trust and its ability to handle crises were suffering,[11] especially by those affected by the economic

---

6 Helen Xanthaki, 'Legislation as Tool for Trust in the EU' in Maria de Benedetto, Nicola Lupo, and Nicoletta Rangone, *Legislation and Citizen Confidence* (2020, Hart, Oxford), 83–102.

7 See L Berg 'Citizens' Trust in the EU as a Political System' in A Bakardjieva Engelbrekt, N Bremberg, A Michalski, L Oxelheim, *Trust in the European Union in Challenging Times* (2019, Palgrave Macmillan, Switzerland), 65, 87.

8 For support to the argument that alerting EU citizens to their personal benefit from the EU can change attitudes and trust, see A Bakardjieva Engelbrekt, N Bremberg, A Michalski, and L Oxelheim, 'Trust in the European Union: What Is It and How Does It Matter?' in Bakardjieva Engelbrekt, Bremberg, Michalski, and Oxelheim, ibid., 1, 19.

9 See G. Maganza, 'Can the Authority of EU law be taken for Granted? A Tale of Principles and Realities' in W. Heusel and J-P Rageade (eds), *The Authority of EU Law Do We Still Believe in It?* (2018, Springer, Berlin), 39–50, 47.

10 See T Raines, M Goodwin, and D Cutts, 'The Future of Europe. Comparing Public and Elite Attitudes', June 2017, Chatham House, The Royal Institute of International Affairs.

11 In a survey for the 40 years of Greek accession to the U, more than half of those surveyed stated that the EU does not understand the needs of EU citizens: see https://www.news247.gr/20-20/ereyna-20-20-oi-ellines-einai-yper-tis-ee-kai-zitoyn-meiosi-ton-anisotiton.9226004.html accessed 13 December 2023. It is worth noting that support for the EU amongst those surveyed continued to register at a very high 70.1 per cent, so the belief that the EU does not understand its citizens cannot be attributed to Eurosceptic sentiments.

and other crises.[12] In the Standard Eurobarometer survey conducted between 18 January and 14 February 2022, Europeans thought that the most important issues facing the EU were the environment and climate change (26 per cent), rising prices, inflation, cost of living (24 per cent) and immigration (22 per cent); 41 per cent of respondents mentioned prices, inflation, cost of living as one of the most important issues facing their country, before health (32 per cent) and the economic situation (19 per cent).[13] In addition, there was a generally reduced trust in political institutions and political actors both at the international and the national level.[14] It is worth noting that in 2017 only 42 per cent of Europeans trusted the EU, as opposed to an alarming 58 per cent that did not.[15] So, there has always been plenty of scope for improvement there.

But the war against Ukraine has turned things around for the EU. In the same survey in 2022, EU membership was declared as positive by no less than two-thirds (65 per cent) of Europeans, which is the highest result since 2007 (then at 58 per cent); 52 per cent of Europeans today have a positive image of the EU, against 12 per cent negative; 59 per cent of Europeans see the defence of common European values such as freedom and democracy as a priority. The perception of the war and what it means for the EU becomes also visible in the citizens' core values they want the European Parliament to defend as a matter of priority. Democracy again tops the list, with an increase of six points compared to Autumn 2021 (38 per cent).[16] In the Spring 2023 Standard Eurobarometer survey, 47 per cent of the EU population tend to trust the EU while 32 per cent tend to trust national governments. 45 per cent tend not to trust the EU. 45 per cent of EU citizens have a positive image of the EU, 18 per cent a negative image and 37 per cent a neutral image. In all Member States, positive perceptions outweigh negative ones.[17]

There is therefore a golden opportunity for the EU to re-establish a direct dialogue with EU citizens and to establish (retain?) the current levels of positivity and trust to the EU. And this can be done via good regulation. As quoted by Margaritis Shoinas, Vice President of the European Commission, 'the best

---

[12] See S B Hobolt and C E de Vries, 'Public Support for European Integration' (2016) 19 *Annual Review of Political Science*, 413, 431.

[13] See https://europa.eu/eurobarometer/surveys/detail/2553 accessed 13 December 2023.

[14] See J R Dalton, *Citizen Politics – Public Opinion and Political Parties in Advanced Industrial Democracies* (2013, Sage Publications, London), 6.

[15] See 'Public Opinion in the European Union (Spring 2017)', Standard Eurobarometer, 87.

[16] See https://europa.eu/eurobarometer/surveys/detail/2792 accessed 13 December 2023.

[17] See https://europa.eu/eurobarometer/surveys/detail/3052 accessed 13 December 2023.

weapon against populism and extremes is good policy, the kind that creates trust and offers real solutions to real problems'.[18]

So, conveying the regulatory rationale in EU legislative texts can render EU citizens participants (rather than suffering pawns) to the regulatory process. It can create collective ownership of the regulatory aims. If these aims continue to be acceptable and shared between the EU and its membership, they can enhance loyalty to the EU as an ideal and as a union. And if the regulatory aims continue to be achieved, they can also enhance trust in the EU as an organisation capable of delivering the common aims to which EU citizens and EU Member States are now loyal.[19]

From this analysis it is now obvious that EU legislation can become a powerful tool for the enhancement of loyalty and trust to a sustainable EU ideal and membership, as well as for the enhancement of the EU's regulatory aims though which the EU ideal is fed and nourished. This requires legislation that can contribute to the EU's regulatory aims.

But what exactly is good legislation?

B. BETTER LEGISLATION: LEGISLATIVE EFFECTIVENESS[20]

Sustainable integration is the political framework for Better Legislation. But, what is the goal of Better Legislation? What is it trying to achieve? It is submitted that the goal for a Better Legislation is legislative effectiveness as a tool for regulatory efficacy. Let us unpeel that statement.

Although the relationship between regulation and legislation is straight forward,[21] it is rarely placed in a functional context[22] thus depriving it of direct practical applicability. Mousmouti and Voermans distinguish clearly between legislation and regulation: 'legislative quality reflects an institutional view of legislation as an issue closely related to the constitutional principles

---

[18] See M Shoinas, Speech at the Conference of the Spanish Peoples' Party on 4 April 2022, https://www.iefimerida.gr/politiki/shoinasto-kalytero-oplo-enantia-sto-laikismo accessed 13 December 2023.

[19] See Y N Harari, *Sapiens: A Brief History of Humankind* (2014, Harvill Secker, London).

[20] This chapter relies heavily on H Xanthaki, *Drafting Legislation: Art and Technology of Rules for Regulation* (2014, Hart Publishers, Oxford).

[21] See H Xanthaki, 'Quality of Legislation: An Achievable Universal Concept or a Utopian Pursuit?' in M Travares Almeida (ed), *Quality of Legislation* (Baden-Baden. Nomos, 2011), 75, 76–78.

[22] See S T Trautmann 'Empirical Knowledge in Legislation and Regulation: A Decision-making Perspective' (2013) 1 *The Theory and Practice of Legislation* 533, 538–539.

of legality, effectiveness and legal certainty, while regulatory quality reflects a more instrumental view of legislation where quality mirrors the success of legislation in promoting economic development'.[23]

Simply speaking, irrespective of the polity of each State, governments are there [elected, appointed, or otherwise established] to run the business of governing the State. They take their place in order to ensure that the agenda that led to their placement in power is actually seen through.[24] Government agendas are seen through via policies,[25] aiming to produce the desired regulatory results:[26] the prevalent measure of policy success is the extent of production of the desired results.[27] Policies are conceived by policy-makers, normally in the first instance at the pre-election/appointment/establishment agenda setting phase and later at the governing phase.[28] Normally policy agendas at the two stages coincide but of course this is not always the case[29] either because a policy is abandoned in between stages, because a policy is not prioritised in the governing stage, or because a policy presents itself after the election/ appointment/establishment to power stage. But, whatever the timing of their appearance, the fate of prioritised policies is to be put to effect.[30] Regulation, in the sense used in this analysis, is the process of putting government policies

---

[23] See M Mousmouti, 'Operationalising Quality of Legislation Through the Effectiveness Test' (2012) 6 *Legisprudence* 191, 194; also, W Voermans, 'Concern about the Quality of EU Legislation: What Kind of Problem, by What Kind of Standards?' (2009) 2 *Erasmus Law Review* 59, 223 and 225; and R Baldwin and M Cave, *Understanding Regulation: Theory, Strategy and Practice* (Oxford, Oxford University Press, 1999) 85.

[24] See OECD, 'Recommendation of the Council on Improving the Quality of Government Regulation', 9 March 1995, C(95)21/Final.

[25] See L Fuller, *The Morality of Law* (1964, Yale University Press, Yale) 106.

[26] The executive branch of government is no longer expected to confine itself to the mere making of proposals: it has to see them through. See J Craig Peacock *Notes on Legislative Drafting* (Washington, REC Foundation, 1961) 3.

[27] See N Staem, 'Governance, Democracy and Evaluation' (2006) 12(7) *Evaluation* 7, 7.

[28] For a contra view, namely that most policies come about in response to sudden needs rather than from the manifesto commitments of the governing party, see M Zander, *The Law Making Process* (Cambridge, Cambridge University Press, 2005), 2, 7.

[29] On the dynamic nature of regulation see C Radaelli and F de Francesco, *Regulatory Quality in Europe: Concepts, Measures and Policy Processes* (Manchester, Manchester University Press, 2007) 36.

[30] OECD notes the importance of public sector management in ensuring policy effectiveness and economic efficiency under conditions of democratic accountability: C(94)125/final.

into effect to the degree and extent intended by government.[31] The regulatory tools available to government vary[32] from flexible forms of traditional regulation (such as performance-based and incentive approaches), to co-regulation and self-regulation schemes,[33] incentive and market-based instruments (such as tax breaks and tradable permits) and information approaches.[34]

More often than not, rule-making takes the form of legislation, although alternative means of rule- or law-making are becoming popular in the form of soft law. But legislation remains a choice offered to governments as a regulatory tool. And this is really what gives law legitimacy: its adoption by a formally authorised legislature.[35] Here the policy process narrows down to a legislative process, namely a process of, for civil lawyers, law-making or, for common lawyers, legislating. Here rules become artifacts with practical authority over enough persons within their scope of application that they can order these persons' affairs.[36] Here the policy becomes translated to legal concept and then expressed as a legislative text.[37]

This latter part is an even narrower circle within the legislative process: the drafting process. It is within the drafting process that drafters undergo each one of Thornton's five stages of drafting.[38] Here policy officers and legal officers see their concept transform into written law, if and where appropriate.[39]

And so legislation is a mere tool for governing, or else a mere tool of regulation. This is the relationship between regulation and legislation. Legislation

---

[31] See National Audit Office, Department for Business, Innovations and Skills, 'Delivering regulatory reform', 10 February 2011, para 1.

[32] See Better Regulation Task Force (BRTF), 'Routes to Better Regulation: A Guide to Alternatives to Classic Regulation', December 2005.

[33] See J Miller, 'The FTC and Voluntary Standards: Maximizing the Net Benefits of Self-Regulation' (1985) 4 *Cato Journal* 897.

[34] See OECD Report, 'Alternatives to traditional regulation', para 0.3; and also OECD, *Regulatory Policies in OECD Countries: From Interventionism to Regulatory Governance* (Paris, OECD, 2002).

[35] See Y Blankt, 'The Reenchantment of Law' (2010–2011) 96 *Cornell Lre*, 633, 639.

[36] See L Alexander and E Sherwin, *The Rule of Rules: Morality, Rules, and the Dilemmas of Law* (USA, Duke University Press, 2001) 188.

[37] A statute is the formal expression of legislative policy: see E A Driedger *The Composition of Legislation – Legislative Forms and Precedents* (Ottawa, MoJ, 1976) xv.

[38] See H Xanthaki, *Thorntons Legislative Drafting* 6th edition, (London, Bloomsbury, 2022).

[39] See National Audit Office, Department for Business, Innovations and Skills, 'Delivering regulatory reform', 10 February 2011, para 2.5.

is one of the many choices[40] offered to governments in their pursuit to put their policies to effect. But legislation cannot be 'reduced' to policy.[41]

If one takes this holistic picture of legislation as a tool for regulation into account, identifying the goal of the drafter as achieving 'quality in legislation' is a rather short sighted and narrowly focused approach.[42] In application of Stefanou's scheme on the three processes,[43] drafters can only aim to perform well in their little, albeit crucial, part in the application of governmental policy better expressed as regulation[44] by pursuing better legislation.

But, if drafters pursue to contribute towards the quality of governmental regulation, what does this contribution really entail? Figure 1.1[45] visualises these goals and their hierarchy.

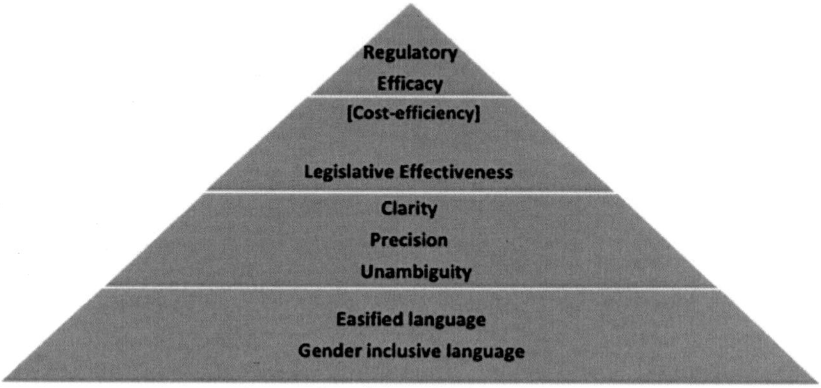

Figure 1.1 *Pyramid of legislative drafting values*

40 See A Flueckiger, 'Régulation, dérégulation, autorégulation: l'émergence des actes étatiques non obligatoires' (2004) 123 *Revue de droit suisse* 159.

41 P Westerman 'Breaking the Circle: Goal-legislation and the Need For Empirical Research' (2013) 1 *The Theory and Practice of Legislation* 385, 411.

42 For a detailed historical analysis of the term 'quality of legislation', see E Albanesi, *Teoria e Tecnica Legislative in Sistema Costituzionale* (Npoli, Editoriale Scientifica, 2013) 45–54.

43 See C Stefanou, 'Legislative Drafting as a form of Communication' in L Mader and M Travares-Almeida (eds), *Quality of Legislation Principles and Instruments* (Baden-Baden, Nomos, 2011) 308; and also see C. Stefanou, 'Drafters, Drafting and the Policy Process' in C Stefanou and H Xanthaki (eds), *Drafting Legislation: A Modern Approach* (Aldershot, Ashgate, 2008) 321.

44 In fact, there is an emergence of a public interest in good quality of rules: see M De Benedetto, M Martelli and N Rangone, *La Qualità delle Regole* (Bologna, SE il Mulino, 2011), 23.

45 The first draft of the figure appears in H Xanthaki, 'On Transferability of Legislative Solutions: The Functionality Test' in C Stefanou and H Xanthaki (eds), above, n 43, 1.

The ultimate goal for regulation is regulatory efficacy. Efficacy is the extent to which regulators achieve their goal.[46] The term effectiveness is also used within the context of regulation, often even within the EU.[47] For example, W Bradnee Chambers offers a unique systematisation of the conceptual spectrum of what he calls effectiveness[48] and really is efficacy: the measure to which the performance data of the legislation match its objectives.[49] Bradnee Chambers distinguishes between rule-based positivist models of efficacy that look at the level of compliance achieved;[50] social legal models[51] that assess efficacy by reference to the compliance of rules with societal norms and values falling within the 'established milieu'[52] or to their legitimacy leading to compliance;[53] the economic legal model that include cost efficiency to the measure of efficacy;[54] and international relations models that call for clearer distinctions between efficacy, implementation, and compliance.

For the purposes of this analysis, efficacy relates to the actual achievement of the desired regulatory results: this delimits the term to the context of regulation, and distinguishes it from legislative effectiveness that refers to

---

46 See ibid., 126.

47 See U Karpen, 'Efficacy, Effectiveness, Efficiency: from Judicial to Managerial Rationality' in K Messerschimdt and D Oliver-Lalana, *Rational Lawmaking under Review. Legisprudence According to the German Federal Constitutional Court* (2016, Springer, New York) 304, 306.

48 Also see A Flückiger, 'L'évaluation législative ou comment mesurer lefficacité des lois' (2007) *Revue européenne des sciences sociales* 83.

49 See W Bradnee Chambers, 'Towards And Improved Understanding of Legal Effectiveness of International Environmental Treaties', 16 (2003–2004) *Geo Intl Envtl L Rev* 501, 531.

50 See H Jones, *The Efficacy of Law* (1968, Rosenthal Lectures, Northwestern University Press) 4; also see A Allot, *The Limits of Law* (1980, Butterworths, London) 11; and L Friedman, *Impact: How Law Affects Behaviour* (2016, Harvard University Press, Cambridge MA), 48.

51 Based on the theory that legislation is a tool for changing behaviour: see H Kelsen, 'Law as a Specific Social Technique' (1941) 9 *University of Chicago Law Review* 75, 79–80.

52 See I Jenkins, *Social Order and the Limits of Law: A Theoretical Essay* (New Jersey, Princeton University Press, 1980) 180.

53 See T M Franck, 'Legitimacy in the International System', (1988) 82 *Am.J.IntlL.*, 705.

54 See O K Young and M A Levy, 'The Effectiveness of International Environmental Regimes' in O R Young et al. (eds), *The Effectiveness of International Environmental Regimes* (Massachusetts, MIT Press, 1999) 1, 4–5; also see OECD, 'Regulatory Policies in OECD Countries; from Interventionism to Regulatory Governance', 2002, OECD, Paris; and also 'Background Note to the OECD Reference Checklist for Regulatory Decision Making' of OECD, 'Recommendation of the Council on Improving the Quality of Government Regulation', C (95) 21 final.

legislation.[55] In order to showcase the difference in contexts between the two concepts, two different terms have been chosen. And so, this analysis uses the terms regulatory efficacy and legislative effectiveness. Taking into account the limited role of the drafter as only one of the many actors in the policy, legislative, and drafting processes of regulation,[56] efficacy in drafting is delimited to the production of a legislative text that has the capacity to achieve the regulatory aims that it is set to address.[57] Thus, efficacy is not a goal that can be achieved by the drafter alone.[58] An unethical, unconstitutional or simply unacceptable (for the constituents) policy cannot be rectified by a good legislative expression. Similarly, good legislative expression cannot hide or rectify the disconnection of bad policy choices with the underlying social phenomenon.[59] Finally, good legislative expression is destined to fail in the event of bad implementation[60] or bad judicial application.[61] Of course, one has to accept that the extent of the margin for incorrect implementation and judicial application is directly linked to the quality of the draft,[62] but it is quite possible that the error in the draft may be attributed to a fault in the content of the pursued policy or in the calculations of the regulatory impact assessment made for the allocation of resources for implementation.

Within the umbrella of regulatory efficacy, the drafter pursues legislative effectiveness.[63] The term is used widely but often without a definition. For

---

55 On legislation as a goal setter, see G Teubner, 'Substantive and Reflexive Elements in Modern Law' (1983) 17 *Law and Society Review* 239.

56 See A E Black, *From Inspiration to Legislation: How and Idea Becomes a Bill* (New Jersey, Pearson Education LTD, 2007) 123.

57 See N Gunningham and D Sinclair, 'Designing Smart Regulation', http://www.oecd.org/dataoecd/18/39/33947759.pdf accessed 13 December 2023, 18; and also R Baldwin, 'Is Better Regulation Smarter Regulation?' (2005) *Public Law* 485, 511.

58 See J P Chamberlain, 'Legislative Drafting And Law Enforcement' (1931) 21 *Am.Lab Leg Rev* 235, 243.

59 See K Tuori, 'Legislation Between Politics and Law' in L Wintgens (ed), *Legisprudence* (2002, Hart Publishing, Cambridge) 99; also see L Wintgens, 'The Rational Legislator Revisited: Bounded Rationality and Legisprudence' in L Wintgens and D Oliver-Lalana (eds), *The Rationality and Justification of Legislation* (2013, Springer, New York), 3.

60 See D Hull, 'Drafters' Devils' (2000) *Loophole*, https://calc.ngo/sites/default/files/loophole/jun-2000.pdf accessed 13 December 2023.

61 See U Karpen, 'The Norm Enforcement Process' in U Karpen and P Delnoy, (eds), *Contributions to the Methodology of the Creation of Written Law* (Baden-Baden, Nomos, 1996), 51; also L Mader, 'Legislative Procedure and the Quality of Legislation' in Karpen and Delnoy, ibid., 62, 68.

62 See G Teubner, 'Regulatory Law: Chronicle of a Death Foretold' (1992) 1 *Social Legal Studies* 451.

63 See C Timmermans, 'How Can One Improve the Quality of Community Legislation?' (1997) 34 *Common Market Law Review* 1229, 1236–7.

example, the EU calls for accountability, effectiveness, and proportionality as a means of achieving better law-making, but the term is not defined at all.[64] Similarly, the UK's Office of Parliamentary Counsel repeat their aspiration to effectiveness as a contribution to or in balance with accuracy, but do not define the term.[65] Mader defines effectiveness as the extent to which the observable attitudes and behaviours of the target population correspond to the attitudes and behaviours prescribed by the legislator.[66] Snyder defines effectiveness as 'the fact that law matters: it has effects on political, economic and social life outside the law – that it, apart from simply the elaboration of legal doctrine'.[67] Teubner defines effectiveness as a term encompassing implementation, enforcement, impact, and compliance.[68] Muller and Ulmann define effectiveness as the degree to which the legislative measure has achieved a concrete goal without suffering from side-effects.[69] Fluckiger defines effectiveness as the achievement of objectives.[70] In Jenkins's socio-legal model effectiveness in the legislation can be defined as the extent to which the legislation influences in the desired manner the social phenomenon which it aims to address.[71] Voermans defines the principle of effectiveness as a consequence of the rule of law, which imposes a duty on the legislator to consider and respect the implementation and enforcement of legislation to be enacted.[72] Mousmouti describes effectiveness as a measure of the causal relations, or under Zamboni

---

64 See 'European Governance: Better Lawmaking', Communication from the Commission, COM(2002) 275 final, Brussels, 5.6.2002; also see High Level Group on the Operation of Internal Market, 'The Internal Market After 1992: Meeting the Challenge – Report to the EEC Commission by the High Level Group on the Operation of Internal Market', SEC (92) 2044.

65 See Office of Parliamentary Counsel, 'Working with OPC', 6 December 2011; and OPC, 'Drafting Guidance', 16 December 2011.

66 See L Mader, 'Evaluating the Effect: A Contribution to the Quality of Legislation' (2001) 22 *Statute Law Review* 119, 126.

67 See F Snyder, 'The Effectiveness of European Community Law: Institutions, Processes, Tools and Techniques' (1993) 56 *Mod L Rev* 19, 19; also F Snyder, *New Directions in European Community Law* (London, Weidenfeld and Nicolson, 1990) 3.

68 See G Teubner, 'Regulatory Law: Chronicle of a Death Foretold' in Lenoble (ed), *Einfuhrung in der Rectssoziologie* (Darmstadt, Wissenschaftliche Buchgesellschaft, 1987) 54.

69 See G Muller and F Uhlmann *Elemente einer Rechtssetzungslehre* (Zurich, Asculthess, 2013) 51–52.

70 See A Flückiger, 'Effectiveness: A New Constitutional Principle' [2009] 50 *Legislação: cadernos de ciência de legislação*, 183, 190.

71 See I Jenkins, *Social Order and the Limits of the Law: A Theoretical Essay* (Princeton, Princeton University Press, 1981) 180; also see R Cranston, 'Reform Through Legislation: The Dimension of Legislative Technique' (1978–1979) 73 *NwULRev* 873, 875.

72 See W Voermans, above, n 23, 230.

the functional link,[73] between the law and its effects: and so an effective law is one that is respected or implemented, provided that the observable degree of respect can be attributed to the norm.[74]

For the purposes of drafting in its narrow sense, therefore, effectiveness is the ultimate measure of quality in legislation.[75] It simply reflects the extent to which the legislation manages to introduce adequate mechanisms capable of producing the desired regulatory results.[76] If one subjects effectiveness of legislation to the wider semantic field of efficacy of regulation as its element, effectiveness manages to hold true even with reference to diverse legislative phenomena, such as symbol legislation, or even the role of law as a ritual. If the purpose of legislation is to serve as a symbol, then effectiveness becomes the measure of achieved inspiration of the users of the symbol legislation. If the legislation is to be used as a ritual, effectiveness takes the robe of persuasion of the users who bow down to its appropriate rituality.

In its concrete, rather than abstract conceptual sense, effectiveness requires a legislative text that can (i) foresee the main projected outcomes and use them in the drafting and formulation process; (ii) state clearly its objectives and purpose; (iii) provide for necessary and appropriate means and enforcement measures; (iv) assess and evaluate real-life effectiveness in a consistent and timely manner.[77]

Cost-efficiency is a parallel concern for drafters. Efficiency is the use of minimum costs for the achievement of optimum benefits of the legislative action.[78] Efficiency refers to the choice of the most financially appropriate solution: as a result, it is a preoccupation for the economists of the multi-disciplinary drafting team. In the context of legislation as a tool of regu-

---

[73] See M Zamboni, 'Legislative Policy and Effectiveness: A (Small) Contribution from Legal Theory' (2018) 9 *European Journal of Risk Regulation*, 416, 418.

[74] See M Mousmouti, above, n 23, 200.

[75] See H Xanthaki, 'On Transferability of Legal Solutions' in C Stefanou and H Xanthaki (eds) *Drafting Legislation, A Modern Approach*, above, n 43, 6.

[76] See Office of the Leader of the House of Commons, *Post-legislative Scrutiny – The Governments Approach*, March 2008, para 2.4; also see A Flückiger, 'L'obligation jurisprudentielle d'évaluation législative: une application du principe de précaution aux droits fondamentaux' in A Auer, A Flückiger and M Hottelier, *Les droits de l'homme et la constitution: études en l'honneur du Professeur Giorgio Malinverni* (2007, Schulthess, Zurich), 170, 172.

[77] This is Mousmoutis effectiveness test: see M Mousmouti, 'Effectiveness as an Aspect of Quality of EU Legislation: Is it Feasible?' (2014) 2 *Theory and Practice of Legislation* 309; also see M Mousmouti, 'Making Legislative Effectiveness an Operational Concept: Unfolding the Effectiveness Test as a Conceptual Tool for Lawmaking' (2018) 9 *European Journal of Risk Regulation* 445.

[78] See R Posner, 'Cost Benefit Analysis: Definition, Justification, and Comments on Conference Papers' (2000) 29 The Journal of Legal Studies 1153.

lation, efficiency is a quality *sine qua non* of the regulation, and consequently the legislation that has been selected as the tool for the achievement of the regulatory goals.[79]

Leaving cost-efficiency aside, effectiveness is achieved by means of three tools: clarity, precision, and unambiguity. Clarity, or clearness,[80] is the quality of being clear and easily perceived or understood.[81] Precision is defined as exactness of expression or detail.[82] Unambiguity is certain or exact meaning:[83] semantic unambiguity requires a single meaning for each word used,[84] whereas syntactic unambiguity requires clear sentence structure and correct placement of phrases or clauses.[85] Clarity, precision, and unambiguity offer predictability to the law. Predictability allows the users of the legislation, including enforcers,[86] to comprehend the required content of the regulation. Predictability of effect is a necessary component of effectiveness and indeed of the rule of law.[87] Thus, compliance becomes a matter of conscious choice for the user, rather than a matter of the users' subjective interpretation of the exact content of the legislation and, ultimately, the regulation.

At the third level of the hierarchy of goals for the drafter comes easified language and gender inclusive language. Easified language is a successor of plain language as a concept encapsulates a qualifier of language, which is subjective to each reader or user.[88] Eagleson defines plain language as clear, straightforward expression, using only as many words as are necessary. It is language that avoids obscurity, inflated vocabulary and convoluted sentence structure. It is

79 See W Voermans, 'To Measure is to Know: The Quantification of Regulation' (2015) 3 *Theory and Practice of Legislation* 91, 110.

80 See Lord H Thring, *Practical Legislation: The Composition and Language of Acts of Parliament and Business Documents* (London, John Murray, 1902) 61.

81 *See Compact Oxford English Dictionary of Current English* (Oxford, Oxford University Press, 2005).

82 Ibid.

83 Ibid.

84 J MacKaye, A W Levi and W Pepperell Montague, *The Logic of Language* (Hannover, Dartmouth College Publications, 1939) chapter 5.

85 For the distinction between semantic and syntactic ambiguity, see R Dickerson, *The Fundamentals of Legal Drafting* (Boston, Little-Brown, 1986) 101 and 104; for an application of rules of logic to resolve syntactic ambiguities, see L E Allen, 'Symbolic Logic: A Razor-edged Tool for Drafting and Interpreting Legal Documents' (1956–1957) 66 *Yale L J* 833, 855.

86 See A Seidman, R Seidman and N Abeyesekere, *Legislative Drafting for Democratic Social Change* (The Hague, Kluwer Law International, 2001) 255.

87 See Sir S Laws, CALC Conference 2009, Hong Kong.

88 See R Sullivan, 'Some Implications of Plain Language Drafting' (2001) 22 *Statute Law Review* 145, 149.

not baby talk, nor is it a simplified version of language.[89] According to Redish, plain language means writing that is straightforward, that reads as if it were spoken. It means writing that is unadorned with archaic, multi-syllabic words and majestic turns of phrase that even educated readers cannot understand. Plain language is clear, direct, and simple; but good plain language has both clarity and grace.[90] Plain language takes into account design and layout, as well as language, and means analysing and deciding what information readers need to make informed decisions, before words, sentences, or paragraphs are considered.[91] A plain language document uses words economically[92] and at a level that the audience of the particular text can understand. Sentence structure is tight. The tone is welcoming and direct. The design is visually appealing.[93] Common problems identified by the plain language movement are long sentences; passive voice;[94] weak verbs; superfluous words; legal and financial jargon; abstract words; and unreadable design and layout.[95] Easified language develops plain language by getting rid of its bi-dimensionality. Plain language requires the drafting of an objectively plain text. Easified language addresses the impossibility of this task by recognising the relativity of communication: each audience carries individual needs of communication and understanding. Easified language therefore departs from an objectively plain text, and seeks a text that is understandable by the specific circle of users of the particular text.

Gender inclusive language requires the elimination of any notion of gender characteristic or classification from the text. It basically requires expression that does not recognise gender as a characteristic relevant to the communication. Gender inclusivity is a development of gender-neutral language, which in

---

[89] See R D Eagleson, *Writing in Plain English* (Commonwealth of Australia, 1990) 4.

[90] See J C Redish, 'The Plain English Movement' in S Greenbaum, *The English Language Today* (New York, Pergamon Press, 1985) 125, 126.

[91] See B A Garner, *Legal Writing in Plain English* (Chicago, The University of Chicago Press, 2001) 10–13.

[92] See R Wydick, *Plain English for Lawyers* (Durham, North Carolina, Carolina Academic Press, 1998) 9.

[93] Ibid., 121–134.

[94] See 'Maine Manual in Legislative Drafting', Chapter 1, Section 7, at http://janus.state.me.us/legis/ros/manual/Webdman-12.htm accessed 13 December 2023.

[95] See 'Guidelines on Process and content of legislation 2001 (including the 2003 Supplement)', May 2001, Updated September 2003, Legislation Advisory Committee, Ministry of Justice, Wellington.

itself is a tool for accuracy, as it promotes gender specificity in drafting[96] and before the courts.[97]

The brief expose of the main principles of drafting and their placement in a pyramid of hierarchy presents interesting conclusions. The pursuit of drafters is their contribution towards efficacy of regulation. This is undertaken within the limited role of the drafter in regulation and is defined as effectiveness. Thus, for drafting in its narrow sense quality in legislation is synonymous to effectiveness. Effectiveness in legislation is achieved via clarity, precision, and unambiguity. Easified language and gender inclusive language are both worthwhile tools for the achievement of clarity, precision, and unambiguity.

C. THE NATURE OF LEGISLATIVE DRAFTING: ART OR TECHNOLOGY?

But what is the nature of rules for regulation? And how are they to be applied? Answering this question depends on the nature of drafting legislation, which is often evasively described as 'serious business'.[98] Dick describes it as 'legal thinking made visible'.[99] Dickerson views legislative drafting as 'the crystallization and expression in definitive form of a legal right, privilege, function, duty, status or disposition'.[100] Salembier distinguishes drafting from other forms of writing, in that its goal is not to entertain, to impress or to explain, but to set out the parameters for legal relationships in the clearest possible manner.[101]

If drafting is considered to be a pure form of art[102] or a quasi craft,[103] then rules and conventions bow down to creativity and innovation. Drafting is a liberal skill that is bound by no rules and is developed through experience

---

96 See Commentary, 'Avoidance of Sexist Language in Legislation' (1985) 11 *Commonwealth L Bull* 590, 590.

97 See W B Hill Jr., 'A Need for the use of Nonsexist Language in the Courts' (1992) 49 *Wash and Lee L Rev* 275.

98 See D Revell, 'Authoring Bilingual Laws: The Importance of Process' (2004) 29 *Brooklyn Journal of International Law* 1085.

99 See R C Dick, *Legal Drafting* (Toronto, Carswell Publishers, 1972) 1.

100 See R Dickerson, *Fundamentals of Legal Drafting,* 2nd edn (Boston, Little Brown, 1986) 3.

101 See P Salembier, *Legal and Legislative Drafting* (Canada Inc. Markham, LexisNexis, 2009) 23.

102 See Sir G Bowman, 'The Art of Legislative Drafting' (2005) *EJLR* 3, 3; also see K Gilberg, 'De l'Art de Mieux Légiférer' *Le Monde*, 17 February 2010, 1.

103 See B G Scharffs, 'Law as Craft' (2001) 45 *VandLRev*, 2245, 2339.

and subjective mentoring.[104] There is therefore no possibility of instruction on how drafting must be done for each possible set of circumstances that may occur in the future, and therefore there are no lessons to be learnt from rules of any kind; moreover, techniques, language and general approach change and must be allowed freedom to do so.[105] This is drafting as traditionally conceived in the common law world of the past, and in the civil law world even currently. Drafting is a liberal skill, which is possessed by enlightened legal scholars who take part in drafting committees on behalf of a variety of governmental Ministries and agencies drafting legislation.[106]

But this traditional approach to legislative drafting ignores its nature as a discipline of law,[107] and the decline of law as art and the rise of technique and regulation.[108] And, even within the ideal of multi-disciplinary drafting teams, drafting remains a mainly legal job. For those who reject the classification of law as art, law is a science: drafting, as a part of the science of law, can only be a science or maybe a technique.[109] And if drafting is indeed a science,[110] then there are rules that apply to it,[111] awareness of them is gained via professional development in courses and seminars,[112] and this awareness is so specialized that drafting is reserved to specialist professionals[113] usually gathered in a special department of the government, such as a Parliamentary Counsels Office.

In our choice of our subjectively preferred approach to law and drafting, Aristotle comes to the rescue. For Aristotle there are three possible options:[114]

---

[104] Some would call it 'intuitive' rather than subjective: see O Korhonen, 'New International Law: Science, Defense or Deliverance' (1996) 7 *European Journal of International Law* 1, 13.

[105] See B G Scharffs, above, n 103, 15.

[106] See C Nutting, 'Legislative Drafting: A Review' (1955) 41 *ABA J* 76, 76.

[107] See F Ost and M van de Kerchove, *Jalons pour une theorie critique du droit* (Brussels, Publications des Facultes universitaires Saint-Louis, 1987) 52.

[108] See Shi-J Lavir, *The Modern Art of Dying: A History of Euthanasia in the US* (2005) 1–14.

[109] See J-C Piris, 'The Legal Orders of the European Union and of the Member States: Peculiarities and Influences in Drafting' (2006) *EJLR* 1, 1.

[110] See 'Editorial Review' (1903) 22 *Can LTimes* 428, 437.

[111] See C Langdell, *A Selection of Cases on the Law of Contracts* (1871), viii.

[112] See M Hoyt, 'Education, Training and Retention of Legislative Draftsmen in Canada' (1979) 5 *CommwLBull* 260, 261; also see M Mulkey, 'Judges and Other Lawmakers: Critical Contributions to Environmental Law Enforcement' (2004) 4 *Sustainable Dev L&Poly* 2, 9.

[113] See R Dickerson, 'Professionalizing Legislative Drafting: A Realistic Goal' (1974) 60 *ABA J* 562, 563.

[114] See M Griffiths and G MacLeod, 'Personal Narratives and Policy: Never the Twain?' (2008) 42 *JPE* 121, 126.

science as episthmh;[115] art as techne; or phronesis[116] as the praxis of subjective decision making on factual circumstances or the practical wisdom of the subjective classification of factual circumstances to principles and wisdom as episthmh.[117]

Phronesis has been translated as practical reasoning, practical wisdom, moral discernment, moral insight, and produce.[118] In Aristotle's words, phronesis is an intellectual virtue that is 'reasoned, and capable of action with regard to things that are good or bad for man'.[119] It is 'the art of judgement'.[120] Phronesis can neither relate to things that are not capable of being changed, nor to goals that cannot be realised.[121] Phronesis is not knowledge about the unchangeable order of the world; it relates only to human affairs and, among them, again only to those which can be objects of meaningful deliberation.[122]

Phronesis concerns values[123] and goes beyond analytical, scientific knowledge of episteme and the technical knowledge or know how of techne. Voegelin writes that phronesis differs from the dianoetic virtues of episteme-science that draws conclusions from principles; from nous-intellect, which recognises first principles; and from sophia-wisdom, which, as a combination of science and intellect, refers to things divine.[124] Phronesis differs from artistic and technical skill-techne, because techne produces artifacts and thus is not action that has its end in itself.[125] Phronesis involves both rational choice and the process of reflective deliberation by which a rational choice is formed, and is a primary

---

[115] Episteme is defined as scientific knowledge: see D W Hamlyn, 'Aristotelian Epagoge' (1976) 21 *Phronesis* 167, 167.

[116] See Aristotle, *Nichomachean Ethics*, bk VI, chs. 5-11 (D Ross trans. 1980).

[117] See S-U von Kirchmann, *Die Werlosigkeit der Jursprudenz als Wissenschaft* (Berlin, Verlage von Julius Springer, 1848).

[118] See J Noel, 'On the Varieties of Phronesis' (1999) 31 *Educational Philosophy and Theory* 273, 273.

[119] See Aristotle, *Nicomachean Ethics*, above, n 116, 1140a24–b12, 1144b33–1145a11.

[120] See G Vickers, *The Art of Judgement: A Study of Policy Making* (London, Sage, 1995).

[121] See Aristotle, *Nicomachean Ethics*, above, n 116, 1140a32 f.

[122] See E Voegelin, 'Phronesis as Deliberation', http://voegelinview.com/from-The-Collected-Works/natural-law-and-aristotle-what-is-right-by-nature-pt-3/Phronesis-as-Deliberation-Phronesis-as-Knowledge-of-What-is-Good.html accessed 13 December 2023; and also see Aristotle, *Nicomachean Ethics*, above, n 116, 1141 b 8 ff.

[123] A person with phronesis cannot fail to act correctly and a person to act correctly must have phronesis: see D Brosnan, 'Virtue Ethics in a Perfectionist Theory of Law and Justice' (1989) 11 *Cardozo Law* Review, 335, 344.

[124] See E Voegelin, above, n 122; and also see Aristotle, *Nicomachean Ethics*, above, n 116, 6.6–7.

[125] See E Voegelin, ibid.; and also Aristotle, ibid., 6.4.

virtue of good citizenship.[126] Phronesis is supreme to episteme and techne as it is able to manage human affairs, including episteme and techne which cannot manage themselves.[127] Phronesis is most important also because it is that activity by which instrumental rationality is balanced by value-rationality.[128]

Episteme is defined by Aristotle as a demonstrative state, (i.e., a state of mind capable of demonstrating what it knows). A person has scientific knowledge when their belief is conditioned in a certain way, and the first principles are known to them because if they are not better known to him than the conclusion drawn from them, he will have knowledge only incidentally.[129] *Episteme* concerns universals and the production of knowledge that is invariable in time and space and achieved with the aid of analytical rationality, and corresponds to the modern scientific ideal as expressed in natural science.[130] And so law as episteme 'would be basic science aiming at universality and searching for generic truths or laws'.[131] Techne is defined by Aristotle as a truly reasoned productive state, whose practice is the study of how to bring into being something that is capable of being or not being.[132] And so techne is a craft or art that is concrete, context-dependent, and variable. Its objective is the application of technical knowledge and skills according to a pragmatic instrumental rationality that Foucault calls 'a practical rationality governed by a conscious goal'.[133] Dunne sees techne as 'the kind of knowledge possessed by an expert maker: it gives him a clear conception of the why and wherefore, the how and with-what of the making process and enables him, through the capacity to offer a rational account of it, to preside over his activity with secure mastery'.[134] And law practiced as techne would be a type of consulting aimed at arriving at better laws by means of instrumental rationality, where 'better' is defined in terms of the values and goals of those who employ the consultants, sometimes

---

[126] See S Heyman, 'Aristotle on Political Justice' (1992) *IowaLRev* 851, 862–863.

[127] See B Flyvbjerg and T Landman, *Real Social Science: Applied Phronesis* (Cambridge, CUP, 2012) 2.

[128] See B Flyvbjerg, 'Phronetic Planning Research: Theoretical and Methodological Reflections' (2004) 5 *Planning Theory & Practice* 283, 285; also M Weber, *Economy and Society* (Berkeley, University of California Press, 1978) 85.

[129] See Aristotle, *Nicomachean Ethics*, above, n 116, 1139b18–36.

[130] See B Flyvbjerg, *Making Social Science Matter: Why Social Inquiry Fails and How it Can Succeed Again* (Cambridge, Cambridge University Press, 2001), chapters 3–4.

[131] Drawn from Flyvbjerg's definition of planning as episteme: see B Flyvbjerg, 2004, above n 128, 283.

[132] Aristotle, *Nicomachean Ethics*, above n 116, 1140a1–23.

[133] M Foucault, 'Space, Knowledge, and Power. Interview with Paul Rabinow' in P Rabinow (ed) *The Foucault Reader* (1984, Pantheon, N. York), 239, 255.

[134] J Dunne, *Back to the Rough Ground: Practical Judgement and the Lure of Technique* (1993, University of Notre Dame Press, South Bend, IN), 9.

in negotiation with the latter.[135] Phronesis focuses on practical knowledge within the realm of ethics: 'phronesis is a true state, reasoned, and capable of action with regards to things that are good or bad for man ... this quality belongs to those who understand the management of households or states'.[136] Persons with phronesis [phronimoi] are moved by a sense of the proper order among the ends pursued, which cannot be conceived as theoretical axioms but only grasped by phronesis.[137] And so phronetic law is concerned with reflection about values and interests with reference to praxis based on practical value-rationality.[138]

Aristotle distinguished the practical wisdom (phronesis) needed to work with practical knowledge (praxis) from the theoretical wisdom (sophia) and theoretical understanding (episteme) needed to carry out enquiry into timeless truths (theoria). Praxis is the kind of practical knowledge needed for the social and moral judgements made by the phronimos (the possessor of phronesis). Aristotle also distinguished practical wisdom (phronesis) from the expertise (techne) needed to apply technical knowledge (poiesis) when making things.[139]

Is law phronesis? It can be.[140] And it predominantly is considered to be such.[141] Law as phronesis encourages continued uniform application, and thus supports certainty and the rule of law in the civil law tradition. Law as phronesis supports prudence or appropriateness, and hence *stare decisis*, in the common law tradition. Phronesis can serve as a concrete guide to anyone wishing to ameliorate justice by urging the subject to answer the following questions: where are we heading to? Who wins and who loses, and by virtue

---

135 Drawn from Flyvbjerg's definition of planning as techne: B Flyvbjerg, 2004, above, n 128, 287.

136 See Aristotle, *Nicomachean Ethics*, above, n 116, 1140a24-b12.

137 See C Taylor, *Sources of the Self: The Making of the Modern Identity* (Cambridge MA, Harvard University Press, 1989) 125 and 148.

138 Drawn from Flyvbjerg's definition of planning as phronesis: B Flyvbjerg, 2004, above, n 128, 287.

139 See M Griffiths and G MacLeod, 'Personal Narratives and Policy: Never the Twain?', above, n 114, 126.

140 But it can also be craft: see especially B G Scharffs, 'Law as Craft' (2001) 54 *Vand LRev*, 2245; or art: see especially S G Pollock, 'The Art of Judging' (1996) 71 *NYU L Rev* 591; or science: see especially P Schlag, 'Law and Phrenology' (1997) 110 *Harv L Rev* 877, 897.

141 See S J Burton, 'Law As Practical Reason' (1989) 62 *Cal L Rev* 747; also, W N Eskridge Jr and P P Frickley, 'Statutory Interpretation as Practical Reasoning' (1990) 42 *StanLRev* 321, 353; and D A Farber, 'The Inevitability of Practical Reason: Statutes, Formalism, and the Rule of Law' (1992) 45 *Van.L.Rev* 533; B Leiter, 'Heidegger and the Theory of Adjudication' (1996) 106 *Yale L.J* 253; R Mohr and D Manderson, 'From Oxymoron to Intersection: an Epidemiology of Legal Research' (2002) 6 *Law Text Culture* 159, 174.

of what mechanisms? What are desirable consequences? What can be done on this topic?[142] Phronesis supports probabilistic reasoning, as opposed to deductive reasoning, which can be defined as the selection of solutions made on the basis of informed yet subjective application of principles on set circumstances.[143] Phronesis is 'practical wisdom that responds to nuance and a sense of the concrete, outstripping abstract or general theories of what is right. In this way, practical wisdom relies on a kind of immediate insight, rather than more formal inferential processes'.[144] Phronesis provides the means to achieve the purpose.[145] And phronesis accommodates both legal *episteme* and *techno*-law.[146]

So, what is the nature of legislative drafting, as a sub-discipline of law? The debate between drafting as art and drafting as science seems to be false. It ignores relativity as the essence of legal science. Law, and consequently drafting as its discipline, is not part of the arts, nor is it part of the sciences[147] in the positivist sense.[148] Law, and consequently drafting is neither episthmh nor techne. It is phronesis, an arty science, with principles and rules that may well apply, but only in principle. Because phronesis supports particularity.[149] In other words, law, and consequently drafting, is a liberal discipline where theoretical principles guide the drafter to conscious decisions made in a series of subjective empirical and concrete choices. And, as it is phronetic, law is context dependent, in the sense that it can only inform on what might work in certain circumstances, but the decision about what to do in any specific circumstance will always depend on normative judgements that have to be made

---

142 See M Deschamps, 'L'acces a la justice, l' affaire de chacun' (2009) 50 *Cahiers de Droit* 248, 253.

143 See E Engle, 'Aristotle, Law and Justice: The Tragic Hero' (2008) 35 *NKyLRev* 1, 4.

144 See C Rideout, 'Storytelling, Narrative Rationality, and Legal Persuasion' (2008) 14 *Legal Writing: J Legal Writing Inst* 53, 75.

145 See J Moss, 'Virtue Makes the Goal Right: Virtue and Phronesis in Aristotle's Ethics' (2011) 56 *Phronesis: A Journal for Ancient Philosophy* 204.

146 See P Cserne 'Introduction: Legislation, Legal Episteme, and Empirical Knowledge' (2013) 1 *The Theory and Practice of Legislation* 387, 391.

147 For an analysis of the contra argument on law as a science, see M Speziale, 'Langdells Concept of Law as Science: The Beginning of Anti-Formalism in American Legal Theory' (1980) 5 *Vt LRev* 1.

148 See R R Formoy, 'Special Drafting' (1938) 21 *Bell Yard: JLSocySchL* 3, 3; but see contra C Langdell, 'Harvard Celebration Speeches' (1887) 3 *LAW Q Rev* 118, 123–124.

149 See S Schwarze, 'Performing Phronesis: The Case of Isocrates Helen' (1999) 32 *Philosophy & Rhetoric* 78, 78.

by those who are there.[150] It is also subject to revision as new perspectives are encountered: it is always revisable.[151]

In applying the description of phronetic social science and its distinction from techne and episteme onto legislative drafting, phronetic legislative drafting is centrally about decisions on how things can and should be done, and actually how to perform the task. It is not theoretical knowledge (episteme) because it is not about only what is true, but also about what would be good under the circumstances. It differs from technical knowledge (techne) in that it is concerned with evaluating and prescribing goals, and setting the means to achieve them.[152]

In other words, the art of drafting lies with the subjective use and application of its science, with the conscious subjective Aristotelian application and implementation of its universal theoretical principles to the concrete circumstances of the problem.[153] Being aware of these principles, the drafter has to decide in a conscious and informed manner, how to apply them to the concrete future choices[154] that form part of their trade. And this can only be done if the drafter is aware of the theoretical principles that need to be applied, and of their hierarchy in the pyramid of principles.

Take for example, the notorious question of limits in the extreme use of plain language: do we need to substitute the term '*mens rea*' in rules of criminal procedure or criminal evidence? If one refers to the hierarchy of principles in drafting, then plain language is clearly a tool for clarity: thus, since the term '*mens rea*' is clear to lawyers and judges as the main users of rules of criminal evidence or criminal procedure, plain language bows down to clarity, and there is no need for a substitution of the term with its plain language equivalent. Moreover, the introduction of a new term may distort clarity and hence effectiveness of the new legislation. Another example of another notorious question: what happens in the event of a clash between clarity and precision? Simply, in application of the pyramid, the criterion of choice is effectiveness: since clarity and precision are in the same grade of the pyramid, the drafter will need to select whichever one of these two principles serves effectiveness best.

150 See M Griffiths and G MacLeod, 'Personal Narratives and Policy: Never the Twain?', above, n 114, 129.

151 See H Arendt, *The Human Condition* (London and Chicago, University of Chicago Press, 1958) 129.

152 See S Schram, 'Phronetic Social Science: an idea whose time has come' in B. Flyvberg, T. Landman, S. Schram (eds.), *Real Social Science: Applied Phronesis* (Cambridge, Cambridge University Press, 2012), 15, 19.

153 See W Eskridge Jr, 'Gadamer/Statutory interpretation' (1990) 90 *ColumLRev* 609, 635.

154 See M Curtis, 'A Better Theory of Legal Interpretation' (1950) 3 *Vand L Rev* 407, 423–24.

In order to achieve good EU legislation, it is necessary to ensure quality both in EU Acts and of course in the national transposition measures. As these form a legislative package, their effectiveness is intertwined, albeit not identical. There is therefore a need to introduce transposition techniques that nurture effectiveness of the national implementing measures. And there is an equally pronounced need to instigate reformed EU drafting techniques that facilitate effectiveness of transposition, and therefore efficacy of national and EU regulation.

The methodology for any analysis of legislative quality lies with Thornton's five stages of legislative drafting, namely understanding the policy proposal, analysing the policy proposal, designing the draft law, composing the draft law, and verifying it internally and externally. This is the structure used in Chapters 2, 3, 4, 5, and 6.

CONCLUSIONS

The war against Ukraine has unified EU citizens under the umbrella of the EU. In contrast to low popularity scores of the past, the EU has the attention and the positive disposition of two-thirds of its citizens. Who are listening. To the EU.[155] To its regulatory messages.

It is time for the EU to talk to its citizens. Directly. Blocking the populist voices of the past. It can do so via its policies using EU legislation as a tool.

It is time for change.

For better transposition legislation.

For better EU legislation.

Let's do this. Starting with transposition.

[155] In 2023 71 per cent of Europeans say that EU actions have an impact on their daily lives: https://europa.eu/eurobarometer/surveys/detail/3093 accessed 13 December 2023.

2. Understanding the transposition task: the intricacies of transposition

The drafting of national implementing measures is crucial for the success of the EU regulatory package as a whole. This synergistic nature of the drafting work undertaken at the EU and the national levels is successfully expressed by the Commission's use of the term 'co-legislators' to describe drafters/law-makers in the Member States.

If one subscribes to the theory of sustainable integration, which requires communication with citizens for the long-term success of the EU,[1] then the role of national drafters and law-makers becomes even more important. It is they who express the EU's regulatory rules in the national legislative language, legislative structure, and legislative form.[2] This can offer EU citizens/nationals of that state the context of national legislative effectiveness that can entice them even further to participate to the EU's regulatory effort[3] and thus contribute to the EU's regulatory efficacy. Moreover, and from the point of view of legislative effectiveness, national drafters can apply the EU policy to the context of their State, with its own legal, political, cultural, and economic eccentricities.[4] This 'nationalisation' of the objectives and rules of EU instruments can enhance effectiveness of the EU text considerably by offering it the national characteristics that entice citizens to apply it fully.

The drafting of legislation presents difficulties under any context. But drafting for transposition is all the more difficult. Transposition pre-supposes *ab*

---

1 EU law is 'for delivering results for citizens and protecting their rights and freedoms': see Court of Auditors, 'Landscape Review, Putting EU law into practice: The European Commission's oversight responsibilities under Art 17(1) of the Treaty on European Union', 2018, 1.

2 See D Roebuck, 'Plain, Clear and Something More? Criteria for Communication in Legal Language' (2014) 16 *European Journal of Law Reform* 633, 650.

3 Non-implementation of EU law affects the credibility of the Union: see European Commission, 'White Paper on European Governance', COM (2001) 428 final.

4 'Dealing with transposition as a mere semi-automatic method, an administrative conveyor belt of implementation, would seriously undermine the legitimacy of the EU legislation in question': W Voermans, 'Transposition of EU legislation into domestic law: Challenges faced by National Parliaments', Policy Department for Citizens' Rights and Constitutional Affairs, Directorate-General for Internal Policies PE 608.845, November 2018, 6.

definitio an existing EU legislative text, with already made decisions on legislative choices, on set objectives, on the structure of the text, and on legislative expression. This renders transposition all the more complicated, as national drafters, at least until now, are forced to undertake their already difficult task with additional restrictive parameters in place. Moreover, the dynamism of the *acquis*, especially when soft law is taken into account, signifies that the goalpost for transposition is inevitably being moved further away as time passes.[5] Every new EU legal instrument, every new judgment of the European Courts, every international agreement signed by the EU are added to the body of rights and obligations that form part of the *acquis* and that Member States must receive in their national legal order. Thus, national drafters and legislators require constant updates on the definition and delimitation of their concept of the *acquis*.[6] Furthermore, EU instruments differ from the form of national, and international, legal measures. This renders the understanding of their legal value, their degree of bindingness, and the depth of their enforcement requirements a rather complex task.[7] Finally, the terminology used in EU instruments tends to have an idiosyncratic meaning[8] with connotations that differ from those awarded to the same term in the national laws of Member States.[9] The identification of the elements of the concept utilised in the *acquis* and the nuances of variation with the national concept adds a layer of extra difficulty to the task of adequate and full transposition. Fourth, as legislative texts are intertwined, the *acquis* may enter into aspects of national law that are outside the fields of regulation covered by the EU. In order to achieve the desired task of full reception and compliance without undue distortion to the national legal system, transposition must take into account the legal system as a whole, thus requiring amendments to all of its fields.[10]

---

5 See R Wainwright, 'Techniques of Drafting European Community Legislation: Problems of Interpretation' (1996) *Statute Law Review* 7, 9.

6 The problem is becoming more pronounced as increasingly emphasis is placed on the use of alternative regulatory instruments, including self-regulation, co-regulation, open coordination, benchmarking, peer pressure, networks, standardisation and soft law: see L A J Senden, 'Soft Law and Its Implications For Institutional Balance in the EC' (2005) 1 *Utrecht Law Review* 77.

7 Even lists in annexes of EU Directives must be transposed either expressly or in preparatory work in national implementing measures; see Case C-478/99, *Commission of the European Communities v Kingdom of Sweden*, [2002] ECR I-4147.

8 See S Chalton, 'The Transposition into UK Law of EU Directive 95/46/EC (The Data Protection Directive)' (1997) 11 *International Review of Law Computers and Technology* 25, 27.

9 See T A Finlay, 'Community Legislation: How Big a Change for the National Judge?' (1996) 17 *Statute Law Review* 79, 80.

10 See W-H Roth, 'Transposing "Pointillist" EC Guidelines into Systematic National Codes – Problems And Consequences' (2002) 10 *European Review of Private Law* 761.

Having spelt out the crucial yet difficult nature of transposition, let us focus on how it is to be done. Transposition is, ultimately, a drafting task. The intellectual process required for the drafting of good legislation is expertly introduced in the holy book of modern drafters, Grant Thornton. Thornton classifies drafting into five stages:[11]

(1) Understanding the proposal.
(2) Analysing the proposal.
(3) Designing the law.
(4) Composing and developing the draft.
(5) Verifying the draft.

In stage 1, the drafter begins with the reading and understanding of drafting instructions, namely the request to draft legislation. In stage 2, the drafter proceeds with an analysis of the drafting request, and its expression in a skeletal outline known as the legislative plan. In stage 3, the drafter begins to identify the design and structure of the legislative text. In stage 4, the drafter puts pen to paper and drafts the requested legislation. In stage 5 the drafter pursues internal and external verification of the first version of the draft legislation delivered within and outside the drafting team.[12]

In the understanding of the transposition task, and consequently the analysis of the transposition task here, Thornton's five drafting stages serve as a useful methodology. The benefits of this method is that it has been tried, tested, and appreciated by modern drafters across the common/civil law divide. Moreover, it compartmentalises the intellectual journey that drafters take, often unconsciously, from the receipt of the EU legislative text to the completion of the national implementing measures, thus offering a practical and applied roadmap for novice and experienced transposition drafters.

It is worth noting, even at this early stage, that the classification of stages is of course a technical one: tasks tend to spread over more than one stage and the drafter tends to revisit decisions made in previous stages whilst pursuing their drafting task. But compartmentalising drafting, even in the knowledge that this is a technical classification, offers exceptional merits not only for the academic presentation of the tasks involved but also, and perhaps more importantly, for the identification of a methodological sequence of tasks that, if followed by the drafter, can lead to good legislation.

The next chapters will analyse the task of drafting for transposition focusing separately in each of Thornton's five drafting stages. Each stage is examined in

---

[11] See H Xanthaki, *Thornton's Legislative Drafting* (5th edn, Bloomsbury, London, 2013), 128–174.

[12] See J Stark *The Art of the Statute* (Littleton, F Rothman, 1996) 52–53.

detail, by analysing the tasks involved in each drafting stage in abstract,[13] and then applying this to transposition *in concreto*. This leads to the identification of what each stage must involve, in pursuit of better legislation.[14] This brings to light best practice for modern transposition drafters and recommendations for the improvement of transposition techniques within the context of sustainable integration via effective co-legislation in the Member States. But, at the same time, by highlighting the challenges faced by transposition drafters in the Member States, the chapters also identify the most prominent sources of these challenges. Some challenges prove inevitable, due to complexity of the drafting tasks involved. But other challenges derive, or are at least enhanced, by the long-established practices and traditions of legislating at the EU level. Thus, each chapter completes with an assessment of current EU legislating practices, and with recommendations on the improvement of the provision offered to national transposition drafters by the EU in its role as the instructing organisation requesting complete transposition. Ultimately, in co-legislating, the EU and Member States must work in harmony and support of each other in order to achieve the whole package of better legislation at the EU and national levels.

A. UNDERSTANDING THE EU LEGISLATIVE TEXT AND THE PARAMETERS OF TRANSPOSITION

1. Drafting Instructions in Legislative Literature

The drafting process begins with the receipt of drafting instructions by policy officers. Drafting instructions begin the unbroken dialogue between policy officers, legal specialists in the substantive field of law, and legislative drafting.[15] These three sets of experts need to translate policy objectives into law reform and into accessible legislative expression.[16] Ideally, these three areas of expertise are represented by three different physical persons,[17] although smaller jurisdictions tend to assign more than one of these tasks to the same

---

[13] For a full analysis on the five drafting stages in abstract, see H Xanthaki, *Drafting Legislation: Art and Technology of Rules for Regulation* (Hart Publishers, Oxford, 2014).

[14] See R Fox and M Korris, *Making Better Law: Reform of the Legislative Process from Policy to Act* (London, Hansard Society, 2010) 86.

[15] See C-A Morand (ed) *Légistique formelle et matérielle* (Aix-en-Provence, 1999) 25.

[16] Lord Goldsmith described the role of a drafter as translating policy into legal text: see Lord Goldsmith KC, 'Parliament for Lawyers: An Overview of the Legislative Process' (2002) 4 *Eur JLReform*, 511, 513.

[17] See P Regan, 'Enacting Legislation – a Civil Servant's Perspective' (2012) 34 *Statute Law Review* 32, 33.

civil servant.[18] At the end of the day, even one officer can adequately complete all three tasks, but they must be aware of which hat they are wearing in each task, and what role they are expected to play.[19] Legislation is the product of many minds[20] but it is the drafter's task to ensure that the drafting process is followed religiously.[21]

Drafting instructions is a broad term to express the request[22] of policy officers to the drafter to draft legislation.[23] There are no real rules on the content of these drafting instructions apart from the necessity to offer the drafter all necessary data to enable them to contribute to legislative effectiveness. Although this seems a rather liberal statement that can allow policy officers to get away with minimal effort offering minimal data in their request to drafters, effectiveness places a heavy burden on drafting instructors.

In order to achieve effectiveness, the drafter need to be aware of the precise and real (not beautified) policy goals,[24] the spirit and intent of the proposed legislation,[25], that the executive is aiming to achieve.[26] This allows them to confirm that legislation is indeed necessary for the purposes of achieving these policy goals, that the selection of the policy solutions can lead to the required goals, and that legislation is able to contribute to their achievement.[27] It is precisely because of the role of drafting instructions in the formulation of

---

18 See T W Cain KC, 'The Legislative Draftsman in a Small Jurisdiction' (1993) 19 *Commw L Bull*, 1237, 1238.

19 See A Seidman, R B Seidman, and N Abeyesekere *Legislative Drafting for Democratic Social Change – A Manual for Drafters* (The Hague, Kluwer, 2001) 280.

20 See G Tanner, 'Confronting the Process of Statute-Making' in R. Bigwood (eds), *The Statute: Making and Meaning* (Wellington, LexisNexis, 2004), 54.

21 See V Vanterpool, 'A Critical Look at Achieving Quality in Legislation' (2007) 9 *European Journal of Law Reform* 167, 170.

22 See B Simamba, *How to Make Effective Legislative Proposals* (Indiana, AuthorHouse, 2012) 8.

23 See R J Martineau and M B Salerno, *Legal, Legislative and Rule Drafting in Plain English* (St Paul, Thomson West, 2005) 93.

24 J. Kobba, 'Criticisms of the Legislative Drafting Process and Suggested Reforms in Sierra Leone' (2008) 10 *Eur JLReform* 219, 228.

25 V C R A C Crabbe, 'The Role of Parliamentary Counsel in Legislative Drafting' 'UNITAR Sub-Regional Workshop on Legislative Drafting for African Lawyers', Kampala, Uganda, 20–31 March 2000. 8; also see S L Trusty, 'The Value of Clear Instructions' (1946–1947) 15 *U Kan City L Rev*, 9.

26 N A Hashim, 'Consultation: A Contribution to Efficiency of Drafting Process in Malaysia' (2012) 14 *Eur J L Reform* 142, 148.

27 See A Flückiger and J-D Delley, 'L'élaboration rationnelle du droit privé: de la codification à la légistique' in C Chappuis et al. (eds), *Le législateur et le droit privé, Mélanges en l'honneur de Gilles Petitpierre* (Geneva and Zurich, Bale, 2006) 125–126; also see D R Miers and A C Page, *Legislation* (2nd edn, London, Sweet and Maxwell, 1990) 11.

good law, that the tradition[28] of brief,[29] oral[30] Ministerial 'orders'[31] to legislate is rejected in effectiveness-driven drafting. The more aware of the regulatory aims the drafter is, the closer the link between the regulatory aims and the legislative tools will be.[32] Going back to the doctrine of legislation as a means of regulation, the more aware of the real regulatory aims the drafter is, the better equipped they are to pursue the legislative choices that best promote the policy and legal choices made by the instructing officers.[33] If the drafting choice is haphazard, and this of course would happen in cases where drafting instructions are a simple order to legislate, then the effectiveness[34] of the legislation can only be haphazard.[35] Unless the instructions are clear on the idea and objectives of the proposal,[36] 'it is sheer waste of time to embark upon drafting a piece of legislation'.[37] Eloquently pictured by J-D Delley and A Flückinger below, the sequence of phases in the drafting process is as follows: the instructing officers define the problem, determine the objectives of the requested law, identify alternative scenarios, and on the basis of 'prospective evaluation' (pre-legislative scrutiny) they choose the right solutions: drafting instructions are there to describe all of the above, thus allowing the drafter to put the chosen solutions to effect in preparation for 'retrospective evaluation' (post-legislative scrutiny) of the passed legislation.[38]

---

[28] See U Karpen, 'Instructions for Law Drafting' (2008) 10 *Eur J L Reform* 163.

[29] On the inadequacy of drafting instructions see N Nand, 'Legislative Drafting, Distance Education and Its Contribution to Good Governance in the Pacific' 2008, https:// oasis .col .org/ items/ 1c7d31b9 -54b1 -42ee -8ebc -2739a37f1273 accessed 13 December 2023; also see A Songa Gashabizi, 'The Challenges of Rwandan Drafters in the Drafting Process for Good Quality Legislation' (2012) *14 Eur JL Reform* 280, 281.

[30] See J-D Delley, M T Christin Jochum and S Ledermann, 'La conception des lois: la démarche légistique entre théorie et pratique', (Geneva, CETEL, 2009), http:// archive-ouverte.unige.ch/unige:2026 accessed 13 December 2023, 23–24.

[31] See R Ikiriza, 'Instructions to Draft Legislation – A Study on Legislative Drafting Process in Rwanda' (2012) 14 *EurJ.L Reform* 225, 226.

[32] See V F Nourse and J S Schacter, 'The Politics of Legislative Drafting: A Congressional Case Study' (2002) 77 *New York University Law Review*, 575, 595.

[33] See D Elliot, 'Preparing Drafting Instructions for Legislation' https://studylib.net/ doc/ 5913046/ preparing -drafting -instructions -for -legislation accessed 13 December 2023.

[34] And this will not be the drafter's fault: see A Ashworth, 'A Crystal Mark for Lawmakers' (1996) *MarCrimL.R.* 149, 149.

[35] See M Mayer, *The Lawyers* (London, Harper and Rowe, 1967) 50.

[36] Clear drafting instructions ultimately serve the citizens: see P Salembier, *Legal and Legislative Drafting,* (Lexis Nexis, Toronto, ON, 2009), p. 1.

[37] See V C R A C Crabbe, *Legislative Drafting* (London, Cavendish Publishing, 1993) 14.

[38] See J-D Delley and A Flückinger, 'La légistique: une élaboration méthodique de la legislation' in *Confection de la loi* (Paris, Presses Universitaire de France, 2005), http://archive-ouverte.unige.ch/unige:8307 accessed 13 December 2023, 83, 84.

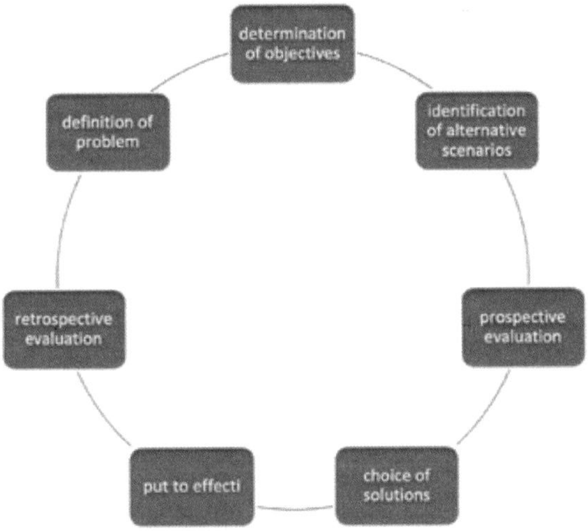

Figure 2.1 *The drafter's journey*

Source: J-D Delley and A Flückinger, La légistique: une élaboration méthodique de la legislation' in *Confection de la loi* (Paris, Presses Universitaire de France, 2005).

It is precisely the necessity for the drafter to fully understand the policy goals and policy choices, which renders the practice of offering drafters raw or ready drafts unacceptable in modern legislative drafting.[39] Instructing officers seem to prefer ready drafts to writing instructions, mainly because they erroneously think that this will speed up the process of drafting, and perhaps guide the drafter to the result that instructing officers hope to achieve.[40] This cannot be further from the truth.[41] A bad ready draft can only start a gradually increasingly frustrating friction between instructing officers and drafters, promoting

[39] A number of jurisdictions reject lay drafts: for the UK see Office of Parliamentary Counsel; for Australia, see 'Guide to Making Legislation'; for Canada see 'Guide to Making Federal Acts and Regulations'; for New Zealand see Cabinet Manual 2008; for Australia also see Giving Written Instructions, https:// www .aph .gov .au/ about _parliament/ house _of _representatives/ powers _practice _and _procedure/ 00 _- _infosheets/infosheet_7_-_making_laws accessed 13 December 2023; also see Sir W Dale, 'Canadian Draftsmanship, and the French Connection' (1984) 10 *CommwLBull*, 1865, 1866.

[40] For a detailed insight in the disruption caused by lay drafts, see P Perry Biribonwoha, 'The Role of Legislative Drafting in the Law Reform Process' (2006) 32 *Commonwealth Law Bulletin* 601.

[41] See D Elliot, 'Getting Better Instructions for Legislative Drafting' at the Pre-Conference Clinic on Writing Laws of the Just Language Conference, 21 October

a power game between offices, and leading to dangerous products.[42] As a result, even the defence of alleged expediency cannot stand at the side of ready drafts:[43] drafters have to undo what is badly done by untrained officers.[44] Without narrative drafting instructions, the architecture of the resulting legislative text can only be of questionable quality.[45] Ready drafts are dangerous, and more often than not useless and misleading.[46]

This is an indicative checklist for legislative instructions:

1. What is the precise problem?
   a. What harm or other undesirable outcome do we want to prevent?
   b. Who or what is being harmed?
2. What is the nature and scale of the risk from the harm?
   a. How frequent or probable is the occurrence of the problem?
   b. How many people or situations are affected, and how seriously, when the problem occurs?
3. What are the options for dealing with the problem?
   a. What are the alternative courses of action, from doing nothing through to, e.g., a complete prohibition of specific activities?
   b. Are there any alternatives that do not involve a governmental body?
   c. Can the matter be dealt with without making any regulation?
4. What is the likely impact of each option?
   a. What is the probable benefit from each option; i.e., how far is it likely to reduce the estimated risk?
   b. To what extent should this be discounted because the reduction in risk is likely to be lessened by persons altering their behaviour in response to the option?

1992, Victoria, British Columbia; also J F Wilson, 'The Preparation of Drafting Instructions'.

42 See J Hertin, J Turnpenny, A Jordan, M Nilsson, D Russel and B. Nykvist, 'Rationalising the Policy Mess? Ex Ante Policy Assessment and the Utilisations of Knowledge in the Policy Process' (2009) 41 *Environment and Planning* 1185; for an interesting example of the tension between evidence-based policy making and political considerations in the drafting of legislation see R.W. Hahn and P.M. Dudley 'The Disconnect between Law and Policy Analysis: A Case Study of Drivers and Cell Phones' (2003) 55 *Admin L Rev* 127, 181.

43 See R Muhamad, 'Instructions to Draft Legislation: A Study on the Legislative Drafting Process in Malaysia' (2011) *EurJLReform* 236, 256.

44 See E A Driedger, *The Composition of Legislation* (2nd edn, Ottawa, Department of Justice, 1957) xix–xx.

45 See Office of the Queensland Parliamentary Counsel, 'A guide for effective legislative drafting instructions', para 37.

46 See G Eorsi, 'Unifying the law (A Play In One Act, With A Song)' (1977) 25 *Am. J. Comp. L.* 658.

   c. To what extent should this be discounted because of indirect side-effects or other harms likely to flow from an option?
5. What administrative mechanisms are needed?
   a. Is the mechanism for implementing each option the most practical and effective?
   b. In so far as the mechanisms involve public services, is that option an efficient use of public resources, given other claims?
6. What is the monetary value of the expected benefits?
   a. In monetary terms, what is the value of the benefits that are expected to accrue from each option?
   b. To what extent is that value likely to be increased by other benefits in respect of which the monetary value cannot be fully calculated (i.e., because they are not marketed)?
7. What are the estimated costs of each option?
   a. Overall, what are the costs (recurring and non-recurring) to the government budget of implementing each option?
   b. What is the cost of providing the administrative mechanisms (in personnel and non-personnel expenditure) necessary for each option?
   c. What are the likely direct costs (recurring and non-recurring) to the private sector in complying with each option?
   d. What are the likely indirect costs to the private sector in complying with each option, e.g., in terms of reduced competitiveness?
8. How cost-effective is each option?
   a. How do the costs of each option compare with the expected benefits? Are they proportionate?
   b. How efficient are the administrative mechanisms necessary for each option, in terms of costs measured against the likely reduction in risk?
   c. Which option is the most cost-effective?
9. What issues of distributive fairness and public perception are relevant?
   a. Are the costs and benefits fairly distributed between different groups in the society?
   b. What are the public perceptions about the extent of the risk and the need to eliminate it?

2. Drafting Instructions and Transposition

The application of international literature on drafting instructions reveals two inherent weaknesses in current transposition processes. The first relates to the difficulty in understanding the policy goals pursued by means of legislation, and the second relates to the inevitable legislative (rather than narrative) style of drafting instructions in transposition. Here lie two grave challenges for national drafters.

For the purposes of achieving effective legislation, legislative literature stresses the crucial need for the drafter to understand the overarching policy goals. Without understanding the real, unbeautified for popular consumption, reasons behind the EU's decision to legislate, it is impossible to comprehend the policy context within which lies the legislative text. Context is important for understanding what the aim of the EU regulatory effort is, as a means of assessing whether these aims coincide with those at the national context, whether they have already been achieved at the national context, or whether they are partially achieved at the national context. In the case of partial or non-achievement at the national level, the EU text offers an excellent model for the road ahead: why legislation was selected amongst the other available regulatory tools, how legislative mechanisms connect with the policy goals, and whether these can be usefully transplanted at the national level.

In the case of transposition, understanding the policy goals is exceptionally tricky because the text of EU legislation does not currently introduce adequately concrete and clearly expressed policy goals. Some inkling on policy goals can be derived from the generic objectives of legislation currently included in the recitals of most EU legislative instruments. But these are drafted mainly to express the legal basis for the legitimacy of EU action. For example, Recital 36 of Directive 2019/904 on the reduction of the impact of certain plastic products on the environment[47] states that:

> Since the objectives of this Directive, namely to prevent and to reduce the impact of certain single-use plastic products, products made from oxo-degradable plastic and fishing gear containing plastic on the environment and on human health, and to promote the transition to a circular economy, including the fostering of innovative and sustainable business models, products and materials, thus also contributing to the efficient functioning of the internal market, cannot be sufficiently achieved by the Member States but can rather, by reason of the scale and effects of the action, be better achieved at Union level, the Union may adopt measures, in accordance with the principle of subsidiarity as set out in Article 5 of the Treaty on European Union. In accordance with the principle of proportionality as set out in that Article, this Directive does not go beyond what is necessary in order to achieve those objectives.

The recital pacifies possible concerns of subsidiarity and proportionality but does not identify the policy goal that the Directive aims to achieve: is it the protection of the environment and human health, or is it the contribution to the internal market by promoting competitive business models? Selecting the main policy goal directs understanding of the legislative measures differently. Thus,

---

[47] See OJ L155, 12.6.2019.

protection of the environment and human health would support the reduction of oxo-degradable types of plastic, whereas promotion of competitive business models would support the reduction of plastic that is not financially competitive. If the goals are equally valuable, then guidance as to how any clashes are to be addressed would have made the task of understanding the context easier. This latter point is not addressed even in the objectives provision of the text of the Directive in Article 1, which introduces them both in parallel and without hierarchy. The understanding and prioritisation of the two goals are necessary for the determination of the timeframe within reduction of plastic is to be undertaken in each Member State. If the context is environmental, then immediate reduction and recall of all such products would be the most effective national implementing measure. If competitiveness is the issue, then a longer period of grace for the transition of relevant businesses to other materials would serve the policy goals best.

Some EU texts carry no objectives at all. An example is Directive 2019/1160 amending Directives 2009/65/EC and 2011/61/EU with regard to cross-border distribution of collective investment undertakings.[48] Recital 1 states that:

> Common objectives of Directive 2009/65/EC of the European Parliament and of the Council (3) and Directive 2011/61/EU of the European Parliament and of the Council (4) include ensuring a level playing field among collective investment undertakings and removing restrictions to the free movement of units and shares of collective investment undertakings in the Union, at the same time ensuring more uniform protection for investors. While those objectives have been largely achieved, certain barriers still hamper the ability of fund managers to fully benefit from the internal market.

Since the objectives of the original EU text have been largely achieved, transposition drafters remain in the dark as to the policy aims of this Directive. A lack of express objectives can lead them to select transposition by means of repealing the previous transposition laws and replacing them with a new law addressing the specific hurdles at hand. The question is whether this would be considered incomplete transposition of the whole regulatory package. Perhaps even worse, this choice could lead to undetected incomplete transposition: as the Member State's obligation is to report the new transposition measures, the repeal of the previous law can legitimately remain unreported, and consequently the incomplete transposition package could inadvertently fall under the carpet.

Policy goals are found in the introductory reports of EU instruments or even in recently the introduced transposition guides, both of which could serve as

---

48 See L188/106, 12.7.2019.

ideal sets of drafting instructions in the context of transposition. Introductory reports are drafted by the initiating EU body, and accompany the text of the draft EU instrument for the purposes of discussion in expert groups. They include the problem that the EU attempts to address, evidence of the cost of inaction, a discussion on the prevalent policy options, the reasoning behind the prevalence of the preferred option, and obviously comments in the necessity, subsidiarity, and proportionality of the proposed measures. Similarly, transposition guides, which are an increasingly frequent transposition assistance tool for Member States, tend to focus on the text rather than the policy goal that it serves. For example, the 2013 Guidance Document related to the transposition and implementation of Directive 2012/29/EU on victims' rights, insists on explaining each provision of the Directive in turn without offering a contextual background or underlying policy aims.[49] When analysing the objectives clause of the Directive, the Guidance document focuses on the scope of the Directive, namely its field of application rather than the policy goal that it aims to achieve.

As a result, the visibility of concrete policy objectives at the EU level is rather low. This is not an ideal place for the quality of EU legislation. Current trends in legislative drafting are expressing loud calls for concrete objectives clauses introducing the measurable criteria for effectiveness to be used in post-legislative scrutiny.[50] In other words, the movement for better regulation that views legislation as tool for the achievement of concrete regulatory goals calls for the introduction of concrete objectives accompanied by measurable criteria for regulatory success within the text of legislation. The concept behind this innovation is that agreement of concrete criteria of successful regulation bind post-legislative scrutiny exercises to the specific effectiveness criteria on the basis of which success of regulation will be assessed. The concept derives from and enhances the holistic image of legislating as a task included in law-making and ultimately regulating. Since legislation is a regulatory tool, regulatory success is measured by means of concrete and quantifiable (albeit not always in numbers) changes in the regulated environment. For example,

---

[49] See DG Justice Guidance Document related to the transposition and implementation of Directive 2012/29/EU of the European Parliament and of the Council of 25 October 2012 establishing minimum standards on the rights, support and protection of victims of crime, and replacing Council Framework Decision 2001/220/JHA, Ref. Ares(2013)3763804, 19/12/2013, https://www.google.com/url?sa=t&rct=j&q=&esrc=s&source=web&cd=&ved=2ahUKEwj188O2wbSDAxW7X0EAHcUaDjIQFnoECBIQAQ&url=https%3A%2F%2Fe-justice.europa.eu%2FfileDownload.do%3Fid%3D05758a3a-9e2e-49a5-a7ec-3737c3ad6876&usg=AOvVaw2wXIYZ8jWq_S3sc3Gos6-v&opi=89978449 accessed 13 December 2023.

[50] See H Xanthaki, above n 13, 185–188; also see D Berry, 'Purpose Sections: Why They are a Good Idea for Drafters and Users' (2011) 2 *The Loophole* 49.

it would be ideal to state that the objective of an anti-money laundering Directive is to increase the number of prosecutions by 20 per cent over a period of three years, to increase the number of convictions for cross-border prosecutions by 25 per cent over a period of five years, and to recover receipts of money-laundering crimes of at least 1,000,000,000 Euros in the same period. From the point of view of transposition, such quantifiable effectiveness criteria in the EU text urge national transposition drafters to draft proportionate and realistic national effectiveness criteria. Of course, a commitment to such concrete policy goals is undoubtedly frightening. But it is the only strategy that can finally give stealth to post-legislative reviews, thus contributing to the effectiveness of the legislative text at the EU and national levels. Moreover, it closes the circle of regulation, legislation, and review by introducing from the start the theme of effectiveness as a measure of quantifiable success. Finally, by already setting out criteria of effectiveness, it prepares those who will undertake post-legislative scrutiny to collect the data that will be deemed necessary for the completion of their task at a later stage.

Ultimately, the onus of accurately identifying the EU's regulatory goals remain with the transposition drafters. From the national perspective, involving transposition drafters in the EU legislative process could guarantee their better understanding of the regulatory context, the regulatory goals pursued by the EU, the position of Member States on aspects of vagueness or ambiguity, and of course the initial national response to draft texts. Ideally, therefore, national drafters can be in the negotiating teams of Member States in expert groups. As resources rarely allow that, at least in smaller Member States, a starting point would be for Member States to offer access to the normally confidential reports on expert meetings. These are commonly drafted by the delegations of Member States in negotiations, are addressed to the delegate's 'centre' and offer brief but valuable records of relevant discussions and decisions. They can be copied to the drafting team along with the request to transpose the relevant EU text.

The second weakness in current transposition processes relates to a flaw in the style of drafting instructions to transposition drafters. Although literature rejects ready drafts in favour of narrative drafting instructions, transposition continues to be based on an existing, already drafted legislative text, and indeed one that is already set in stone. Having been passed by the initiators of EU legislation, the EU text, in the form of a ready draft, binds national drafters in many aspects of their drafting. This restricts their creativity in designing their national legislative solution and endangers the effectiveness of the national implementing measures. By offering national drafters a ready legislative text, the EU invites the faithful copying of the text verbatim as a transposition strategy. From the point of view of understanding the legislative proposal, which is the focus of this chapter, this can be detrimental to the quality of the resulting national legislation because it serves as a good excuse for the omission of most of Thornton's drafting methodology. By tempting national drafters to omit the understanding of the legislative proposal, it deprives the drafting process from an analysis of the regulatory goals that must be achieved at the EU level. In turn, this deprives the process from the identification of the national regulatory goals. Which in turn, disintegrates the regulatory foundations of the legislative building. Ineffectiveness and non-compliance are real dangers. If proof is needed, perhaps one should take a closer look at the effectiveness records and compliance rates of EU legislative texts.

And so, better transposition legislation requires national transposition drafters to insist on identifying the real and quantifiable regulatory aims of the EU legislators, either via EU or national resources. And to persist with Thornton's Stage 1 by utilising the EU text as a set of drafting instructions rather than as a model law that can be light-heartedly and quickly copied into national legislation.

3. Addressing the Challenges of Transposition (Thornton's Stage 1)

With reference to Stage 1 of the transposition process, valuable lessons can also be learnt for the senders of drafting instructions, namely for the drafters of the EU instrument, its introductory report, and any transposition guidelines. These are documents that are used by national drafters to understand what the transposition task requires and entails.[51]

The analysis of Stage 1 has demonstrated the need for the introductory report and transposition guidelines, where available, to be fine-tuned to also cover the need of national drafters for complete drafting instructions. The drafters of the introductory report must become aware that, apart from its main scope as a policy document justifying the necessity, subsidiarity, proportionality, and context of the proposed draft, the report also serves an additional purpose. It offers national drafters necessary data for the understanding of the EU text, a purpose crucial for the adequate completion of Stage 1 of the transposition process, and, ultimately, the effectiveness of transposition from national co-legislators.

To achieve this additional purpose, introductory reports need to identify the concrete policy goals of the legislation. This is necessary in order to allow national drafters to understand what the regulatory goals are. It is imperative,

[51] For an analysis of the inevitability of lay drafts in certain jurisdictions, see P Perry Biribonowoha, 'Efficiency of the Legislative Process in Uganda' (2005) 7 *EurJLRef* 135, 146–147.

therefore, that introductory texts include tangible, concrete, and achievable goals.

Moreover, concrete and measurable effectiveness criteria for the EU text are necessary in order to direct national drafters towards the goal that they are co-legislating for. It is not necessary to apportion these measurable criteria per Member State. Even placing them as EU-wide objectives alert national drafters to the need to achieve proportionate measurable success, to secure that the criteria are proportionately met at the Member State level, and to collect the relevant data.

Finally, it is commendable that EU drafters persist with the use of sunset clauses in EU legislation, especially in combination with a review clause of the effectiveness of the text. Further, EU drafters can foresee that the EU text will expire unless EU legislators decide to extend its life, subject to an evidence-based post-legislative review on the achievement of the measurable criteria of effectiveness. This would reflect the nested cycles of legislation within law within regulation and would enhance the link between legislation as a tool for regulation.

EU citizens are of course at the forefront of law-making. Thornton's Stage 1 is a technical stage of drafting and is therefore infertile for citizen participation. However, conveying to EU citizens the message that EU drafters also contribute to the effectiveness of transposition measures through evidence-based, transparent, and open data to national drafters can only instil positivity and trust to the EU and its regulatory efforts. And this can serve sustainable integration greatly.

CONCLUSIONS

The analysis of Stage 1 of the transposition process refers to the understanding of the proposal to transpose an EU legislative text. This constitutes the start of the intellectual process that leads to the completion of a draft text ready for parliamentary scrutiny and passing.

The first stage involves the receipt and understanding of the following data:

1. What is the precise regulatory problem?
    a. What harm or other undesirable outcome does the EU want to prevent?
    b. Who or what is being harmed?
2. What is the nature and scale of the risk from the harm?
    a. How frequent or probable is the occurrence of the problem?
    b. How many people or situations are affected, and how seriously, when the problem occurs?
3. What are the options for dealing with the problem?

   a. What are the alternative courses of action, from doing nothing through to, e.g., a complete prohibition of specific activities?
   b. Are there any alternatives that do not involve a governmental body?
   c. Can the matter be dealt with without making any regulation?
4. What is the likely impact of each option?
   a. What is the probable benefit from each option; i.e., how far is it likely to reduce the estimated risk?
   b. To what extent should this be discounted because the reduction in risk is likely to be lessened by persons altering their behaviour in response to the option?
   c. To what extent should this be discounted because of indirect side-effects or other harms likely to flow from an option?
5. What administrative mechanisms are needed?
   a. Is the mechanism for implementing each option the most practical and effective?
   b. In so far as the mechanisms involve public services, is that option an efficient use of public resources, given other claims?
6. What is the monetary value of the expected benefits?
   a. In monetary terms, what is the value of the benefits that are expected to accrue from each option?
   b. To what extent is that value likely to be increased by other benefits in respect of which the monetary value cannot be fully calculated (i.e., because they are not marketed)?
7. What are the estimated costs of each option?
   a. Overall, what are the costs (recurring and non-recurring) to the government budget of implementing each option?
   b. What is the cost of providing the administrative mechanisms (in personnel and non-personnel expenditure) necessary for each option?
   c. What are the likely direct costs (recurring and non-recurring) to the private sector in complying with each option?
   d. What are the likely indirect costs to the private sector in complying with each option, e.g. in terms of reduced competitiveness?
8. How cost-effective is each option?
   a. How do the costs of each option compare with the expected benefits? Are they proportionate?
   b. How efficient are the administrative mechanisms necessary for each option, in terms of costs measured against the likely reduction in risk?
   c. Which option is the most cost-effective?
9. What issues of distributive fairness and public perception are relevant?
   a. Are the costs and benefits fairly distributed between different groups in the society?

b. What are the public perceptions about the extent of the risk and the need to eliminate it?

The main challenges of current transposition practices in Stage 1 are the low visibility of the EU's concrete regulatory goals, and the provision of a final legislative text as drafting instructions to transposition drafters. These challenges blind the transposition drafters as to the direction that their legislative efforts should take and encourage a religious copying of the EU legislative text within the national legal system of the Member State.

In order to produce better transposition legislation, national drafters must dig deep to identify concrete, quantifiable EU regulatory aims either in the text of EU legislation or in transposition tools. As these are currently ineffective in serving as drafting instructions, national drafters can mobilise national resources in the form of the national confidential reports of national delegations to the 'centre' during negotiations on the draft EU text.

In order to facilitate better transposition legislation, EU institutions must fine-tune the introductory report of draft EU texts and any transposition guidelines to also serve as complete drafting instructions. To this effect, they must include the data required in drafting instructions within those texts.

Concrete and measurable effectiveness criteria within the EU text can guide national drafters both on the context of the EU legislation and on the data to be collected for the purposes of post-legislative review of the transposition texts.

Keeping EU citizens aware of the transparent exchange of drafting data and the openly joint and cordial legislating efforts between the EU and its Member States can contribute to sustainable integration via the instilment of cooperation and participation of EU citizens and their elected representatives in the production of legislation as a regulatory tool.

3. Analysing the transposition task

Having received the brief for the drafting of transposition legislation and have understood the request, transposition drafters now get into action. In Thornton's Stage 2 they move to the analysis of the transposition task.

The chapter begins with the presentation of trends and innovations in modern legislative drafting in this topic. These are applied to transposition. They are followed by best practices and recommendations for transposition drafters. The chapter ends with any lessons learnt for the EU institutions as facilitators of the co-legislative efforts of Member States.

A. THE LEGISLATIVE PLAN IN LEGISLATIVE LITERATURE[1]

In Stage 2 drafters analyse their drafting instructions. This is the time when, having understood the drafting instructions and being aware of the regulatory goal to be achieved, drafters translate policy and law reform into legislative choices. Also known as designing a legislative solution, Stage 2 marks the compilation of a legislative scheme,[2] a research report,[3] a commentary,[4] or a report.[5] Via a list of questions and answers, the report confirms the need for legislative action and places the concept of the legislative solution within the current legislative environment. The latter is characterised by inherent legal,

---

1 See H Xanthaki, on 'Transferability of Legislative Solutions' in C Stefanou and H Xanthaki (eds), *Drafting Legislation. A Modern Approach* (Ashgate 2008) 1–18, 17; also see H Xanthaki, *Drafting Legislation. Art and Technology of Rules for Regulation* (Hart Publishers, Oxford, 2014) ss7.

2 See R Muhamad, 'Instructions to Draft Legislation: A Study on the Legislative Process in Malaysia' (2011) 13 *EurJLRef* 236, 241; also see L Levert, 'Bilingual and Bijural Legislative Drafting To Be or Not To Be' (2004) 25 *Statute Law Review* 151; and E A Driedger, *The Composition of Legislation – Legislative Forms and Precedents* (Ottawa, MoJ, 1976) 1.

3 See A Seidman and R B Seidman, 'ILTAM: Drafting Evidence Based Legislation for Democratic Social Change' (2009) 89 *Boston University Law Review* 435, 479.

4 Office of Parliamentary Counsel UK, 'Working with Parliamentary Counsel', 6 December 2011, https://www.gov.uk/government/uploads/system/uploads/attachment_data/file/62668/WWPC_6_Dec_2011.pdf accessed 13 December 2023, para 260 ss.

5 See B R Atre, *Legislative Drafting* (Dehli, Universal Law Publishing Co, 26) 88–89.

political, cultural, and economic intricacies, which must be taken into account for the design of an optimal legislative solution that can entice behaviour change within the selected jurisdiction at the specific moment in time. In that respect, the effectiveness of the final draft relies heavily on the quality of the legislative report.[6]

Stage 2 affords drafters creativity.[7] Here drafters begin to interpret policy goals expressed in policy terms into law reform goals expressed in legal terms into legislative options expressed in legislative forms. This is not a matter of translation, the drafter is not just a scribe. The passing from one set of choices undertaken by one set of experts and expressed in their own jargon into the second and then the third requires not just creativity but great expertise in the environment within which the proposed law is to be placed. This creative interpretation allows a small degree of policy to creep into the otherwise purely legislative task of drafters.[8] An element of quality control over the choices of instructing policy officers is also present.[9]

Parkinson describes quite accurately the elements of the intellectual task involved in drafting: knowledge of conditions proposed to be regulated, and determination of the exact evils requiring regulation; determination of the nature of the regulation required and the precise principles or rules which will effect such regulation; and phraseology of the new principles or rules and of necessary administrative provisions in apt and precise language which will fit them into existing principles of constitutional and statute law and make them reasonably clear to the executive and judicial officers who are to enforce them:[10] in other words, policy/law/legislative expression. It is worth noting that this translation, albeit necessary carries risks of introducing obtuseness due to: (i) the necessary incompleteness of legislation; (ii) the communication risks from extrapolating a legislative solution from a failed non-legislative solution;

---

6 Law Drafting Division, Department of Justice, *Legislative Drafting in Hong Kong – Crystallization in Definitive Form*, 2001, http://www.doj.gov.hk/eng/public/pdf/ldhkv2e.pdf accessed 13 December 2023; also see E Page, 'Their Word is Law: Parliamentary Counsel and Creative Policy Analysis' (2009) *Public Law*, 790, 797.

7 See R J Martineau and M B Salerno, *Legal, Legislative and Rule Drafting in Plain English* (St Paul, Thomson West, 2005) 95.

8 But the current prevalent view is that the drafter's work on policy instructions is political: see D A Marcello, 'The Ethics and Politics of Legislative Drafting' (1995–1996) 70 *TulLRev* 2437, 2441.

9 Driedger advocates non-political drafting: see E A Drieger, 'The Preparation of Legislation' (1953) 31 *Canadian Bar Rev* 33, 36.

10 See T Parkinson, 'Legislative Drafting' (1913) 3 *Proceedings of the Academy of Political Science in the City of New York* 142, 191, http://www.jstor.org/stable/1193363 accessed 13 December 2023.

(iii) the precedent trap, and (iv) the difficulty of hitting a moving target from a moving platform.[11]

In view of the inherent complexity of this translation from policy to law to legislation, constant and open communication amongst the member of the drafting team is greatly beneficial. Stefanou pictures expertly this communication during stage 2 of the drafting process, and beyond, in Figure 3.1 below:

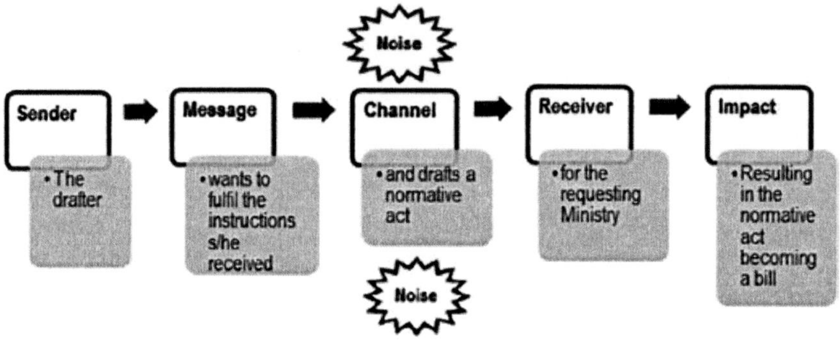

Figure 3.1 *Communication within the drafting team*

Source: C Stefanou, 'Is Legislative Drafting a Form of Communication?' (2011) 37 *Commonwealth Law Bulletin* 407, 414.

The legislative report is the record of this communication and the main points of agreement within the drafting team. The advantage of a legislative report at this early stage of drafting ensures that, within the members of the drafting team, there is agreement on the very basic concepts of the drafting task, and the way in which the legislation will put them to effect. Instead of waiting to discover such an unpleasant surprise at the verification stage of the first draft, the compilation of a legislative plan allows instructing officers to confirm that the drafting choices are agreeable to them, before any wastage of time and resources.[12] In turn, this agreement amongst the team prevents disruption of drafting.[13] Moreover, the legislative plan assists with the division of long instruments into distinct parts; with the introduction of a logical relationship between the parts

[11] See Sir S Laws, 'Giving Effect to Policy in Legislation: How to Avoid Missing the Point' (2011) 32 *Statute Law Review* 1, 6.

[12] See R van Gestel and J Vranken, *Kwaliteit van beleidsanalytische wetgevingsadviezen van de Raad van State* (The Hague, Boom Juridische Uitgevers, 2008), ch. 2.

[13] Sir G Engle, ''Bills are Made to Pass as Razors are Made to Sell': Practical Constraints in the Preparation of 'Legislation' (1983) *Statute Law Review*, 7, 14 ss.

and the whole; and with the identification of a rational sequence of normative provisions focusing only on the questions within the scope of the problem.[14] Seidman also suggests that, by identifying the elements of the legislative solution, the design ensures that the drafter examines all relevant evidence and facts and that these facts are classified logically.[15]

The elements of the legislative plan correspond to the content of drafting instructions, although the focus here is more at the drafting language and concepts rather than the policy and substantive law concepts.[16] They include:

- Analysis of the existing law
- Analysis of the necessity of legislation
- Analysis of potential danger areas[17]
- Analysis of the policy options and the preferred legislative solution
- Analysis of the practical implications of the legislative proposal, including projected statutory interpretation issues and an analysis of matters for which secondary legislation is likely to be needed to implement the draft law.

The analysis of the existing law is one of the main starting points for the drafter. Having read the drafting instructions, having understood the gap in regulation and its evaluation, the drafter begins to translate the regulatory gap to a legal one. In other words, the drafter analyses the existing law (not just legislation) as a means of confirming that there is no other legal rule that can respond to the 'mischief' identified by policy officers in their drafting instructions. Such rules can derive not only from existing legislation, but also from administrative or legal practices or from jurisprudence. The whole framework of the legal position is to be assessed, namely the relevant current law, as interpreted, implemented and supplemented by court decisions and academic opinion.[18]

---

[14] See J C Dernbach, R V Singleton II, C S Wharton, J M Ruhtenberg and C J Wasson, *Legal Writing and Legal Method* (Austin, Woletrs Kluwer, 2007) 62.

[15] See A Seidman, R B Seidman and N Abeyesekere, *Legislative Drafting for Democratic Social Change – A Manual for Drafters* (The Hague, Kluwer, 2001) 88.

[16] See H W Jones, 'Notes for a Legislative Research Checklist' (1950) 36 *ABA J* 685.

[17] See H Xanthaki, *Thornton's Legislative Drafting* (West Sussex, Bloomsbury, 2013) 153.

[18] For an eloquent analysis of the failings in the process of understanding the law before law reform, see N Des Rosiers, President Law Commission of Canada, 'A Just Law for All – Equality and Law Reform', Notes for a speech delivered at the 2001 Canadian Congress on Criminal Justice, Halifax, Nova Scotia, 21 June 2001, https://epe.lac-bac.gc.ca/100/206/301/law_commission_of_canada-ef/2006-12-06/www.lcc.gc.ca/president/speeches-en.asp@id=26&content_type=2 accessed 13 December 2023.

In addition to this, the drafter must consider which relevant rules could be affected by the proposed new legislation. Thornton says that all laws are amending laws. And he is right, in the sense that in our current complex system of legislation, every new insertion in the statute book is bound to somehow amend existing legislation. And so, the analysis of the existing law must also respond to the following questions:

- What must be amended?
- What must be repealed? And how: express or implied repeals?
- What must be preserved?
- What must be added?

And this is exactly one of the points in the drafting process where drafting instructions in the form of a ready draft fail to provide the necessary background information to allow the drafter a head start in understanding the legal position.

Once the current legal position and any mischief is identified, the drafter now looks to establish the necessity of the proposed legislative text. Legislation is a solution of last resort, and indeed one that should not be undertaken lightly. Even within Wintgren's concept of relative freedom,[19] legislation chews away a small bit of citizens' freedom to act as they choose. Legislation is restriction. 'Far from being paid for productivity, therefore, drafters should be paid for non-productivity.'[20] Moreover, new legislation adds to the unbearable volume of the statute book whose consequences include increasing complexity leading to incomprehensibility and ultimately ineffectiveness, and to an increasing loss of the value and importance of legislation when used as a ready and easy regulatory tool.[21]

It is therefore necessary for the drafter to assess whether the identified social need can be addressed[22] by use of alternative means of regulation,[23] such as

---

[19] See L J Wintgens, 'Legitimacy and Legitimisation from the Legisprudential Perspective' in L J Wintgens, *Legislation in Context: Essays in Legisprudence* (Aldershot, Ashgate, 2007) 3, 20.

[20] See D Greenberg, *Laying Down the Law* (London, Sweer and Maxwell, 2011) 155.

[21] See Department for Business, Innovation and Skills, 'Delivering Regulatory Reform', Report by the Comptroller and Auditor General, HC 758, Session 2010–2011, 17 February 2011, 31, para 3.5 ss.

[22] The drafter must aim to diminish the 'uneven correspondence of lawmaking purpose and social outcome': see H W Jones, *The Efficacy of the Law* (Evanston, Northwestern University Press, 1969), 48.

[23] Legislation is often an insignificant instrument of control when compared to extra-legal means of social control: see S F Moore, 'Law and Social Change: The Semi-autonomous Social Field as an Appropriate Subject of Study (1973) 7 *Law and*

contracts and voluntary agreements, self-regulation, economic incentives and wider dissemination of information.[24] Drafters who strive to be faithful to their trade must begin with an instinctive negation to any request for further legislation, even though the process of legislating has already begun and the preliminary decision to proceed with legislation has already been taken.[25] Every drafter's response must be 'how can I avoid drafting this bill?'.[26] The crucial importance of necessity in all new legislation has been recognised by the regulators of the EU, who require that any new piece of legislation passes the necessity test.[27]

Having established the mischief and the necessity for the proposed legislation, the drafter then focuses on potential danger areas. These are issues of political, legal, cultural, or financial nature that can stand in the way of legislative effectiveness. With a mind to implementation and enforcement, the drafter explores what can create impediments to the desired unhindered application of legislation via user participation to the regulatory effort. It is only when these issues are identified that the drafter can formulate an opinion on the appropriateness of legislation as an adequate means of regulation. And it is only when these issues are identified fully that the drafter can, with cooperation from the other members of the Bill team, fine-tune the policy choices to either accommodate any sensitivities and danger areas, or to steer clear of them. Which of the two prevails is a policy choice. The drafter's duty is to raise the issues of concern, to explain how these sensitivities or danger areas may impede user application and ultimately implementation. But the choice to proceed, nonetheless, or to proceed with amendments in the previously selected policy choices lies with the policy officers of the Bill team.

Society Rev 719; also R D Schwarz, 'Social Factors in the Development of Legal Control: A Case Study of the Two Israeli Settlements (1954) 63 *Yale LJ* 471; and P Selznick, 'Legal Institutions and Social Controls' (1963) 17 *VandLRev* 79.

[24] See OECD, 'Law drafting and regulatory management in Central and Eastern Europe', OCDE/GD(97)176, SIGMA PAPERS: No. 18, Paris, 14.

[25] See A Nicolaï, 'Schoonheid en effectiviteit: enkele observaties bij de kwaliteit van wetgeving' (2002) *RegelMaat* 39.

[26] See Marcello, above, note 8, 2444.

[27] See in particular, *The Internal Market After 1992: Meeting the Challenge.* Report presented to the Commission by the High Level Group on the Functioning of the Internal Market (The Sutherland Report), EC COM (1992); also see *The Brussels Programme*, COM (93) 545; *The Molitor Report, The Report of the Group of Independent Experts on Legislative and Administrative Simplification* , COM SEC (95) 1379; *Simpler Legislation for the Internal Market*, http://publications.europa.eu/resource/cellar/b38fc89b-c072-4932-9e93-da04356df5d2.0004.01/DOC_19; *Better Regulation – Simplification Initiative*, http://www.europa.eu.int/comm/enterprise/regulation/better_regulation/simplification.htm; and Smart Regulation in the European Union: Communication from the Commission COM(2010) 543 final, 8.10. 2010.

Possible danger areas include, but are not restricted to, issues of constitutionality, legality, adherence with regional and international law, and effectiveness. Constitutionality related issues[28] include issues of competence; proposals affecting adversely personal rights, such as social benefits, pensions, access to justice, freedoms, non-discrimination; proposals ignoring or clashing with established case law; and proposals with powers for delegated legislation. Legality issues include proposals for retrospective[29] or extra-territorial legislation.[30] Issues related to compliance with regional or international law include proposals clashing with an international treaty to which the jurisdiction has acceded; and proposals clashing directly or indirectly with legally binding regional legislation, such as EU law. Issues related to best practices for effectiveness include proposals that are unnecessarily bureaucratic. Issues of ethical or political sensitivity in specific jurisdictions may include proposals for the de-criminalisation of abortion in strictly religious States; the de-criminalisation of homosexuality and the legalisation of gay marriages in most of Africa; the introduction of no-fault divorce in strict Catholic States; legislation related to minorities and minority rights; and legislation tackling issues of migration.

Having analysed the existing law, having confirmed the necessity of legislation, and having addressed sensitivities and danger areas, the drafter now possesses a clear concept of regulatory efficacy.[31] The mischief is confirmed, the necessity of legislation is confirmed, and danger areas are balanced against the persistence of policy officers to proceed with the proposal. With this at hand, the drafter now begins to grapple with the conceptual effectiveness of the proposed legislation. Here the drafter translates the policy choice to a preferred legislative solution.[32] The drafter's main task at this stage is to guarantee accuracy in the translation of policy language into legal language and ultimately

---

28 For an analysis on the relevance of constitutional constraints to the drafter's basic legislative design, see J Zurcher, 'Basic Rules of Legislative Drafting' (1976–1977) 7 *Man. L.J.*, 131, 132.

29 Criminal retrospective legislation must be viewed with extreme caution; civil retrospective legislation can be accepted if the law is certain and stable, it is general in character, and it is not subject to alteration in regard to specific individuals: see Prof. Goodhard 66 *Law Quarterly Review* 314.

30 In principle, extra-territorial legislation is a shock to the legal system; however, it may be imposed in the case of transnational social needs, such as for the regulation of transnational legislation.

31 Policy-makers decide in principle of the basis of efficiency and equity: see R O Zerbe Jr, 'An Integration of Equity and Efficiency' (1998) 73 *WashLRev* 349, 350.

32 See R F Cranston, 'Reform Through Legislation: The Dimension of Legislative Technique' (1978–1979) 73 *NwULRev* 873, 874; also see W Bussmann, 'Evaluation of Legislation: Skating on Thin Ice' (2010) 16 *Evaluation* 279; D L Faigman, 'To Have and Have Not: Assessing the Value of Social Science to the Law as Science and Policy' (1989) 38 *EmoryLJ* 1006, 1052 ss and 1079 ss.

into legislative expression. This is one of the moments where the required creativity, and consequently the effectiveness of the legislative text, is nurtured by narrative drafting instructions rather than ready drafts.

It is worth noting here that selecting the most appropriate legislative solution is not a purely legal task. As is the case with most aspects of drafting, open communication amongst the Bill team is crucial. In their pursuit of the most appropriate legislative solution drafters are entrusted to identify the regulatory solution that is best served by legislation. More often than not, the drafter's task ends up being the expression of the preferred policy choice into the most appropriate legislative choice. But it is useful to point out that the drafter can utilise a number of methods in their own selection of the legislative choice. In end-means analysis the drafter attempts to reach the most socially cost-effective means[33] of achieving the predetermined[34] end result desired by the regulators. Although the end-means analysis has been accused in literature for its susceptibility to serve blindly those in power[35] thus possibly leading to legislative solutions of doubtful ethical or moral standing,[36] within a modern polity respecting the rule of law and human rights, end-means analysis can be a good choice for the drafting team. It allows, in fact it invites, members of the team to on the table every conceivable legislative solution, which is assessed for effectiveness and prioritised on the same basis. Another option for drafters is incrementalism or gradual legislative action, giving credit to precedent and history[37] and encouraging experimental legislation or legislation in stages with regular post-legislative scrutiny cycles that can guarantee the almost inevitable damage limitation. Incrementalism can prove extremely useful[38] when the gap between the current mischief and the final stage of the legislative solution renders the solution difficult to accept and or doubtfully implementable by citizens. Reason informed by experience is a method of selecting the most appropriate legislative solution under the realm of drafting as phronesis. Here

---

[33] See E L Rubin, 'Legislative Methodology: Some Lessons from the Truth-in-Lending Act' (1991) 80 *Georgetown Law Journal* 233.

[34] See B Comly French, 'Council of the District of Columbia, Legislative Drafting Manual Revised Edition' (1982) 25 *How L* 735.

[35] See R B Seidman, 'The Memorandum of Law' (1991)15 *Seton Hall Leg. J.* 334; also see Edward Rubin 'Legislative Methodology: Some Lessons from the Truth-in-Lending Act' in Ann Seidman, R B Seidman and Thomas Waelde (eds), *Making Development Work: Legislative Reform for Institutional Transformation and Good Governance* (1999), 157.

[36] See A E Anton, 'Legislation and Its Limits' (1979) 5 *Dalhousie LJ* 233, 233.

[37] S Levmore, 'Interest Groups and the Problem with Incrementalism' (2010) 158 *University of Pennsylvania Law Review* 815, 815.

[38] See Y Listokin, 'Learning Through Policy Variation' (2008) 118 *Yale LJ* 480, 519–22.

the drafter conducts research both in the jurisdiction and abroad as a means of developing new ways of doing things by reflecting on the facts presented by experience.[39] The questions asked are: (a) what is the social problem and whose behaviour creates it?; (b) what are the explanations for this behaviour?; (c) what are the proposed solutions?; and (d) how these will be implemented and monitored?[40] In other words, the drafter makes use of evidence-based policy analysis undertaken by the instructing department.[41] This policy analysis assesses the effectiveness and cost of each policy option, thus leading by way of practical reasoning to the most appropriate one for the social problem at hand.[42] Reason informed by experience recognises the degree of subjectivity involved in the selection of legislative solutions,[43] and therefore invites all disciplines and experts to contribute to the common aim, which is of course the identification of the solution that has the most probability to lead to efficacy of the underlying regulation.

Having analysed the existing law, the necessity of the legislation, the danger areas and sensitivities, and the preferred legislative solution, the drafter now completes their intellectual journey into Stage 2 by attempting to precipitate possible issues of interpretation.[44] The drafter takes into account general principles of law, Interpretation Acts, and court precedents in an attempt to identify any issues of conceptual or terminological vagueness or ambiguity. Especially in the context of teleological or purposive interpretation, where meaning is derived from within and outside the words of the text, addressing possible interpretation issues guarantees that the text will be used in the way that the regulators, as expressed by the drafters, require.

This completes Thornton's Stage 2 of the drafting process, analysing the proposal for legislation. This is where the tri-alogue between policy, legal, and

---

39 See A Seidman, R B Seidman and Nalin Albeyesekere, *Legislative Drafting for Democratic Social Change: A Manual for Drafters* (Kluwer Law International, The Hague, 2001), 90.

40 R B Seidman, A Seidman and N Makgetla, 'Big Bangs and Decision-making: What Went Wrong?' (1995) 13 *Boston University. Int'l L J* 435, 458–460.

41 R B Seidman, 'Justifying Legislation: A Pragmatic Introduction to the Memorandum and Law, Legislative Theory, and Practical Reason' (1992) 29 *Harv J On Legis* 1.

42 And law has been successful in effecting social change: see Y Dror, 'Law and Social Change (1959) 33 *TulLRev* 787, 796–801; and W M Evan, 'Law as an Instrument of Social Change (1962) 2 *Estudios Sociologicus* 167.

43 See R Munday 'In the Wake of 'Good Governance': Impact Assessments and the Politicisation of Statutory Interpretation' (2008) 71 *MLR* 386.

44 See W N Eskridge Jr, 'Dynamic Statutory Interpretation' (1987) 135 *U.Pa.L.Rev.* 1479; J R Macey, 'Promoting Public-Regarding Legislation Through Statutory Interpretation: An Interest Group Model' (1986) 86 *ColumLRev* 223; W D Popkin, 'The Collaborative Model of Statutory Interpretation' (1988) 61 *SCalLRev* 543.

drafting officers is established. Translation here encapsulates creativity that can, and often does, fine-tune or change the underlying policy.[45] In the process of their analysis, the drafter explores the existing law, the necessity of legislation, any danger areas or sensitivities, the legislative solution, and any issues of interpretation. All these elements are recorded in the legislative plan, which serves as a basis of agreement in the basic conceptualisation of the proposed legislation within the Bill team. The team will have plenty of opportunity to fine-tune their agreed points as the process of drafting evolves, and their elaboration of details progresses deeper and further.

B. ANALYSING THE PROPOSAL FOR TRANSPOSITION OF EU LAWS

The completion of Thornton's Stage 2 on the transposition of EU legislation is further complicated by the parallel presence of two contexts, namely the EU and the national one. Completing the task of understanding the proposal requires analysis of both EU and national laws. The content of analysis remains the same: analysis of the existing law, analysis of the necessity of legislation, analysis of potential danger areas, analysis of the policy options and the preferred legislative solution, and analysis of the practical implications of the legislative proposal, including projected statutory interpretation issues and an analysis of matters for which secondary legislation is likely to be needed to implement the draft law. But the interplay and interconnection of the EU and the national legal orders creates issues eccentric to transposition.

The analysis of the existing law is one such example. In a national drafting exercise, the drafter only needs to understand one law: context of the mischief and placement of the legislative solution overlap within the same legal system. In transposition, the system identifying the mischief and the system hosting the legislative solution differ. The drafter needs to analyse two sets of existing laws: the complex EU[46] and the national one. The understanding of EU law is necessary in order to grasp the full extent of the mischief addressed at the EU

---

45 D Hull, 'Drafters' Devils' (2000) *Loophole*, https://calc.ngo/sites/default/files/loophole/jun-2000.pdf accessed 13 December 2023.

46 The main factors blamed for the risk of infringements of EU law by MS are: the size of the body of law to be monitored and the complexity of many legal instruments; the specificities of policy areas, including the availability of EU funds and alternatives to the infringement procedure; and certain features of Member States' legislative and oversight arrangements, including the length of the legislative procedure, transposition preferences and administrative capacity: see Court of Auditors, 'Landscape Review, Putting EU law into practice: The European Commission's oversight responsibilities under Article 17(1) of the Treaty on European Union', 2018, 5.

level. But the understanding of the national legal system is equally necessary both as a means of confirming that the same mischief applies and also that the proposed legislative solution is equally useful in the national context also. Of course, it must be noted that most EU legislative proposals come as result of a common mischief identified not just by the EU but by Member States though investigatory questionnaires as early as before the stage of policy formulation. This open consultation, and its consequent opportunities to communicate an updated national position, continues until the end of the agreement on the text by the technical experts of Member States' delegations. It is therefore unusual for a Member State to have adequately dealt with the mischief already. But the theoretical possibility exists, and, in the interest of effectiveness, the process of understanding both the EU and national laws must be repeated every time transposition is attempted.

Similarly, assessing legislative necessity carries duality in transposition. Necessity of legislation at the EU level does not necessarily signify necessity of legislation at the national level. It is possible that the national legal system already addresses the mischief by legislative or even by non-legislative means of regulation. And although established past case law of the European courts is adamant that administrative practices do not suffice for complete transposition of EU law, the rationale of the courts was not to exclude alternative means of regulation, but to reject regulatory practices that, by their nature, lack bindingness to non-discriminatory application and consequently endanger uniform application to all EU citizens. One must note that in our current era of de-regulation led by the Better Regulation Agenda of the EU, non-legislative means of transposition with some certainty in the uniformity of their application may no longer be as readily rejected by the Commission and the CJEU.

The analysis of danger areas and sensitivities is more relevant if undertaken solely within the national context. It is the jurisdiction of placement of the national implementing measure that will have to accommodate any intricacies of the legislative environment that may hinder implementation of the EU text there. The same principle applies with practical implications, including powers for delegated legislation and statutory interpretation. Having said that, in both cases it is important to remember that national implementing measures complete an EU regulatory package. Cross-border application and application to citizens from the whole of the EU form part and package of transposition measures. Taking into account sensitivities and practical implications present in other cultures and peoples of the EU contribute to the effectiveness and accessibility of the national transposing measure by other EU nationals, in application of the principle of non-discrimination that is enshrined in the totality of EU law.

The analysis of the drafting proposal in transposition is a rather complex task. Burdened by the presence of a complete and agreed EU text, as opposed to narrative drafting instructions, and without, in most cases, the wisdom of participation in national negotiating teams, national drafters need to somehow unearth the EU regulatory aims and the EU policy choices,[47] the EU gap in the law, the necessity for EU legislation, and any sensitivities and danger areas. As these are rarely included, at least expressly and to the required amount of detail, in EU legislative texts, the role of national drafters in Stage 2 likens that of an ex ante legislative assessor. To this end, Mousmouti's test, with its focus on objectives, content, context, and results,[48] can be of great value as a methodology. Purpose tests the link between the purpose of the law and the policy objectives. Content tests the responsiveness of the legislative choices to the underlying social phenomenon, and the consistency and alignment between the choice of rules, enforcement mechanisms and communication. Results test the monitoring mechanisms in the law. And context tests the integration of the new legislation within the existing system of laws. The value of the test lies in its originality as the first test of effectiveness, and its innovative concretization of effectiveness. The test is an excellent tool in scrutinising legislation and can be of great assistance as a guide for the analysis of existing EU law in Stage 2 of the transposition process.

An enlightened pre-legislative scrutiny at the national level includes answering the following questions in sequence and as 'sudden death', as failure in one test puts a stop to the exercise, and is evidence of ineffectiveness of the text:

1. Testing the conceptual effectiveness of the regulatory concept via empirical data[49]
   a. Which are the desired regulatory results?
   b. How can they be measured?
   c. Within how long are they to be achieved?
   d. Can the selected enforcement mechanisms produce the desired regulatory results within the set times?
   e. Can the text be implemented without stumbling on socio-legal hurdles?
2. Testing the effectiveness of the legislative concept

---

[47] M Zamboni, 'Legislative Policy and Effectiveness: A (Small) Contribution from Legal Theory' (2018) *European Journal of Risk Regulation* 6 eloquently asks 'effective in relation to what?'.

[48] M Mousmouti, 'Operationalising Quality of Legislation through the Effectiveness Test' (2012), 6:2 *Legisprudence* 201.

[49] O D Oliver-Lalana, 'Due Post-Legislative Process? On the Lawmakers' Constitutional Duties of Monitoring and Revision' in K Messerschimdt and A D Oliver-Lalana (eds), *Rational Lawmaking under Review. Legisprudence According to the German Federal Constitutional Court* (Springer 2016) 259; also see J Rachlinski, 'Evidence-Based Law' (2011) 96 *Cornell Law Review* 901–923, 910.

   a. What is the legal mischief and how is it connected to the desired regulatory goals?
   b. Is this addressed by non-legislative means in the jurisdiction?
   c. How is the new legislation expected to address the mischief?
3. Testing the effectiveness of the legislative communication
   a. Which are the main groups of possible users of the text?
   b. What level of awareness of the topic do they have?
   c. What is their level of legal awareness?
   d. What questions does each group ask?
   e. Does the current structure provide accessible answers the specific questions of each of the user groups?
   f. Does the current structure facilitate the unhindered identification of the relevant answers?
4. Testing the effectiveness of legislative expression
   a. Does the language of each provision communicate its message to each of the intended user groups in a manner that they can understand (topic and law)?
   b. If this is difficult, what tools have been used to address complexity?
      i. Examples
      ii. Definitions or interpretation
5. Testing the effectiveness of presentation
   a. Is the layout simple?
   b. Does the text refer the user to relevant provisions, perhaps via:
      i. Hyperlinks
      ii. Explanatory notes
6. Testing the effectiveness of monitoring
   a. How often?
   b. With which results?[50]

The rationale behind Xanthaki's holistic effectiveness lies with Sir Stephen Laws's holistic depiction of effectiveness as a concept that brings together policy, law, and drafting.[51] The test also conforms with Zamboni's theory of three pillars of effectiveness, ideal, situation, results,[52] in that it encompasses policy ideals, socio-cultural-economic-political-legal parameters of the legislative environment, and internal and external results (change in the law and in behaviour).

---

50 See H Xanthaki, 'An Enlightened Approach to Legislative Scrutiny: Focusing on Effectiveness' (2018) *European Journal of Risk Regulation* 431–434, 438–439.

51 Sir S Laws, 'Legislation and Politics' in D Feldman, *Law in Politics, Politics and Law* (Hart Publishers, Oxford, 2013), 90.

52 M Zamboni above n 47, 6–7.

When applied to transposition in specific, Xanthaki's effectiveness test requires an analysis of the EU context by answering the sequence of the following questions:

1. Which are the desired regulatory results of the EU?
2. How will they be measured by the EU?
3. Within how long are they to be achieved by the EU?
4. What is the legal mischief at the EU level, and how is it connected to the desired regulatory goals?
5. How is the new EU legislation expected to address the mischief at the EU level?
6. Does the language of each EU provision communicate its message clearly?
7. If this is not the case, what tools are available to address complexity?
   i. The Introductory report (often in the form of a White or Green Paper) that accompanies the draft proposal in expert groups and details the regulatory rationale behind policy choices;
   ii. definitions in the EU text;[53]
   iii. any EU transposition guidelines;
   iv. any explanatory documents;
   v. any Transposition and Implementation plan (which is prepared in the initial stages of the Commission's proposal and identifies weaknesses and challenges for MS); and
   vi. any meeting-based pre-transposition tools (networks, expert groups, package meetings,[54] scoreboards etc).

Once this exercise has been completed and national drafters have analysed the EU text, analysing the proposal for its transposition within the Member State can begin by answering the following questions in sequence:

1. Which are the desired regulatory results for the Member State? These do not always coincide with the EU's and this diversity may lead to transposition problems.[55]

---

[53] Terms can have a different meaning in EU law. See e.g., Case 283/81, *CILFIT* [1982] ECR 3415, para. 19; and the interpretation of terms differ between the EU officials and MS officials: see Court of Auditors, above n 46, 15.

[54] These were scored as the most effective transposition aids by Member State, along with explanatory documents with correlation tables: see Court of Auditors, 'above n 46, 44; also see 'Framework Agreement on relations between the European Parliament and the European Commission', OJ L304.

[55] See Court of Auditors, ibid., 20.

2. Do they coincide with those of the EU or must they be fine-tuned to apply to the concrete national regulatory environment of the Member State?
3. How can they be measured by the MS, in order to provide both the data needed for the purposes of evidencing EU regulatory success and Member State success?
4. Within what timeframe are they to be achieved at the EU level, as normally this will be the time set for the Member State also?
5. Can the selected enforcement mechanisms produce the desired regulatory results within the set time at the level of the Member State?
6. Can the text be implemented without stumbling on socio-legal hurdles within the Member State or in connection to other EU nationals within the Member State?
7. What is the legal mischief in the Member State and how is it connected to the desired regulatory goals of the Member State?
8. Can this be addressed by non-legislative means that secure uniform application in the Member State? If so, checking the national position with the Commission can prevent unnecessary drafting of national measures.
9. How is the proposed national legislation expected to address the mischief?
10. Which are the main groups of possible users of the national text?
11. What level of awareness of the topic do they have?
12. What is their level of legal awareness?
13. What questions does each group ask?
14. Does the current structure provide accessible answers the specific questions of each of the user groups?
15. Does the current structure facilitate the unhindered identification of the relevant answers?
16. Does the language of each provision communicate its message to each of the intended user groups in a manner that they can understand (topic and law)?
17. If this is difficult, what tools have been used to address complexity?
    a. Examples
    b. Definitions or interpretation
18. Is the layout simple?
19. Does the text refer the user to relevant provisions, perhaps via:
    a. Hyperlinks
    b. Explanatory notes
    c. When will the new national text require monitoring, and with which results?

Conducting this lengthy exercise may seem superfluous at a time when drafting resources are very limited and time is particularly precious for national drafters. But this is the architectural foundation of an effective national implementing text, which contributes greatly to EU effectiveness also. Perhaps even more importantly, this exercise would contribute to a closure of the current gap between legislative intent and legislative effect.[56] By securing an in-principle agreement to the Member State's legislative plans at this early stage of drafting, national drafters can remain content that their legislative plan meets the requirements of the Commission and the EU's regulatory package. Moreover, any problems can be identified early and addressed without much disruption or without the inevitable aggression of the prospect of infringement proceedings at a much later stage.

But, of course, this is one of the many challenges of transposition with reference to Thornton's Stage 2.

C. ADDRESSING THE CHALLENGES OF TRANSPOSITION (THORNTON'S STAGE 2)

Indeed one of the main challenges of transposition is that, admittedly as is the case with national legislation, national drafters are in the dark as to whether they are meeting EU requirements or not. The current methodology of co-legislating for the EU prevents extensive EU intervention to national drafting strategy and transposition practice. Admirable as the rationale of this non-intervention was in the distant past when it was established, namely, to show trust and respect to national policy and legal structures, the current focus on regulatory success under Better Regulation[57] requires a revisit of this practice. Since national drafters are EU co-legislators, this trust and respect to national drafting offices is now a given. Moreover, the new acknowledgement of their role as co-legislators invites, some would say requires, continuous communication amongst what is now fast becoming a joint drafting team with EU and national officers. Within that extended drafting team, early communication on the appropriateness of national legislative plans in Stage 2 of the transposition drafting process enhances greatly both the effectiveness of the national text (by linking the EU's legislative intent to the Member State's

---

[56] E R Beerworth, 'The Evaluation of Legislation' in R Tomasic (ed), *Legislation and Society in Australia* (Allen and Unwin, 1980) 66, 68.

[57] Increasing transposition rates has been a priority for the Commission since 2009: see Commission Communication, 'A Europe of results – Applying Community Law', 2009, 9; European Commission, 'Monitoring the application of European Union law', 2016 Annual Report, COM(2017) 370 final, 28; European Commission, 'Monitoring the application of European Union law: 2015 Annual Report', COM(2016) 463 final, 27; '29th Annual Report on monitoring the application of EU Law' (2011), COM (2012) 714, 7; '30th Annual Report on Monitoring the Application of EU Law (2012)', COM(2013) 726 final, 22.10.2013, 7; Commission 'Monitoring the application of European Union law: 2015 Annual Report', COM(2016) 463 final, 27.

transposition effect), but also the effectiveness of the EU text (which in turn contributes to the efficacy of the EU regulatory strategy in this field[58]). And Member States express thirst for more contact during the transposition phase.[59]

This transposition challenge would greatly benefit from a submission of the Member State's legislative plan to the Commission for comments, in principle.[60] Although this seems to be an additional level of bureaucracy that may cause further transposition delays, it does benefit the process in balance, as it will prevent the resource-heavy and politically unpleasant prospect of infringement proceedings post transposition. That would be in line with the principle of loyal cooperation to assist Member States to carry out their tasks, under Article 4(3) TEU. Moreover, transposition delays may actually be prevented by the new obligation of national authorities to submit a legislative plan quite some time before the expiry of the transposition deadline. In fact, in view of the frequent rush of Member State to legislate just before the expiry of the transposition deadline, the submission of a legislative plan could gently nudge national drafters to start their transposition task much earlier. Finally, the transposition legislative plan could divert Member States from simply copy/pasting the text of EU legislation by inviting them to assess the text creatively, and to address the intricacies of effectiveness within their own legislative environment much more completely. A win-win situation all round.

But of course, this is not the only transposition challenge. Perhaps the greatest one for Stage 2 is the detachment of EU legislative texts from transposition. Although awareness of the need for transposition has been repeated by the EU in recent Better Regulation policy documents, legislative texts themselves have little to show by way of change. And, although there is now increasingly frequent availability of transposition guidelines in separate Commission documents, their content as regulatory, rather than technical drafting documents, is not focused on the transposition drafting task. After all, transposition guidelines documents appear to be missing a set, drafting focused methodology. To introduce that, for the facilitation and coordination of transposition, focus must be placed on the provision of the questions required by the first part of Stage 2 of the transposition drafting process.

EU legislative texts and their accompanying transposition guides, where available, need to provide authentic answers to the seven questions of

---

58 See European Parliament, 'Monitoring the implementation of EU law: tools and challenges', 2017, 5.

59 See Court of Auditors, above n 46, 47.

60 Currently a transposition report can be requested by the MS post-facto: see 'Joint Political Declaration of 28 September 2011 between the Commission and the Member States', OJ 2011/C 369/02; and Joint Political Declaration of 27 October 2011 between the European Parliament, the Council and the Commission, OJ 2011/C 369/03.

Xanthaki's test. One, which are the desired regulatory results of the EU. These must be introduced in a list of concrete, achievable, and measurable regulatory results, against which the effectiveness of the EU text is to be assessed. This can link pre-legislative scrutiny to legislation and to post-legislative scrutiny. Two, how will the desired regulatory results be measured by the EU? A list of measurable empirical data that will be used by the EU to assess effectiveness on a post-legislative scrutiny exercise can direct national drafters to the collection of that data at the national level, thus enhancing the quality of evidence-based Better Regulation. Moreover, national drafters can replicate the type of data used by the EU with data used for the assessment of effectiveness of the transposition measure at the national level. Three, how long is the regulatory deadline, and therefore within what period of time are results expected? Four, what is the mischief at the EU level? This type of analysis of EU law and why it does not currently cover the mischief in question is already found in introductory texts of draft EU texts. Five, how can the new EU legislation expected to address the mischief at the EU level? Drawing the link between the legislative solution and the current gap in EU legislation can play a dual role. In showcasing the rationale behind the EU text, it can persuade national drafters of the soundness of the EU strategy, thus enticing them to participate in the co-legislative effort and guiding them to a similar solution at the national level, using the EU text as a model law, where appropriate. Six, does the language of each EU provision communicate its message clearly? Seven, if not, how can national drafters achieve a sound national terminology. Although this seems to be a task for national drafters, often Commission fonctionnaires who have followed the text through negotiations can shed light into the vagueness of EU terms used in the text.[61] These often come as a result of an impasse in negotiations resulting from diversities and clashes of terminology or concepts in national legal systems. Offering national drafters a menu of possible choices can guide them to the one that is more familiar to them.

And this leads to a final remark on the challenges of Stage 2. In view of the frequency of such diversities and even conflicting positions in the national legal orders of 27 Member States, effectiveness of transposition leads the Commission to revisit the way in which such clashes resolve in EU texts. The current position of introducing a vague term that can encompass most national positions and allow the text to proceed further in the EU legislative process may facilitate progression to the next stage of passing but will inevitably come back to haunt effectiveness via incomplete or even erroneous transposition by

[61] Complexity of the *acquis* and lack of clarity of EU texts are implicated as the main factors behind problems of non-implementation both by Member States and by EU officials: see Court of Auditors, above n 46, 15.

the co-legislators. One wonders whether it now makes regulatory sense to note the richness of national terms that fall within the scope of the EU's legislative intent, thus exposing this danger area or national sensitivity, alerting national drafters to the issue, and consequently inviting them to either remain with the existing national term and concept or to adhere to the EU's complete legislative intent by introducing the EU generic term with a definition that draws the distinction between the two. The latter will facilitate complete transposition but, perhaps equally importantly, complete implementation of the transposing text.

CONCLUSIONS

Stage 2 of the drafting process reveals the inherent complexities of legislating for transposition both as a drafting task per se but also as a process within the EU context. The analysis of the transposition task hovers over two levels of regulation, and consequently legislation, with diverse concrete regulatory aims, diverse legislative means for the effective achievement of these diverse aims, and very little pre-emptive interaction between the EU and Member States' drafting teams.

The analysis of the transposition task can be adequately achieved if national transposition drafters apply Xanthaki's effectiveness test. The test requires separate and subsequent analysis of the EU and national context. For the former, drafters must be confident of their appreciation of the desired regulatory results of the EU, their measurement by the EU, the period of time for their achievement by the EU, the mischief at the EU level and its link with the desired regulatory goals, and any issues of linguistic expression in the EU text. Having completed the first part of Xanthaki's effectiveness test, transposition drafters move to appreciate the national desired regulatory results and their link with those of the EU, their effectiveness criteria, the time period within which they are to be achieved, the adequacy of any enforcement mechanisms, any socio-legal hurdles, the legal mischief in the MS and its link to the desired regulatory goals of the MS, the choice of the appropriate regulatory tool for the task, the necessity and adequacy of legislative approaches, the identification of national user groups, and linguistic and structural choices supporting their unhindered access to the national transposition measures.

The compilation of a legislative plan or report addressing these difficult questions may seem gratuitous, especially if the usual haste for transposition is taken into account. However, literature and experience has shown that such a plan can save national drafters from future problems. For the purposes of transposition in specific, the availability of such a document can innovate the legislative approach of the EU to transposition by fostering a pre-emptive rather than punitive approach.

Instead of allowing transposition to take its course in the dark and intervene by means of infringement proceedings when national choice leads to an alleged incomplete or partial implementation of EU law, the EU can reflect the concept of co-legislation and participate, albeit minimally, in the transposition process from as early as Stage 2. Joint exchange of transposition legislative plans with a structured brief answer to the questions introduced by Xanthaki's effectiveness test can aid national drafters to ascertain whether their subjective take on the task and its elements would meet the EU's in-principle agreement. Of course, this cannot be a legalistic or formalistic exercise. Within a setting of cooperation joint drafting teams with drafters from the EU and the Member States can discuss the transposition drafters' understanding of the EU context, and correct it, where necessary. On that basis, national drafters can offer their EU colleagues a brief description of their intended legislative approaches with a justification for any diversity identified in their report. Within this forum, resolution of any misunderstandings and misconceptions can serve both parties incredibly well. For the national drafters, this exercise can offer some applied guidance as to their transposition plans. For the EU drafters, this exercise can serve a dual aim. First, it can assist them to pre-empt any issues of incorrect transposition and nip them in the bud without the animosity and cost of an infringement case before the CJEU. Second, it can serve as a feedback exercise by identifying the areas of vagueness or ambiguity in the EU text, thus feeding into joint drafting sessions with other Member States also. These can be further addressed in transposition guidance documents, thus addressing textual weaknesses before transposition and application.

And this leads to a final point for EU drafters. Transposition guidance documents are currently drafted without a concrete methodology. If Xanthaki's effectiveness test is used as a methodology and structure for transposition tools, then national transposition drafters would have, at least in principle, the data that they require in order to draft their national transposition legislative plans. They would know which are the concrete desired regulatory results of the EU, how these will be measured empirically, the link between the new EU legislation and the mischief at EU level, and any issues of linguistic expression or terminology.

From the point of view of EU citizens and sustainable integration, the analysis of Stage 2 shows the seeds for their participation in the legislative process. National drafters require an understanding of the concrete user groups of the transposition text in order to begin designing their unhindered communication with them via the proposed transposition text. This point will be explored further in the next chapter, on the design of the law.

4. Designing the transposition law

A. DESIGN AND STRUCTURE IN LEGISLATIVE LITERATURE[1]

Having understood the proposal in Stage 1, having analysed the proposal in Stage 2, drafters embark on the creative side of drafting. Stage 3 involves the design of the law. It is fair to say that most of Thornton's drafting stages have fluid boundaries, and that drafting requires constant revisiting and retuning of each stage as the work progresses. This is mostly relevant to Stage 3, where the draft seems to be on the move between conceptual design and textual design.

In the conceptual design, the drafter formulates an initial vision of the drafting task ahead, and, based on the understanding of the drafting instructions and their translation to legislative expression via law reform, begins to weed out irrelevant aspects of the topic and to glue down relevant ones. The conceptual design involves a decision on the concepts that will form part of the text, and their prioritisation in a sequence that enhances effectiveness. The question is, what are the criteria for setting the sequence of concepts in a draft?

Traditionally, drafters were asked to produce a draft with a 'logical'[2] sequence of provisions that 'facilitates communication of the content at the same time as it achieves the objects of the instructions'.[3] Thus, the concept of structure in traditional legislative drafting is text-focused: which concept logically goes first, and which follows. For example, Lord Thing's Five Rules of Drafting[4] offer precedence to provisions declaring the law versus provisions relating to the administration of the law; to simpler versus the more complex proposition; and to principal versus subordinate provisions. Exceptional, tem-

---

[1] For the original version of this topic, on which this analysis is based, see H Xanthaki, 'The Limits of Legislation as a Product' Hukim (2018) 11 *The Israeli Journal on Legislation* 153–172.

[2] See 2016 Interinstitutional Guide, http://publications.europa.eu/code/en/en-000100.htm.

[3] See H Xanthaki, *Thornton's Legislative Drafting* (5th edn, Bloomsbury, London, 2013), 138ss.

[4] See Lord Thring, *Practical Legislation, The Composition and Language of Acts of Parliament and Business Documents* (London, 1902), 38; also see V C R A C Crabbe, *Legislative Drafting* (Oxford, Cavendish Publishing, 1998), 148–150.

porary, and provisions relating to the repeal of Acts, and procedure and matters of detail should be set apart. The rules are familiar to most drafting styles in Europe and beyond.

However, modern drafting recognises the relativity of the concept of rational or logical sequencing. What is logical or expected for one user is not so for the next. The relativity of user accessibility has, until recently, remained a rather theoretical discussion due to the lack of empirical data on the profile of users of legislation, and the nature of answers that each user expected to find in legislation. This crucial lack of user profiling data has been overcome, to a great extent, by the 2013 Good Law initiative led by the UK's National Archives in cooperation with the UK's Office of Parliamentary Counsel, the Sir William Dale Centre for Legislative Studies and the University of Cambridge.[5] The project revealed at least three categories of people constitute the audience of legislation, and these are lay persons reading the legislation to make it work for them,[6] sophisticated non-lawyers using the law in the process of their professional activities, and lawyers and judges. In more detail in the UK there are three categories of users of legislation:

a. Non-lawyers who need to use legislation for work, such as law enforcers, human resources professionals, or local council officials; the 'Mark Green' of the survey represents about 60 per cent of users of legislation;
b. Lay persons who seek answers to questions related to their personal or familial situation; 'Heather Cole' represents about 20 per cent of users of legislation; and
c. Lawyers, judges, and senior law librarians; the 'Jane Booker' persona represent about 20 per cent of users of legislation.[7]

The significance of the survey for plain language and good legislation cannot be understated. The survey provides, for the first time in European legislative practice, empirical evidence from a huge sample of the 2,000,000 visitors of

---

5 See https://www.gov.uk/good-law accessed 13 December 2023.

6 See J J E Gracia, A *Theory of Textuality: The Logic and Epistemology* (Albany, State University of New York Press, 1995), 159–163, and 164–165; also see G L Pi and V Schmolka, 'A Report on Results of Usability Testing Research on Plain Language Draft Sections of the Employment Insurance Act: A Report to Department of Justice Canada and Human Resources Development Canada' (unpublished, August 2000); and V Schmolka, 'Consumer Fireworks Regulations: Usability Testing, TR1995-2e (Department of Justice Canada, unpublished, 1995).

7 See A Bertlin, 'What Works Best for the Reader? A Study on Drafting and Presenting Legislation' (2014) *The Loophole*, https://assets.publishing.service.gov.uk/government/uploads/system/uploads/attachment_data/file/326937/Loophole_-_2014-2__2014-05-09_-What_works_best_for_the_reader.pdf accessed 13 December 2023, 27–28.

www.legislation.gov.uk per month. The survey, whose data relate to users of electronic versions of the free government database of legislation only, destroys the myth that legislation is for legal professionals alone. In fact, legal professionals are very much in the minority of users, although their precise percentage may well be affected by their tendency to use subscription databases rather than the government database, which is not annotated and often not updated. Whatever the exact percentages of each category are, there is significant empirical evidence that legislation in at least one European country speaks to three distinct groups of users, whose legal awareness varies from none, to some, to much.

How is structure affected by this revolutionary revelation? Modern drafters attempting to communicate with all users of legislation could be led to introducing three versions of the same legislative text, structured and expressed for the purposes of communicating with Group 1 or Group 2 or Group 3. But this would be a recipe for disaster, on moral, ethical, constitutional, practical grounds. There are evident rule of law issues, issues of interpretation between versions, identifying which version corresponds to each user, using that version as opposed to the one selected by the user, who subjects each user to their corresponding persona, ethical and moral consequences of the application of a diverse version for each user. And the parallel existence of three different texts could be counter-productive: users currently choose to use the complex but official legislative text over any of the many interpretation aids offered by government. If the plethora of attractive user-friendly manuals and policy documents are shunned in favour of legislative texts, what makes it probable that users will go to the simple Heather Cole text as opposed to the legal Jane Booker one that reflects users' perception of legislation? And so remaining with a single text is really the only option. But this is exactly what has imprisoned legislative drafters in the struggle for simplicity within legislative texts.

It is now possible to see that each user group has its individual requirements for legislative information that are distinct from those of the other user groups. Identifying the needs for legislative information for each user group at a provision, rather than text, level would allow drafters to imitate oral communication, and pitch the legislative text to specific abilities and requirements. Drafters of legislative texts can now begin to think what regulatory or legal message is relevant to each group, and structure the text accordingly. This formulates the basis of the layered approach to structure,[8] which promotes the division

---

[8] See H Xanthaki, *Drafting Legislation: Art and Technology of Rules for Regulation* (Hart Publishers, Oxford, 2014), 77–79. It must be noted that the term, and to a certain extent, the concept is attributed to John Witing, Tax Director at the Tax Simplification Office. I am very grateful to John for his inspiration and the generosity with which he has shared it with me.

of legislation into three parts, corresponding to each of the three profiles of legislative users. Part 1 can speak to lay persons: the content is limited to the main regulatory messages, thus conveying the essence of law reform attempted by the legislation, focusing gravely on the information that lay persons need in order to become aware of a new regulation, to comply with new obligations, or to enjoy new rights. Part 2 can speak to non-legally trained professionals who use the legislation in the course of their employment. Here one can see scope for further detail in the regulatory messages introduced, and for language that is balanced [technical, yet approachable to the professionals in question]. Part 3 of the legislation can then deal with issues of legislative interpretation, issues of procedure, and issues of application, in a language that is complex but not quite legalese, as there is nothing to prevent all groups from reading all parts.

The layered approach is revolutionary, as it shifts the criterion for legislative structure from the content and nature of provisions to the profile of the users. It switches on a user-centred structure, thus promoting both a link between policy and its effecting legislative text but also enhancing and personalising the channel of communication between drafters and users. And it applies and reflects the modern doctrine of contextualism in language and philosophy. But it cannot be viewed as a complete departure from tradition, as it continues to apply Lord Thring's five rules. By requiring that Part 1 includes the primary regulatory message, it promotes Lord Thring's rules that give precedence to the simpler proposition. And by structuring legislation into three parts, the layered approach complies with the other Thring rules that require division of provisions declaring the law [in Part 1 or 2] with provisions administrating the law [in Part 2 or 3 accordingly]; that principal provisions should be separated from subordinate [in Parts 1 and 2]; that exceptional, temporary, and provisions relating to the repeal of Acts should be separated from the other enactments, and placed by themselves under separate headings [in Part 3]; and that procedure and matters of detail should be set apart by themselves [either in Part 3 of the layered approach, or in a Schedule].

The layered approach seems to be one of the promising initiatives in the field of legislation. But there are three points that need to be clarified. First, the layered approach may, but will not necessarily, lead to a partial, fragmented, or incomplete legislative communication to Heather Cole. There is no doubt that an erroneous application of the approach could result in that. But the placement of the main messages in Part 1 per se must be seen as an added bonus to lay users compared with the current state of affairs: in the layered approach the now frequently elusive main regulatory message will be easily identified, will be brought forward in a pronounced place at the beginning of the legislative text, and will be expressed in a language that is accessible to lay users. Compared to the current state of affairs, where the main message is communicated somewhere within the legislative text and is expressed in the layered approach's Part 2 or 3 language, this is certainly an improvement. And of course, there is nothing preventing Heather Cole from reading the rest of the text: in fact, an inviting Part 1 can only encourage Heather Cole to keep reading, whilst offering her a clear context within which her understanding of complex and detailed messages can only be enhanced.

Second, although Part 1 carrying the main regulatory message is distinctly different from Parts 2 and 3, it may be unclear what really distinguishes between Part 2 data and Part 3 data: both Mark Green and Jane Booker are able to handle complexity and technicality of legislative data. However, they do not both require the same data, as demonstrated by their motives when using www.legislation.gov.uk: Mark Green is interested in answers that allow him to perform his professional but non-legal duties, whereas Jane Booker seeks legal information. As a result, what Mark Green needs is a clear understanding of substantive and procedural requirements imposed by the legislation, whereas Jane Booker seeks deeper statutory interpretation often coupled with a holistic view of the statute book. As a result, Part 2 of the layered approach involves answers to questions such as who must do what by when, and what happens if they do not. Part 3 will delve deeper into intricate distinctions and possible exceptions that relate to statutory interpretation and interconnections between legislative texts within the statute book. There are two caveats here. One, Mark Green must still read the text as a whole. And Part 3 cannot be viewed as a mere shell of definitions, repeals, and consequential amendments: this would deprive the readers from at least part of the benefits of the layered approach.

Third, it would be inappropriate to consider that the simplification serviced by the layered approach would result in an abolition of the need for explanatory materials for legislation. In fact, as the layered approach results in an inherent fragmentation of data, it renders the use of explanatory materials and notes reinstating the fluidity of information and the cross-fertilisation between parts an ever so crucial requirement. The new style of explanatory notes[9] introduced by Good Law and showcased in the Armed Forces (Service Complaints and Financial Assistance) Bill [HL] Explanatory Notes[10] enhances the layered approach by introducing a clear table of contents that is thematic rather than provision based, with information on the policy and legal context of the Act,

---

[9] See Office of Parliamentary Counsel, 'Explanatory Notes Pilot: Response to Consultation', April 2015, https:// assets .publishing .service .gov .uk/ media/ 5a7ff e9840f0b62 302690e0b/ explanatory _notes _response _to _consultation _on _pilot .pdf accessed 13 December 2023.

[10] See https://publications.parliament.uk/pa/; and https://assets.publishing.service .gov.uk/media/5a7e2e25ed915d74e6224a09/new-format-explanatory-notes.pdf accessed 13 December 2023.

and with simple narratives on the main regulatory messages for all three user groups.[11]

B. DESIGN AND STRUCTURE IN TRANSPOSITION

EU Member States have their own traditions in the structure of national implementing legislation.[12] There is little scope in interfering with this, or diverting from it, even in exclusive application for the purposes of transposition. Legislative effectiveness requires accessibility of the regulatory message by the legislative users. Predictability of the location where the relevant data is commonly found in national legislative texts promotes easy access for users, and therefore legislative effectiveness. Moving to a different structure may be counter-productive, as it could affect the level of predictability for users. Let us explore the principles for the design of transposition texts.[13]

In this task, national drafters are guided by the principles of subsidiarity, proportionality, adequacy, synergy, and adaptability.[14] The application of these principles does not signify a qualification of the principle of autonomy for national authorities that are still of course entitled to make their own choice in the selection of the transposition means of their choice.[15] However, the choice of national authorities[16] is by no means beyond the scrutiny of EU authorities,

---

[11] See http://www.publications.parliament.uk/pa/bills/lbill/2014-2015/0003/en/15003en.htm.

[12] For an analysis of the national law-making traditions of the Member States, see U Karpen and H Xanthaki, *Legislation in Europe: A Handbook for Scholars and Practitioners* (Hart Publishers, Oxford, 2017); also see U Karpen and H Xanthaki, *Legislation in Europe: A Country by Country Handbook for Scholars and Practitioners* (Hart Publishers, Oxford, 2020).

[13] This analysis is heavily based on H Xanthaki, 'Technical Considerations in Harmonization and Approximation: Legislative Drafting Techniques for Full Transposition' in M Andenas (ed), *Theory and Practice of Harmonisation* (Edward Elgar Publishing, 2012), 536–550; also see H Xanthaki, 'Transposition Techniques' in C Stefanou and H Xanthaki, *Drafting for EU Approximation* (2005, UK Department for International Development -IALS- Ministry of Justice of Ukraine, Kiev), 9–10; and M Kaeding, 'In Search of Better Quality of EU Regulations for Prompt Transposition: The Brussels Perspective' (2008) *European Law Journal* 583.

[14] For a full analysis of this point, see H Xanthaki, 'Transposition of EC Law for EU Approximation and Accession: The Role of National Authorities' (2006) 4 *European Journal of Law Reform*, 89, at 97–100.

[15] In fact, the application of these principles to non-Member States is questioned by some authors: see W-H Roth, 'Transposing "Pointillist" EC Guidelines Into Systematic National Codes–Problems And Consequences' (2002) 6 *European Review of Private Law*, 761.

[16] J A Usher, 'The Reception of General Principles of Community Law in the United Kingdom' (2005) 16 *European Business Law Review*, 489, at 495.

in the form of Commission officials in the pre-accession stage and in the form of the ECJ at the post-accession stage.[17] It must therefore be accepted that the principle of autonomy, as qualified by the equally important principles of subsidiarity, proportionality, adequacy, synergy and adaptability, now allows national drafting authorities to make their preferred selection from the pool of choice offered to them after the application of the relevant principles of EU law. After all, accountability applies to both the EU and MS.

The principle of subsidiarity dictates that the highest level of action is justifiable only when lower levels of legislative action are inefficient for the achievement of the goal.[18] When applied to transposition, subsidiarity encompasses two parallel concepts: legal subsidiarity is an economy of approaches, whereas legislative subsidiarity is an economy of measures. Legal subsidiarity signifies that legislation is utilised as a means of harmonisation with the relevant EU policies, if, and only if, all other possible forms of harmonising regulation are deemed to fail in the production of the required results.[19] Legislative subsidiarity demands that, if a choice for legislative action is made, national authorities select the lightest possible form of national legislation for the purposes of harmonisation.

The application of the principle of subsidiarity to its extreme could lead to a Spartan method of transposition, which carries the inherent danger of ineffective harmonisation. This danger is mitigated by the principle of propor-

---

[17] C-107/97, *Criminal Proceedings against Max Rombi and Arkopharma SA, the party liable at civil law, and Union federale des consommateurs 'Que Choisir?' and Organisation generale des consommateurs (Orgeco), Union departementale 06,* [2000] ECR I-3367, para 65; see also Case 145/88, *Torfaen Borough Council v B&Q plc.* [1989] ECR 3851; *24 Shrewsbury and Atcham BC v B&Q* [1990] 3 CMLR 535; C-20/00 and C-64/00, *Booker Aquaculture v The Scottish Ministers* [2003] ECR I-7411.

[18] European Commission (2005), Report from the Commission 'Better Lawmaking 2004' Pursuant to Article 9 of the Protocol on the Application of the Principles of Subsidiarity and Proportionality (12th report), COM (2005) 98 final and SEC (2005) 364, Brussels, 21 March 2005, at 2; also G Davies, 'Subsidiarity: The Wrong Idea, in the Wrong Place, at the Wrong Time' (2006) 43 *Common Market Law Review* 63, at 67; B Rodger and S Wylie, 'Taking the Community Interest Line: Decentralisation and Subsidiarity in Competition Law Enforcement' (1997) 18 *ECLR* 485; K Lenaerts, 'The Principle of Subsidiarity and the Environment in the European Union: Keeping the Balance of Federalism' (1994) 17 *Fordham International Law Journal* 846; N Farnsworth, 'Subsidiarity – A Conventional Industry Defence: Is the Directive on Environmental Liability with Regard to Prevention and Remedying of Environmental Damage Justified under the Subsidiarity Principle?' (2004) 13 *European Environmental Law Review* 176.

[19] J O'Keeffe, 'Making A Silk Purse Out of a Sow's Ear' (2006) *Law Society's Gazette* 14.

tionality. As the choice of regulatory instrument, and, if necessary, the choice of legislative instrument is made, one has to take account of the additional consideration of balancing the aim to be achieved with the choice made. In its positive sense, proportionality within this context requires selection of the form of harmonisation that can achieve the required standard. In its negative sense, and this is where the extreme application of subsidiarity is averted, proportionality rejects all forms of harmonisation that are too light for the achievement of the standards required.[20] Legislative proportionality supplements legislative subsidiarity[21] and demands that the choice of form of the national implementing measure reflects its purpose.[22]

Proportionality in its negative sense as the rejection of ineffective measures for harmonisation is also expressed as the principle of adequacy. Adequacy balances subsidiarity in that it prevents harmonisation choices that are too light for the purposes of transposition. Adequacy accentuates proportionality by ensuring that policy-makers and drafters strike an adequate proportionate balance between the need to harmonise and the choice made: over-regulation and under-regulation are therefore averted. Legal adequacy demands that the chosen means of regulation is capable of achieving the effect pursued. Legislative adequacy secures that the chosen form of legislation is capable of achieving the effect pursued. Although adequacy is a value to aspire to in the legislative process, true adequacy in legislative drafting can only be secured post hoc through a prospective evaluation of the proposed law,[23] namely

---

[20] J A Usher, 'The Reception of General Principles of Community Law in the United Kingdom' (2005) 16 *EBLR* 489, at 506; Case 11/70, *Internationale Handelsgesellschaft*, [1970] ECR 1125, at 1148; Report from the Commission 'Better Lawmaking 2004', above n 18 at 2; The Law Society (2005) 'EU Better Law-Making Charter, Better Law-Making Programme' 5.

[21] J Snell, 'True Proportionality' (2000) 11 *European Business Law Review* 50.

[22] G De Burca, 'The Principle of Proportionality and its Application in EC Law' (1993) 13 *YEL* 105; J Jans, 'Proportionality Revisited' (2000) 27 *LIEI* 239.

[23] Where the legislature is obliged to assess the future effects of rules to be adopted and those effects cannot be accurately foreseen, its assessment is open to criticism only if it appears manifestly incorrect in the light of the information available to it at the time of the adoption of the rules in question: Case C-150/94, *United Kingdom v Council* [1998] ECR I-7235, para 49; Case T-54/99, *max.mobil Telekommunikation Service GmbH v Commission of the European Communities* [2002] ECR II-313, para 84.

through a cost benefit analysis and a retrospective evaluation[24] in the form of monitoring of passed laws.[25]

The principle of synergy promotes a holistic approach to the legal system.[26] Legal synergy promotes coherence and interrelated functioning of diverse fields of law within the national legal system of the aspiring Member State. Legislative synergy promotes a holistic approach of the law on a concrete social phenomenon, thus ensuring that the new instrument falls smoothly into place upon its entry into force and that it combines its forces for the achievement of the aim of legislation on the social phenomenon in question. The role of synergy in achieving effective harmonisation is often underestimated: synergy can prima facie be seen as a quality that benefits exclusively the implementing national system. However, effective harmonisation cannot be achieved without effective national implementing legislation: it is therefore crucial to note that synergy is a quality that benefits the national legal system directly and harmonisation indirectly.

The principle of adaptability takes into account the practicalities of the national legislative processes. Legislative practice often requires flexibility in the choice of the appropriate instrument: parliamentary time is valuable[27] and the selection of form may be based on the lighter procedural requirements of a form.[28] When combined with subsidiarity and proportionality, adaptability can reach dangerous extremes of under-regulation or under-authorised regulation produced without resort to parliamentary legitimatisation. An example of this could be the Irish approach to transposition which is commonly left to delegated legislation with the pretext of urgency.[29] However, when delimited by

---

[24] D Kaufmann, A Kraay and M Mastruzzi, 'Governance Matters VI: Aggregate and Individual Governance Indicators 1996–2006' (2007), World Bank Policy Research Working Paper No. 4280; Centre for European Studies Bradford University (2004) 'Final Report on Indicators of Regulatory Quality', report for DG Enterprise, European Commission.

[25] See Law Society, above, n 20 at 8; also, H Schaeffer, 'Evaluation and Assessment of Legal Effects Procedures: Towards a More Rational and Responsible Lawmaking Process' (2001) 22 *Statute Law Review*, 132.

[26] See Law Society, ibid., at 15.

[27] G Ciavarini Azzi, 'The Slow March of European Legislation: The Implementation of Directives' in K Neuenreither and A Wiener (eds), *European Integration after Amsterdam: Institutional Dynamics and Prospects for Democracy* (Oxford University Press, 2000).

[28] Factors include the lourdeur of parliamentary procedures and the lack of parliamentary time: J Usher, 'The Legal Framework for Implementation in the United Kingdom' in T Daintith (ed), *Implementing EC Law in the United Kingdom: Structures for Indirect Rule* (Wiley, 1995) 101.

[29] K Mooney, 'The Work of the Office of Parliamentary Counsel to the Government in Ireland' (2001) 22 *Statute Law Society* 133, at 138; also, The Supreme Court 1993

adequacy and synergy, adaptability can serve national governments to achieve results legitimately but without a waste of resources. Adaptability allows for experimental legislation or legislation in stages.

However, EU law is not the only factor that contributes to choices made for the purposes of achieving effective harmonisation. The coin of harmonisation has two sides, the EU and the national side. And so, the decision whether the national legal order can indeed borrow the EU legislative solution as a means of achieving harmonisation is by no means to be taken for granted.[30] After all, effective harmonisation can only be achieved if the national legal order can utilise the proposed solution and absorb it in the national legal order seamlessly and painlessly. But is this truly possible? Can national legal orders really borrow from the EU, and, if so, on what basis?[31]

Despite the commonality of the transplant practice,[32] national legislators cannot be expected to simply adopt the EU's legislative solution without falsifying or verifying the relationship between the policy choice under consideration and the results of the application of that policy choice.[33] For the Watsonists amongst us, borrowing is never a real issue, as one can borrow practically anything[34] from anywhere.[35] But the followers of Legrand,[36] Kahn

---

No. 127 *John Meagher v The Minister for Agriculture and Food, Ireland and the Attorney General*, 18 November 1993 [Judgment of the Court delivered pursuant to the provisions of Article 34.4.5° by Finlay CJ].

[30] For an analysis of the 'good to fit approach' see M Haverland, 'National Adaptation to European Integration: The Importance of Institutional Veto Points' (2000) 20 *Journal of Public Policy*, 83.

[31] H Xanthaki, 'On Transferability of Legislative Solutions: The Functionality Test' in C Stefanou and H Xanthaki (eds), Drafting Legislation: A Modern Approach – in Memoriam of Sir William Dale (Ashgate-Dartmouth, 2008), 1.

[32] A Watson, *Legal Origins and Legal Change* (Hambledon Press, 1991) at 73; also, J Fedtke, 'Legal Tranplants' in J Smits (ed), *Elgar Encyclopedia of Comparative Law*, (Edward Elgar, 2006), 434.

[33] J H M Van Erp, 'The Use of Comparative Law in the Legislative Process' *Netherlands Reports to the 15th International Congress of Comparative Law*, E. H. Hondius (ed), (Bristol, 1998) 36.

[34] A Watson, 'Legal Transplants and Law Reform' (1976) 92 *LQR*, 79, at 80; also, A Watson, *Legal Transplants: An Approach to Comparative Law*, (Scottish Academic Press, 1974); A Watson, 'Legal Transplants and European Private Law', Ius Commune Lectures on European Private Law, no 2.

[35] E Öcürü, 'Critical Comparative Law: Considering Paradoxes for Legal Systems in Transition' (1999) 59 *Nederlandse Vereniging voor Rechtsvergelijking*; E Öcürü, 'Law as Transposition' (2002) 51 *ICLQ*, 205, at 206.

[36] P Legrand, 'The Impossibility of Legal Transplants' (1997) *Maastricht Journal of European and Comparative Law*, 111.

Freund[37] and the Seidmans[38] object rather radically to the utility of borrowing altogether, whether Schlesinger concludes that the future belongs to integrative comparative law and puts forward the EU's ius commune as an example of integration of similar and different legal systems.[39] Jhering, and Zweigert and Kötz[40] view the question of comparability through the relative prism of functionality,[41] namely of usefulness and need.[42]

It is the theory of functionality that seems to serve borrowing legislative solutions from the EU with an aim to harmonise. As the evident current legal globalisation[43] required global, or at least regional transnational solutions, integrative transnational approaches seem to be no longer a luxury but a realistic response. Does it really matter where these responses are borrowed from? Not in principle. However, a qualifier to Watson's liberal approach can be introduced via Zweigert and Kötz's functionality theory. What matters when deciding if the national legal order can borrow from the EU is not the similarity of their characteristics, but the functionality of the proposal at the national level. If the policy, concept or legislation of the EU can serve the receiving national system well, then the origin of the transplant is irrelevant to its success.[44]

This line of analysis can be used to justify the seemingly unfair demand upon national governments to implement the same policy and legislative choices irrespective of the nature of legal system, its stage of development, and its national intricacies.[45] For the purposes of this analysis, however, it simply

---

[37] O Kahn-Freund, 'On Uses and Misuses of Comparative Law' (1974) 37 *Mod. L. Rev.* 1, at 7.

[38] A Seidman and R Seidman, State and Law in the Developing Process: Problem Solving and Institutional Change in the Developing World (Macmillan Publishers, 1994), 44–46.

[39] R B Schlesinger, 'The Common Core of Legal Systems: An Emerging Subject of Comparative Study' in K Nadelmann, A von Mehren and J Hazard (eds), *XXth Century Comparative and Conflicts Law, Legal Essays in Honour of Hessel E. Yntema* (Leiden: A. W. Sijthoff, 1961); R B Schlesinger 'Research on the General Principles of Law Recognised by Civilised Nations' (1957) (51) *AmJIntL*, 734.

[40] K Zweigert and H Kötz, *Einführung in die Rechtsvergleichung*, 3. neubearbeitete Auflage, (J C B Mohr, 1996).

[41] K Zweigert and K Sier, 'Jhering's Influence on the Development of Comparative Legal Method' (1971) 19 *AmJComLaw* 215.

[42] K Jhering, *Geist des römischen Rechts*, (1955) at 8–9.

[43] L A Mistelis, 'Regulatory Aspects: Globalization, Harmonization, Legal Transplants, and Law Reform – Some Fundamental Observations' (2000) 34 *International Lawyer*, 1059.

[44] S Zhuang, 'Legal Transplantation in the People's Republic of China: A Response to Alan Watson' (2006) *European Journal of Law Reform* 215, at 223.

[45] I Maher, 'Community Law in the National Legal Order: A Systems Analysis' (1998) 36 *Journal of Common Market Studies* 237.

proves that the adoption of whatever policy or legislative solution is required by the EU should not, at least not in principle, lead to problems in the national legal orders of the Member State. The functionality of the EU solution is by definition formulated on the basis of common functionalities represented in the negotiations, and subsequent agreement, on EU policies and EU legislative texts. Since the functionality of the EU solution is shared with that of national requirements, harmonisation may not be viewed as a pure transplant exercise with its inherent common dangers for the receiving legal system.

So, how can national drafters design their national legislative solution? Here a number of factors come into play. First, there are normative criteria. Is this area reserved for a special form of legislation? Minor areas are not considered worthy of legislative intervention and are regulated by Administrative acts; Internal circulars; or Lower forms of regulation. Factors in favour of a primary legislation in the formal sense[46] include special needs of democratic legitimacy, serious compromise of fundamental rights, introduction or attribution of important authority and powers, a wide circle of addressees, significant political, economic and social consequences, or controversial political character of the proposed solutions. In contrast to this, factors in favour of subordinate national legislation include a need for flexibility of regulation, the technical nature of the normative mater, or repetitive acts.[47]

National legislatures have choices, within limits.[48] For example, the scope of application of the national measure cannot depart from the EU one, unless expressly provided otherwise within the EU measure.[49] Clarification of ambiguous or vague terms within the EU instruments can make up for the flaws of EU text.[50] Moreover, identification of provisions already present in national law and avoidance of their inclusion in the implementing measure can reduce 'double banking', namely an unnecessary parallel regulation of the same topic

---

[46] H Xanthaki, 'Drafting for Transposition of EU Criminal Laws: the EU Perspective' (2003) *European Current Law Review*, xi.

[47] B Steunenberg and W Voermans, 'The Transposition of EC Directives: A Comparative Study of Instruments, Techniques and Processes in Six EU Member States' (2006), Leiden/ Research and Documentation Centre (WODC) of the Ministry of Justice, http://ssrn.com/abstract=1215542 accessed 13 December 2023.

[48] See R Král, 'On the Choice of Methods of Transposition of EU Directives' (2016) *European Law Review* 220.

[49] See Case 40/69 *Hauptzollamt Hamburg-Oberelbe v Firma Paul G. Bollmann* [1970] ECR 69, 79; also see Case 74/69 *Hauptzollamt Bremen-Freihafen v Waren-Import-Gesellschaft Krohn and Co* [1970] ECR 451, 459-460.

[50] On the flaws of EU texts, and Directives in specific, under the prism of implementation see: M Kaeding, 'In Search of Better Quality of EU Regulations for Prompt Transposition: The Brussels Perspective' (2008) 14 *European Law Journal* 583.

in two legislative sources.[51] And exclusion of over-drafting in the national legislative text can avoid gold-plating, where this is not within the government's intent.[52] Gold-plating increases the burden resulting from EU legislation, and endangers the competitiveness of national actors.[53] Drafters must ensure that: the national implementing measure does not extend the scope, concepts, or substance of the EU legislative text; and all derogations are taken into account. Piecemeal implementation is not good practice. But if the application of the system depends on a combination of a number of provisions adopted at Community, national and regional level, it is permissible for regional laws to incorporate some elements of the Community Regulations involved, for the sake of coherence, and in order to make them comprehensible to those to whom they apply: at the end of the day the imperative is that 'the EU nature of the regulations, their direct applicability, and their direct effect are not disguised or otherwise compromised'.[54]

So, how can national authorities select the appropriate normative level?[55] Three main considerations are taken into account for the application of the principles to the choice of form for the national implementing measures: the extent of legislative intervention required for full transposition; the type of the main EU instrument for transposition; and the object of the national implementing measure.

The extent of legislative intervention required for the reception of EU instruments by the national law relates to the choice of a legislative, rather than an alternative,[56] means of regulation and to the choice of the legislative level.[57] If national law does not regulate the main object of the EU instrument

---

[51] See Davidson Report, 1996, https://www.regulation.org.uk/library/2006_davidson_review.pdf accessed 13 December 2023.

[52] See P Kellett, 'Is the Better Regulation Agenda Producing Better Regulation?' (2009) *Journal of Planning and Environment Law* 24, 25.

[53] See HM Government, 'Transposition Guidance: How to implement European Directives effectively', April 2013, 2.2; also see L Ramsey, 'The Copy Out Technique: More of A Cop Out Than a Solution?' (1996) *Statute Law Review* 218, 222 and 227; L Etherington, 'Digging Beneath the Surface: Transposition, Implementation and Evaluation of European Environmental Law' (2006) *Journal of Environmental Policy and Planning* 107, 121; K Atthoff and M Wallgren, 'Clarifying Gold-plating: Better Implementation of EU Legislation', Swedish Better Regulation Council, Board of Swedish Industry and Commerce for Better Regulation, 2012, 31.

[54] See Case 272/84, *Commission v Italy* [1985] ECR 1057, 1074.

[55] This analysis is heavily based on H Xanthaki, above n 8, 152–168.

[56] See HM Government, above note 53, 2.5–2.6.

[57] For a sociological analysis of compatibility of national norms and transposition, see A Dimitrova and M Rhinard, 'The Power of Norms in the Transposition of EU Directives' (2005) 9 *European Integration online Papers* N° 16, https://ssrn.com/abstract=856124.

under transposition, the need for regulation is undisputed.[58] In this case the five tests of legislative subsidiarity, proportionality, adequacy, synergy and adaptability have been passed at the EU level when the EU institutions produced the regulatory legal instrument in pursuance of a legislative process. Thus, the need for legislative regulation in the field must be taken for granted. Member States would have extreme difficulty[59] in making a legitimate and objectively plausible case for a refusal to proceed with legislative regulation on the basis of national intricacies.[60] As for the choice of national implementing legislative instrument, here selection is also limited exclusively to legally binding national forms of legislative texts. Delegated legislation could not commonly respond to the need for legal regulation in the cases of lack of former regulation at the national level, as – by definition – lack of prior regulation signifies lack of a primary instrument that would introduce the necessary authorising or enabling clause. As a result, primary legislation would be required for proportionate and adequate regulation. It would be uncommon for the task of transposition to end with the passing of a law, as transposition is a mere part of implementation. For reasons of synergy, the main law may commonly be supplemented by secondary legislative instruments that will deal with technical details arising from the application of the law. In this case delegated legislation would contribute to achieving legal proportionality and legal adaptability. Supplementing the main law with secondary legislation is absolutely necessary for reasons of adequacy with specific reference to compliance with the Madrid administrative criterion. But the problems of piecemeal transposition must also be taken into account: lack of clarity and incomplete implementation.[61]

---

[58] However, transposition does not necessarily require EU provisions to be reproduced verbatim in a specific, express law or regulation; a general legal context may be sufficient, provided that it does effectively ensure the full application of the directive in a sufficiently clear and precise manner. See C-49/00, *Commission of the European Communities v Italian Republic* [2001] ECR I-8575. Nevertheless, faithful transposition is often required: see Case C-38/99, *Commission of the European Communities v French Republic* [2000] ECR I-10941.

[59] In Case C-327/98, *Commission of the European Communities v French Republic* [2000] ECR I- 1851, paras 22–23, the ECJ held that national difficulties in transposition was not a plausible excuse for not passing implementing measures.

[60] National legislation is needed even when the activity regulated by the EU instrument does not take place in the member state: see Case C-441/00, *Commission of the European Communities v United Kingdom of Great Britain and Northern Ireland* [2002] ECR I-4699; see also Case C- 214/98, *Commission v Greece* [2000] ECR I-9601, at para 22. However, national legislation may not be needed when the EU instrument is pointless for reasons of geography; see Case 420/85, *Commission v Italy* [1987] ECR 2983, para 5.

[61] See S Bell and L Etherington, 'Out of Sight, Out of Mind: A Study of the Transposition and Implementation of the Groundwater Directive in the United Kingdom Environmental Law Review' (2007) *Environmental Law Review* 6, 11.

The same principles apply in the case of prior national regulation that is archaic or in radical and direct clash with EU law. In such cases the options available for national implementing measures are limited to the passing of a core law supplemented by delegated legislation dealing with technical and administrative details.

In cases where there is prior national legislation in the field under transposition, national authorities tend to have a wider selection of options. At the regulatory level, the five tests are applicable to ensure that further regulation is indeed necessary. When prior national regulation is complete when compared with EU regulation, each of the tests must be repeated applying national circumstances. In view of prior national laws, is further regulation required? If so, would further regulation be proportionate to the aim that EU regulation sets out to achieve? Could it be that current national regulation is adequate for the achievement of EU aims? Would the proposed new regulatory measures be received smoothly? Is it necessary to regulate further or can a wider interpretation of current regulatory measures, perhaps with a simple addition of a reference to the EU instruments, lead to the desired effect? The answer to these questions will depend on the results of the comparative analysis between national and EU regulation.

If, and only if, the five tests are not passed at the regulatory level, will national authorities proceed with the same five tests at the legislative level. The extent of incompatibility of national law with EU legislative text under transposition dictates the position of the selected national legal instrument in the hierarchy of sources of national law. Existence of prior national law in the field does not guarantee smooth transposition.[62] If the existing national law is incomplete, supplementing the existing law is necessary. This can be undertaken either via a repeal and re-enactment or by an amendment of the existing legislative text. Delegated legislation could be appropriate, where accommodated by an enabling clause in existing primary legislation, if complete transposition requires that: the aim of primary legislation is taken further; or that technical or detailed provisions implement the primary legislation; or that administrative arrangements are set; or that primary legislation is brought in force; or that the existing primary legislation is supplemented or amended.[63]

Moreover, the form of the EU instruments under transposition influences the choice of national authorities to a great extent. From a regulatory point of

[62] See M Kaeding, 'Determinants of Transposition Delay in the European Union' (2006) 26 *Journal of Public Policy* 229, 249.

[63] Nevertheless, national authorities cannot take adequacy to an extreme. This would be the case with transposition of Directives through administrative circulars previously used in France and the UK: see R Kovar, P Lagarde and D Tallon, 'L'éxécution des directives de la CEE en France' (1970) 6 *Cahiers de Droit Européen* 288.

view, at least in theory, the five tests of subsidiarity, proportionality, adequacy, synergy and adaptability have already been met, and a decision to proceed with legislative regulation has been made at the EU level. Similarly, the level of legislative form selected by the EU has already taken into account the legal basis of the instrument but also the order of the selected form in the hierarchy of sources of EU law. And so, the EU instrument under transposition has already passed, at least in theory, the five tests. These choices of EU institutions in the EU legislative process direct the choices of national authorities in the national legislative process for the introduction of implementing measures.[64]

And so, provisions of the constituting treaties are generally suitable for inclusion in national constitutions or constitutional principles. The logic behind this lies with the nature of treaty provisions as general: they are fundamental rules of law drafted in the vague style accommodated by national constitutions or constitutional documents. Most treaty provisions tend to introduce general principles of EU law that influence the interpretation and application of EU law in its entirety[65] and can be considered part of the general principles of national law. But most treaty provisions apply exclusively to EU citizens: and so there is an argument against express transposition of treaty provisions in the national constitutions that apply to both EU and third-country nationals equally. So, when it comes to the provisions of the constituting treaties, the task of national authorities is dual: the negative task is to take out of the legislative equation articles related exclusively to the functioning of the EU; and the positive task is to identify articles that introduce rights and obligations that the treaties award to EU citizens but which subsequent EU law has extended to third-country nationals. These are mainly provisions related to fundamental freedoms rather than to freedoms related to the internal market. It is only the former that require express inclusion to the constitution or constitutional principles. All other treaty provisions require silent transposition through their application to the interpretation and reception of all sources of EU law.

Regulations are directly applicable.[66] As they form part of the national laws of the Member States, they do not normally require transposition. In pursuance of the principle of synergy, Regulations are drafted in a manner that allows

---

64 See J-L Sauron, *L'Application du Droit de L'Union Europèene en France* (Paris, La documentation française, 2000) 40.

65 The lack of any express provision to the same effect in the precise EC text does not mean that the general principle does not apply: see Case T-18/97, *Atlantic Container Line AB and Others v Commission of the European Communities* [2002] ECR II-1125, para 39.

66 See Case 50-76, *Amsterdam Bulb BV v Produktschap voor Siergewassen* [1977] ECR 137; also Case 39-72, *Commission of the European Communities v Italian Republic* [1973] ECR 101.

their smooth reception by national laws as they stand. But this does not relieve national authorities from the task of evaluating Regulations against existing national law.[67] Generally speaking there are four main types of national normative implementing measures for the transposition of Regulations: concretising and/or complementing substantive measures; institutional and/or competence measures; procedural, controlling or penal measures; or adapting or derogating measures.[68] If Regulations are in complete contrast with prior national legislation, the latter must be amended or repealed altogether. Implied amendment may be considered adequate for the purposes of transposition via statutory interpretation. But it hinders clarity in the national law of the Member State, and it cannot be condoned. Moreover, it may leave ground to judicial interpretation and application contrary to EU law,[69] which in turn may lead to judicial State liability claims. If Regulations affect existing national law in part, the task of national authorities is to evaluate the extent and manner in which national law is changed by the reception of the Regulation. In this case amendments via alteration, substitution, or incorporation ensure synergy, while respecting adaptability. In the rare case where the Regulation complies fully with prior national law, Member States may: remain inactive; or add a reference to the Regulation in the purpose clause or explanatory materials of the national legal instrument; or introduce a national legislative text with a sole enacting provision cross-referring to prior national laws and annex the Regulation. The choice is subjective and depends on the extent of the need to draw the user's attention to the connection between the Regulation and the national law.

Directives[70] require attention by national authorities, as they merely set aims to be achieved allowing national authorities to exercise their autonomy in the process of implementation.[71] According to the recent Landscape Review of the

---

[67] See Case C-177/95, *Ebony Maritime SA v Prefetto della Provincia di Brindisi* [1997] ECR I-1111.

[68] See R Král, 'National Normative Implementation of EC Regulations. An Exceptional or Rather Common Matter?' (2008) *European Law Review* 243, 245.

[69] See A J Gil Ibáñez, *The Administrative Supervision and Enforcement of EC Law: Powers, Procedures and Limits* (Oxford, Portland, Hart Publishing, 1999); on the political aspect of judicial interpretation see F Snyder, 'The Effectiveness of European Community Law: Institutions, Processes, Tools and Techniques' (1993) 56 *Modern Law Review* 27.

[70] For a thorough analysis on every aspect of transposition of Directive see B Steunberg and W Voermans, *The Transposition of EC Directives* (Leiden, Universiteit Leiden, 2006).

[71] For an analysis of autonomy in the national legislative process, see J H Jans, 'National Legislative Autonomy? The Procedural Constraints Of European Law' (1998) *Legal Issues of European Integration* 25; also see C-48/75 *Belgium v Royer*

Court of Auditors, Member States have their own preference in approaching transposition: whilst some prefer amending national legislation, others introduce new transposition texts;[72] and whilst some opt for primary legislation, others prefer secondary legislation (delegated or subordinate).[73] Of course autonomy is not boundless.[74] The implementation of a directive requires 'the adoption of general measures of a legislative nature'.[75] National authorities must ensure full application,[76] not only in fact but also in law.[77] In application of this principle, for the transposition of Directives national authorities cannot find refuge in a mere circular that can be amended by the administration at will,[78] or to a simple general provision in national legislation referring to EU law,[79] or to existing administrative practices,[80] or to the tolerance exercised by the administration under existing national rules and administrative rules that do not confer any right on individuals capable of being relied on before

---

[1976] ECR 497; [1976] 2 CMLR 619, para 73; C-194/01 *Commission v Austria* [2004] ECR I-4579; [2004] Env. L.R. 48, paras 38 and 39.

72 Directives do not need to be transposed verbatim: see C-50/09 *Commission v Ireland* [2011] ECR I-873; [2011] PTSR 1122, para 46; also see C-214/98 *Commission v Greece* [2000] ECR I-9601, para 98; and C-433/93 *Commission v Germany* [1995] ECR I-2303, para 18. But see *contra* 38/77 *Enka BV v Inspecteur der Invoerrechten en Accijnzen* [1977] ECR. 2203; [1978] 2 CMLR 212, paras 12 and 17.

73 See Court of Auditors, 'Landscape Review, Putting EU law into practice: The European Commission's oversight responsibilities under Article 17(1) of the Treaty on European Union', 2018, 5.

74 Where the definition in the EU text is so specific that even a slight change could alter their meaning, then verbatim transposition is the only way forward: see C-9/92 *Commission v Greece* [1993] ECR I-4467; [1997] STC 601, paras 8, 10 and 14.

75 See S Prechal, *Directives in European Community Law. A Study of Directives and Their Enforcement in National Courts* (Oxford, Oxford University Press, 1995), 5.

76 See Case C-365/93, *Commission v Greece* [1995] ECR I-499, para 9; see also Case C-144/99, *Commission v Netherlands* [2001] ECR I-3541, para 17: Member States may not justify breach of EC law on the basis of failure of other Member States to perform their obligations; see also C-38/89, *Ministere public v Guy Blanguernon. Reference for a preliminary ruling: Tribunal de police d'Aix- les-Bains* [1990] ECR I-83.

77 See Case C-339/87, *Commission v Netherlands* [1990] ECR I-851.

78 See Case 239/85, *Commission v Belgium* [1986] ECR 3645.

79 See Case C-96/95, *Commission v Germany* [1997] ECR I-1653.

80 See Case C-152/00, *Commission of the European Communities v French Republic* [2002] ECR I- 6973. Member States may not plead provisions, practices or circumstances existing in its internal legal system in order to justify its failure to comply with obligations and time-limits resulting from Community directives. See Case C-310/89, *Commission of the European Communities v Kingdom of the Netherlands* [1991] ECR I-138.

national courts.[81] Moreover, clarity and precision to terminology used cannot be relied upon on the definitions in preparatory materials.[82] And case law cannot fulfil the requirement of legal certainty of the provisions of a Directive.[83] And of course national rules of statutory interpretation cannot be relied upon to complete the implementing measure indirectly.[84] The rationale behind these restrictions to the autonomy of national authorities lies with the fact that the five tests were met at the time of the passing of the Directive, and as a result the need for legislative regulation has been verified.[85] National authorities may leave the implementation of the objectives of the Directive to social partners through collective agreements; but national authorities are still responsible for ensuring that the Directive is fully implemented by adopting the appropriate legislative or administrative measures.[86] In the absence of prior national regulation, or when prior national legislation clashes with the provisions of the Directive, the Directive requires full transposition via legislative measures.[87] In cases of prior partial regulation, and in view of the detailed technical nature of most Directives, they are commonly transposed via delegated legislation. But the power to use delegated legislation for the purposes of transposition must be included in the ratification of the Accession Act. In cases where the national legal system already secures the aims pursued by the Directive, implementing measures are not necessary. This may be the case where the necessary legislation already exists in national law, or where principles of constitutional or administrative law render specific national legislation superfluous.[88] The condition for this is that the legal position arising from such principles is sufficiently precise and clear, and may be relied upon by individuals before

---

[81] See Case 102/79, *Commission v Belgium* [1980] ECR 1473; Case 145/82, *Commission v Italy* [1983] ECR 711.

[82] See Case 143/83 *Commission v Denmark* [1985] ECR 427; on clarity also see C-281/11 *Commission v Poland* [2013] ECR 855, para 60.

[83] See Case C-236/95 *Commission v Greece* [1996] ECR I-4459.

[84] See Case C-162/99 *Commission v Italy* [2001] ECR I-0541.

[85] Even where the settled case law of a Member State interprets the provisions of national law in a manner deemed to satisfy the requirements of a Directive, that cannot achieve the clarity and precision needed to meet the requirement of legal certainty. See Case C-144/99, *Commission of the European Communities v Kingdom of the Netherlands* [2001] ECR I-3541.

[86] See Case 143/83, *Commission v Denmark* [1985] ECR 427.

[87] See Cabinet Office, Regulatory Impact Unit, Transposition Guide: How to Implement European Directives Effectively 14 (2005).

[88] However, even where the settled case law of a Member State interprets the provisions of national law in a manner deemed to satisfy the requirements of a Directive, that cannot achieve the clarity and precision needed to meet the requirement of legal certainty. See Case C-144/99, *Commission of the European Communities v Kingdom of the Netherlands* [2001] ECR I-3541, para 21.

the national courts.[89] A transposition tool commonly used by Member States is the transposition of several Directives via a single national legal instrument, known as 'the national transposition package approach'. Although these are helpful for the reduction of the costs of coordination within the Ministries,[90] their value as technical drafting tools is questionable as they break the express link between a Directive and 'its' national implementing measure. But they can also serve as an antidote to the extensive fragmentation of EU regulation.

Decisions are transposed via administrative acts or delegated legislation. The addressees of the Decision are the subjects of the implementing measure, and this must be reflected in the national implementing measure. Recommendations and Opinions require no transposition, as they are not legally binding. However, they do serve as an authentic interpretation of stronger, legally binding legislative texts,[91] and they are subject to judicial review before the CJEU.[92] Last but not least, judgments of the European courts, and especially persistent case law, is binding on Member States and must be included in national implementing measures.

Apart from the extent of legislative intervention required for full transposition and the type of main EU instrument for reception, national authorities base their choice of national implementing measure on the nature and object of the field under treatment. In other words national authorities take into account the legal and legislative drafting criteria applicable for the selection of legal form in customary national legislative drafting. After all, transposition is ultimately a legislative drafting exercise. Legal criteria relate to the substantive field of law to which the implementing measure refers. Legislative drafting criteria refer to technical requirements for the classification of the national implementing measure as primary or executive legislation.

When it comes to legal criteria for the choice of form of the national implementing measure, national authorities identify the substantive field of law of the proposed measure. First, national legal custom[93] may require that regulation in specific areas of activity is reserved for special legal forms. This

---

89 See Case 29/84, *Commission v Germany* [1985] ECR 1661.

90 See M Kaeding, 'Lost in Translation or Full Steam Ahead: The Transposition of EU Transport Directives across Member States' (2008) 9 *European Union Politics* 115, 123.

91 See M Gardeòes Santiago, Las 'comunicaciones interpretativas' de la Comisión: Concepto y valor normativo, (1992) 3 *Revista de Instituciones Europeas* 933.

92 See Cases C-322/88, *Grimaldi v Fonds des Maladies Professionnelles* [1989] ECR 4407; see also Case C-325/91, *France v Commission* [1993] ECR 3283.

93 For an empirical study demonstrating the huge discrepancies in the national choices of implementing measures, see B Steunenberg, 'Turning Swift Policy-making into Deadlock and Delay National Policy Coordination and the Transposition of EU Directives' (2006) 7 *European Union Politics* 293, 295.

would be the case with the introduction of new crimes in the national legal order: this is traditionally reserved for criminal legislation. Second, areas of minor importance are rarely considered worthy of legislative intervention via primary legislation. In this case, regulation takes the form of delegated legislation, internal circulars, or other lower forms of regulation. An example of such an area concerns the levels of compensation awarded to farmers whose crops have been destroyed by natural phenomena. Third, areas of increased significance are commonly reserved for primary legislation. This refers to legislation affecting issues falling within the exclusive competence of the constitution and constitutional provisions, restrictions of citizens' rights, taxation, electoral issues or the establishment of a public body. But politics and economics also seem to play a role: governments tend to opt for primary legislation for the purposes of transposition in the beginning of their term; and wealthier countries seem to use primary legislation more.[94]

When it comes to legislative drafting criteria national authorities take into account technical drafting issues that affect the choice of form of the national implementing instrument. The main factor in favour of primary legislation refers to the need for parliamentary legitimatisation of the proposed measure in cases when there are special needs of democratic legitimacy: for example, a serious compromise of fundamental rights; or when important authority or powers are introduced and attributed; or when the measure is expected to have significant political, economic or social consequences; or when the proposed solutions are controversial politically. Another factor in favour of primary legislation refers to the characteristics of the proposed measure: a wide circle of addressees; general application;[95] or legal bindingness. The main factor in favour of delegated legislation is an enabling clause. The constitution or constitutional principles must not prohibit the delegation. The enabling clause must be introduced in primary legislation. The clause must delimit precisely the scope of the delegation. The clause must determine the aim and the means of the delegated instrument. Another factor in favour of delegated legislation

---

[94] See D Treutlein, 'What Actually Happens to EU Directives in The Member States?: A Cross-country Cross-sector View on National Transposition Instruments', CESifo working paper, No. 2098, 2007, http://hdl.handle.net/10419/26143.

[95] The wide circle of addressees and the wide application of the measure is judged on the basis of its true characteristics and not on the basis of its title. See Case T-17/00, *Willy Rothley and Others v European Parliament* [2002] ECR II-579, para 61; the mere fact, however, that the number and even the identity of the persons to whom a measure applies can be determined in no way implies that those persons must be regarded as individually concerned by that measure, where that measure applies to them as a result of an objective situation of law or fact specified by the measure at issue: see Case 6/68 *Zuckerfabrik Watenstedt v Council* [1968] ECR 409, para 415; see also Case C-10/95, *P Asocarne v Council* [1995] ECR I-4149, para 30.

is the characteristics of the proposed measure, namely the need for flexibility of regulation, the technical or detailed nature of the normative mater, or the need for repetitive acts. What is surprising and therefore noteworthy is that the choice of primary legislation as a means of transposition does not delay the process at all.[96] But, whatever the choice on the form of the national measure, the drafter as an agent of the State cannot draft 'any measure which would conceal the Community nature and effects of any legal provisions from the person to whom it applies'.[97] And as a result, there must be visibility of the connection between the EU and the national legislative texts.

At the end of the day the choice of format of the national implementing measure, choices related to context of the national legislative texts, and choices related to the policy and, if necessary, the legislative solution can only serve harmonisation if they are made on the basis of one criterion: that of effectiveness. Effectiveness is the legislator's contribution to the efficacy of national implementing measures. Effective meaning that the norm produces effects, that it does not become a dead letter.[98] Parkinson describes effective legislation as reasonable legislation.[99] Mader defines effectiveness as the extent to which the observable attitudes and behaviours of the target population correspond to the attitudes and behaviours prescribed by the legislator.[100] Effectiveness seems to reflect the relationship between the results produced by the national implementing or transposing measures and the purpose of these measures: consequently, it links national measures to the achievement of harmonisation. Effectiveness is not simply the elaboration of legal doctrine.[101] It includes but is not limited to implementation, enforcement, impact and compliance.[102] Thus, effectiveness may include both the effects of legal norms and the follow-

---

[96] See E Borghetto, F Franchino and D Giannetti, 'Complying with the Transposition Deadlines of EU Directives – Evidence from Italy' (2006) 1 *Rivista Italiana di Politiche Pubbliche* 7.

[97] See Case 50-76, *Amsterdam Bulb BV v Produktschap voor Siergewassen* [1977] ECR 137.

[98] See P Delnoy, *The Role Of Legislative Drafters in Determining the Content of Norms*, The International Cooperation Group, Department of Justice of Canada, 2005, at 6, https://canada.justice.gc.ca/eng/rp-pr/csj-sjc/ilp-pji/norm/index.html at 3.

[99] T I Parkinson, 'Functions of Administration in Labour Legislation' (1930) 20 *AmLabLegRev*, 143, at 144.

[100] L Mader, 'Legislative Procedure and the Quality of Legislation' in U Karpen and P Delnoy (eds), *Contributions to the Methodology of the Creation of Written Law* (Nomos Verlagsgesellshcaft, 1996), 62, at 68.

[101] F Snyder, *New Directions in EC Law* (Weidenfeld and Nicholson, 1990) at 3.

[102] G Teubner, 'Regulatory Law: Chronicle of a Death Foretold' (1992) 1 *Soco-Legal Studies*, 451.

ing of such norms.[103] However, one could distinguish in general between two prevailing models of effectiveness, often described as the positivist and the socio-legal models. In his positivist approach Jacobson links effectiveness to implementation and compliance.[104] In his socio-legal model of effectiveness, Jenkins relates the statute to the social reform attained.[105] Irrespective of which of the two models one favours, the fact of the matter is that drafters are in pursuit of effectiveness of the measure that they draft. And, although stating that a drafter can single-handedly achieve effectiveness in legislation would signify a complete ignorance of the interrelation between actors in the policy process, the truth of the matter is that the drafter can, and must seek to, achieve attainment of the purpose and objectives set in the statute under construction. Ultimately, effectiveness is the criterion of choice for any dilemma related to transposition, including design.

Having analysed the principles of law guiding transposition choices for the structure of the national transposition text, and before finalising the analysis of Thornton's Stage 3 (Design), let us revert to the first comment on design namely that there are considerable benefits in predictability of structure and respect to drafting traditions on design and structure. Does the valid, albeit generic, comment, namely that structure must normally stay within the traditional style of structure in each Member State, also apply to transposition legislation? Member States often copy verbatim either the whole of the EU legislative text or at least large chunks of it.[106] Moreover, a large chunk of the *acquis* remains in effect without any national implementation measures as a result of the principles of direct applicability and direct effect. On the basis of the frequency of both these parameters, is it accurate to state that users may be adversely affected by a new structure in national implementing texts? After all, the structure of EU texts is outside their comfort zone already. Perhaps balancing the inherent risk of unpredictability with the accessibility benefits a new structure, facilitating access of user groups to the particular information that they mine for, would tilt the balance to the latter. Accepting that the current structure of national transposition legislation, which copies that of EU

---

[103] F Snyder, 'The Effectiveness of European Community Law: Institutions, Processes, Tools and Techniques' (1993) 56 *Modern Law Review*, 19, 19.

[104] H Jacobson, 'After Word: Conceptual, Methodological and Substantive Issues Entwined in Studying Compliance' (1998) 19 *MichJIn L*, 569, at 573.

[105] I Jenkins, *Social Order and the Limits of the Law: a Theoretical Essay* (Princeton University Press, 1981) at 180; also R Cranston, 'Reform Through Legislation: The Dimension of Legislative Technique' (1978–1979) 73 *NwULRev*, 873, at 875.

[106] See B Steunenberg and W Voermans, *The Transposition of EC Directives: A Comparative Study of Instruments, Techniques and Processes in Six EU Member States* (Leiden University/the Hague, WODC of the Ministry of Justice, 2006); also see L E Ramsey, 'The Copy Out Technique' (1996) *Statute Law Review* 218, 223–224.

texts, is already foreign to the users of national legislation opens the ground for considerations of innovation in that field. Perhaps even more interestingly, this can apply to the EU texts themselves.

Thus, the introduction of a new approach to the structure of, at least, transposition legislation may not disturb certainty and predictability after all. The layered approach can apply to transposition texts as part of the revolution already in action via the Better Regulation movements at the EU and the Member State levels. Transposition legislation is fully informed by the results of the Good Law survey: national legislation, and transposition legislation in specific, is read by three user groups. Group 1 encompasses lay persons who, in the process of seeking answers to their everyday questions, stumble upon a legislative text that is either based on or copied from an EU legislative text. The latter is frequently referred to in the national legislation and often attached to it as an annex or schedule. Group 1 users need to know what rights the EU introduces for them and how to enjoy them, and what obligation are being imposed and how to meet them. They also need to know the rationale behind the new legislation in order to ascribe to it and become willing, and why not eager, participants in the EU's regulatory efforts. Group 2 encompasses non-lawyers but professional users, who use national transposition legislation and its deriving EU text in the course of their professional duties. To exercise those adequately, these expert users dig deep into the legislation to understand both the regulatory messages addressed to Group 1 but also the intricacies of that application, and the procedures through which they can administer the award of rights or the imposition of obligations. Group 2 users are aware of the topic and are used to EU legislation but the legal nuances are not necessarily accessible or perhaps not even relevant to them. Examples of such users would be staff working in personnel offices in private or State-owned companies, equal opportunities units, local authorities, government units, members of the regulated professions, bankers and financiers, fishing or agriculture offices, etc. Group 3 encompasses legal experts, who use national and EU legislation to resolve within or outside national courts in the case of disputes brought to them by Groups 1 and 2. They are expert users called to interpret or apply legislation to address vagueness or ambiguity at a conceptual, structural, or semantic level.

In view of the existence of these three user groups and the variations in their background subject- and legal-related expertise, a creative and innovative layered structure would require that national drafters divide transposition legislation into three parts. Part 1 could include the main regulatory messages, namely, (a) why legislate, (b) how this benefits the user, and (c) what is the gist of law reform introduced by the text. The rationale behind legislation must be concrete and relevant to the user. There is little scope in replicating the current trend of stating that this law is implementing an EU legislative text or, even worse, that this meets the obligation of the jurisdiction to implement/transpose an EU legislative text. The second expression, accurate as it may factually be, already predisposes the user to view an exciting new regulatory effort through the prism of yet another imposition on their freedom, thus failing to incite excitement and participation. The rationale of the national implementing measure must state what the EU legislation attempts to achieve for the citizen in the short and longer term, and what particular value this will have at the national level. For example, stating that 'This law meets the obligation of our country to transpose Regulation (EU) 2017/920' is user-unfriendly, dry, and empty of meaning for most users. However, 'This Law stops roaming charges within the EU', or 'This Law relieves citizens from charges when phoning abroad within the EU' explains the value and topic of the legislation to users, invites them to read further, and spells out the benefit that citizens now enjoy on the basis of their citizenship. Stating that this is an EU initiative would extend user understanding that this new benefit comes as a direct result of their EU citizenship and could instigate or confirm sharing of the EU vision. In the case of the Roaming Regulation, such a legislative expression addresses both points of why legislate and how this benefits the user. In cases where the benefit is not as obvious as in the Roaming Regulation, perhaps because the link with the underlying policy is not as obvious or because the benefit is longer term and may require short-term imposition, the two points must be separated and expressed clearly in separate provisions. For example, '1. This Law prohibits the cultivation of those species of cucumbers that are prone to disease. 2. The objectives of this Law is: a. to enhance the income of cucumber farmers by 20 per cent over a period of three years; and b. to protect crops from disease, thus saving the economy 2,000,000 Euros per year.' It is probable that this type of provision could have prevented or discredited the populist voices who attributed the cucumber cultivation prohibition to an intrusion to farmer choices caused by a distorted regulatory joy in prohibiting bent vegetables. Similarly, if the main regulatory message is not covered by the provision stating why legislation and how this benefits the users, as was the case with the previous two examples above, a third statement is necessary. This can be placed at the beginning of the Group 1 provisions, where it acquires prominence, and thus has optimal chances to be read and understood. For example:

> 1. This Law introduces the right of victims of crime in another EU Member State to receive immediate assistance, interpretation of oral legal processes, and translation of legal documents in their own language. 2. The objective of this law is to benefit the 15 per cent of European citizens who fall victims of crime elsewhere in the EU by offering them easy and immediate access to services and legal processes in a language that they understand. 3. The Law offers the same rights of access to assistance and legal processes everywhere in the EU, thus enhancing citizen safety and security within the whole of the EU, and ensuring full participation in the legal processes.

It is hoped that these first few phrases can explain much better the necessity, rationale, and main regulatory message of the Victim's Rights Directive 2012/29/EU than the current spread of Articles 1–4 coming after no less than 19 recitals of questionable value to Group 1.[107]

Part 2 can include the regulatory messages, and enforcement mechanisms. Regulatory messages are found in the text of the source of EU law under transposition. So, a good completion of Stages 1 and 2 of the drafting process can already provide the national drafters with a good basis upon which design will take place. The national drafter brings together the whole picture of the *acquis* on the topic, not just the text under transposition but the whole of the *acquis* including other relevant EU documents plus interpretation provided by the European courts, and juxtaposes it to the similarly complete picture of national law. Again this is not a juxtaposition of legislation alone: the whole of the law needs to be examined so that the awareness of the national drafter of both EU and national law, as implemented already, can form the intellectual basis of the design of the national implementing measure. The content of Part 2 can include most of what is provided for in the EU legislative text but, of course, adapted to the national context. Plus, of course, the administrative and enforcement mechanisms that can render the text effective in the national context. Although most EU texts indicate the need for 'nationalisation' of these provisions by using the term 'Member States must' or 'national authorities must', there is still need to elaborate on requirements, to identify the particular 'relevant authority', and to

---

[107] For the purposes of juxtaposition, after 19 recitals, the current text, as copied out in the majority of EU MS reads:

Article 1

Objectives

1. The purpose of this Directive is to ensure that victims of crime receive appropriate information, support and protection and are able to participate in criminal proceedings. Member States shall ensure that victims are recognised and treated in a respectful, sensitive, tailored, professional and non-discriminatory manner, in all contacts with victim support or restorative justice services or a competent authority, operating within the context of criminal proceedings. The rights set out in this Directive shall apply to victims in a non-discriminatory manner, including with respect to their residence status.
2. Member States shall ensure that in the application of this Directive, where the victim is a child, the child's best interests shall be a primary consideration and shall be assessed on an individual basis. A child-sensitive approach, taking due account of the child's age, maturity, views, needs and concerns, shall prevail. The child and the holder of parental responsibility or other legal representative, if any, shall be informed of any measures or rights specifically focused on the child.

The Directive then moves on to Article 2: Definitions, and then on to each right.

ensure that the provisions fall smoothly in place with those already in national law.[108] The content and sequence of provisions in Part 2 will be analysed in detail below but, before proceeding to that, let us complete the analysis of the overarching theme for the structure of the transposition text by exploring Part 3 of a layered national transposition text.

Part 3 encompasses everything that is left out of Parts 1 and 2. Legal issues, issues of interpretation, deadline, reviews and sunset clauses are all left for the perusal of legal experts, who will use them to offer expert professional legal services in the event of disputes arising from the transposition laws. This is the part of the legislation, where drafters can use expert terminology freely. Group 3 users are able, and in fact accustomed to, using complex terms, juxtaposing texts in EU and national law, and completing the gaps by linking the threads between interconnected texts and issues. This is where the use of necessary terminology and complexity is allowed, simply because the use of alternative perhaps simpler term will lead the expert users to seek alternative interpretations. The disclaimer here is that the rule of law, so prominent in EU law, does not relieve drafters from the task of drafting a text that is generally, and therefore inclusively of Part 3, accessible. However, one must accept that legal nuances and issues specific to Part 3 may have to be expressed in an expert manner, as a means of guiding the lay user to seek expert help for their correct application and interpretation.

An example of the layered approach applied to transposition legislative can be offered using Cypriot Law 18/I/2014 on the Right to Interpretation and Translation in the criminal trial.[109] The Law states as its objective the transposition of Directive 2010/64/EU. The Law faithfully copies most of the Directive. It starts with definitions, and interestingly defines the 'relevant authority' as 'any one' of a list of bodies ranging from the police to courts without specifying which of the four types of relevant authorities applies in each of the references of the Law to this term. After the scope of application of the Law and its interrelation with prior relevant Cypriot Laws, no earlier than page 4 of the text introduces the right to interpretation and then moves on to translation. The text deals with all aspects of each right. And then ends with a power awarded to the Ministerial Council to issue delegated legislation in order to elaborate further on the text. This legislative text is actually one of the more creative examples of transposition of the Directive, as it at least delves into the identification of the 'relevant authority' and departs from the text of the Directive in a number of provisions. For the purposes of complete interpretation, if one sets aside

[108] See R Thomas and G Lynch-Wood, 'Transposing European Union Law in the United Kingdom' (2008) *European Public Law* 177, 188.

[109] See EE, para 1.I, no 4430, 21.2.2014.

the confusion of the relevant authority in each provision, the Law seems to produce complete transposition of the Directive. But this does not mean that it serves effectiveness to the fullest.

The application of the layered approach to the transposition Law showcases the great contribution of the method for the accessibility of legislation and of course in the incitement of trust to EU citizens/users to the European ideal. Without changing the words or provisions used in the text, a layered Law would begin direct communication with EU citizens by detailing the new rights offered to them by the EU. This would allow them to both understand their right to interpretation and translation, whom to contact to exercise these rights, and what the rights entails. The layered Law would then move to the right to submit an appeal against any decision of national authorities that prevent their rights to interpretation and translation. Note that this provision would be expressed as a right for EU citizens rather than as an appeals process as expressed in the current Law. The layered Law would then move to the legal process of such appeals, and complete with the power of the Ministerial Council to issue delegated legislation. Simple but effective!

To sum up on the design of transposition measures, it can be stated that national drafters can be influenced by a multitude of parallel layers of consideration: their own traditional style of structure of legislative texts, principles of EU law applicable to their task, text-focused considerations of extent, type, and nature of the text under transposition, and the user-centred layered approach. Complex as their task is, design holds a crucial role for the accessibility of the resulting national legislative text, especially for the 80 peer cent of its users, who do not have legal training. Innovative choices of design can deliver the Better Regulation policy to a much greater extent than any choices of legislative expression. Yet, design remains the drafting Stage that suffers the most from an unquestioned, religious replication of persistent erroneous practices, such as the non-transposition of Regulations, and the catastrophic (for effectiveness) yet seemingly safe (for Member States) use of the copy out technique of transposition. Yet, the prominence of effectiveness in the Better Regulation agenda of the EU remains, and the road to regulatory innovation is already paved. Perhaps it is the EU, rather than Member States alone, that can start the ball rolling with the layered approach?

C. ADDRESSING THE CHALLENGES OF TRANSPOSITION (THORNTON'S STAGE 3)

The ideological debate between the effectiveness of elaboration[110] in the national transposition legislation and the practicability of the copy out transposition method has tilted with practicability in at least Denmark, France, Germany, Greece, Estonia, Ireland, Italy, Poland, Portugal, Romania, Spain (albeit to a lesser extent), and, albeit perhaps no longer so importantly, the UK. If anything, Member States are moving away from elaboration and are beginning to test non-transposition altogether on the basis that Accession Acts combined with the supremacy of EU law can allow transposition by reference only without even the need to copy out the text of the EU legislation under transposition. This is being debated in Luxembourg, Cyprus (here it is rarely used), the Czech Republic, Germany, Latvia, the Netherlands (where it is actually used in practice), in Slovenia, and in Spain. The French *Conseil d'Etat* has been resisting continuing attempts to introduce the practice in France.[111] It is therefore evident that, despite considerable opposition from academia,[112] Member States seems reluctant to depart greatly from EU legislative texts. The design and structure of EU legislation ends up being replicated in national transposition legislation, in an increasing majority of Member States.

At the same time, the design and structure of EU legislation remains completely unexplored as a tool for delivering the Better Regulation goals. Inter-institutional Agreements and documents on the style of EU Acts simply re-iterate the axiom of chapter/part/section as a reflection of the 'logical' division of EU documents.[113] And, thus, the purely text-focused 70-year-old

---

[110] Also known as re-write: see D Greenberg, 'The "Copy-Out" Debate in the Implementation of European Union Law in the United Kingdom' (2012) *Legisprudence* 243.

[111] See B Steunenberg and W Voermans, 'The Transposition of EC Directives: A Comparative Study of Instruments, Techniques and Processes in Six EU Member States', Leiden/ Research and Documentation Centre (WODC) of the Ministry of Justice (2006), http://ssrn.com/abstract=1215542.

[112] See L Ramsey, 'The Copy Out Technique: More of a "Cop Out" than a Solution?' (1996) 17 *Statute Law Review* 218; also see National Audit Office, 'Lost in Translation? Responding to the challenges of European law', HC 26 Session 2005-2006, 26 May 2005; Cabinet Office Regulatory Impact Unit, 'Transposition guide: how to implement European directives effectively, 2005; L Etherington, 'Digging Beneath the Surface: Transposition, Implementation and Evaluation of European Environmental Law' (2006) *Journal of Environmental Policy and Planning* 107.

[113] See Inter-institutional Agreement, http://publications.europa.eu/code/en/en-250600.htm accessed 13 December 2023.

traditional structure of EU legislation is the one communicated to EU citizens via the EU and the national transposition legislative texts.

Yet, design can serve as one of the most successful tools for the accessibility of EU legislation. Design can be used to convey the real EU regulatory goal and the benefit that it offers to EU citizens in the short or longer term. This can lead to create or confirm support and loyalty to the EU vision. Design can effectively offer all three user groups answers to their questions directly, thus ensuring that the right message is received by the right group, as the EU legislative text intended. This can identify rights and obligations clearly, thus enhancing correct application of EU legislation. In turn, this can lead to the desired social behavioural change that is sought by the regulators, which, if the regulatory choices were correct at the time of legislating, can produce the desired regulatory results. Design is crucial for the legislative effectiveness of EU legislation, and, consequently, the regulatory effectiveness (what literature calls efficacy) of EU policies.

In view of the Commission's continued emphasis on Better Regulation, and the EU institutions continuing dedication to the cause, this may be opportune time for the EU institutions collectively to discuss whether the current design of EU legislative texts is fit for purpose. Taking into account the age of the design, the innovations already paved in EU regulation, and the reality of replication of the EU design in the national transposition texts, there is little doubt that change is urgently needed. And that it can deliver miracles.

In the citizen-focused EU a user-focused design can reflect the great value now expressly placed on EU citizens and their following of the EU as an ideal and as an organisation. The optimal tool to express this in legislative design is the layered approach. In order to apply this to EU legislation, it is necessary to identify the users of EU legislation. Traditionally, EU law was referred to as a *droit diplomatique*. But this is no longer a valid approach. The identity of EU legislation is no longer defined by the compromises made in its passing. In application of sustainable integration, the new identify of EU legislation clearly expressed in Better Regulation already, is defined by effectiveness to the longer-term benefit of EU citizens. And this identity is best reflected in a layered text offering prominence to EU citizens as participants to the regulatory agenda of the legislative text.

Before presenting the design of a layered EU Act, it is necessary to identify the user groups of EU legislation. There is no doubt that Member States and the national authorities remain a solid user group of EU legislation: they are entrusted with the provision of the administrative framework for the application of EU legislation at the national level; they may not necessarily have legal training, but they certainly have great sophistication both in the subject matter and in handling EU legislation. They therefore fall in the layered approach's Group 2 users. Moreover, there is also little doubt that lawyers and judges continue to user EU legislation: they are entrusted with the interpretation and application of EU legislation in the national and European courts; they have expert sophistication in EU legislation. Therefore, they fall in to the layered approach Group 3 users. So far, so good. The question is, whether EU legislation is actually used by lay users? In other words, is there a Group 1 type of users in EU legislation? There certainly is a Group 1 user group in national transposition legislation. But, since in an increasing number of Member States EU legislation is simply copied and pasted, or just referenced, in the national transposition measures, Group 1 users end up using the EU text either in its form as an EU text or in its copied out form as a national transposition text. And, although in the past the EU could be forgiven for relying on Member States to bring the text to its national users creatively, there is now enough evidence to pull that safety net from under the institutions' feet altogether. There is little doubt therefore that EU legislation now has a group of lay users that read EU legislative texts in order to understand what the new legislation is offering them in the form of rights, or what it is asking them to do in the form of obligations. In fact, one wonders whether the actual usage of EU legislation by lay users should be a factor in the design of EU legislation at all. After all, the objective of Better Regulation to regain direct communication with EU citizens in order to convey the EU regulatory messages accurately, and away from populist interpretations, requires that the text talks to EU citizens directly. Even if they do not read it now, making it more user friendly will entice them to read it, and its regulatory messages, in the future. And so the objectives of Better Regulation surpass even one's position in the debate on whether current usage includes a Group 1 user group. It does, but, even if it does not, it should. And the layered structure of EU texts can bring this in for the EU institutions.

Having established that EU legislation is addressed to three user groups, the layered division of EU legislation becomes much easier. In fact, it tends to fall clearly in the lap of EU drafters. In application to the layered division presented above, Part 1, addressed to Group 1 lay users, can contain the main regulatory messages, namely, (a) why legislate? (b) how this benefits citizens and enterprises, and (c) what are the awarded rights and imposed obligations? These must be expressed concretely, simply, and accurately.

For example, Regulation (EU) 2017/920 can start with 'This Regulation relieves EU citizens from charges when phoning abroad within the EU.' The rather unfortunately named round cucumbers and bent bananas EC Commission Regulation No 2257/94 (now repealed) could start with;

> 1. This Regulation prohibits the cultivation of those species of bananas and cucumbers that are prone to disease. 2. The objectives of this Law is: a. to enhance the income of banana and cucumber farmers by 20 per cent over a period of three years;

> and b. to protect crops from disease, thus saving the economy 2,000,000 Euros per year.

Finally, Victim's Rights Directive 2012/29/EU could start with:

> 1. Directive introduces the right of victims of crime in another EU Member State to receive immediate assistance, interpretation of oral legal processes, and translation of legal documents in their own language. 2. The objective of the Directive is to benefit the 15 per cent of European citizens who fall victims of crime elsewhere in the EU by offering them easy and immediate access to services and legal processes in a language that they understand. 3. Directive offers the same rights of access to assistance and legal processes everywhere in the EU, thus enhancing citizen safety and security within the whole of the EU, and ensuring full participation in the legal processes.

Placing these crucial regulatory messages in the very beginning of the text, when the attention span of lay users is in its prime time (think advertising) would promote awareness of EU citizens on what the EU is offering them, short or longer term, why legislation is necessary, and what the new provisions are about. One final point for Part 1 could be the inclusion of the effect of the EU text on EU citizens. This would require the identification of the date of entry into force, and an explanation of direct applicability and direct effect in lay terms. For example, 'This Regulation is the law in all EU Member States after 31 December 2019, even without further national implementation.' Or 'This Directive is the law in all Member States after 31 December 2019, and EU citizens can rely on it before the national courts even if their state has not legislated any further.' Or;

> Articles 1, 3, 5, and 10 of this Directive are the law in all EU Member States after 31 December 2019, and EU citizens can rely on these provisions before the national courts even if their state has not legislated any further. Articles 2, 4, and 5 of this Directive are the law in the EU but EU citizens cannot rely on them before their national courts without further legislation in the Member State.

Part 2, addressed to Member States and national authorities, can include the detailed list of regulatory messages. The content, and even language, here would not change from the existing EU legislation. Perhaps it would make sense to divide in separate lists the duties of Member States and their powers: Member States must, as opposed to Member States may. This will facilitate complete transposition, by identifying in a clear list the obligations of Member States. This is where national authorities can focus, and these can be replicated in correlation tables like the one currently used by the Commission. Duties could be enhanced by including specific national implementation action, such as the identification of an agency to administer the law, the provision of enforcement mechanisms, and any monitoring requirements. This would promote effective implementation of the EU legislation at the national level and effective monitoring of implementation at the EU level. Of course, as duties are necessary elements for the completion of the regulatory package, duties must come with a clear deadline. This is already provided for as the transposition deadline. But taking it away from the variety of dates at the end of the EU text would both draw Member States' attention to what they are expected to do by that time, and it would alleviate the confusion of lay users on the date of entry into force of the EU legislative text. Powers of Member States, namely transposition options, could be a new element in EU legislation. They are currently found in Transposition Guidance. The advantage of placing them in the text of the legislation would be that the choices of Member States would be limited to the ones included in the legislation. This could dramatically prevent gold-plating, and would enhance a level of harmonisation by steering Member States to manageable groups of trends in legislation and practice.

Part 3, addressed to EU and national lawyers and judges, can include everything that is left out of Parts 1 and 2. Recitals, definitions, legal issues, issues of interpretation, reviews and sunset clauses can be collected in Part 3. This would involve simply transferring these types of provisions from the beginning of the EU texts to the bottom. This is the part of the legislation, where drafters can use expert terminology freely provided that the rule of law is still served.

Applying the layered approach to EU texts seemed a daunting task, in theory. But in practice, it proved to be a minor tweak in the current structure of EU legislative texts. It involves creating a new Article 1 with the three regulatory messages requested by Group 1 lay users: why, how, and what, in concrete terms. Then dividing current content into duties and powers for Member States and authorities. And transferring recitals, definitions, and interpretation from the start of the text, and bundling them to the bottom along with the rest of final provisions. Not a bad price for enhanced effectiveness, in delivery of Better Regulation.

CONCLUSIONS

Stage 3 in the transposition drafting process plays perhaps the most significant role in the production of an effective legislative text. The prerequisites of understanding in Stage 1 and analysis in Stage 2 feed into the real creativity of the transposition process that begins and takes roots in Stage 3. Here the transposition task is expressed in a legislative design that will be applied in Stage 4 and verified in Stage 5. And so, despite the prevalent but erroneous view that drafting is all about writing and words, it is the design that constitutes the heart of drafting. Once the design is compiled, words and syntax will fall into place. In fact, if the design is not fit for purpose, any perfection in the legislative communication will be lost in a legislative text that cannot contribute to the achievement of the desired regulatory results and, as such, is ineffective. If the design does nurture effectiveness, then erroneous choices of legislative expression (words and syntax) can be salvaged by clarity of context, clarity of structure, and clarity of objectives.

Yet, there is little focus on the design of the transposing text. At the national level, transposition drafters blindly copy the design of the EU text. At the EU level, the legislative text is chained by archaic traditions of legislative style from a bygone era when EU law was a *droit diplomatique* whose effectiveness was considered to be the successful completion of yet another political agreement. But this is no longer the case. Europe, and its citizens, are seeking results. The achievement of the desired regulatory results, as a measure of effectiveness, requires that the legislative text conveys to the users of EU legislation all regulatory messages using a legislative expression that is correctly pitched at their level of subject and legal sophistication. Similarly, this is the task of transposition drafters, only their concrete user groups may differ from those of the EU level. And their levels of sophistication may also differ. For the purposes of achieving effectiveness at the national and at the EU levels, the use of the same legislative design is therefore inherently infertile.

In the compilation of their own legislative design in Stage 3 of the transposition process, national drafters look to their own traditional style of structure of legislative texts, principles of EU law applicable to their task, text-focused considerations of extent, type, and nature of the text under transposition, and the user-centred layered approach. In their inevitably subjective choices national drafters are guided by the concept of effectiveness at the national level as contributor to effectiveness at the EU level. A prerequisite and enhancer of this effectiveness is the unhindered communication of the regulatory messages to the concrete users of the specific legislative text. The layered approach is an innovative tool that can serve them very well indeed.

But the layered approach can also serve EU drafters. By dividing EU legislative texts into three parts addressing each of the main three user groups of EU legislation, they can speak directly to lay users, to the national authorities of the Member States, and to lawyers and judges. Using the layered approach can greatly contribute to the direct communication between the EU and its citizens, thus creating a 'personal' relationship of dialogue and nurturing understanding of the rationale behind the regulatory efforts of the EU and heir added value for EU citizens. This can foster participation of users in the regulatory process, ultimately inciting better implementation and the creation of a vested interest of regulatory success for legislative users. If this cannot be the best route towards sustainable integration, it is difficult to see what can.

5. Composing and developing the transposition law

In the previous chapter, emphasis was placed on design and the crucial importance that this serves for an effective transposition text. Indeed, Stage 3 may well be the most important stage in the drafting process in general and the drafting process of transposition texts in specific. But, of course, this does not detract from the significance of Stage 4, which refers to the composition of the draft transposition law. Here design acquires bones and flesh by its application to choices of legislative expression.

This Stage is rather jurisdiction specific. Composition, syntax, and language are perhaps the most jurisdiction eccentric features in legislative drafting, and transposition drafting is no exception. However, there still are principles that can guide transposition drafters in making their national choices. This chapter will focus on this aspect whilst respecting the national intricacies of composition in the legislations of the Member States.

A. COMPOSITION IN LEGISLATIVE LITERATURE: THE LEGISLATIVE EXPRESSION[1]

In the same way in which appropriate structure can inform quick comprehension,[2] language choices can also inform clarity, precision, and unambiguity.[3] In turn, these promote and contribute to effectiveness, the ultimate goal for legislative drafters. They enhance predictability,[4] accessibility especially by

---

1 This is heavily based on H Xanthaki, *Drafting Legislation: Art and Technology of Rules for Regulation* (Hart Publishers, Oxford, 2014), 85–102.

2 See J Stark, 'Should the Main Goal of Statutory Drafting be Accuracy or Clarity?' (1994) 15 *Statute Law Review* 207, 208.

3 Clarity causes are volume, quality, and perceptions of legislation: see Cabinet Office, Office of Parliamentary Counsel *When Laws Become Too Complex*, 16 April 2013, https://www.gov.uk/government/publications/when-laws-become-too-complex accessed 14 December 2023, para 3.

4 See E Majambere, 'Clarity, Precision and Unambiguity: Aspects for Effective Legislative Drafting (2011) 37 *Commonwealth Law Bulletin* 417, 417.

lay users,[5] and clarity via certainty[6] in what the law states.[7] This allows users to understand what is required of them,[8] and thus comply with the legislation[9] and contribute to effectiveness of implementation.[10] Moreover, clarity, precision, and unambiguity is a tool[11] for achieving transformation[12] via legislation expressing regulatory goals contributing to transforming law reform:[13] unclear laws are the worst form of tyranny.[14] Finally, clarity, precision, and unambiguity offer officers of the law the opportunity to understand correctly and fully the law, and consequently to apply it appropriately, as required under the rule

---

5 See B Bekink and C Botha, 'Aspects of Legislative Drafting: Some South African Realities (or Plain Language Is Not Always Plain Sailing)' (2011) 28 *Statute Law Review* 34, 65.

6 On clarity via a balance of continuity and change, see Sir S Laws, 'Plus ça change? Continuity and Change in UK Legislative Drafting Practice' (2009) 11 *Eur. J.L. Reform* 139.

7 See Sir S Laws, 'Consistency v Innovation', CALC conference, 2009, Hong Kong.

8 See J Paul Martin, 'Development and Rights Revisited: Lessons from Africa' (2006) 3 *SUR: International J Human Rights* 97.

9 In *R v Royal* (1993) 10 CRNZ 4 (HC), J Penlington noted it is not a beach of the accused's right to legal assistance that they could not mount a sound defence without legal training where the accused has access to a lawyer; the question is whether this argument can be reversed where no access to a lawyer is possible.

10 See M J Rizzo, 'Which Kind of Legal Order? Logical Coherence and Praxeological Coherence' (1999) 9 *Journal des Economistes et des Etudes Humaines* 1, 2; also see R Craswell and J E Calfee, 'Deterrence and Uncertain Legal Standards' (1986) 2 *Journal of Law of Economics and Organization* 279, 281.

11 See S Krongold, 'Writing Laws: Making Them Easier to Understand' (1992) 24 *Ottawa L. Rev.* 495, 501; for a direct link between democracy, the rule of law, and clear laws see *Mercur Island Shipping Co v Laughton* [1983] 1 All E.R. 334, [1983] 2 W.L.R. 45.

12 In the context of South Africa, see K Klare, 'Legal Culture and Transformative Constitutionalism' (1998) *South African J Human Rights* 147, 178–79.

13 The clarity of law means overall consistency of their justificatory grounds and their intelligibility as justice-based reasons: see T Inoue 'The rule of Law as Legislation' in L J Wintgens, *Legislation in Context: Essays in Legisprudence* (Aldershot, Ashgate, 2007) 55, 71.

14 See Lord Oliver of Aylmerton, 'A Judicial View of Modern Legislation' (1993) 14 *Statute Law Review* 1, 2; also see Parliamentary Counsel Office, *Public Access to Legislation, A Discussion Paper for Public Comment* (New Zealand, 1998), 6–8.

of law.[15] Finally, clarity, precision, and unambiguity avoid the hefty costs of vagueness.[16]

Clarity is defined as 'clearness or lucidity as to perception or understanding; freedom from indistinctness or ambiguity'. For Gérard Caussignac clear means easy to understand, intelligible, unequivocal, or unambiguous. For Majamberee 'it is not possible to separate, clarity, precision and ambiguity when drafting'. Kabba juxtaposes clarity and unambiguity, and finds that the latter is part of the former, as they share similar characteristics. Clarity, precision, and unambiguity all serve as techniques used for effectiveness, which have equal standing. And so in a dilemma, the drafter will implement whichever of these virtues best serves effectiveness based on the type of legislation that is being drafted, and the audience that it is drafted for.

At the end of the day the drafter's tool is perfect words. They are units of grammar whose semantic field is a fully closed circle: the meaning that they express is received exactly as it was sent, because the hermetically closed boundaries of their sematic field prevent additional referents from creeping in. The word 'tree' conveys the message of a tall plant with leaves: it is not a bush nor an animal. But, unfortunately, perfect words do not really exist: it is not the word that defines the meaning, it is people who define a meaning.[17] And perfect communication in legislation is an even rarer phenomenon:[18] legislation is an expertise;[19] the high number and diversity of recipients leads to inherent possibilities of misunderstanding; and legislation as a form of written communication lacks the luxury of gesture and elaboration often afforded in oral face to face communication. And so, words tend to suffer from breaks in the boundaries of their semantic fields that allow additional referents to creep

---

15 See A Seidman, R Seidman and N Abeyesekere, *Legislative Drafting for Democratic Social Change* (The Hague, Kluwer Law International, 2001), 255; for specific reference to human rights related legislation see M Arden, 'Modernising legislation' (1998) *Public Law* 65, 75; also see L L Fuller, *The Morality of Law* (New Haven and London, Yale University Press, 1969), 39.

16 See G K Hadfieldt, 'Weighing the Value of Vagueness: An Economic Perspective on Precision in the Law' (1994) 82 *California Law Review* 541, 546.

17 See J Waldront, 'Vagueness in Law and Language: Some Philosophical Issues' (1994) 82 *California Law Review* 509, 510.

18 See L Del Duca, 'Introduction Symposium on the UCC, SEC, ALI, Federal Rules and Federal Government Simplification Experiences – Is It Time for a Model Set of Drafting Principles?' (2001) 105 *Dickinson Law Review* 205, 211; also see J McBaine, 'The Rule Against Disturbing Plain Meaning of Writings' (1942–1943) 31 *Californi Law Review* 145, 147.

19 See F Bennion, 'The Readership of Legal Texts', https:// www .yumpu .com/ en/ document/ read/ 38055018/ 1993001 -the -readership -of -legal -texts -francis -bennion accessed 14 December 2023.

in (vagueness); or from overlapping sematic fields that can attribute more than one meaning to it (ambiguity).

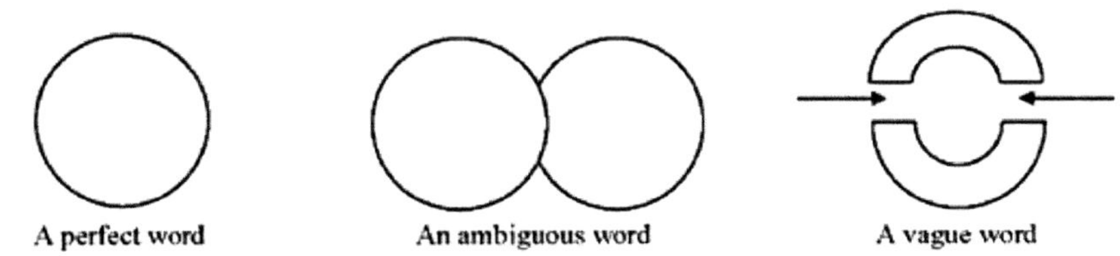

Figure 5.1 *Perfect and diseased words*

Source: See R Dickerson, 'The Diseases of Legislative Language' (1964) 1 *Harv J on Legis* 5.

Vagueness exists when there is doubt about where a word's boundaries are. Here the disease is one of inadequate communication: the user is offered such a generic term, that their legitimate unilateral insertion of referents can lead to numerous semantic fields and numerous meanings. Vagueness is a choice of any meaning, and so it is legislative chaos. For example, the term 'blind': what degree of visual impairment is required? Or the term 'vehicle': does it mean mechanical vehicle or are animals used for transport also included in the semantic field? But vagueness is benign chaos: unlike ambiguity it does not pretend to convey a specific message only to trap the recipient to one message only; instead, it invites the recipient to think exactly what is intended to convey, thus allowing conscious choices of referents. It is precisely its benign nature that renders vagueness a useful disease for drafters and legislators. Vagueness can be forgiven, if a political compromise is needed,[20] if there is a disagreement between policy officers and drafters,[21] or if an intransitive legislative text is needed to allow post enactment individualisation of the legislation at the moment of application.[22] In these exceptional cases, vagueness seems

[20] After all, the drafter's primary aim is to award effect to government policy: see E Sutherland, 'Clearer Drafting and the Timeshare Act 1992: A response from Parliamentary Counsel to Mr. Cutts' (1993) 14 *Statute Law Review* 163, 163.

[21] See R Dickerson, *Fundamentals of Legal Drafting* (Boston, Little Brown and Company, 1986) 11.

[22] See G Christie, 'Vagueness and Legal Language' (1963–1964) 48 *Minnesota Law Review* 885, 889.

justifiable, or even desirable,[23] but not ambiguity.[24] Let us draw the difference between the two concepts, described by Dickerson as the diseases of words.[25]

Ambiguity exists when a word can be interpreted in more than one way,[26] or when it can admit two or more meanings, or when it can be understood in more than one way, or when it refers to two or more things at the same time.[27] Ambiguous words invite semantic diversity: is a 'light' truck light in weight or light in color? Does 'shall' mean 'must' or 'will'? These terms can be legitimately used to convey either of the two messages. A number of authors feel that all words are ambiguous and that the 'one word, one concept' notion is a fallacy,[28] and that 'often more than one interpretation is possible'.[29]

In an attempt to form perfect words, drafters can fall into the trap of over-exhaustiveness: long exhaustive lists of referents per term used. This may promote precision of meaning. But at its extreme it can lead to an inadvertent exclusion of classes of concepts that the drafter intended to include in the semantic field conveyed. Over-precision, over-exhaustiveness, or (in the words of a former Chief Parliamentary Counsel to the Government in Ireland) over-drafting may result in redundancy, verbosity, and unintended loopholes.[30] Striking the balance between over-drafting and vagueness (under-drafting) requires careful consideration of the boundaries of the words used.

But it is ambiguity that really plagues legislative expression, as it guarantees legislative mis-communication. Ambiguity can be sematic, syntactic, or contextual.

---

[23] See R Dickerson, 'Some Jurisprudential Implications of Electronic Data Processing' (1963) 28 *Law and Contemp. Prob.* 53, 62.

[24] But see contra A Miller, 'Statutory Language and the Purposive Use of Ambiguity' (1956) 42 *Virginia Law Review* 23; G Fraser, 'In Praise of Ambiguity' (2000) *Policy Options* 21, 25; and P Thomas, 'Legal Skills and the Use of Ambiguity' (1991) 42 *Northern Ireland Legal Quarterly* 14, 22–23.

[25] For a detailed analysis see R Dickerson, 'The Diseases of Legislative Language' (1964) 1 *Harv J on Legis* 5.

[26] See J Evans, *Statutory Interpretation: Problems of Communication* (Oxford, OUP, 1988) 73; also see F A R Bennion, *Bennion on Statutory Interpretation: A Code* (London, LexisNexis, 2008) 444–56.

[27] See *Webster's Third New International Dictionary* (Chicago, Encyclopedia Britannica, 1976), Vol. I, 66.

[28] See J Frank, 'Words and Music: Some Remarks on Statutory Interpretation' (1947) 47 *Columbia Law Review* 1259, 1263.

[29] See Lord Dilhorne, in *Black-Clawson International Ltd v Papierwerke Waldhof-Aschaffenburg AG* [1975] AC 591 at 622.

[30] See 'Legislative Drafting Manual' (unpublished, Dublin, 2001), para 4.4.

Semantic ambiguity[31] occurs when a single word has more than one meaning.[32] It is defined as the phenomenon where a word's inherent multiplicities of meaning derive from lexicographical usage and exist independently of context.[33] There are words that are inherently ambiguous. 'May' and 'shall' are often used interchangeably in language.[34] The problem of the false imperative, namely the use of 'may' for the imposition of an obligation, plagues legal language.[35] The ambiguity created by the erroneous use of 'may' is enhanced in legislation, and so it is the drafter's duty to ensure that 'may' is only used for the purposes of introducing a discretionary action.[36] 'Shall' is one of the most dangerous ambiguous words. To lay users it can convey the future tense,[37] whereas to lawyers it conveys an obligation.[38] This is exactly why the use of 'shall' is not recommended,[39] and must be eliminated altogether.[40] 'Shall' can be easily replaced by 'must', 'it is the duty of', or 'is to'.[41] And the use of the present tense as an alternative would make exceptional sense since legislation carries the context of a duty or obligation anyway.[42] But in amending laws there is an argument for the retention of the dreaded 'shall', if it is present

---

[31] For an analysis of the concept of semantic ambiguity, see J MacKaye, *The Logic of Language* (London, Russell and Russell, 1965), chapter 5.

[32] For example, the parties to *Frigaliment Importing Co v International Sales Corp.* (190 F. Supp. 116, S.D.N.Y. 1960) disagreed over the meaning of 'chicken'. Did the word 'chicken' in their contract include only broilers and fryers, or did it include stewing chickens as well?

[33] See S Kloepfer, 'Ambiguity and Vagueness in the Criminal Law: an Analysis of Types' (1984–1985) 27 *Crim L Q* 94, 98.

[34] For an example of a case confusing may with must see R Carter 'Statutory Interpretation in New Zealand's Court of Appeal: When "May" Means "Must", Section Heading Affect Interpretation, and Latent Acts Have Effect' (2001) 22 *Statute Law Review* 20.

[35] See J Payne, 'The False Imperative' (2010) *The Legislative Lawyer*.

[36] See R J Martineau, *Drafting Legislation and Rules in Plain English* (St Paul, West, 1991) 81.

[37] See M M Asprey, 'Shall Must Go' (1992) 3 *Scribes J Leg Writing* 79, 79.

[38] See R Eagleson and M Asprey, 'Must We Continue With "Shall"?' (1989) 63 *Australian L J* 75.

[39] See A Watson-Brown, 'Do We Still Need "Shall"?' (1998) 28 *Hong Kong LJ* 29, 44.

[40] See P Butt, *Modern Legal Drafting: A Guide to Using Clearer Language* (Cambridge, Cambridge University Pres, 2013) 269; also see J Kimble, *Lifting the Fog of Legalese* (St Paul, Carolina Academic Press) 159–160; B Garner, *Dictionary of Legal Usage* (Oxford, Oxford University Press, 2011) 954; M Asprey, *Plain Language for Lawyers* (Australia, Federation Press, 2010) 218.

[41] See R Redux, '"Shall" in Legislative Drafting' (1987) 104 *South African Law Journal* 186, 194.

[42] On the imperative of legislation, without reference to 'shall' see generally D Greenberg, 'Nothing Will Come of Nothing' (2010) 30 *New Law Journal* 1084.

in the original text: the possibility of ambiguity created by the use of two synonym terms endangers the effectiveness of the amending law enough to tip the balance towards clarity as opposed to plain language.

'And' and 'or' are words often causing confusion if it is unclear whether they reflect conjunction or disjunction.[43] As a result they are by their very nature ambiguous.[44] 'And' is normally[45] conjunctive. For example, 'This Act applies to doctors and nurses' indicates that both groups are within the field of application of the legislation. 'Or' is normally disjunctive. For example, 'Exchange of contracts may take place before or after payment' means that either options are acceptable. But 'or' has two possible meanings: it can either mean 'either...or', or it can be 'or/and', thus causing ambiguity.[46] When it comes to 'and' or 'or' issues often arise simply because the drafter uses the terms wrongly, or because the placement of 'and' or 'or' as a means of expression of the legislative sentence is ambiguous,[47] or because courts fail to respect the general rule.[48] And so it is advisable for the drafter to trench on over-precision when using 'and' or 'or': often breaking the possibilities into three separate options, also foreseeing the combination of the two obvious options, helps the reader. Although verbose and superfluous, it is much clearer to state that 'A doctor, a nurse, or a doctor with a nurse may conduct HIV tests in maternity wards with or without the subject's consent.' Moreover, 'and/or' is to be avoided.[49]

Words setting boundaries or exceptions also cause ambiguity, if the exception or the precise boundary is not regulated. For example, unless/except,[50] less than, more than, not exceeding; exceeding; above; below; over; under; before; after. The danger with scale indicators is that they do not automatically provide for the benchmark itself. For example, 'Less than X, then A; and more than X, then B' provides for cases falling less and above X, but do not provide for

---

[43] See L Allen, 'Symbolic Logic: A Razor-edged Tool for Drafting and Interpreting Legal Documents' (1956–1957) 66 *Yale L.J.* 833, 858.

[44] See M B Kirk, 'Legal Drafting: The Ambiguity of and Or' (1970) 2 *Tex. Tech L. Rev.* 235.

[45] See T J Richards and R A Girlie, '"Or" and "And/or": a discussion' (1989) 10 *History and Philosophy of Logic* 29.

[46] See L Goddard, 'The Exclusive "or"' (1960) 20 *Analysis* 97.

[47] See S Wisotsky, 'How to Interpret Statutes – Or Not: Plain Meaning and Other Phantoms' (2009) 10 *J App Prac and Process* 321, 327.

[48] In case *Re H (a minor)* [1994] 1 All ER 812 CA 'and' in 'Recognition and enforcement' was held to be disjunctive.

[49] See B A Garner, *Legal Writing in Plain English* (Chicago and London, University of Chicago Press, 2001), 112.

[50] See J Zurcher, 'Basic Rules of Legislative Drafting' (1976–1977) 7 *Manitoba Law Journal* 131, 144.

Table 5.1 *Dickerson's time expression*

Instead of...	Say...
From 1 July 2020, to ...	After 30 June 2020, and before ...
Between 1 July 2020, and ...	After 20 June 2020, and before ...
To (or until or by) 30 June 2020 ...	Before 1 July 2020 ...
... between the ages of 17 and 4 5...	... 17 years old or older and under 46 ...
... who is more than 17 years old ...	... who has passed their 17th birthday [or who is 17 years old or older] *unless you mean* ... who is 18 years old or older ...

Source: Dickerson as cited by V R A C Crabbe *Legislative Precedents – Volume II* (London, Cavendish Publishing Ltd, 1998) 14.

cases that fall spot on X. And so the question is, what happens if it is X itself. The drafter needs to provide for these cases also. And so it would be clearer if the provision stated 'Less than *or at* X' or 'X *or more than* X'. There is a trend in defusing the situation by providing for –X as a means of ensuring that X does not come into play at all. This is better expressed in ranges of numbers, ages, and dates, such as to, through, between, and from. The problem with these words is that they do not adequately convey when exactly is the start and end of the range that they express.[51] But it is crucial for the drafter to convey exactly that information, and indeed in a very clear manner. Convention helps here, but not always. Reed Dickerson offers good advice:

Similarly, 'that' and 'which' create confusion because they are used interchangeably. They are not. 'That' is used to introduce restrictive clauses: it restricts and defines the word that it modifies and so it is not set off by commas. For example, 'The court retains the weapon that was used in the alleged offense until the conclusion of the trial.' Here the drafter defines which weapon it is that the court must retain: it is none other than the particular weapon used in the alleged offence. 'Which', with commas, introduces non-restrictive clauses, which provide additional or descriptive information about the word modified. For example, 'The Commission establishes the hearing date, which may be changed upon the request of either party.' Here the drafter does not attempt to define which is the hearing date established by the Commission, and does not prohibit the Commission from establishing other dates. Ambiguity arises when the drafters uses 'which' without a comma:[52] 'A report which is required to be available for inspection must be in a form convenient for photocopying.' The

[51] See B Simamba, *How Laws are Written and Applied* (Indiana, Author House, 2010) 32–33.

[52] Example from the Minnesota Legislative Drafting Manual, para 10.11.

user is left with two possible messages: Either, 'A report, which is required to be available for inspection, must be in a form convenient for photocopying' meaning that all reports must be made available for inspection, and all have to be in a certain form. Or, 'A report that is required to be available for inspection must be in a form convenient for photocopying' meaning that of all reports only those that are required to be available for inspection must be kept in a form available for photocopying.

Syntactic ambiguity[53] or ambiguity at the sentence level[54] arises from the way in which the meaning of a sentence is influenced by the intended relationships between individual words and phrases used in the sentence, as distinct from the way in which the meaning of the sentence is influenced by the meaning of the individual words and phrases.[55] A statement is syntactically ambiguous where its grammatical structure gives rise to uncertainties of reference. Syntactic ambiguity is the principal cause of the fallacy of amphiboly,[56] and expressions in which it occurs are often not without aspects of humour, intended or not.[57] Here ambiguity arises out of a loose combination of words, such that it is not clear which word or phrase refers to which other word of phrase.[58] In legislative drafting this phenomenon, also known as syntactic discontinuity, is connected with the frequent use of the so-called qualifications in legislative provisions: there are simply too many adverbial constructions aiming to establish the scope of application of legislative rules, and often these are all fitted into a single sentence.[59] These constructions aim to promote clarity and precision; but attaching them all at the various words that they identify is a recipe for ambiguity. There is no doubt that to a certain extent syntactic discontinuity contributes to a greater complexity of the text and makes greater demands on the interpreter. The reason for this is that due to syntactic

---

53 See J L Montrose, 'Syntactic (formerly amphibolous) Ambiguity' (1962) *M U L L* 65, 69, 70; also see P J Fitzgerald, 'Law and Logic' (1963–1964) 39 *Notre Dame L* 570.

54 Martineau and Salerno also talk about contextual ambiguity, namely situations where it is unclear which of the two or more available alternatives are intended: see R J Martineau and M B Salerno, *Legal, Legislative and Rule Drafting in Plain English* (St Paul, Thomson West, 2005); but this seems to be included in ambiguity at sentence level.

55 See R Engholm, 'Logic and Laws: Relief From Statutory Obfuscation' (1975–1976) 9 *U Mich J L Reform* 322, 324.

56 Also known as ambiguity of reference or amphibolous: see Copi, *Introduction to Logic* (UK, Collier Mack, 1953), 70.

57 See S Kloepfer, above n 33, 102.

58 See L Allen, above n 43, 860.

59 See V K Bhatia, 'Cognitive Structuring in Legislative Provisions' in J Gibbons (ed), *Language and the Law* (New York, Longman Group UK Ltd, 1994) 136, 147–148.

discontinuity, the relations between individual clause elements throughout the legislative provision are less transparent and less explicit. The interpretation thus requires much analytical thinking and experience.[60] For example, a sign about refunds at a local hardware store reads 'Store credit only after 90 days.' Does this mean that after 90 days, the customer can receive a refund only in the form of store credit? Or is the point that store credit is not available as a form of refund until 90 days have elapsed? The placement of 'only' makes the reader unsure.[61] Combinations of nouns and their modifiers (the *escaped* prisoner; the executive officer *of the county*; an order *that has been signed by the governor*; an order *signed by the governor*; a document *stating the name of the accused*) within the same sentence leads to complexity, because the sentence itself becomes longer,[62] but also because it becomes increasingly difficult for the reader to retain the subject-verb-object structure without being distracted by the modifiers. Also, modifiers invite syntactic ambiguity due their dubious placement in the sentence and attachment to structural words. For example, the adjective 'married' is semantically clear but syntactically ambiguous in the clause 'A married woman or man may….' The question is whether the drafter meant married man or any man. The rule of last antecedent says that ambiguities like these are to be resolved by taking the problem phrase as applying only to the last item in the series.[63] But this is of little help to lay users. Punctuation can also cause semantic ambiguity, even when the sentence presents no semantic ambiguities at word level. Thornton's advice on this is paramount. His four rules are to punctuate sparingly and with purpose; to punctuate for structure and not for sound; to be conventional; and to be consistent.[64]

Contextual ambiguity occurs when the regulatory message is amphibolous despite its unequivocal words and syntax. Contextual ambiguity is an issue arising of errors in the policy itself or in the design of the law, and not in the composition of the legislative text.

Finally, clarity is enhanced by gender inclusive language. Gender-inclusive, rather than gender-neutral, language contributes to clarity of the legislative text, and thus ultimately serves legislative effectiveness and legislative quality.

---

[60] See J Mackinlay, 'Syntactic discontinuity in the language of UK and EU legislation' (2004) 3 *English for Specific Purposes World*, http://esp-world.info accessed 13 December 2023.

[61] See D R Woodworth, 'Musings on Precision in Legal Writing' (1966) 41 *J. St. B. of Cal.* 910, 911–912.

[62] See Sir W Dale, 'A London Particular' (1985) *Statute Law Review* 11, 20.

[63] See T Myers, 'Clearing up ambiguity from a series modifier' (2011) 90 *Mich. B.J.* 52.

[64] See H Xanthaki, *Thornton's Legislative Drafting* (West Sussex, Bloomsbury, 2013) 37–39; also see R Wydick, 'Should Lawyers Punctuate?' (1990) *1 Scribes Journal of Legal Writing* 7, 23.

Gender-neutral language (GNL) refers to language that includes all sexes and treats women and men equally.[65] Gender-neutral language, also called non-sexist, non-gender-specific, or inclusive language, attempts to redress the balance.[66] Gender-inclusive language (GIL) puts to effect the principle that every citizen is equal before the eyes of the law, and deletes sex and gender from legislative expression.

In Europe and in the English-speaking world, gender neutrality and its successor gender inclusivity are gaining ground as tools of clarity.[67] Although internationally gender neutral language has been adopted by the New South Wales Office of Parliamentary Counsel in 1983, by New Zealand in 1985, by the Australian Office of Parliamentary Counsel in 1988, by the UN and the International Labour Organization roughly around 1989, by Canada in 1991, by South Africa in 1995, and by the US Congress, albeit not consistently, in 2001, European drafters are lagging behind.[68] GNL refers to language that includes all sexes and treats women and men equally. GIL language takes the argument further. In an attempt to put to effect the principle that every citizen is equal before the eyes of the law, it aims to delete sex and gender from the expression of the subjects of legislation. Therefore, instead of ensuring that both men and women are within the scope of legislative expression, as is the case with GNL, GIL aims to eliminate the consideration of sex and gender altogether. As a result, it differs from GNL in that it avoids any classification of sex and gender. With GIL the subject does not need to be classified or to identify as any sex or gender. A GI draft simply renders sex and gender irrelevant as a consideration. The preferred technique for real gender inclusivity is the use of the singular noun followed by the plural 'they' rather than singular pronouns 'he' or 'she': for example, 'a doctor, who fails their examination'. This technique was favoured by authors prior to the nineteenth century in

---

[65] See D Greenberg, 'The Techniques of Gender-Neutral Drafting' in C Stefanou and H Xanthaki (eds), Drafting *Legislation: A Modern Approach* (Aldershot, Ashgate, 2008) 63.

[66] See 'Guidelines on Gender-Neutral Language', UNESCO 1999.

[67] See H Xanthaki, 'Gender-inclusive Legislative Drafting in English: A Matter of Clarity', in: A Flückiger (ed), *La rédaction administrative et législative inclusive, la francophonie entre impulsions et résistances* (Berne, 2019) 57.

[68] See the statement of the Leader of the House of Commons HC Deb 8 March 2007, c146 WS. See also the debates in the House of Lords in 2013 and 2018: HL Deb 12 December 2013 cols 1004–1016; HL Deb 25 June 2018 cols 7–9.

English and French[69] and is still common in contemporary English.[70] An example is in the UK Counter-Terrorism Act 2008: 'References in this Part to a person being dealt with for or in respect of an offence are to their being sentenced ... in respect of the offence.' A further example comes from the Local Democracy, Economic Development and Construction Act 2009, Schedule 1, paragraph 2(5)(b): '...the chair holds office... in accordance with the terms of their appointment'. The technique is rather innovative, since it uses a grammatical error to draw the reader's attention to gender inclusivity. But at the same time it demonstrates quite rightly that drafters must use grammar without being its slave. It is better to be inelegant than uncertain.[71]

B. COMPOSITION IN TRANSPOSITION: THE LEGISLATIVE EXPRESSION

Having explored the main modern trends on the composition of legislation, let us explore the composition of transposition laws. Composition and legislative expression in transposition laws does not, or should not, differ from that in other national legislative texts. Although drafting styles may differ within the Member States,[72] they all pursue clarity.[73] Clarity is nurtured by familiarity of style (predictability). It enhances the accurate communication of the legislative message, which expresses the regulatory message.[74] Users understand what is requested of them and, if they are so inclined, can successfully follow legislative demands, thus participating in the implementation of the transposition legislation. In fact, the Court of Justice has repeatedly linked complete and full transposition to users who understand fully what rights and obligations they have.[75] Offering a clear expression of the regulatory messages in transposi-

---

69 See A Bodin, 'Androcentrism in Prescriptive Grammar: Singular "they", Sex Indefinite "he", and "he or she"' (1974) 4 *Language in Society* 129, 131–133; also see S Petersson, 'Gender Neutral Drafting: Historical Perspective' (1998) 19 *Statute Law Review* 93.

70 See C Miller and K Swift, *The Handbook of Non Sexist Writing* (New York, Lippincott and Crowell, 1980) 38–40.

71 See J K Aitken and E L Piesse, *The Elements of Drafting* (Sydney, The Law Book Company Ltd, 1995) 57.

72 See M Hernandez Ramos and V Heydt, 'Legislative Language and style' in U Karpen and H Xanthaki (eds), *Legislation in Europe: A Handbook for Scholars and Practitioners* (Hart Publishers, Oxford, 2017), 129.

73 See A Watson, 'Legal Change: Sources of Law and Legal Culture' (1983) 131 *University of Pennsylvania Law Review* 1121, 1154.

74 See D Roebuck, 'Plain, Clear and Something More? Criteria for Communication in Legal Language' (2014) 16 *European Journal of Law Reform* 633, 650.

75 See Case C-29/84 *Commission v Germany* CJ 23 May 1985, C(1985) 229, para 23; also see Case C-144/99 *Commission v The Netherlands*, C(2001)257, para 17; Case C-478/99 *Commission v Kingdom of Sweden*, C(2002)281, para 18.

tion legislation contributes to the regulatory success not only of the national transposition legislation but also, indirectly, of the EU text. Following the national drafting style offers the transposition text predictability. Users find the structure and concepts familiar, they know exactly where to look for the information that they need, and they can easily identify the legislative messages and their underlying regulatory messages. This entices them to implement the transposition legislation, and, thus, to contribute to the effectiveness of the EU regulatory package as a whole. From the point of view of the rule of law, predictability enhances accessibility of the legislative text by its users, thus nurturing transparency and democracy.[76] And all these nurture sustainable integration.

Unfortunately, this familiarity of drafting style is snatched away by transposition users. Despite the repeated reassurances of the European courts that copying out is not necessary,[77] most transposition texts simply copy verbatim the text of the EU legislation. But copying the EU legislative text allows the EU legislative expression to creep into national legislation, thus creating issues of unpredictability and interpretation.[78] For example, the inclusion of definitions within the EU text, when copied to the national transposition instrument, can create confusion to civil law jurisdictions where definitions are not commonly found in legislation.[79]

Moreover, copying provisions of the EU legislative text may lead to ineffectiveness at the national level.[80] More precisely, copying the terms used in the EU legislative text blindly can lead to serious transposition gaps.

Let us take the example of the Victim's Rights Directive and observe the possible outcomes of copying out the term into the national legal orders of the Member States. A depiction of the term 'victim' in the legal orders of the

---

[76] See Spanish Constitutional Court stC 150/1990, 4 october 1990, § 8; also see stC 96/2002, § 5; stC 235/2000, § 8; stC 104/2000, § 7.

[77] See Case C-59/89 *Commission v Germany*, C(1991)225, para 18.

[78] See Case 363/85 *Commission v Italy*, C(1987)196, para 7.

[79] See P Giliker, 'The Transposition of the Consumer Rights Directive into UK Law: Implementing a Maximum Harmonization Directive' (2015) *European Review of Private Law* 5, 13.

[80] See C Twigg-Flesner, 'Comment: The Future of EU Consumer Law – The End of Harmonisation?' in J Devenney and M Kenny (eds), *European Consumer Protection: Theory and Practice* (2012, CUP, Cambridge), 8; but see contra M W Hesselink, 'The Ideal of Codification and the Dynamics of Europeanisation: The Dutch Experience' (2006) 12 *European Law Journal* 279, 300; also see E Ramsey, 'The Copy Out Technique: More of a "cop out" than a Solution?' (1996) 17 *Statute Law Review* 218.

Member States (outside the Directive and its transposition) is shown in Table 5.2.[81]

In Table 5.2, the term 'victim' in the Directive has a different meaning to that in a number of Member States. For example, in Cyprus the prevalent term is complainants. In Belgium one distinguishes between victims, registered victims, and civil actors in a criminal trial. In the Czech Republic there are both victims and injured parties with overlapping and interrelated rights: victims are viewed holistically whereas injured parties are viewed under the prism of the criminal trial. In Denmark the more neutral word 'aggrieved' (*forurettede*) is used. In Estonia there is a parallel existence of victims in the Victim Support Act (*ohver*) and in the Code of Criminal Procedure (*kannatanu*), and many victim support services and types of, including different types of compensation are open only to victims as defined by CCrP. In Spain terms used are 'hurt', 'offended', or 'injured' but these concepts have been used without much precision, which has led to a huge uncertainty in what refers to their concrete significance. In Finland victim is usually defined as a person who owns the case (*asianomistaja*) but the term 'injured party' describes rather well the essence of the Finnish concept. In France the term victim is used along with *partie lésée* (aggrieved party) or *partie civile*: it is the latter term that best represents victims under the Directive. In Hungary, victims are called harmed/injured parties. In Italy the concept of 'passive subject' can coincide with the 'damaged person', but not always: in a murder case the passive subject is the deceased whereas the damaged person is their relatives. In Malta both victim and injured party are used but there is no definition for either of them. In Poland both the term injured party and victim are used: if proceedings are terminated there is no injured party but they remain victims. In Slovenia injured party is the prevalent term but the term victims is also used in the law. In the Slovak Republic the term aggrieved party is used.

And so, the correlation between EU and national terms is not always evident, and national authorities have to assess whether the term victims can be equated to the national term or not. If it can, then the national term must be used in transposition, thus ensuring a smooth transplantation of the content of the Directive into national law. The disadvantage of this practice is that the correlation is not immediately evident to the foreign victim or indeed to the Commission for the purposes of the assessment of the national transposition.

---

[81] See Centre for European Constitutional Law and Institute of Advanced Legal Studies, 'Study: Protecting Victims' Rights in the EU: the theory and practice of diversity of treatment during the criminal trial – Comparative Report and Policy Recommendations', https://www.cecl.gr/en/category-projects/research/2012/11/15/protecting-victims-rights-in-the-eu-the-theory-and-practice-of-diversity-of-treatment-during-the-criminal-trial/ accesed 14 December 2023.

Table 5.2 Definition of victims

Country	Definition of victims	Family member as victims	Do victims have priority over the accused	Is the place of crime relevant to victims	Are victims only relevant to criminal proceedings	Special categories of victims
Austria	Wider than D	Yes	No, balanced	No	Yes	No
Belgium	D plus registration as victim	Yes	No, balanced	For jurisdictional purposes only	Yes	No
Bulgaria	Wider than D but vague	No	No	No	Yes	Yes, those on protected grounds
Cyprus	Wider than D but vague	No	No	No	Yes	No
Czech Rep	D but with restrictions	Yes	No	No	No	Yes but stricter than D
Denmark	Wider than D but vague	Yes	No	No	No	No
Estonia	Narrower than D	No	No	No	Yes	No
Finland	Wider but vague	Yes but with restrictions	No	No	Yes	Yes for specific crimes
France	Wider but vague	Yes	No, balanced	Yes	Yes	Yes
Germany	Wider but vague	Yes	No, the contrary	Yes	Yes	Yes for specific crimes
Greece	Wider but vague	Yes	No, the contrary	Yes	Yes	Yes for specific crimes
Hungary	Wider but vague	Yes but with restrictions	No	Yes	Yes	Yes
Ireland	No definition	Yes	No	Yes	Yes	Yes for specific crimes
Italy	No definition	Yes	No	Yes	Yes	Yes

Country	Definition of victims	Family member as victims	Do victims have priority over the accused	Is the place of crime relevant to victims	Are victims only relevant to criminal proceedings	Special categories of victims
Latvia	Multiple definitions	Yes	No	Yes	No unless they wish to take part in them	No
Lithuania	Wider but vague	Yes	No, to the contrary	Yes	Yes	No
Luxembourg	Wider but vague	Yes	No	Yes	Yes but in practice services maybe offered outside criminal proceedings	Yes
Malta	No definition	No	No, to the contrary	Yes	Yes	No
The Netherlands	Wider but vague	Yes	No	Yes	Yes	No
Poland	Narrower definition	Yes but only in death	No, to the contrary	No	Yes	Yes
Portugal	A number of definitions	Yes but with restrictions	No, to the contrary	Yes	Yes	Yes
Romania	A number of definitions	Yes but with restrictions	No, to the contrary	Yes	Yes	Yes for specific offences only
Slovak Republic	Narrower than D	No	No	No	No	No
Slovenia	None	Yes but with restrictions	Yes but in specific offences	No	Yes	Yes, for specific offences only
Spain	None	No	No	No	Yes	Yes, for specific offences only

Country	Definition of victims	Family member as victims	Do victims have priority over the accused	Is the place of crime relevant to victims	Are victims only relevant to criminal proceedings	Special categories of victims
Sweden	Narrower than D	No	No	Yes	Yes	No
United Kingdom	Wider than D	Yes	No	Yes	No	Yes

It is advisable therefore that the nationally prevalent term and the Directive's 'victim' is introduced as synonymous in the definitions section of the national legal instrument, where definitions are used, or at least in any explanatory materials escorting the legal instrument. If the nationally prevalent term cannot be equated to that of the Directive, it is worth keeping the term victims within the purposes of the transposition measure, in which case it is imperative that the distinction between the two parallel terms is made expressly. What is particularly concerting is that in a large number of Member States two terms already exist in parallel, and the introduction of a third term of victims in the sense of the Directive can and will complicate things enormously. Ideally, one would have preferred that the Directive used a generic comparative term not found in national legal orders thus showing the specific generic content of the semantic field of victims in the sense of the Directive. Unfortunately this was not done in the drafting of the Directive and one of the main tasks of transposing Member States is to finally clarify who it is that actually benefits from the Directive.

A number of Member States offer no unique definition of victim and the term is defined by means of statutory interpretation deriving from the combination of a number of instruments and case law. This is the case in Belgium, Germany, Denmark, Estonia, Spain, Ireland, Luxembourg, Malta, Portugal, Romania, and the Slovak Republic. In Latvia the term victim encompasses two different meanings: the actual person who has suffered damage as a result of an offence; and the party to criminal proceedings. In Swedish Code of Judicial Procedure (SFS 1942:740) uses the procedural term '*målsägande*' (the injured person), but the term victim is used in other laws. This creates grave concerns on the transposition front. The lack of a unique definition in national law may well allow for the recognition of persons as victims under specific conditions introduced by special criminal provisions, laws, or case law. This is highly disconcerting as the victim, much more so the foreign victim, and the Commission have no way of knowing for sure whether a person is classified as victim in the specific circumstances of the case. Moreover, the lack of a detailed definition creates opportunities for inequalities but also corruption for *male fide* officials: the choice of classifying a person as a victim or not must not be left to the discretion of government agencies or NGOs but must be clearly and expressly introduced in the law to which victims and their advisers have easier access.

A large number of Member States define victims by virtue of a wide but vague reference to persons suffering harm as a result of a criminal offence. This is the case in Bulgaria, Cyprus, Germany, Estonia, Finland, France, Greece, Italy, Lithuania, Luxembourg, the Netherlands, Slovenia, the Slovak Republic, and the UK. This is rather problematic as many of these Member States do not have a single definition of victims. The fragmentation of definitions and the vagueness of any existing fragmented definitions leave ground for restrictions to the circle of persons recognised as victims and is in direct clash with the Directive and the inclusive definition of victims. The lack of a unified definition and the introduction of a vague definition carry similar concerns for transposition: uncertainty in the law allows for the possibility of inequalities, and corruption in the case of *male fide* officials.

A number of Member States offer a definition of victims that is stricter than the definition of the Directive. In Cyprus, family members are not included in the definition. In the Cypriot Compensation of Crime Victims Law No. 51(I)/1997, a victim is 'any person who has suffered serious bodily injury or damage to his health, directly caused by the commission of a violent crime or who died as a result of such crime'. Section 2 of the Anti-Trafficking Law No. 87(I)/2007 defines victim as 'the physical person who suffered detriment, including physical or psychological damage or economic loss, which is the direct result of the commission of offences which are punishable under this Law'. For the purposes of compensation the definition is much stricter than that of the Directive and does not recognise any damage other than serious bodily harm or damage to health. In the Czech Republic, victims are family members only in the case of death of the victim, and they include relatives in direct line of descent, brothers and sisters, adoptive parents and adoptive children, spouses, registered partner and partner, or persons living in a family relationship or similar type of relationship if the harm suffered could be considered as own harm by the other person. The Czech national expert identifies two areas of restrictions: in the definition of the disabled as vulnerable victims the Czech legislator requires disability imposing various obstacles preventing the full and effective exercise of rights of this person in the society. Moreover, the group of victims at risk of secondary victimisation is restricted to victims of crime against human dignity in the area of sexuality and crimes that included violence or the threat of violence. Furthermore, Czech law limits protection to victims of violent crimes or sexual crimes thus excluding organised crime and exploitation, hate crimes and crimes committed in close relationships (not only those that include violence). And the Czech legislator has omitted to mention 'gender identity' among the factors leading to secondary victimisation, as explicitly mentioned in Recital 56 of the Directive. In Germany, family members and the victim's heirs can be victims only under certain conditions. And the right to receive information and communication is exercised by them only if they are exceptionally authorised to be co-plaintiffs. An example of this is the family co-plaintiff in the sense of § 395 Section 2 No. 1 CPC for capital offences, when the affected victim has died. The parents of a child who has been sexually abused, are, however, not injured in the sense of the Code of Criminal Procedure. In Estonia, family members are not included in the definition. Moreover, a victim does not self-declare: proceedings are needed to identify and declare a person as a victim. In Spain, victims do not include family members, and the actual circle of persons recognised as such depends on the specific crime occurred. In Finland, the term parents and children of the victim, other family members, first responders, but not necessarily same-sex partners of the victim: some experts indicate that the term would not cover same-sex partners but the Constitution of Finland prohibits discrimination on the basis of sexual orientation.

In France, victims must have suffered individual harm directly and personally; in addition, they need to register as civil parties within criminal proceedings before the investigating judge, or through the claim for restitution or for damages during the police investigation with a judicial police officer, or at the hearing by a statement recorded by the clerk, or by the deposit of pleadings, or before the hearing with the court office. In Greece, partners or same-sex partners are not considered family members and are excluded from the definition of victims. Also, victims are synonymous to civil action plaintiffs and therefore the definition only applies to them within the course of criminal proceedings. In Hungary, the definition of victims is narrower than that of Article 2 of the Directive since siblings are not considered family members for the purposes of their classification as victims, whereas the status of direct relatives living in the same household is ambiguous. But the definition of victims also includes the victim's legal representative or ecclesiastical superior. Moreover, the classification of a person as a victim is directly linked to the location of the crime and also, for most offences, to their nationality as Hungarian and EU citizens. In Ireland, despite an attempt to transpose the definition of the Framework Decision, victims do not expressly include family members or other indirect victims. In Lithuania, the definition of victims does not cover persons suffering indirect damage or indirect economic loss. Moreover, the status of a victim is awarded by the pre-trial officer on application from the victim, a process that is questionable both because it requires a final call of judgment by a pre-trial officer who is not necessarily a judicial authority but also because there is no time limit for the processing of the victim's application. In Latvia, the definition of victims, for the purposes of participating in criminal proceedings and enjoying most of the rights of the Directive, requires a special decision of the body in charge of proceedings made on application of the victim and accepting that they have suffered individual moral, physical, or financial loss. Moreover, the implementation of the wide definition of victim in practice seems to indicate that partners are not considered victims. In Malta victims are only direct victims and only during criminal proceedings. In Poland, victims are persons whose property or rights have been directly violated or threatened. Moreover, family members not including partners only come into play in the case of death of the direct victim. In Portugal victims do not include partners. In Romania, relatives are not always considered victims; they are awarded the status by means of express special provisions. In Slovenia family members may be indirect victims, but only when their property rights have been indirectly jeopardised. In the Slovak Republic aggrieved parties do not include family members even when the aggrieved party's rights cannot be exercised by the victim. If a victim is deceased, the rights of the aggrieved party are transferred to their legal representative. In Sweden, victims may include family members but only on the basis of their individual claim as persons suffering pain and suffering as a personal injury in the case of death of a close relative.

The long list of direct or indirect restrictions to the circle of persons considered victims under current national law depicts an image of fragmented legislative regime. Combined with the prevalent perception that the national law already complies with the definition of victims in the Directive (by virtue of a vague national definition or by virtue of a parallel extension of the definition in other circles of persons within the same national legal order), the narrow national definitions of victims endanger directly and crucially the core of the effectiveness of the Directive.

So, as each Member States has its own challenges to address, copying the term of the Directive verbatim is far from a guarantee of complete transposition. Admittedly, there are some noted trends in Member States: some restrict victims to those directly harmed by the offence; others allow family members as victims, but only as successors in the case of death of the direct victims; others allow family members as victims generally, but do not include partners or non-traditional family members in the definition of family members. But there are restrictions that only apply to one or two Member States, for example the Slovakian link of family members as victims is solely when property rights are affected. And there are many cases of Member States where restrictions go hand in hand with cases of wider elements of victims. The danger here is that the wider categories absorb the legislator's attention to the restrictions, some of which are identified by means of statutory interpretation or awareness of implementation in practice.

A number of Member States offer a definition of victims that is wider than that of the Directive. This is the case in Austria, Belgium, Germany, Poland, and Slovenia, where legal persons can also be victims. The Austrian definition of victims includes legal persons represented by its organs, but not shareholders or association members. And it also includes indirect damages of the offence, as long as they are explicitly eligible for compensation by instruments of civil law. Moreover, the Belgian definition includes family members ('*leur proches*') who have a particular affective relationship with the victim. In Germany, the definition includes an authority or a government. In Latvia family members are considered victims even without the occurrence of death of the victim. In Poland victims can be a legal person, a public government, a local government, a social institution, the Social Security Agency, the National Labour Inspectorate, or other agencies. In Romania victims can be also persons that suffered moral or material injuries as a consequence of administrative or civil acts. In the UK, according to the Draft Code 'close relatives' can be victims, and the term includes the next of kin, spouse, partner, parents, guardian and/or children of the victim, as well as the carer of a vulnerable adult, if applicable. Other family members may be considered close relatives at the discretion of the service provider. There is little doubt that wider national definitions of victims do not harm in transposition: however, the problem is that these wider definitions in the majority of cases go hand in hand with restrictions. It is only the UK Draft Code that seems to hold, when holistically scrutinised, as going beyond the definition of the Directive.

And there are some Member States with national eccentricities. For example in Belgium victims include their successors: for example in the case of a deceased victim their heirs, or in the case of an insured victim the compensating insurance. In Hungary the scope of Act CXXXV of 2005 on assistance of victims of crimes and state compensation (*Ást.*) includes victims of crime committed in the territory of the Republic of Hungary, natural persons victims of an offence against property committed in the territory of Hungary, and any natural persons who have suffered injuries as a direct consequence of these criminal acts, in particular bodily or emotional harm, mental shock or economic loss (hereinafter collectively referred to as 'victims'), on condition that they are Hungarian citizens, citizens of any EU Member State, citizens of any non-EU country lawfully residing in the territory of the EU, stateless persons lawfully residing in the territory of the Republic of Hungary, victims of trafficking in human beings, and any other persons deemed eligible by virtue of international treaties concluded between their respective states of nationality and the Republic of Hungary or on the basis of reciprocity. A similar link to compensation and Lithuanian or EU nationality is traced in Article 2(2) of the Lithuanian Law on Compensation for Harm Caused by Violent Crimes. In Sweden children are victims in their own right if they have witnessed violence in a close relationship provided that there is harm to the child's confidence and trust to a person with whom they are in a close relationship. The UK Code and Draft Code introduce clear categories of victims, namely vulnerable or intimidated victims, victims of the most serious crime, and persistently targeted victims: all these are offered enhanced services. There is no harm in national eccentricities, especially since these do not seem to clash with the Directive. But it is questionable whether the Directive's scope, albeit as an EU instrument, is limited to EU citizens alone. There seems to be no reason why victims are discriminated by nationality, even when the discrimination is outside EU nationalities. One also wonders whether having to prove an EU nationality is an additional burden for EU victims that puts inevitable hurdles before them in the process of accessing services and rights allegedly made available to them by virtue of the same national laws that attempt to offer them preferential treatment compared to third-country nationals.

It is unfortunate that the Directive uses a term already in existence in some national legal orders but with variable semantic meanings: the EU term inevitably antagonises the national term thus harbouring clashes, consequential amendments to national legislation, or, if left in parallel, ineffective transposition. The transposition of the definition of victims in the Directive seems to be one of the most fundamental yet most complicated issues. Definitions are easily by-passed, especially in Member States who are not familiar with them from their national drafting styles, or who do not have the luxury of placing them within a definitions section in their national transposition instruments. It is therefore imperative for the effectiveness of the Directive that the definition is introduced in a meticulous, detailed, and almost pedantic manner by all Member States. And so, copying the term 'victim' as defined in the Victim's Rights Directive would negate the purpose of the Directive itself, which is to harmonise the level of rights offered to victims of crime in other Member States.

In addition, as the criminalisation of some acts (road traffic offences or discrimination, hate or bias conducts or stalking) varies to a large degree between the Member States, using the term 'victims of crime' without specifying which crimes fall into the scope of the Directive will create further diversity within EU Member States rather than instil harmonisation.[82] In turn, instead of arming EU citizens with the same victims' rights irrespective in which other Member

---

[82] See DG Justice Guidance Document related to the transposition and implementation of Directive 2012/29/EU of the European Parliament and of the Council of 25 October 2012 establishing minimum standards on the rights, support and protection of victims of crime, and replacing Council Framework Decision 2001/220/JHA, Ref. Ares(2013)3763804, 19/12/2013, https://www.google.com/url?sa=t&rct=j&q=&esrc=s&source=web&cd=&ved=2ahUKEwj188O2wbSDAxW7X0EAHcUaDjIQFnoECBIQAQ&url=https%3A%2F%2Fe-justice.europa.eu%2FfileDownload.do%3Fid%3D05758a3a-9e2e-49a5-a7ec-3737c3ad6876&usg=AOvVaw2wXIYZ8jWq_S3sc3Gos6-v&opi=89978449 accessed 13 December 2023, note 9, 7.

State they find themselves in, these diversities will render the discrepancies in their treatment as victims even more pronounced. Citizens will now expect a harmonised treatment but in reality they will get something different. From the point of view of sustainable integration this is catastrophic: in the process of selling citizens the added value of EU harmonisation, the application of the EU text will simply showcase how little added value there is. And this will have occurred when EU citizens victims of crime would need the EU the most. The same issue will occur when victims come to learn that the definition of their family members may not include their same sex-spouse in Member States where same-sex marriages are not yet recognised. And, although the ideal solution would be to have had these issues resolved within the EU text by offering lists of crimes or family members, national transposition drafters can certainly use their drafting creativity to transpose the relevant terms with a different definition or a term that is not tautonymous to, for example, victim of crime or family member.

The analysis of the Victims' Directive as a case-study shows that copying the EU text and its terms conceals a risk of ineffectiveness, which may only become visible after some application. Copying out the EU text is therefore rarely good practice.[83] It may appear safe, in that a superficial scrutiny may brand it as complete transposition. However, application of the national transposition legislation inevitably reveals those hidden drafting issues. At that point, the seeming safety net of copying out the EU text disappears. The application-fuelled proof of incomplete or partial transposition in practice leads ultimately to infringement proceedings.

It is important for transposition drafters to fully comprehend why their transposition task does not end with the wise selection of the most appropriate form of the national implementing measure. To nurture full transposition, national drafters must bravely create a new transposition text. Their legislative choices are influenced by national eccentricities, often classified as institutional, political, and substantive.[84] Whatever the national eccentricities are, they cannot detract from the requirement that national legislative texts adhere to the EU standards of legislative quality.[85] Unfortunately, there is no magic formula for achieving quality in legislation.[86] Each country has its own rules

---

[83] See E Öücü, 'Law as Transposition' (2002) 51 *International and Comparative Law Quarterly* 205, 207.

[84] See D G Dimitrakopoulos, 'The Transposition of EU Law: "post-decisional politics" and Institutional Autonomy' (2001) 7 *European Law Journal* 442.

[85] See W Robinson, 'How the European Commission Drafts Legislation in 20 Languages' (2004) 53 *Clarity* 4, 6.

[86] Nevertheless, national drafting guidelines introduce similar standards of quality: see H Xanthaki, 'The Problem of Quality in EU Legislation: What on Earth is Really Wrong?' (2001) 38 *Common Market Law Review* 651.

that are affected by the type of its legal system (is it a civil or a common law system?), the type of its polity (federal state?) and the main aim of its legislators (to promote economic development, in which case legislation must serve corporations, or to protect its citizens, in which case legislation must be simple and approachable by all?).[87] Most EU Member States introduce rules of legislative drafting which bind the professional drafters or legal experts who participate in the process of drafting.[88] Austria,[89] Belgium,[90] Bulgaria,[91] Croatia,[92] the Czech Republic,[93] Cyprus,[94] Denmark,[95] Estonia,[96] Finland,[97] France,[98]

---

[87] See Rt Hon Lord Renton, 'The Preparation and Enforcement of Legislation in the Enlarged Community' (1996) 17 *Statute Law Review* 1, 3.

[88] For the synthesis of national drafting conventions in this chapter, see H Xanthaki and C Stefanou, 'Drafting for Transposition of EU Criminal Laws: the EU Perspective' (2003) *European Current Law Review* xi–15.

[89] See *Legistische Richtlinien*, 1990, https:// www .justiz .gv .at/ web2013/ home/ verfassungsdienst/legistik/e-recht-und-legistische-richtlinien/legistische-richtlinien~2c94848a60c158380160e4e3747c0c33.de.html accessed 14 December 2023.

[90] See *Principes de technique legislative – Guide de rédaction des textes législatifs et réglementaires,* Conseil d'Etat, http://www.raadvst-consetat.be/?page=technique_legislative&lang=fr accessed 14 December 2023, which replaces the *Traité de légistique formelle*, Circular of the Prime-Minister of 23 April 1982.

[91] See Law on Normative Acts, Promulgated, State Gazette No. 27/3.04.1973, amended and supplemented, SG No.65/21.07.1995, supplemented, SG No. 55/17.06.2003, effective 18.12.2003, amended and supplemented, SG No. 46/12.06.2007, SG No. 34/3.05.2016, effective as of 4.11.2016, https://www.legislationline.org/documents/ id/22269 accessed 14 December 2023.

[92] See Croatian Guidelines for Legislative Drafting, June 2015.

[93] See Resolution of the Government no. 188, 19 March 1998, https://www.vlada .cz/cz/ppov/lrv/dokumenty/ legislativni-pravidla-vlady-91209/ accessed 14 December 2023.

[94] See Legal Service of the Republic, *Guidelines for the drafting of national and transposition legislation*, March 2017.

[95] See Zahle, Dansk forfatningsret I (2001) 263 an Zahle (4).

[96] See Regulation 279, Regulatory Rules on draft Normative Acts, RT 1, 1999, 73, 695; 2004, 10, 61.

[97] See *Bill Drafting Instructions* (2006, Ministry of Justice publication 2006:3, Helsinki), https://oikeusministerio.fi/en/bill-drafting-instructions accessed 14 December 2023.

[98] See *Circulaire relative à la codification des textes législatives et réglementaires*, Circular of Prime Minister of 30 May 1996, JORF n°129 du 5 juin 1996 page 8263, https://www.legifrance.gouv.fr/affichTexte.do?cidTexte=JORFTEXT000000742705&categorieLien=id accessed 14 December 2023; also see *Circulaire relative aux règles d'élaboration, de signature et de publication des textes au Journal Officiel*, Circular of the Prime Minister of 2 January 1993.

Germany,[99] Greece,[100] Italy,[101] Latvia,[102] Luxembourg,[103] the Netherlands,[104] Poland,[105] Portugal,[106] Romania,[107] Spain,[108] and the UK[109] have introduced texts that include some guidelines or standards of quality for national drafters. For the rest of the Member States drafting principles derive from their legislative traditions. These guidelines and principles are applicable to all national texts, irrespective of their role as implementation documents of purely national policy or as transposition documents. Clarity, simplicity, precision, accuracy and plain language are common standards of good quality of legislation both in

---

[99] See *Handbuch der Rechtsförmlichkeit*, 1991 and 2008 (revised).

[100] Manual for the procedures of Inter-ministerial coordination of the Greek Government, June 2018, http://www.ggk.gov.gr accessed 14 December 2023.

[101] See N Jotti e Camera dei Deputati, 'Formulazione tecnica dei testi legislative' [1986] 109 *Il Foro Italiano* 139 and 147; also see *Regole e suggerimenti per la redazione dei testi normativi*, 1992 and 2007, http://web.consiglioveneto.it/qualita/manuale%20drafting.pdf accessed 14 December 2023; also *Istruttoria legislativa nelle commissioni*, 1997, https://www.senato.it/1057?testo_generico=28&voce_sommario=62.

[102] See *Normatīvo aktu projektu izstrādes rokasgrāmata*, https://tai.mk.gov.lv/book/1/chapter/178 accessed 14 December 2023.

[103] See M Besch, *Traité de légistique formelle* (2007, Service Central de Législation, Luxembourg).

[104] See *Aanwijzingen voor de regelgeving or Ar*, 1992, https://www.kcwj.nl/kennisbank/integraal-afwegingskader-beleid-en-regelgeving/verplichte-kwaliteitseisen/aanwijzingen-1 accessed 14 December 2023; also see C. Borman (ed), *Aanwijzingen vor de Regelgeving* (1993, Zwolle, the Netherlands).

[105] See Regulamin Pracy Rady Ministrów, Regulamin RM, Law on Normative Acts, Promulgated, State Gazette No. 27/3.04.1973, amended and supplemented, SG No. 65/21.07.1995, supplemented, SG No. 55/17.06.2003, effective 18.12.2003, amended and supplemented, SG No. 46/12.06.2007, SG No. 34/3.05.2016, effective as of 4.11.2016.

[106] See Assemblea da Republica, *Regras de Legistica a Observar na Elaboração de Actos Normativos da Assembleia da República*, http:// ialorg .wpengine .com/ wp -content/uploads/2018/02/RegrasLegistica-AR.pdf accessed 14 December 2023; also see Deliberation of the Council of Ministers of 8 February 1989 on the approval of the general principles for the elaboration of projects for normative acts.

[107] See Law No. 24 Of 27 March 2000 On The Rules Of Legislative Technique For The Preparation Of Normative Acts (LEGE nr. 24 din 27 martie 2000 privind normele de tehnică legislativă pentru elaborarea actelor normative), https:// www .global-regulation.com/law/romania/3071730/-lege-nr.-24-din-27-martie-2000-privind -normele -de -tehnic -legislativ -pentru -elaborarea -actelor -normative .htmLaw24/ 2008 accessed 14 December 2023.

[108] See Directives on the form and structure for the schemes of projects of laws, 1991; also see Norms on the consultation regime of the *Congreso de los Diputados e del Senato*, 1989.

[109] See Consolidation of Enactment (Procedure) Act 1949, 41 *Statutes* 741; also see Statutory Instruments Act 1946, 41 *Statutes* 717; Interpretation Act 1978, 41 *Statutes* 899.

the common and in the civil law drafting styles.[110] Consideration of the circle of persons which are the main users of the legislative texts,[111] consideration of any interpretative problems arising from the text,[112] the need for consistency with existing legislation, avoidance of irrelevant provisions and the use of uniform terminology are all rules of drafting that are common in the legislative guidelines of EU Member States.[113]

Legislative action as a means of regulation must be selected only if it is an essential and effective means of ending legal uncertainty. This is expressly the case in Belgium, France, Germany and Portugal.[114] However, even in the rest of the Member States this principle would apply as it is ensuing to the principle of proportionality: only proportional measures are necessary and efficient means of attaining the aim of the law and, consequently, only proportional measures may fulfil the imposed national tests of necessity and efficiency.

The principle of legality is expressly introduced in Germany and Portugal.[115] In the other Member States the principle is consequential to the hierarchy of sources of law, which invariably place EU and the Constitution or constitutional laws higher than laws or executive decrees.

Drafting for a circle of users is reflected in the Austrian and German appreciation that legislative texts are mainly used by lay persons whose lack of legal knowledge does not allow for complicated, specialised texts full of legal terminology,[116] as well as in the German requirement for the clear determination of

---

[110] See G C Thornton, *Legislative Drafting* (1996, Butterworths, London/Dublin/Edinburgh), 52–54; also see R Pagano, *Introduzione alla legistica: l'arte di preparare le leggi* (1999, Giuffrè Editore, Milano), 26–30.

[111] See M Ainis, *La legge oscura* (1997, Laterza, Bari), 103.

[112] See V Fronsini, *Lezioni di teoria dell' interpretazione* (1993, Bulsoni, Roma), 1993; also see W A Leitch, 'The Interpretation Act: Ten Years Later' (1958) 16 *Northern Ireland Legal Quarterly* 215, at 236–237.

[113] See R Pagano, 1999, above n 110, 37–39.

[114] See the French Circular of 2 January 1993 on the rules for the elaboration, signature and publication of texts in the Official Journal and to the coming into force the particular procedures of the Prime Minster, Art 2.1.1.1; German *Gemeinsame Geschäftsordnung der Bundesministerien*, 15 October 1976 as modified, Art 40; German Manual of judicial formalities, 1991, paras 26–28; Portuguese Deliberation of the Council of Ministers of 8 February 1989 on the approval of the general principles for the elaboration of projects of normative acts, Art 1a.

[115] See the German Manual of judicial formalities, 1991, paras 31–32; Portuguese Deliberation of the Council of Ministers of 8 February 1989 on the approval of the general principles for the elaboration of projects of normative acts, Art 4.

[116] See Austrian *Legistische Richtlinien*, 1990, Art 9; also see the German *Gemeinsame Geschäftsordnung der Bundesministerien*, 15 October 1976 as modified, Art 35; German Manual of judicial formalities, 1991, para 34.

the new duties and rights introduced by the legislative text.[117] An expression of this rule can be found in the common rule for plain language and unambiguity.

Clarity of legislation is a principle common to the laws of the Member States which is expressly introduced in Austria, Belgium, France, Germany, the Netherlands, Portugal, Spain and the UK.[118] Unambiguity is required from Belgian, German, Italian, Portuguese, Spanish and UK drafters.[119] Simplicity is a rule of drafting in Austria, Belgium, Germany, Portugal, and Spain.[120] In the UK simplicity is also pursued but not to the detriment of certainty.[121] Plain language, as an expression of the rule for the consideration of the language

---

[117] See the German Manual of judicial formalities, 1991, para 59.

[118] See Austrian *Legistische Richtlinien*, 1990, Art 7; Belgian *Circulaire de Premier Ministre*, 23 April 1982, Art 1; German *Gemeinsame Geschäftsordnung der Bundesministerien*, 15 October 1976 as modified, Art 35; German Manual of judicial formalities, 1991, paras 33–39; Italian *Regole e suggerimenti per la redazione dei testi nomativi*, 1991, Art 2; Dutch *Aanwijzingen Voor de Regelgeving*, 1992, Art 218; Portuguese Deliberation of the Council of Ministers of 8 February 1989 on the approval of the general principles for the elaboration of projects of normative acts, Art 7c; Spanish Guidelines on the form and structure of projects of laws, 1991, approved by the Decision of the Council of Ministers of 18 October 1991, OJ of 18 November 1991, no 276, disposition 27774, pp. 37235–37, at 37235; also see L Neville-Rolfe, 'Good Regulation: Weighing-up the Risks', in A Kellermann, G Ciavarini-Azzi, S Jacobs and R Deighton-Smith, *Improving the Quality of Legislation in Europe* (Kluwer Law, The Hague, 1998), 245–249; Thornton, above n 110, 53–54.

[119] See Belgian *Circulaire de Premier Ministre*, 23 April 1982, Art 1; *Gemeinsame Geschäftsordnung der Bundesministerien*, 15 October 1976 as modified, Art 35; German Manual of judicial formalities, 1991, para 37; Italian *Regole e suggerimenti per la redazione dei testi nomativi*, 1991, Art 2; Portuguese Deliberation of the Council of Ministers of 8 February 1989 on the approval of the general principles for the elaboration of projects of normative acts, Art 7c; Spanish Guidelines on the form and structure of projects of laws, 1991, approved by the Decision of the Council of Ministers of 18 October 1991, OJ of 18 November 1991, no 276, disposition 27774, pp. 37235–37; for an analysis of ambiguity under British law see Black, *The Labyrinth of Language* (Pelican Press, London, 1972), 107.

[120] See Austrian *Legistische Richtlinien*, 1990, Art 1; Belgian *Circulaire de Premier Ministre*, 23 April 1982, Art 1; German *Gemeinsame Geschäftsordnung der Bundesministerien*, 15 October 1976 as modified, Art 35; German Manual of judicial formalities, 1991, para 33; Portuguese Deliberation of the Council of Ministers of 8 February 1989 on the approval of the general principles for the elaboration of projects of normative acts, Art 7c; Spanish Guidelines on the form and structure of projects of laws, 1991, approved by the Decision of the Council of Ministers of 18 October 1991, OJ of 18 November 1991, no 276, disposition 27774, pp. 37235–37.

[121] See The Preparation of Legislation – Report of a Committee appointed by the Lord President of the Council (Renton Report) of May 1975, ch.XI, Art 14.

accessible by the lay persons who will be the main users of the particular legislative text is expressly introduced in the Netherlands, Portugal and the UK.[122]

The requirement of the use of the same term when referring to the same concept is an expression of the principle of unambiguity and is expressly introduced in Austria, Belgium, Italy, the Netherlands and Portugal.[123] On the basis of the same principle of unambiguity, unnecessary abbreviations are to be avoided not only at the EU level, but also in Germany and Italy.[124] As an expression of the need for clarity and unambiguity, lack of pointless repetitions of existing provisions which is often followed by the use of different terms to reflect the same concept is to be avoided not only under the EU rules, but also under the Austrian, Italian and Dutch guidelines.[125] Long sentences must be avoided in Austria, Germany, and Italy.[126] It is noteworthy that the UK does not introduce a general rule against long sentences; nevertheless, a similar result is achieved through restrictions in the use of subordinate sentences (especially before the subject of the phrase or between the subject and the verb of the sentence)[127] and against long sentences which are not split into paragraphs.[128] Moreover, imprecise references to other legal texts are expressly prohibited in the Austrian, German, Italian, Dutch, and Portuguese guidelines.[129]

---

[122] See the Dutch *Aanwijzingen Voor de Regelgeving*, 1992, Arts 54 and 218; Portuguese Deliberation of the Council of Ministers of 8 February 1989 on the approval of the general principles for the elaboration of projects of normative acts, Art 7a; for the UK see M Faulk and I M Mehler, *The Elements of Legal Writing* (Macmillan Press, London, 1994).

[123] See Austrian *Legistische Richtlinien*, 1990, Art 31; Belgian *Circulaire de Premier Ministre*, 23 April 1982, Art 3a; Italian *Formulazione tecnica dei testi legislativi*, 1986, G.U., no. 123 of 29 March 1986, Ordinary Supplement, no. 40, Art 16a; Italian *Regole e suggerimenti per la redazione dei testi nomativi*, 1991, Art 16; Dutch *Aanwijzingen Voor de Regelgeving*, 1992, Art 58; Portuguese Deliberation of the Council of Ministers of 8 February 1989 on the approval of the general principles for the elaboration of projects of normative acts, Art 7a.

[124] See *Gemeinsame Geschäftsordnung der Bundesministerien*, 15 October 1976 as modified, Art 34; Italian *Formulazione tecnica dei testi legislativi*, 1986, G.U., no. 123 of 29 March 1986, Ordinary Supplement, no. 40, Art 9.

[125] See Austrian *Legistische Richtlinien*, 1990, Art 3; Italian *Regole e suggerimenti per la redazione dei testi nomativi*, 1991, Art 19; Dutch *Aanwijzingen Voor de Regelgeving*, 1992, Art 78.

[126] See Austrian *Legistische Richtlinien*, 1990, Art 18; German Manual of judicial formalities, 1991, para 51; Italian *Regole e suggerimenti per la redazione dei testi nomativi*, 1991, Art 1.

[127] See The Preparation of Legislation – Report of a Committee appointed by the Lord President of the council (Renton Report) of May 1975, Art 16.

[128] See ibid., Art 8.

[129] See Austrian *Legistische Richtlinien*, 1990, Art 56; German Manual of judicial formalities, 1991, paras 97–109; Italian *Regole e suggerimenti per la redazione dei*

In parallel to these, there still are EU standards to be observed, and these offer great guidance to transposition drafters. From the point of view of composition, the EU has a rich set of rules. In their purity these drafting rules bind the EU and its institutions. However, as early as in 1998 the Commission in its *Better Lawmaking Report 1998: A Shared Responsibility*[130] the role of Member States in the process of improving the quality of EU legislation was fully established. The correct transposition of EU Directives was one of the eight main guidelines for action introduced by the Report.[131] Transposition legislation must be clear,[132] unambiguous and simple. Clarity includes the use of plain language and the avoidance of too many cross-references, and political statements without legislative character.[133] Unambiguity covers the use of the same term throughout the text, lack of unnecessary abbreviations, and lack of pointless repetition of existing provisions. Simplicity incorporates lack of jargon, long sentences and imprecise references to other legal texts.[134] In principle, national transposition laws must be capable of leading to effectiveness of national and, as a member of the implementing collective,[135] to effectiveness of EU regulation.

And so, in Stage 3 national drafters have to depart from the easy yet unproductive safety blanket for copying the EU legislative text that they set to transpose. Effectiveness requires the compilation of a new, nation-focused legislative package, which serves national effectiveness via clarity, precision, and unambiguity. There are choices for drafters in the compilation of the national transposition legislation. These require subjective decisions fuelled by

---

testi nomativi, 1991, Art 55; Dutch *Aanwijzingen Voor de Regelgeving*, 1992, Art 78; Portuguese Deliberation of the Council of Ministers of 8 February 1989 on the approval of the general principles for the elaboration of projects of normative acts, Art 6c.

[130] See COM (1998) 715 final.

[131] See Bulletin EU 5-1998, point 1.8.3.

[132] When it comes to transposition, individuals should have the benefit of a clear and precise legal situation enabling them to ascertain the full extent of their rights and duties and, where appropriate, to rely on them before the national courts: see C-49/00 *Commission of the European Communities v Italian Republic* [2001] ECR I-8575.

[133] See Opinion of the Economic and Social Committee of 5 July 1995 on plain language, OJ 1995 C 256/8.

[134] See Resolution of the EP of 4 July 1996 on the report of independent experts on simplification of Community legislation and administrative provisions, COM(95)288 fin.; see also A-4 0201/96, OJ 1996 C 211/23.

[135] See L J O'Toole Jr, 'Multi-organizational Policy Implementation: Some Limitations and Possibilities for Rational Choice Contributions' in F W Scharpf (ed), *Games in Hierarchy and Networks: Analytical and Empirical Approaches to the Study of Governance Institutions* (Frankfurt am Main/Boulder, Colo., Campus Verlag/ Westview Press, 2003) 27.

the design of the national transposition text that serves its concrete user groups identified in Stage 3.

A creative approach to transposition requires courage and a willingness to shoulder responsibility for the choices of legislative expression that transposition drafters have to take. In some cases, a creative approach is encouraged by the Commission in their transposition guidance. For example, in the Explanatory Memorandum of Network and Information Systems Directive,[136] the Commission urges transposition drafters to go beyond the focus of the Directive on companies and services that are of particular critical importance, and to expand to holistic and consistent 'comprehensive national strategies which go beyond the minimum requirements of the NIS Directive'. However, in most cases, such a creative approach is not nurtured by the currently mainly formalistic monitoring exercises at a post-scrutiny level undertaken mainly by the Commission.[137] This allows some Member States to choose a 'quick and dirty' superficial transposition method.[138] Having said that, if the recommendation for pre-legislative joint co-legislating committees during the previous drafting stages is accepted, the main elements of the Member State's transposition plans will have been approved by the scrutinisers of the transposition process. Liberating national drafters from the terror of making a mistake and dragging their jurisdiction to infringement proceedings would unleash their creative talent for drafting for effectiveness. Entrusting national drafters requires a change of mentality both at the EU and the Member States levels. But it is very much in application of the Better Regulation policy of the EU. And it fosters sustainable integration, which serves the longevity of the EU's success. So, although it cannot be undertaken single-handedly, it can come about gradually and seamlessly if both national drafters and EU monitoring officers focus on effectiveness in substance rather than form.

It is encouraging that seeds for such a re-channelling of the nature of transposition scrutiny is found in recent documents. For example, the REFIT Platform

---

[136] See Explanatory Memorandum to COM(2017)476 – Making the most of NIS – towards effective implementation of Directive (EU) 2016/1148 on measures for a high common level of security of network and information systems, COM(2017)476, 13/09/2017, https://www.eumonitor.eu/9353000/1/j4nvhdfdk3hydzq_j9vvik7m1c3gyxp/vkhlg270lwyq accessed 14 December 2023, para 4.

[137] See L Collins, *The European Civil Code: The Way Forward* (CUP, Cambridge, 2008) 196; also see L Prete and B Smulders, 'The Coming of Age of Infringement Proceedings' (2010) 47 *Common Market Law Review* 9.

[138] See T König and L Mäder, 'Non-conformable, Partial and Conformable Transposition: A Competing Risk Analysis of the Transposition Process of Directives in the EU15' (2013) 14 *European Union Politics* 46.

Opinion on Transparent Transposition by a member of the Stakeholder group[139] invites the Commission to make national transposition text and guidelines publicly available via the EUR-LEX website (including information about the use of regulatory choices stipulated in the directive or any national discretion used by a Member State to implement directives or provisions of directives that are based on minimum harmonisation).

C. ADDRESSING THE CHALLENGES OF TRANSPOSITION (THORNTON'S STAGE 4)

The linguistic tools used by national drafters in the composition of national legislation do not vary dramatically. Clarity, simplicity, plain language are popular drafting goals based on the equally common principles of the rule of law, constitutionality, and legality. Even drafting styles are breaking the boundaries of the civil/common law divide.[140] EU integration has resulted in a rapprochement between civil and common law drafting styles within the EU.[141] In fact, legislative expression, within or outside transposition, has been adequately explored and amended into a modern style in most Member States. It would be accurate to say that linguistic expression is the Stage of Thornton's drafting process where change is needed the least. This is because, until recently, legislative drafting was viewed as a science of words. In that respect, the plain language movement, which prevailed in legislative theory and practice over the last fifty years, has produced results. But innovations in linguistic expression in the Member States seem to be de facto blocked at the EU level. The frequent replication of the legislative expressions used by the EU text within the transposition texts deprive the latter from the creative composition that decorates other national legislative texts. From the point of view of the EU this practice can be reversed if monitoring of the effectiveness of national transposition measures is transformed.

A principled, in-depth and in-substance monitoring of the capacity of the text to produce the agreed desired regulatory results at the national level contributes greatly to the achievement of the desired regulatory results at the EU level. This is precisely what monitoring the implementation of the EU

---

[139] See 'REFIT Platform Opinion on Transparent Transposition by a member of the Stakeholder group' of 14/3/2019, https://commission.europa.eu/system/files/2020-08/annual_burden_survey_2019_4_digital.pdf accessed 14 December 2023, 6.

[140] See H Xanthaki, 'Editorial: Burying the Hatchet Between Common and Civil Law Drafting Styles in Europe' (2012) 6 *Legisprudence* 133–148.

[141] See M Hernández Ramos and V Heydt, 'Legislative Language and Style' in U Karpen and H Xanthaki (eds), *Legislation in Europe: A Handbook for Scholars and Practitioners* (Hart Publishers, Oxford, 2017), 129, at 142.

text by Member States should measure. Of course, the current superficial box-ticking monitoring exercise is an established practice for the EU. It may well be justified by the limited resources in most institutions. However, a shift of focus, and hopefully resources, from a punitive post-legislative review of national transposition legislation with questionable contribution to sustainable integration[142] to a pre-emptive pre-legislative joint co-legislative review of national transposition plans could fertilise the ground for creative composition of transposition texts. In fact, there are calls for joint cooperation between the Commission and national authorities to continue after transposition, thus allowing national authorities to interpret the EU legislative text more accurately, to explain the provisions to EU citizens correctly, and to be up to date with developments arising from judicial interpretations of the legislation.[143]

Moreover, EU legislative expression must be selected also by reference to national terminology. Loading the EU text with terms already existing in the national legal orders of Member States creates ambiguity within the holistic co-legislative regulatory package of EU and transposition legislation. Taking transposition into account when choosing terms in the EU text would go a long way in avoiding such ambiguities, which (as is the case with the Victims' Rights Directive) can gravely affect the effectiveness of EU legislation.

CONCLUSIONS

Admittedly, the right choice of words, and the right legislative expression by itself cannot lead to effectiveness of regulation and legislation. Perhaps the biggest innovation in legislative studies has been the recognition of the link between regulation and legislation. Seeing legislation as a tool available to regulators to communicate their regulatory messages has led to the identification of the three user groups of legislation, and to the easification of legislative expression. This requires pitching the legislative expression to each user group at a level appropriate for their legal and subject sophistication.

Easification[144] applies to legislative expression, to design, to conceptualisation. And so, the biggest challenge of Stage 4 of Thornton's drafting stages

---

[142] See M Smith, 'Enforcement, Monitoring, Verification, Outsourcing: The Decline and Decline of the Infringement Process' (2008) 14 *European Law Review* 777; also see C Harlow and R Rawlings, 'Accountability and Law Enforcement: The Centralised EU Infringement Procedure' (2006) 12 *European Law Review* 447.

[143] See e.g., DG for Internal Policies, 'Study on Transposition of the Directive on the recognition of professional qualifications', IP/A/IMCO/ST/2009-05, PE 416.238, Recommendation 4.

[144] On easification see G Pennisi, 'Legislative Provisions in Context: A Linguistic Approach' (2016) *Statute Law Review* 101, especially 103.

(composition) is to mobilise the legislative expression that can best communicate each transposition regulatory message to each concrete user group. But of course this demands the prerequisite of understanding the legislative proposal, and designing it in a way that promotes easy access to the answers sought by each user group.

Whether the drafter has managed to achieve this is a matter for Stage 5, verifying the draft.

6. Verifying the transposition draft law and completing the transposition task

A. VERIFICATION IN LEGISLATIVE LITERATURE

Verification of the legislative draft is a procedure inherent, albeit informally, in the processes of most drafting offices. It involves the presentation of the draft for discussion within or outside the drafting team.[1] It can be internal, within the drafting team, or external, outside the drafting team. Ideally it should be both because internal and external verification exercise serve two different purposes. Internal verification satisfies the drafting team that at the end of the drafting process the regulatory messages are expressed appropriately and adequately in the draft legislative text. External verification satisfies the drafting team that the regulatory messages, as expressed by the draft legislative text, will be received by the users in the way that they were intended by the policy-makers.

Academic literature outside the discipline of legislative studies can be used to define verification and determine what it pursues. Verification is the process of proving or disproving the correctness of the legislative text against the underlying regulatory goals.[2] In other words, verification reviews, and verifies or falsifies the potential of the legislative text to contribute to the achievement of the regulatory goals. And thus, verification requires 'human-directed proof' that 'can be automated to some extend'.[3]

---

[1] See C-A Morand (ed), *Légistique formelle et matér*ielle (Aix-en-Provence, 1999) 25.

[2] For a definition of verification in general, see D Zhang, R Vishnuvajjala and W T Tsai, 'Verification and Validation of Knowledge-Based Systems' (1999) *IEEE Transactions on Knowledge and Data Engineering*, 202, 203.

[3] See E Plaza, 'Validation and Verification of Knowledge-based Systems' (1993) *IEEE Transactions on Knowledge and Data Engineering*, 45; also see T M van Engers and E J J Glassée, 'Facilitating the Legislation Process Using a Shared Conceptual Model' (2001) IEEE Intelligent Systems, 50–58; T M Engers, 'POWER: Programme for an Ontology Based Working Environment for Modeling and Use of Regulations and Legislation' (2000) *Proceedings 11th International Workshop on Database and Expert Systems Applications* 327–334.

Literature has not explored this drafting stage. This can be attributed to the erroneous perception that by this stage the drafting task is complete, or that verification is achieved in the public consultations offered either at the very start of the regulatory process by the executive or at the very end of the legislative process by parliaments. This is incorrect. Policy consultations offered at the start of the regulatory cycle gauge public perception on possible policy alternatives: they are useful for the selection of the regulatory solution, which will then form part of the drafting instructions of Stage 1 of the drafting process. Legislative consultations offered at the end of the legislative process by parliaments gauge public acceptance of the legislative text as a plausible regulatory tool for the efficacy of the underlying regulation. They are useful to ascertain public agreement with the obligations imposed or rights offered by means of the legislative text, to ensure that sensitivities are adequately addressed, and to alert parliamentarians to the views of their constituents. User testing does not really serve participation, legitimacy, and democracy, at least not directly. User testing, in the sense used here, is a tool of technical quality assurance of the legislative text.

The conceptual basis of user testing lies with the notion of effectiveness as a measure of legislative quality. Within the context of legislation as a tool for regulation, the drafting task does not end with the composition of a legislative text. Drafting legislation, or indeed passing legislation through parliament, is not an achievement as such. Since drafting is a form of communication, the drafting task spreads far beyond the text's entry into force. It extends to ensuring that the communication sent will be received as intended. Without user testing, this assumption cannot be ascertained, at least not in practice and with empirical data showing that way. In the current ethos of better regulation, where legislation is a tool for the achievement of regulatory results, it is nonsensical to leave the receipt of the regulatory message to chance by allowing the legislative text to sail away in pursuit of its sea of users. Any empirical data showing how representative groups of the main user groups perceive the text, and how they apply it in practice contains valuable information that must be actively pursued by the drafting team. Moreover, the better regulation ethos requires that the drafting team double-check that every step in the regulatory process serves its aim and that it dovetails beautifully with the rest of the regulatory process. So, quality assurance of the drafting process is also a mechanism of review and evaluation of the legislative process and ultimately the regulatory process. And there is a direct link between product reviews in Stages 2 (analysing the proposal), 3 (designing the draft), 5 (verifying the draft) and post legislative scrutiny exercises. Ultimately, as the process develops, the same questions are answered with a different focus. In Stage 2 answers relate to comprehending the proposal fully, in Stage 3 answers related to how the text can serve the proposals, in Stage 5 answers relate to how the text serves the proposals, and in post-legislative scrutiny how the legislation has actually worked in practice. The earlier these issues come about, the earlier they can be resolved, thus eliminating them from the subsequent stages (as issues, not as questions posed). Stage 5, verification, is therefore a crucial moment of self-reflection for the drafting team that can easily resolve quality issues before the legislation is passed and post-legislative scrutiny reveals their existence. It is important to keep in mind that early resolution is not just a matter of pride and prestige for the drafting team. Early detection of quality issues in Stage 5 prevents the text from being passed as it stands, thus thwarting a bad legislative text from being put to circulation, and therefore blocking unintended consequences for citizens in the implementation of the legislation.

Enhanced rates of regulatory success is not the only advantage of verification. Early participation of users in the legislative process invokes legitimacy.[4] And it can enhance voluntary compliance for two reasons: first, because changes are announced in a timely manner and there is time to adjust to changes, and second, because the sense of legitimacy and shared ownership offered by early information motivates affected parties to comply.[5] It is on that basis that post-legislative scrutiny is so pronounced. And why early involvement of users nurtures effectiveness and efficiency.[6]

The rich fruit of verification justify its conduct at the early stage of the end of the drafting process compared to the legislative process before parliamentary scrutiny. There is no reason for regulators to avoid acquiring crucial indications of legislative quality until the legislation is already passed, especially since they have the opportunity to intervene and prevent any issues before the draft is submitted to the law-makers.

Verification in Stage 5 of the drafting process can serve this purpose. Although scrutiny of the legislative text is a continuous process throughout the drafting, it is best practice to subject each version of a draft to internal scrutiny of legal form, clarity and comprehensibility. Much more so the final draft. Internal verification basically is the process by which the drafter re-takes the steps taken in the four stages of drafting and seeks positive answers of success to each task by the other members of the drafting team. In other words, in internal verification, the drafter seeks confirmation that the draft reflects accurate understanding of the regulatory request in Stage 1, appropriate legislative

---

[4] See European Governance – A White Paper, COM(2001) 428 final, 11 https://eur-lex.europa.eu/EN/legal-content/summary/white-paper-on-governance.html accessed 8 January 2024.

[5] See OECD, 'Background document on public consultation', http://www.oecd.org/mena/governance/36785341.pdf accessed 14 December 2023.

[6] See 'European Governance – A White Paper', COM(2001) 428 final, above n 4, 7.

solutions to address the request in Stage 2, appropriate design for the three user groups in Stage 3, and appropriate choices of legislative expression for each part of the draft in Stage 4. In other words, the drafting team undertakes a short effectiveness check within the team. Internal verification serves as a tool precipitated regulatory quality. But it does not aid participation.

This is served by external verification. Here the drafting team reaches out to user groups to seek their confirmation that the regulatory message has been accurately translated to legislation.[7] To confirm this, the team conduct user testing. It is a sign of good management in government in general to ensure that well-designed quality and internal control procedures and good user testing are not bypassed or undertaken without sufficient time and attention within a public management with short-term productivity pressures.[8] User testing asks users to apply the legislation,[9] and to provide answers to concrete questions of application, based on the level of information offered to them by the legislative text.[10] If the answers offered by the users are correct, the drafting team can be assured that the users received the intended message accurately.[11] If the answers are wrong, then the legislative expression chosen is not correct for the user group in question, and the team need to fine-tune the text to dilute any ambiguity and correct any erroneous expression.[12] For example, in user testing, users are asked to read the, hypothetically still draft, Victim's Rights Directive. They are asked whom to approach if they are mugged in the streets of a Member States, when assistance starts, and what happens if they cannot read the trial documents. If user answers are that they must ring their own national authorities to find assistance, or that they must wait until the prosecution starts to be approached by NGOs for help, or that they need to hire a local lawyer to be able to follow the legal process abroad, then the team

---

7 This is the full meaning of accessibility of legislation: see R Sullivan, 'The Promise of Plain Language Drafting' (1992) 24 *McGill Law Journal* 97, 188.

8 For the importance of user testing in government, see T Poysti, 'Information Government in Practise: Functional Gains and Legal Perils' (2010) 56 *Scandinavian Studies in Law* 91, 120.

9 See R Heaton, 'Innovation and Continuity in Law Making – 13th Sir William Dale Memorial Lecture' (2015) 17 *European Journal of Law Reform* 369, 376 and 382; also see J Sheridan, 'Using Data to Understand How the Statute Book Works' (2014) 14 *Legal Information Management* 244, 246.

10 See V Aubert, 'Contributions to the Sociology of Law' (1966) 10 *Acta Sociologica* 98, 100.

11 See A Nkunika, 'The Role of Cognitive Reasoning and Decision Making and User Testing in the Enhancement of Communication Of Legislative Messages in a Digital Age' (2015) 2 *IALS Student Law Review* 26, 29.

12 See S Krongold, 'Writing Laws: Making Them Easier to Understand' (1992) 24 *Ottawa Law Review* 495, 499.

know that the text is not pitched correctly for the user group represented in the user testing exercise. And they need to go back to the drawing board, and re-state these three points in a clearer manner. If the answers provided in user testing are correct, then external verification is completed successfully. In this case, the regulatory messages are received by the users loudly and clearly, and, with the synergy of the other actors in the regulatory process, legislative, and ultimately regulatory, effectiveness is on track to being achieved.[13]

It is important to state here that user testing is not synonymous with consultation. Consultation signifies participation of the public in decision-making by offering views and opinions. User testing does not offer the public an opportunity to share views or comments on the text. In that sense user testing is not a method of participation *stricto sensu*, it is simply a verification tool for drafters. User testing allows the drafters to ascertain whether their selected legislative expression transmits the correct regulatory message to the users of the legislative text. User testing tests the text by setting its provisions to hypothetical scenario of future application. If users are led to the solution intended by the drafters, external verification of the legislative text is achieved. If not, drafters must identify the mismatch between sender and receiver of the legislative communication, and amend the legislative expression accordingly. In view of its nature as a mere testing tool user testing in Thornton's drafting Stage 5 gauges future application. Any regulatory choices are considered to have been made already. Consultation at the policy formulation stage addressed regulatory choices before the drafting team embarked on the resource-heavy task of drafting legislation.[14] In Stage 5 verification involves legislative, not regulatory choices.[15] Perhaps the soundest statement of the interrelation between consultation and user testing is offered by Popelier, who views user testing as serving one of the functions of consultation: the control function of consultation, operated by an independent external body, helps to identify possible deficiencies of a technical, budgetary or legal nature.[16]

---

[13] See E Onoge, 'Structure of Legislation: A Paradigm for Accessibility and Effectiveness' (2015) 17 *European Journal of Law Reform* 440, 445.

[14] Basic questions must be asked early on: see S Bell and L Etherington, 'The Role of Consultation in Making Environmental Policy and Law' (1999) 8 *Nottingham Law Journal* 48, 67.

[15] See N A Hashim, 'Consultation: A Contribution to Efficiency of Drafting Process in Malaysia' (2012) 14 *European Journal of Law Reform* 142, 150.

[16] See P Popelier, 'Consultation on Draft Regulation: Best Practices and Political Objections' in L Mader et al. (eds), *Quality of Legislation: Principles and Instruments* (Nomos, Baden-Baden, 2011) 136, 138.

B. VERIFICATION IN TRANSPOSITION

Having discussed the modern trend of user testing in Stage 5, let us apply it to transposition. The treatment of national transposition legislation does not differ from that of other legislation in Stage 5. Internal and external verification can be sought in the same process that applies to all national laws. In fact, it is all the more important to undertake both types of verification, in view of the additional intricacies of transposition identified in the other stages of the drafting process. The problem with transposition is that not all Member States assign to user testing and therefore to external verification of the text.

External verification with user testing can reassure drafters that their transposition text has managed to convey the correct regulatory messages, despite the involvement of two legal orders, diverse legislative choices, and the EU foreign legislative expression. External verification at the national level ensures that the transposition text, be it elaborated or copied out from the EU text, is accessible to the national users of the jurisdiction in question. One could be tempted to state that, in cases of copied out texts or EU texts that are expected to apply without further national implementation, user testing can be undertaken at the EU level. But this would go against the whole ethos of better regulation, which recognises the relativity of effectiveness. As the latter requires accessibility of the text by each user group within each Member State, true external verification can only be achieved via user testing by representatives of the three user groups within each national jurisdiction. Resource-heavy as this process may be, it is the only secure way of ensuring that the EU regulatory messages will be received as intended, by all three user groups in the Member State in question.

Internal verification ensures that the EU regulatory goals have been successfully translated to national law reform in the transposition Member States, and that this law reform has been expressed by means of appropriate legislative expression in the transposition Member State. The latter part is achieved in external verification via user testing. But the first part, the translation of EU regulatory goals to national law reform can only be verified by the EU regulators, who are aware of what is being sought, with the assistance of national regulators, who are aware of the regulatory effect expected from their transposition choices. Making the correlation between these two regulatory aspects and their expression in national legislative choices requires an open channel of communication between EU institutions and national drafters at the pre-legislative transposition phase. This can ensure that issues of incomplete or bad transposition can be addressed and rectified before the national transposition text becomes law, and before punitive intervention is necessary in the form of infringement proceedings against the Member State. Aggression, embarrassment, and costly legal processes can be prevented, if scrutiny of transposition is moved to the verification stage of drafting as opposed to the post-legislative stage of correlation tables and informal letters and infringement proceedings before the CJEU and the imposition of fines. Better Regulation has matured the concept of co-legislation. Within that context, internal verification of transposition must be introduced not as a substitute for infringement proceedings but as a collaborative prevention of infringement proceedings, wherever possible.

C. ADDRESSING THE CHALLENGES OF TRANSPOSITION (THORNTON'S STAGE 5)

This preventative verification of national transposition drafts is the main challenge for the Commission in Stage 5. This could be introduced to supplement and 'personalise' transposition Guidance by use of one of the most popular transposition aids, expert meetings. In a lighter version of the proposed solution, the Commission can offer the opportunity to national teams to bring forward their transposition drafts, allowing experts to comment and benefit from peer review of the drafts by EU and Member States' experts. Such a discussion could inform national teams of best practices or common errors, which can supplement transposition Guidance documents. In a heavier, and ideal, version of the proposed solution, the EU can offer channels of communication, such as an appointed member of staff or meetings where necessary, where technical experts can present their drafts and seek advice. Although the resources of EU institutions are not limitless, there is an argument to support the view that moving transposition monitoring from prevention to intervention could balance the work between the two, thus allowing current resources to cope with the new requirement. Perhaps more importantly, the move will finally showcase the departure from the current ethos of rushing through a legislative texts for its completion whatever its quality.[17] It is essential for all those involved in shaping Union legislation to be reminded that their political concerns and desire for results must not be allowed to override the need for clear and precise legislation, as already suggested by the Mandelkern Group.[18] After all, true co-regulation enhances EU legitimacy.[19]

In view of the technical nature of such meetings, perhaps the most suitable Chair would be a member of the Better Regulation team, whose expertise in

[17] See G Sandström, 'Knocking EU Law into Shape' (2003) 40 *Common Market Law Review* 1307, 1309.

[18] See W Robinson, *Drafting EU Legislation: Note*, 2012, 25.

[19] See P Verbruggen, 'Does Co-Regulation Strengthen EU Legitimacy?' (2009) 15 *European Law Journal* 425.

effectiveness can guide discussion to the correlation between EU regulatory goals, national effectiveness goals, and national choices of design and legislative expression in the draft transposition text. To alleviate the constraints of formality that can inhibit substance, the conclusions of such meetings can be advisory only, thus allowing a frank and risk-free exchange of views without concerns on their possible contribution to binding decisions at the end of the meeting. Such meetings can only work if there is a strict Better Regulation methodology, perhaps that of Stage 2, with an ethos of cooperation within the co-legislating drafting team of EU and national drafters. Otherwise, the meetings could be usurped for the purposes of strengthening national positions.[20]

CONCLUSIONS

Good transposition legislation is legislation that achieves effectiveness at two levels: the EU level and the national level. National drafters pursue the achievement of the desired regulatory results as introduced in the EU legislative text and as translated within the national legal order. Drafting transposition legislation is one of the most difficult drafting tasks because the drafter serves two masters: two sets of regulatory goals, two texts, two sets of legal concepts, two sets of common and legal languages, and two drafting styles.

These difficulties are exacerbated by the inherent lack of freedom in the performance of the transposition task. Currently, transposition remains chained to the choices of the EU legislator. The tests of necessity, proportionality, adequacy, synergy, adaptability and subsidiarity have been passed, albeit at the EU level. The choice of legislation as the appropriate regulatory tool has already been made and alternative regulatory choices have been rejected. The type of legislative instrument has been decided, at least for the EU text. And the model law has been drafted. It is quite possible for national drafters to simply copy the EU text. Equally explicable is the safety sought by national drafters in the faithful repetition of the EU text: within a formalistic scrutiny exercise, the Commission is expected to accept the text drafted by its staff as a plausible legislative solution. However, effectiveness as a value of legislative quality demolishes the image depicted above. Effective transposition requires that the national drafter repeats all the tests of necessity, proportionality, adequacy, synergy and adaptability. Repeating of these tests is necessary because the national drafter does not conduct them against the policy, legislative, financial, administrative or cultural environment of the EU as a whole, but rather against the national environment. It is possible that national law already provides for

[20] See A Meuwese, *Impact Assessment in EU Lawmaking* (Kluwer, The Hague, 2008), 144.

the desired EU regulatory aims rather successfully. But what is necessary at the EU level may not be necessary at the national level. What is adequate at the EU level may require a more forcible legislative message in Member States where culture or societal values are adverse to the desired regulatory reform. Of course, reservations on synergy, subsidiarity or proportionality have little role to play here, as one would have expected them to arise at the level of passing of the EU text. Nevertheless, proportionality against existing national legislation may well be relevant where EU legislation offers a level of discretion above the required minimum.

In the transposition process, the choice of legislation as the appropriate regulatory tool must also be assessed against national laws. It is plausible for the national drafter to demote the regulatory tool for the achievement of the desired regulatory result in jurisdictions where legislation is not communicating with citizens adequately and non-legislative tools are successful in regulating behaviours. If the EU rejects a formalistic box-ticking scrutiny of transposition, the national drafters' arguments for effective transposition by alternative means of regulation can be truly effective. Of course, agreed monitoring mechanisms and agreed regulatory goals within set review times would be required, but the option is there and is quite plausible.

The same approach applies to the type of legislative instrument selected for transposition. It is not always necessary to provide a national implementing text whose type corresponds to that of the EU text. Regulations may require further legislative intervention. Directives may require transposition by means of a national law or even by a selection of diverse national texts of diverse types for the various regulatory parts of the EU text. Judgments of the European courts may well require legislative transposition. At the end of the day, the choice is one of effectiveness, not of formal correspondence between the EU and transposing laws.

Finally, the EU text is not a model law whose role is to be copied and pasted. Effectiveness demands that EU laws are used by the national drafters as legislative instructions, not model laws. They are there to state the desired regulatory result, to identify the policy tools promoted as most appropriate to achieve them, to draw the drafter' s attention to the elements that must be transposed compulsorily, and to alert the drafter to discretion in the transposition process. Although currently these elements are not easily identifiable by the existing legislative structure of EU texts, these are nevertheless the elements that the national drafter must extract in order to transpose effectively. This process, if conducted adequately, can lead to an effective national text, which in turn can lead to correct implementation and ultimately to true regulatory success for the EU and national legislators.[21]

These profound intricacies of transposition invite for early detection of any regulatory and legislative errors. Stage 5 of the drafting process aims to achieves exactly that. Internal verification controls the legislative solution against the desired regulatory results, identifies any mismatches, and incites their correction before the draft is presented to the legislators. External verification, in the form of user testing, ascertains that the regulatory message expressed by the legislative text is received by the users as indented by the drafters. Transposition requires internal and external verification even more. Especially in the rather common occurrence of copied out legislative texts, internal and external verification ensures effectiveness of the EU text within the diverse environment of the Member State.

National transposition drafters must invest in properly conducted internal and external verification exercises, much more so if they chose the copy out transposition technique.

The Commission, in its move from pre- to post-legislative transposition monitoring can instigate external verification by offering meetings as opportunities of ensuring that the proposals of EU regulators are adequately and accurately expressed by the national drafters.

[21] H Xanthaki, 'Improving the Quality of EU Legislation: Limits and Opportunities?' in Sasha Garben and Inge Govaere (eds) *The Better Regulation Agenda: A Critical Assessment* (Hart, Oxford, 2018) 28–47, 44–46.

7. Legislating for EU accession and approximation

The previous chapters analysed in great detail the task of legislating for transposition of EU legislation into the laws of Member States. Transposition requires full, complete and timely reception of EU legislation into the legal order of the transposing jurisdiction. However, perfection in reception is not always the goal set for national drafters. Using EU legislation as a model for national legislation is often undertaken outside EU membership.

The obvious example for approximation (rather than transposition) is that of applicant countries. They undergo a drafting exercise within which preparations are made for transposition with effect starting from the possible future event of accession, whenever in the future that will occur. Until that still undetermined date of accession, national drafters approximate national legislation, in preparation for the moment of accession. Moreover, to a looser degree, and consequently as a lighter drafting exercise, approximation also takes place outside membership and accession, in jurisdictions where compliance with EU legislation allows for and facilitates the diversity of close relationships between the EU and countries with special agreements. EFTA, Switzerland, countries with bilateral or multilateral agreements with the EU and its Member States fall in this category. Finally, approximation is also undertaken when, in the absence of any special relationship or bilateral agreement, countries seek to enhance trade with the EU and therefore receive EU legislation as a prerequisite for access to the EU market. This chapter will focus on approximation for future accession.[1]

Whichever level of approximation is sought and for whatever reason, the EU assesses the quality of national approximation legislation using the same concept of effectiveness that is applied on transposition. But, of course, the extent and consequences of the capacity of national authorities to comply with the EU effectiveness model are lighter than in the case of transposition.

[1] For a fuller analysis on drafting for accession, with focus on Cyprus, see H Xanthaki, 'The Route to EU Accession' in C Stefanou (ed), *Cyprus and the EU: The Road to Accession* (Ashgate, Aldershot, 2005), 11.

Applying effectiveness, as the EU's regulatory and legislative goal, requires the structure of the approximation drafting task using Thornton's[2] methodology.

A. STAGE 1: UNDERSTANDING THE PROPOSAL – THE ROUTE TO EU ACCESSION FOR ASPIRING MEMBER STATES

The national drafter's task to approximate national legislation with that of the EU cannot be viewed separately from the policy goal set holistically for the relationship of the jurisdiction with the EU, carrot, stick and all.[3] Although drafting to focus on individual drafts, understanding the proposal to draft approximating legislation requires an understanding of the whole national strategy. In Thornton's Stage 1 of drafting for accession, the drafter needs to familiarise themselves with the intricacies of the process for accession. This is necessary for effective drafting choices that contribute to the whole accession exercise within the timeframe set by policy officers.

Accession to the EU is not a purely political decision.[4] The three main criteria for accession to the EU were introduced by the Copenhagen European Council in June 1993.[5] Membership of the EU is dependent upon fulfilment of a political, an economic, and a legal criterion. Compliance with the political requirements signifies the existence of stable institutions, which guaranteed democracy, the rule of law, human rights and respect for minorities in the aspiring country. These are now reflected in Article 2 TEU, which confirms the political values of the EU as human dignity, freedom, democracy, equality, rule of law and human rights, including those of persons belonging to minorities. Compliance with the economic requirements signifies a functioning

---

[2] See H Xanthaki, *Thornton's Legislative Drafting* (5th edn, Bloomsbury, London, 2013), 128–174.

[3] See F Schimmelfennig and U Sedelmeier, 'The Europeanization of Eastern Europe: The External Incentives Model Revisited', Paper for the JMF@25 conference, EUI, 22/23 June 2017, https://www.eui.eu/Documents/RSCAS/JMF-25-Presentation/Schimmelfennig -Sedelmeier -External -Incentives -Revisited -JMF .pdf accessed 14 December 2023, 3.

[4] See D Phinnemore, 'The Stabilization and Association Process. A Framework for European Union Enlargement' in A Elbasani (ed), *European Integration and Transformation in the Western Balkans. Europeanization or Business as Usual?* (Routledge, London, 2013) 25, 31.

[5] See European Council, 'European Council in Copenhagen, 21–22 June 1993, Conclusions of the Presidency', 22 June 1993, DOC/93/3, http:// www .consilium .europa.eu/ueDocs/cms_Data/docs/pressData/en/ec/72921.pdf accessed 14 December 2023, 14.

market economy in the aspiring country.[6] The legal criterion requires the full adoption of the *acquis communautaire* before accession, as a means of securing that the candidate country already shares the EU's political, economic and monetary goals detailed in the constituting treaties, primary and secondary EU legislation. The December 1995 Madrid European Council added that the three Copenhagen criteria must not only met but also enforced. This requires the adoption of the necessary administrative structures for the gentle integration of the aspiring country within the EU.[7]

The first step towards the start of negotiations for accession is the evaluation of the candidate country's national legislation as a means of identifying areas of discrepancy. On the basis of this evaluation, which is undertaken by the Commission, a work programme is agreed and negotiating positions are defined.

The second step towards the start of negotiations is the inclusion of the work programme, negotiating positions and priorities for each sector of legislation in an accession partnership. The aim of accession partnerships is to set clear goals for the reception of the *acquis*. This is defined as a dynamic body of stipulations that engulfs the content, principles and political objectives of the constituting treaties; secondary legislation adopted in application of the treaties and the case law of the European courts; the declarations and resolutions adopted by the EU; measures relating to the common foreign and security policy; measures relating to justice and home affairs; and international agreements concluded by the EU and those concluded by the Member States between themselves in the fields of the EU competence. In other words, the acquis covers not only legislation (law *strictu sensu*) but all sources of EU law. Applicant countries have to transpose all of the *acquis* before they can join the EU. This obligation is of course subject to specific and expressly agreed derogations or periods of grace clearly introduced in the accession treaty for the particular country. Implementation of the acquis by the new Member States begins on the date of their formal accession to the EU.

---

6 Subject areas include free movement of goods; freedom of movement for workers; right of establishment and freedom to provide services; free movement of capital; public procurements; company law; intellectual property law; competition policy; financial services; information society and media; agriculture and rural development; food safety, veterinary and phytosanitary policy; fisheries; transport policy; energy; taxation; economic and monetary policy; statistics; social policy and employment; enterprise and industrial policy; Trans-European networks; regional policy and coordination of structural instruments; customs union; financial control; financial and budgetary provisions.

7 See I Kawka, 'Approximating Macedonian Legislation to the EU's Acquis' (2014) 30 *Politeja* 175, 179.

The third step towards the start of negotiations is the conclusion of a detailed programme for the adoption of the *acquis*. The programme takes into account the Commission's evaluation of the legislation of the country and the identification of areas of discrepancy with the *acquis* as detailed in the accession partnership. The aim of the programme is to organise the implementation of the priorities identified in the accession partnership, the introduction of a realistic and adequate timetable for the transposition of the *acquis* into national law, and the identification of the human and financial resources needed to achieve compliance with the timetable and final compliance with the Copenhagen legal criterion as a requirement for EU accession. Programmes and indeed accession partnerships are re-evaluated and adjusted regularly upon agreement of the Commission and the candidate country.

The main framework for accession remains the same and is based on Article 49 of the EU Treaty.[8] Negotiations with candidate countries can only begin if all three central EU institutions are in agreement. What is required is support from the European Commission, agreement of the European Parliament and finally unanimous agreement of the Council. In other words, all existing Member States and all EU institutions must be in agreement before even the lengthy period of negotiations for accession can begin. Apart from this *conditio sine qua non*, each candidate country must comply with the specific requirements for its own accession as negotiated and agreed in each particular case. Thus, specific conditions for admission, transitional periods and adjustments to the constituting treaties must be determined before negotiations for accession can begin and at a time when the candidate country has little, if any, negotiating powers. The legal nature of the agreement between the candidate country and the EU is that of an international treaty. National ratification requirements for all signatories must therefore be completed before the agreement acquires legal force.

Once this is done, a structured dialogue of approximation begins. Here the national authorities and representatives of EU institutions meet to explore similarities and differences in the policies, economies and laws of the two legal orders, and to introduce proposals for the facilitation of gradual closer cooperation. A record of the status quo is expressed in a Commission White Paper, which includes an initial, indicative and incomplete table of the *acquis* that has to be transposed before accession to the EU, but prioritisation and planning for the achievement of this aim is left to the national authorities.[9] After a positive

---

8 See Treaty on European Union, consolidated version, *OJ* C 326/1 (2012).

9 For examples of such plans, see 'Закон за Владата на Република Македонија, 22.07.2000', Сл. весник/година, No. 59 (2000); also see A Hronec, 'The Approximation of EU Environmental Legislation in the Czech Republic' (1999) 8 *European Energy and Environmental Law Review* 17.

response by the European Commission and assent of the European Parliament, the Council can allow negotiations to begin, and determine the legal instruments that will form the basis for negotiations: normally, this is an accession partnership that then forms the framework for other pre-accession instruments, including joint assessments of medium-term economic policy priorities, pacts on organised crime, national development plans and other sectoral programmes necessary for participation in the Structural Funds after accession and for the implementation of the Instrument for Structural Policies for Pre-Accession and the Special Accession Programme for Agriculture and Rural Development. Accession negotiations are normally undertaken via bilateral inter-governmental conferences between the EU and the applicant country.

From the point of view of the national drafter attempting to understand the request to draft for accession, it is important to be aware that the national accession strategy requires complete transposition of EU law before accession. Priorities are set by the national authorities and drafters must be aware of where their accession draft lies within this context. If it is within the areas of priority, then prompt and complete transposition will allow prompt closure of negotiations in this field and consequently prompt progress towards accession. If it is outside the areas of priority, the drafter can expect difficulties and discrepancies between national and EU legislation. Time is more generous here, but it is required to achieve the task.

The problem with Thornton's Stage 1 in the drafting process for approximation is that, instead of the long checklist of issues raised in drafting instructions, national drafters receive a finished EU legislative instrument, which is in the EU style and language, and which offers very little information on its regulatory context. At least as EU texts stand, there is little reference to concrete regulatory goals, to the criteria of effectiveness to be applied in post-legislative scrutiny, to options examined and costed, to the expected costs and benefits of the preferred choice, to the identified audiences of the EU legislative text, and to linguistic choices made as part of the legislative expression. National approximating drafters are being asked to produce effective national approximating legislation without being offered an analysis of the overarching policy goals, the link between them and regulatory and legislative and linguistic choices made, the criteria of effectiveness of the EU text, and the administrative mechanisms required to make this an implementable and enforceable piece of national legislation. Moreover, approximation, just as is the case with transposition, inherently suffers from the provision of a ready legislative text instead of proper drafting instructions. For approximation in specific, this flawed is accentuated by the *ab definitio* lack of any direct or indirect involvement of the approximating drafter in the formulation of the EU text, which could have offered them a degree of context behind the rationale of policy, legal and legislative choices.

The advantage of approximating drafters in this stage is that Member States have already transposed the EU text. There are, therefore, a great number of models that approximating drafters may identify to try and understand the task ahead. But, of course, these replicate the flaws of the EU text in that they are ready-made drafts, and they provide little insight in the elements of effectiveness of the national transposition measures. And again the reality of transposition is that, more often than not, the transposition text simply copies the EU one, thus replicating their problems as drafting instructions for the purposes of approximation.

Reforms proposed here on the transposition process can also help approximation. Thus, the introduction of an introductory report and transposition guidelines covering the need of national drafters for complete drafting instructions would address the needs of approximating drafters also. Moreover, the introduction of effectiveness measurements in these reports would assist approximating drafters to understand what effect is being sought by the EU text, when this will be measured, and on what basis. This would allow them to identify the correlating effect at the national level, thus promoting national effectiveness. The combination of this with sunset clauses in EU texts would accentuate the understanding of effectiveness as a concept, and its significance in EU law-making as a condition *sine qua non* of EU legislation: without it, EU texts die.

Injecting the concept of effectiveness in Stage 1 of approximation drafting would have long-term effects too. First, approximating drafters would come into contact with the concept of Better Regulation from the very start of their engagement with the EU. As this is an innovative concept for most legislatures, exposure to it from the very start of engagement with the EU would mentor national approximating drafters to the concept of processes of effective law-making, thus, in turn, injecting more technical expertise in the transposition drafting community post accession. Perhaps even more importantly, conveying to aspiring EU citizens the message that EU drafters contribute to the effectiveness of transposition through evidence-based, transparent, and open data to national drafters can only instil positivity and trust to the EU and its regulatory efforts. And this relationship of communication and openness with aspiring citizens can bear the invaluable fruits of trust, loyalty, and participation before and after accession.

B. STAGE 2: ANALYSING THE PROPOSAL

Thornton's Stage 2 involves analysing the proposal. Drafters must be aware of what the request of approximation really entails. The main aim of accession negotiations is to achieve the highest possibly compliance of the national law of the applicant country with EU law.[10] Complete transposition is not limited to the incorporation of the *acquis* to the national law of the applicant country. Implementation and enforceability of the *acquis* upon accession is an equally important part of transposition[11] and indeed one that is often neglected by the applicant countries. It is the most technical and intricate part of their preparation for accession, as it requires the strengthening of the administrations and the legal system of applicant countries, as well as their drastic adaptation as a means of complying with EU standards. This is often a rather painstaking exercise especially in the very technical areas of agriculture, transport, energy and the environment. As a means of facilitating the intricate and often unbearable task of the radical prompt reform of the administration and the legal system to accommodate these requirements, the EU provides to applicant countries pre-accession aid.

Negotiations identify areas of difficulty, the measures required for transposition of the *acquis* and the timetable to be followed for complete compliance before the accession date. Moreover, negotiations look at the human and financial resources noted in the accession partnership in order to determine the nature and extent of pre-accession aid that the EU will award to the applicant country to support the gentle and effective incorporation of the *acquis* to the existing body of national laws. Lack of complete and timely transposition will signify failure of the applicant country to fulfil the legal Copenhagen criterion and therefore failure to accede to the EU. As a result, partial compliance is only acceptable if so agreed by the EU institutions. This can only occur in the minimal cases of derogation from the *acquis* or for transitional measures.

The role of the national authorities of the applicant country in accession negotiations is to clarify existing national law, to explore to which extent this complies with the *acquis* and to accept fully or partially the recommendation of the Commission on new measures to be introduced for the achievement of complete and timely transposition. Within this framework of negotiations national authorities have the opportunity to argue for favourable terms for the adoption, implementation and enforcement of the *acquis* by their legislatures, executive and judiciary. They may also request limited transitional arrangements when more time is needed for the full reform of legislation in a particularly difficult area or where the nature and extent of discrepancy between the existing national law and the *acquis* in a particular area of very limited scope could allow a derogation from the *acquis* which would not disturb the

---

[10] On compliance see H Jacobson, 'After Word: Conceptual, Methodological and Substantive Issues Entwined in Studying Compliance' (1998) 19 *Michigan Law Journal* 569, 573.

[11] See F Snyder, 'The Effectiveness of European Community Law: Institutions, Processes, Tools and Techniques' (1993) 56 *Modern Law Review* 19, 19.

full integration of the applicant country to the EU. Traditionally, arguments for derogations and periods of grace are received with much scepticism from the Commission. Nevertheless, in a small number of cases genuine difficulties of the applicant country are recognised. Each applicant country draws up its position on each of the 35 negotiable chapters of the EU *acquis*; these form the basis of negotiations.[12]

The subjects of negotiations are the existing Member States and the applicant country. The applicant country appoints a Chief Negotiator, with a supporting team of experts. On the EU's side the subject of negotiations is neither the EU nor EU institutions: subjects are the existing Member States. As a result, negotiating positions are presented by the President of the European Council as the representative of national governments and not the European Commission which, however, is very much involved in the actual meetings. Meetings at the level of Ministers or their deputies are also chaired by the Council. The Presidency rotates every six months and applicant countries have the opportunity to push their positions forward under the Presidency of a number of existing Member States. The role of the European Commission in negotiations is to propose the draft negotiating positions on the basis of pre-accession documents and outcomes of negotiations in the 29 chapters of the *acquis*. The Commission acts both as a facilitator of the applicant countries in the accession process but also as a guarantor of compliance with the *acquis* by the applicant country. The Commission is therefore in close cooperation with national authorities in order to advise them on solutions to problems and difficulties but also to apply pressure for the finalisation of all necessary measures for the timely and full transposition, implementation and enforcement of the *acquis*. In view of the role of the European Commission within the EU, this is not a task unknown to them. Although all Directorate Generals of the Commission take an active role in the accession process for applicant

[12] These are: 1. Free movement of goods; 2. Freedom of movement for workers; 3. Right of establishment and freedom to provide services; 4. Free movement of capital; 5. Public procurement; 6. Company law; 7. Intellectual property law; 8. Competition policy; 9. Financial services; 10. Information society and media; 11. Agriculture and rural development; 12. Food safety; 13.Veterinary and phytosanitary policy; 14. Fisheries; 15. Transport policy; 16. Energy; 17. Taxation; 18. Economic and monetary policy; 19. Statistics; 20. Social policy and employment; 21. Enterprise and industrial policy; 22. Trans-European networks; 23. Regional policy and coordination of structural instruments; 24. Judiciary and fundamental rights; 25. Justice, freedom and security; 26. Science and research; 27. Education and culture; 28. Environment; 29. Consumer and health protection; 30. Customs union; 31. External relations; 32. Foreign, security and defence policy; 33. Financial control, Financial and budgetary provisions; 34. Institutions; 35. Other issues.

countries, it is the Directorate General for Enlargement that has overall responsibility for the coordination of the effort on the part of the Commission.

However, administrative/secretarial support for accession negotiations is provided for by the General Secretariat of the Council and by the applicant countries themselves. At the negotiating stage the role of the European Parliament is to watch the work undertaken by the Council and the Commission and to evaluate the progress of the applicant countries. The European Parliament, as indeed national Parliaments of the accession countries, acquire an active role in enlargement only at the final stage of assent to the resulting accession treaties in the case of the European Parliament and the stage of ratification of the resulting accession treaties in the case of national Parliaments. The citizens of the EU are represented by the Council and the Parliament in the accession process and are awarded a direct active role in enlargement only in countries where a referendum is a constitutional necessity for the final approval of the accession treaties.

Negotiations for EU accession are conducted on the basis of four main principles. The principle of specificity limits the scope of negotiations exclusively to the terms under which the applicant country can adopt, implement and enforce the *acquis*. The principle of leniency allows transitional arrangements but delimits them in scope and durations as a means of ensuring that integration of the applicant country will not be harmed by them. The principle of differentiation prohibits the dependence of progress in negotiations from processes of negotiation undertaken in parallel with a group of candidate countries. Finally, the principle of catching up allows candidate countries to proceed quicker than previous applicants should their progress merit quicker advancement.

The task of transposition begins with the detailed analysis of the *acquis*. Although it would be tempting for a future Member State to conduct this analysis internally, experience has shown that the presentation of EU law by the Commission and its interpretation by the CJEU constitute the only reliable source of information in this area. National legal officers from third countries tend to lack the know-how necessary for the correct identification of the sources of EU law, the appreciation of the hierarchy of these sources, and the objective determination of discrepancies between national laws and the acquis. Often the starting point for this process is different and the priorities of the EU and the Commission only become evident after the screening process has begun. Future Member States have additional guidance in their initial efforts to familiarise themselves with the *acquis*. Firstly, the Commission's guide to negotiations presents the main points of each chapter for future negotiations and presents an accurate picture of EU law as it currently stands. Nevertheless, this is a very two-dimensional picture of the *acquis*, which quickly becomes inadequate for long-term use: EU law is a dynamic, ever-changing set of rules under constant review and interpretation by the European courts. Secondly, the route to transposition is signposted by the efforts, faults and successes of the 2004 enlargement and subsequent accession by Croatia: future Member States have access to complete reports on the Commission's priorities per chapter and the criteria for their evaluations. Thus, work towards EU accession begins long before negotiations are even contemplated. Aspiring Member States must have a strategy for accession even at the time that the initial international agreements with the EU are signed. Approximation pacts are far from the common perception of mere international agreements aiming to draw the country's attention to points of concern for the EU in exchange of hefty financial assistance. They constitute the basis upon which the assessment of the country's suitability as a future Member State will be undertaken. In fact, points of concern identified in these instruments are often at the forefront of negotiations for EU accession as they reflect the EU's points of priority in the event of future enlargement. The agreement of the aspiring country in these pacts is often interpreted as an initial consent as to the existence of a problem in the areas identified in the text.

Negotiations for accession are crucial. They are not cosmetic and they cannot be taken lightly. Experts participating in the screening process should be very much aware that their views will be binding for their country. Their presentation on the existing national provisions will be scrutinised very closely and any discrepancies will be brought to light. The best service that negotiators could offer to their country is to be frank and present the full picture of the existing legal provisions. Although compliance will have to be achieved, the Commission is more likely to agree on realistically longer deadlines and on understandable delays in full transposition, if the intricacies of the applicant country's national legal system are made know to the Commission delegation. As the Commission' role is to facilitate transposition, their experience from negotiations with a number of applicant countries may well lead to an innovative solution to any problems.

Of course, the precise measures to be taken for complete and timely compliance with the *acquis* are determined and taken by the applicant country. The Commission advises on the points that the applicant country must address and expects adequate measures to be taken within the agreed deadlines. In theory, the applicant country may ignore all Commission recommendations. The Commission's power in negotiations is only indirect: power is there only if the applicant country wishes to proceed with its application for accession to the EU; and the Commission's power lies on its instrumental role in the assessment of the applicant country's transposition of the *acquis*.

It would be fair therefore to state that the process of negotiations with aspiring Member States begins long before the application for EU membership is submitted. The pre-accession strategy of aspiring Member States must engulf any initial international agreements and approximation pacts with the EU. The route to EU accession is long and painful. Very often the required radical changes can prove destructive for the legal system of applicant countries. However, if accession is desirable, the route to it offers an invaluable opportunity to the applicant countries to acquire a realistic and insightful taste of the internal mechanisms of the EU, its legal system, its institutions and its values. National drafters cannot afford to ignore the totality of the accession process and deal solely with the approximation task that they have been assigned. This is just a piece in the puzzle of approximation. Fragmentation of approximation leads to a box-ticking exercise of correlation tables, which does not guarantee full approximation and certainly not implementation and enforcement. If one takes into account the progress of innovation brought in by Better Regulation, the balance of EU demand versus applicant State capacity to produce effective national approximation legislation will always tend to tilt towards the EU.

For the purposes of achieving effective national approximating legislation, as required for the purposes of accession, national approximating drafters need to respond to drafting instructions by means of a legislative plan. The elements of the legislative plan include the analysis of the existing law, of the necessity of legislation, of any potential danger areas, of the policy options and the preferred legislative solution, and of the practical implications of the legislative proposal. Xanthaki's effectiveness, applied to the transposition task in Chapter 9, also applies to approximation with minor changes. Understanding the EU proposal for the purposes of approximation inevitably leads to the same requirements as understanding for the purposes of transposition. The only difference here is that guidance tools for approximation drafters are much less than those offered to drafters in existing Member States. They have experience and training in handling EU legislation, and their legal systems and styles have been taken into account (and actually contributed) in the formulation of the EU text. This does not apply to approximation drafters whose exposure to EU structures and law may be minimal. The first part of Xanthaki's effectiveness test requires an understanding of the EU context by answering the sequence of the following questions:

1. Which are the desired regulatory results of the EU?
2. How will they be measured by the EU?
3. Within how long are they to be achieved by the EU?
4. What is the legal mischief at the EU level, and how is it connected to the desired regulatory goals?
5. How is the new EU legislation expected to address the mischief at the EU level?
6. Does the language of each EU provision communicate its message clearly?
7. If this is not the case, what tools are available to address complexity?

i. The Introductory report (often in the form of a White or Green Paper) that accompanies the draft proposal in expert groups and details the regulatory rationale behind policy choices;
ii. definitions in the EU text;
iii. any EU transposition guidelines;
iv. any explanatory documents;
v. any Transposition and Implementation plan (which is prepared in the initial stages of the Commission's proposal and identifies weaknesses and challenges for Member State); and
vi. any meeting-based pre-transposition tools (networks, expert groups, package meetings, scoreboards etc).

Once part one of this exercise has been completed and national drafters have understood the EU text, part two (understanding the proposal for its approximation) can begin by answering the following questions in sequence:

1. Which are the desired regulatory results for the State? These do not always coincide with the EU's, as they are dependent upon the national regulatory environment, but they must contribute to the EU's.
2. Do they coincide with those of the EU or any of the existing MS?
3. How can they be measured by the State, in order to provide both the data needed for the purposes of evidencing regulatory success?
4. Within how long are they to be achieved?
5. Can the text be implemented without stumbling on socio-legal hurdles within the State?
6. What is the legal mischief in State, and how is it connected to the desired regulatory goals?
7. Can this be addressed by non-legislative means? If so, checking the national position with the Commission can prevent unnecessary drafting of national measures.
8. How is the proposed national legislation expected to address the mischief?
9. Which are the main groups of possible users of the national text?
10. What level of awareness of the topic do they have?
11. What is their level of legal awareness?
12. What questions does each group ask?
13. Does the current structure provide accessible answers the specific questions of each of the user groups?
14. Does the current structure facilitate the unhindered identification of the relevant answers?
15. Does the language of each provision communicate its message to each of the intended user groups in a manner that they can understand (topic and law)?

16. If this is difficult, what tools have been used to address complexity?
    a. Examples
    b. Definitions or interpretation
17. Is the layout simple?
18. Does the text refer the user to relevant provisions, perhaps via:
    a. Hyperlinks
    b. Explanatory notes
    c. When will the new national text require monitoring, and with which results?

Perhaps the biggest hurdle for approximating drafters in Stage 2 of the approximation task is one of drafting mentality. The application of Thornton's drafting stages may seem superfluous, the need to put pen to paper and get on with an approximation text quickly is inevitably urgent, and the whole mentality of effectiveness and legislation as a tool of regulation aiming to produce regulatory results may be missing from the approximating State. Becoming familiar with the concept and mechanics of effective law-making is perhaps the biggest reform required in the approximation process.[13] And Stage 2, with its long list of difficult questions, is the most challenging point of the effectiveness process for approximating drafters. However, it needs to be done, and it needs to be completed properly, if the resulting approximating text is to be affective, and therefore adequate for the purposes of approximation. Although effectiveness was not formally monitored by the Commission in that 2004 wave of mass accessions, Better Regulation has progressed greatly, and EU institutions are both attuned to its requirements, and entrenched in its application. Moreover, the move from a mass accession in 2004 to a selective accession of ready applicant countries affords the Commission time and capacity to achieve full reception of EU law by the future accession countries, effectiveness and all. On that basis, rushing to copying the EU text into national approximating texts is not a wise move for aspiring Member States. And engagement with full effective approximation starts with understanding the proposal, and designing the national approximating legislation. These are the most crucial stages of the approximation drafting process. And following them religiously can prevent a myriad of problems down the line, when time and effort have been spent to provide a draft already.

---

[13] And most of the relatively newer Member States report improvement in implementation and enforcement: see OECD, Sigma Paper – 'Regulatory management capacities of Member States of the European Union that joined the Union on 1 May 2004, Sustaining regulatory management improvements through a Better Regulation policy', Sigma Paper No 42, GOV/SIGMA(2007)6, http:// www .sigmaweb .org accessed 14 December 2023, 90.

C. STAGE 3: DESIGNING THE NATIONAL APPROXIMATING LAW

Of course, approximating drafters have the benefit of a degree of hindsight. Member States have already transposed the EU text, and there may already be assessments by the Commission on monitoring and implementation, thus showcasing best practices. But simply replicating a national implementing measure is not necessarily a good idea. Legal transplants can work but only if the two jurisdictions share the same concepts of need and usefulness.[14] In other words, copying a national implementing measure is no guarantee for regulatory success. Drafters need to assess the similarity of the regulatory goals between the two jurisdictions. Even where the mischief is the same and the regulatory goals are identical, the usefulness of the proposed regulatory solution in the approximating State may not be the same as in the model jurisdiction.

In fact, against the current trend of integrative legal globalisation,[15] approximating drafters need to tread carefully when using the EU or national transposition texts as models of approximation laws. In a drafting ethos promoting effectiveness, such as that of the EU and its Member States, comparability is not synonymous to convenience or familiarity with the legislation of an existing Member State. Policy choices, concepts, terms and legislative solutions can be borrowed from other legal systems, but only on the basis of functionality. For the completion of a transplant, the use of EU or Member State policies, concepts and legislative choices must be undertaken through the relative prism of functionality[16] introduced by Jhering, Zweigert and Kötz.[17] It is the theory of functionality that seems to serve drafting teams in the current period of integrative legal globalisation, although currently the use of social analysis in legislation is minimal.[18] What matters when selecting the model law of the EU or a Member State is not the similarity of its characteristics with that of the approximating jurisdiction, but the functionality of the proposal. If the policy, concept or legislation of the source law can serve the approximating

---

14 See H Xanthaki, 'Legal Transplants in Legislation: Defusing the Trap' (2008) 57 *International and Comparative Law Quarterly* 659.

15 See L A Mistelis, 'Regulatory Aspects: Globalization, Harmonization, Legal Transplants, and Law Reform – Some Fundamental Observations' (2000) 34 *International Lawyer* 1059.

16 See K Zweigert and K Sier, 'Jhering's Influence on the Development of Comparative Legal Method' (1971) 19 *Am J Comp Law* 215.

17 See K Zweigert and H Kötz, *Einführung in die Rechtsvergleichung*, 3. neubearbeitete Auflage (J.C.B. Mohr, Tübingen, 1996).

18 See J Brown, A Kudan and K McGeeney, 'Improving Legislation Through Social Analysis: A Case Study in Methodology from the Water Sector in Uzbekistan' (2005) 5 *Sustainable Development Law and Policy* 49, 49.

State well, then the origin of the transplant is irrelevant to its success.[19] As long as the transplant can serve the social need to be addressed, the transplant can work well in the new legal ground. In fact, it is this transfer of the transplant to national contexts that promotes indigenisation of positive transplants as a block to indiscrete globalisation and modern legal colonialism.[20]

Far from resolving the drafting team's problems, the qualifier of functionality demands an answer to a rather difficult question: which is social need that the draft law addresses? In an ideal legislative process, which involves drafting instructions with the identification of the social problem to be addressed and a discussion of various solutions,[21] the drafting team can immediately link the phenomenon to be addressed with the selected solution. In cases where the purpose of the original law is clearly explained in explanatory materials, the issue of functionality as a qualifier for compatibility can be easily resolved. However, legislative practice is not necessarily ideal. Often drafting instructions refer to the solution opted for by policymakers rather than to the social need to be addressed. More often than not, the social need to be addressed is hidden and may only appear in explanatory materials, whose use is by no means wide.[22] Under such circumstances the task of the drafting team to identify the underlying social need and to use it as a criterion of comparability and a safeguard for transplants seems rather intricate, especially if one takes into account the dominance of pure lawyers in drafting teams.[23] And of course these issues are all the more prevalent in an approximation context where drafting instructions are simply non-existent, regulatory data are buried in EU sources with which approximating drafters are unfamiliar, and the pressure of quick and accurate replication of the EU or national transposing texts are grave. Add to this the lack of interaction at the pre-legislative stage, and national approximating drafters are really in the dark as to whether they are meeting EU requirements, at least until a post-legislative approximation assessment reveals all. But, by that time, time and effort would have already been wasted

---

19 See S Zhuang, 'Legal Transplantation in the People's Republic of China: A Response to Alan Watson' (2006) *European Journal of Law Reform*, 215, 223.

20 See R Petrella, 'Globalization and Internationalization: The Dynamics of the Emerging World Order' in R Boyer and D Drache (eds), *States Against Markets: The Limits of Globalization* (Routledge, London and New York, 1996),132.

21 See D E Elliott, 'Getting Better Instructions for Legislative Drafting', *Just Language Conference*, 21 October 1992, Victoria, British Columbia.

22 See Sir G Bowmann, 'Legislation and Explanation' (2000) *Loophole*, https://calc.ngo/sites/default/files/loophole/jun-2000.pdf accessed 14 December 2023.

23 For an analysis of causality in sociological research see C Ragin and D Zaret, 'Theory and Method in Comparative Research: Two Strategies' (1983) 61 *Social Forces* 731.

in compiling an approximation text that, in view of the inherent weaknesses above, will often suffer from basic faults of understanding and design.

More often than not, it is precisely design that can salvage approximation drafts. This is where demands for effectiveness are most relevant. As is the case with transposition, the crucial job of the national drafter is not with the choice of words and legislative expression, but with structural choices related to the translation of regulatory demands into a legislative text that will be implemented in practice.[24] To achieve such a text, approximating drafters can either copy a transposition instrument that serves the same concepts of need and usefulness, or they can create a new approximation text tailored to the eccentricities of their own legal system and requirements. To achieve that, national drafters can replicate the transposition methodology.

First, approximating drafters must identify the regulatory messages that the text needs to convey to users. In other words, they must answer the difficult question of what it is that the text is saying to users. Answers to that question produce the regulatory messages, namely the regulatory commands with which users must comply in order to contribute to the achievement of the desired regulatory results[25] (namely, the efficacy of the regulation).[26] In contrast to transposition, in approximation the desired regulatory results will always differ from those of the EU text. For example, the EU food labelling standards aim to protect public health within the EU, whereas the aim of the relevant approximating text is simply to open the way to the sale of national products within the EU market. A diversity of regulatory aims leads to a diversity in the mechanisms by which these aims are to be achieved. To follow the same example, in the EU text can foresee periodic sample analysis of ingredients in food as a means of ensuring that foods comply with public health requirements. In approximation, the frequency and depth of testing can be much lighter, and simply serve the need to ensure trust of the importing foods from the EU authorities and its consumers. A diversity of regulatory mechanisms may then lead to a diversity of post-legislative assessments. In the case of the EU text, a post-legislative scrutiny of the text would have to prove

---

[24] On the detachment between policy formulation and legislative drafting in pre-accession Slovakia, see K Staronova and K Mathernova, 'Public Policy Process Recommendations for the Improvement of the Legislative Drafting Process in Slovakia', Final Policy Paper, 2002.

[25] On legislation as a tool for changing social behaviour see I Jenkins, *Social Order and the Limits of the Law: A Theoretical Essay* (Princeton University Press, Princeton, 1981), 180; also see R Cranston, 'Reform through Legislation: The Dimension of Legislative Technique' (1978–1979) 73 *Northwestern University Law Review* 873, 875.

[26] See G Teubner, 'Regulatory Law: Chronicle of a Death Foretold' (1992) 1 *Socio-Legal Studies* 451.

that the change in labelling has indeed reduced incidents of disease in the EU population. In contrast to this, there would be no need for post-legislative scrutiny of the approximating text other than perhaps to assess if food labelling has led to increased trade with the EU, and if an update of EU labelling rules requires an amendment to the approximating law.

Second, approximating drafters must identify the user groups for the approximating law. Identifying those concretely plays a crucial role in the effectiveness of the approximating law. Group 1 would be lay persons who will be using the law in their everyday life. In the food labelling law for example, lay users would be producers, distributors, and exporters of foods imported in the EU. Group 2 would be users whose professional duties relate to the inspection of foods and exports. And Group 3 would be lawyers and judges involved in the resolution of any disputes. Identifying the user groups concretely will guide approximating drafters to an accurate assessment of the level of subject and legal sophistication. This will guide them as to prioritisation of the regulatory messages per user group, thus affecting structure. Part 1 of the approximating law will include regulatory messages relevant to Group 1 users, Part 2 for Group 2, and Part 3 for Group 3. This exercise will offer approximation drafters a structure for their national approximating legislation.

Third, approximating drafters must decide on the type of national instruments to be used for approximation. If accession is planned, then choice of instrument is led by the form of the EU text and by national sources of law. If accession is not an immediate goal, then the form of the EU instrument is irrelevant. What matters is exclusively the effectiveness of the national law. So, in approximation for accession, a Treaty article will have to be addressed in a constitutional text, whereas in approximation for trade, a Treaty article can be largely ignored. An example for a need for constitutional reform for the purposes of accession is the amendment of the constitution of North Macedonia in compliance with the Ohrid Agreement, which resulted in constitutional amendments recognising some ethnicities, replacing the term 'minority' with 'community' or 'communities not in the majority', recognising the language of national minorities accounting for more than 20 per cent of the population in particular municipalities, and offering equitable representation to all communities.[27]

---

[27] See 'Рамковен договор' (Охридски рамковен договор), 13.08.2001, https://peacemaker.un.org/sites/peacemaker.un.org/files/MK_010813_Frameword%20Agreement%20%28Orhid%20Agreement%29.pdf accessed accessed 8 January 2024.

D. STAGE 4: DEVELOPING THE DRAFT

Once design has been completed, approximating drafters can move on to the composition. National styles are prevalent here, as they ensure that users are familiar with the approximating law and can implement it as easily as possible. For the purposes of approximating for accession, the style of the EU text is equally, if not more, relevant. In pre-accession negotiations time has always been a factor. And the Commission's capacity to delve into the scrutiny of each text has its boundaries. Scrutiny for accession is not as intense as scrutiny for transposition, and this is evident by the number of infringement proceedings faced by new Member States soon after accession.

Legislative expressions selected by the EU in the EU text can be copied, if they are not already used in the national legal order of the approximating jurisdiction or can be elaborated on. The latter requires the introduction of a new term that reflects the meaning of the EU one[28] but distinguishes it from the national usage of the existing term. It is worth noting here that full equivalence of a term in two legal systems is only possible when the source and target language relate to the same legal system when translating within a bi- or multi-lingual legal system, such as that of Belgium, Finland, Switzerland and, to some degree, Canada.[29] This is hardly the case between the EU and its Member States, where preserving the source term is the least desirable option.[30] Often, a bridging definition would do the trick. For example:

> In this law the term automated compilation of data has the same meaning as the term database used in Directive 96/9/EC of the European Parliament and of the Council of 11 March 1996 on the legal protection of databases, and means a collection of independent works, data or other materials arranged in a systematic or methodical way and individually accessible by electronic or other means.

The drafter can go further and clarify the difference between the new term and the existing term 'database' as used in national law, in order to settle any confusion.

Copying provisions from the EU text is by no means an anathema. But the decision to copy a provision must be justified by means of need and usefulness. If the provision serves the national regulatory message and the national legisla-

---

[28] On hybrid EU terms that derive from languages and cultures in contact see A Trosborg, 'Translating Hybrid Political Texts' in A Trosborg (ed), *Text Typology and Translation* (John Benjamins, Amsterdam/ Philadelphia, 1997), 145.

[29] See G-R de Groot, 'Translating Legal Information' in G Zaccaria (ed), *Translation in Law* (Lit Verlag, Münster-Hamburg-London, 2000) 131.

[30] See D Yankova, 'On the Concept of Term Equivalence' (2015) 1 *English Studies at NBU*, 4, 17.

tive message well, then there really is no reason to depart from it. The criterion to be used here is that of effectiveness: if the EU provision is considered effective for the approximating environment, then it can of course stay as it is. But effectiveness, rather than convenience, should be the basis of that decision.

Copying the EU text as a whole is very rarely a good option. Effectiveness is relative and the EU and approximating policy, regulatory, financial, social, and cultural environments are bound to differ. Elaborating a text on the basis of the national parameters seems the best option in most cases.

If elaboration is the way forward, the pyramid of drafting values is of guidance to approximating drafters also. Clarity, precision, and unambiguity support legislative effectiveness, which enhances regulatory efficacy.

E. STAGE 5: VERIFICATION

Internal verification of the approximating text can be undertaken within the drafting team, and with the negotiating officers of the accession country, as a means of ensuring that the level of effectiveness achieved complies with that pursued by policy. For approximation legislation verification touches upon constitutional compliance, compliance with the existing law and legal system, level of EU approximation, compliance with international obligations, implementation checks, checks as to legal form, clarity and comprehensibility and post-drafting policy checks.[31]

External verification in the form of user testing can be undertaken both as an effectiveness tool but also as a provider of empirical data on the effectiveness of the text in post-legislative scrutiny of the approximating laws by the Commission, at a pre-accession stage, and by the CJEU in future infringement proceedings.

CONCLUSIONS

Approximation with EU legislation takes place for the purposes of future accession to the EU, of compliance with bilateral or multilateral agreements with the EU, or for access to the EU market without any aspiration to further integration. Whatever the reason behind it, approximation demands the production of a legislative text that is capable of contributing to the production of the desired regulatory results overarching the EU text.

In other words, approximation does not end with the passing of a legislative text in the approximating State. This text must comply with the EU's vision for

---

[31] See OECD, *Sigma Paper – Checklist on Law Drafting and Regulatory Management in Central and Eastern Europe*, Sigma Paper No 15, 22.

Better Regulation and better legislation. Effectiveness of the approximating text as a contributor to regulatory efficacy is demanded by the national approximating drafters, irrespective of whether their national legal order shares the EU vision or not.

Understanding the concept of effectiveness and drafting an effective text is perhaps the biggest demand on approximating drafters. Perhaps the biggest challenge for them is to comprehend and share fully the concept of effectiveness by departing from the religious focus on words and expressions. Real legislative drafting in pursuit of legislative quality emphasises the first three stages of the drafting process: understanding the proposal, analysing the proposal, and designing the law.

Here innovative practices come into play: linking legislation to regulation, using legislation as a means for regulation, drafting a legislative plan as a record of the translation of regulation into legislation, viewing legislation as a means of communication of regulatory messages directly to the users of legislation, identifying the concrete user groups of the specific legislative text, and communicating the regulatory message that is relevant to each group using legislative expressions that are pitched correctly to their level of subject and legal sophistication.

Approximation is a drafting task, and, as such, is a tool for the production of regulatory results. Setting those clearly and concretely from the start focuses the drafting mind to the intricacies of the dossier. And ensuring that these results can, and later on have, been produced closes the cycle of legislation as a means for regulation. This would be successful approximation.

8. Drafting for exit from the EU

This chapter of the book examines the process of drafting for exit from the EU. Its purpose is to introduce a sound methodology for exit rather analyse what happened in practice with Brexit. Before engaging with the analysis of the drafting for that purpose it is worth noting that exit from the EU should not be viewed as a failure or an embarrassment. The EU is an organisation based on the willingness of its Member States to subscribe to its ideals, and to sacrifice part of their sovereignty in order to act collectively for the achievement of these ideals. The process is a voluntary one. If, at any point in time, a Member State ceases to desire participation to the collective actions or subscription to the EU ideals,[1] exit is a regrettable but respected decision with wider repercussions.[2] Membership to the EU is not a result of the fear of repercussions in the event of exit.[3] It is a conscious decision that can, subject to Article 50, change at any moment in time.[4]

The policy decision to exit the EU inevitably creates a rather complex task for legislative drafters both at the exiting Member State and at the EU. This chapters aims to analyse these tasks, drawing empirical examples from the only, so far incomplete, exit process. Brexit is therefore used as a case study simply because it is unique. The methodology used remains that of Thornton's five stages of legislative drafting, namely understanding, analysis, design, composition, and verification.

The process starts, as is always the case, with drafting instructions. In the case of exit from the EU drafters require instructions on the policy aim to be

---

1 This is often attributed to a legitimacy crisis often as a result of the failure of EU institutions to establish the trust of the electorate and to purposively channel debate and dissent in constructive ways: see U Steiger, 'The Heart of the Matter: Emotional Politics in the New Europe' in B Martill and U Staiger (eds), *Brexit and Beyond Rethinking the Futures of Europe* (UCL Press, London, 2018), 230, 238.

2 See M Cini and A Verdum, 'The Implications of Brexit for the Future of Europe' in Martill and Staiger, ibid., 63, 66; also see E Jones, 'Four Things We Should Learn from Brexit' (2018) *Survival* 35.

3 See K Nicolaïdis, 'Sustainable Integration in A Demoicratic Polity: A New (or not so new) Ambition for the EU after Brexit' in B Martill and U Staiger, ibid., 212.

4 For an analysis of the need for campaign deliberation arising from the Brexit campaign, see J Organ, 'Legal Regulation of Campaign Deliberation: Lessons from Brexit' (2019) *Politics and Governance* 268.

achieved. And here there are plenty of choices.[5] One option lies with a complete radical divorce from the EU, in the form of complete disengagement including trade relations. This would signify a return to a third-country status, without any special agreements. This is the WTO model.[6] A second option is departure from the EU core but maintenance of some degree of relationship, for example, for the purposes of continuing trade or the offer of services with EU partners. This would be the Swiss or Canadian model, where the relationship with the EU is based on tailor-made bilateral agreements. A third option is soft exit with participation to core EU policies as a budget contributing, non-voting, and non-EU participating country. This would be the Iceland and Norway models. Here participation in the Single Market and Schengen, for example, is wholesale and replicates the obligations of Member States. But it is a membership à la carte in that, for example, the Common Agricultural Policy and the Common Foreign Policy are outside the scope of the relationship with the EU.[7]

For the purposes of drafting and an exiting legislative policy, the precise scenario of the relationship between the EU and the exiting country is not relevant: what is important is the qualitative diversity between policies where participation remains and policies where participation ceases post-exit.

A. DRAFTING FOR EXIT AND COMPLETE DISENGAGEMENT FROM THE EU

If the intent of the government is to proceed with a complete break from any relationship with the EU, the desired regulatory effect is a complete break from the pre-exit legal regime. This is not a mandate that can be undertaken lightly. Complete disengagement and detachment is a rather radical decision that seems to clash with rationality in decision-making. For the purposes of

---

[5] For a classification and analysis of these options, see P Koutrakos, *EU International Relations Law Second Edition* (Hart, Oxford and Portland Oregon, 2015) 379 ss; also see M Maresceau, 'Bilateral Agreements Concluded by the European Community' (2004) 309 *Recueil des Cours de l'Academie de Droit International de la Haye*, 125; and S Peers, 'EC Frameworks of International Relations: Co-operation, Partnership and Association' in A Dashwood and C Hillion (eds), *The General Law of EC External Relations* (Sweet & Maxwell, London, 2000) 160.

[6] On the WTO exit option, see R Adlung, 'Brexit from a WTO/GATS Perspective: Towards an Easy Divorce?' (2018) *Journal of World Trade* 721.

[7] For an analysis of the possible Brexit models, see 'Alternatives to membership: possible models for the United Kingdom outside the European Union', HM Government, 2016, https://www.gov.uk/government/publications/alternatives-to-membership-possible-models-for-the-united-kingdom-outside-the-european-union accessed 15 December 2023.

this analysis, the regulatory and drafting task imposed by such a decision would be rather difficult to fathom, let alone complete. As EU law constitutes a supreme source of national legislation during the period of membership to the EU, a sudden complete collapse of all regulatory and legislative measures deriving from the EU would be expected to lead to circumstances assimilating a sudden change of regime. The difference here would be that such sudden and complete regime changes tend to be a result of a coup. And the 'advantage' of a coup is that its leaders will often dismantle the democratic process thus enabling them to fill in legislative gaps with emergency measures fast. In contrast, a complete detachment from the EU by a rule of law government would require a complete departure from the pre-exit legal regime and a smooth transition to a new regime basically overnight.

Difficult as it is to imagine such a complete detachment from the EU, for the purposes of a complete analysis of all possible exit scenarios, it is important to still deal with this highly hypothetical scenario.

The task of legislative drafters in such circumstances lies with ensuring that they understood the legislative proposal. To analyse its intricacies policy officers must clarify what the regulatory aim of the overarching policy strategy is. Although stopping all relationship with the EU is a concrete policy aim, perceived regulatory choices can range from removing the capacity of all national agents from all aspects of EU cooperation, including trade, services, and employment; or to maintain current cooperative relations whilst preventing new ones, at least as a transitional measure.

If the regulatory aim is to remove the capacity for all cooperation, the corresponding legislative mandate would be to server the legislative framework for such cooperation. The legislative design would involve identifying all EU derived or EU compatible laws, repeal them, and either allow a legislative gap or re-enact a legislative framework that is completely adverse to EU law and therefore cannot possibly harbour any cooperation. At the composition stage, drafting choices could be to repeal all legislation enacted between the date of accession and the date of exit, and replace what is needed with new legislation. This would seem a rather disproportionate measure with emphasis on ensuring that all possible EU-related (not just EU-derived) laws would disappear. The side-effect would be a severe and dangerous legal gap that would be expected to appear upon application of the new laws, irrespective of how meticulous the re-enacting work has been. Possible problems could arise from the break in statutory interpretation of terms and provisions used during that period time, and the still debatable application of that in the new legislation; from the mammoth task of redrafting how many years' worth of legislation; and of course, from the difficulty in attaching the new legislation to the legislative framework as it existed before accession. One would hope that even militant anti-EU decision-makers would be at least puzzled, if not derailed, by the insanity of the inevitable ineffectiveness of the legislative task.

If the regulatory aim is to maintain current cooperative relations whilst preventing new ones at least as a transitional measure, then the legislative design would be to maintain the pre-exit legal framework for existing cooperation but pull it out for any new cooperation. Drafting choices can be the introduction of an umbrella provision along these lines, by stating that EU derived legislation continues to apply to existing trade, services, and employment contracts until expressly repealed. Such a generic provision could cover all possible measures (implemented by national legislation or not) and all existing cooperation, but would exempt new cooperation from its field of application. It would be inevitably vague but it would buy the drafters and legislators the luxury of time to address each piece of legislation separately. And it would avoid legislative gaps. From the point of view of composition, the provision could be drafted as a transitional, as a saving, or as an application provision, with a corresponding heading and of course legislative expression. A transitional umbrella provision could state that 'For a period of five years starting from the start date of this Law, EU derived legislation continues to apply exclusively to existing trade, services, and employment cooperations with EU persons.' A saving umbrella provision could state that 'EU derived legislation applies to trade, services, and employment cooperations with EU persons, save for new cooperations.' And an application provision in the relevant law could state that 'This Law does not apply to cooperations with EU persons formed after its coming to effect.' The choice will depend on the prioritisation of the main regulatory message. If that is the brevity of the period of time within which such arrangements will apply, a transition provision would express it best. If priority is to exclude new cooperation, then a saving provision would be clearer. And if the priority is to delimit the field of application of the new law, then an application provision would be more appropriate. Needless to say that in the process of drafting any one of the three provisions identified here the terms 'EU derived legislation' and 'cooperations', used here generically, would have to be specified depending on the specific areas of cooperation envisaged, and the national terminology for that purpose.

In any case, verification of the provision within and outside the drafting team would direct drafters to the choice of the most appropriate terms within the national context.

B. DRAFTING FOR EXIT AND THE MAINTENANCE OF SOME DEGREE OF RELATIONSHIP WITH THE EU

The second, and more credible scenario, invites drafting for exit and the maintenance of some degree of relationship with the EU. The former Member State departs from the Union but intends to continue to trade or cooperate with the EU or its Member States in the foreseeable future. So, the desired regulatory result is the continuation of adherence with those aspects of the *acquis* that are required for the maintenance of opportunities for cooperation.

In understanding the proposal, policy officers need to specify the extent and breadth of cooperation envisaged with the EU. Although theoretically possible, the scenario where a former Member State continues to apply all of the *acquis* is rather unrealistic. If that remains the case, one would wonder what would be the purpose, scope, and object of exit. A more probable scenario is one where the former Member State departs from part of the whole of the core of the *acquis* (the four freedoms) but continues to pursue cooperation in aspects of the EU, for example under certain instruments or in certain policies. In designing the legislative strategy for exit, drafters must provide a clear legislative statement detailing these arrangements. From a design perspective, this objective could be served either by a positive or by a negative provision. And the provision could be a generic one, what is known as an umbrella provision, or a compilation of concrete provisions addressing each and every one of the pre-exit laws separately.

In the composition of the law, drafters could provide that EU law instruments and their national implementing measures continue to apply after exit, unless expressly repealed. Drafters here can also offer an alternative legal basis for EU law instruments, since the Accession Act would presumably be repealed, although the provision above could be adequate for that purpose. This affirmative umbrella provision ensures that there is a smooth transition from the pre- to post-exit regimes, and averts legal gaps in the transitional and immediate post-exit period. It also offers drafters the luxury of time to assess the application of the affirmative umbrella provision in each specific case, and address each mischief with empirical evidence of application in practice. The alternative option to an affirmative umbrella provision is a negative umbrella provision, where drafters provide that after exit EU law instruments and their national implementing measures are repealed, unless expressly saved. It is also possible, but not advisable, to use an implied repeal, and provide simply that the EU Accession Act is repealed after the exit date. Since the Accession Act constitutes the basis for implementing delegated legislation, at least all the delegated instruments implementing EU law would lose their enabling clause and would consequently expire. Technically, the latter option would cover most of the national implementing legislation, as it is mainly delegated acts that implement EU law. However, it would not cover primary legislation, and it would require a rather hefty drafting undertaking to replace the massive body of repealed enactments with new ones. From a drafting perspective, the only advantage of a negative umbrella provision therefore is the loud and clear conveyance of the regulatory message that exit is done.

The advantages of umbrella provisions are evident to see: no risk of legislative gaps, no hectic rush in covering each and every one of the thousands of primary and delegated acts that derive from EU law, no violent break in the legal framework for cooperation with the EU, and no radical change in the actual cooperation mechanisms in everyday practice. But umbrella provisions like the above present equally pronounced disadvantages. An umbrella provision is by definition vague. By stating that all EU law and implementing measures continue to be in effect or are repealed after exit day, drafters send users on a wild goose chase for the purposes of identifying exactly which acts fall within the scope of application of the provision. In a complex labyrinth of intertwining legislative texts as that of EU membership, it is often difficult to assess which is the source of the provision, especially in jurisdictions where reference of the corresponding EU legislative text is not present. Moreover, the term 'EU law' covers not only the EU legislative texts that have been transposed in the national legal order but also these that have not yet formed part of national law due to the principle of direct applicability. Finally, the provision is vague with reference to EU legislative acts that were issued after the former Member State's decision to exit or national implementing measures that have been drafted and passed but perhaps with a post-dated entry into force that now falls after exit.

These rather intricate issues can be dealt with adequately if the drafting technique used is not an umbrella provision but a compilation of concrete repeal or saving provisions applied to each and every one of the EU legislative instruments and national implementing measures. Here there is no vagueness at all, and thus certainty in the law and the rule of law are served adequately. The downside is that this task is mammoth and entails a real risk of legislative gaps or errors. Moreover, since the process takes place before exit, any provisions replacing the pre-exit ones are drafted without the benefit of empirical data on the mischiefs arising from the repeal of the previous regime and on the new needs of the legislative users.

The most appropriate way forward seems to be a combination of the two techniques, namely a compilation of concrete provisions dealing with each previous enactment separately along with the safety net of a positive umbrella provision. This allows a balance between the clarity of the exit message with the surgical intervention into every aspect of exit. This is the route promoted in the UK's government preparations for Brexit, which constitutes the sole, and therefore representative, case study of a legislative strategy for exit from the EU.

Leaving the politics aside,[8] Brexit, from a legislative drafting perspective, constitutes a model approach for a sudden divorce from a body of supranational legislation that overarches the national legal system as a whole. The UK Office of Parliamentary Counsel disengaged themselves from judgements on the wisdom of political decisions and applied to the letter the methodology proposed in Chapter 2 of this book.

In Thornton's Stage 1 they received instructions on drafting first for the intent to exit the EU, and then for exit. Perhaps not unusually in the drafting world, but still in a rather pronounced manner here, their drafting instructions were de facto so vague that it seemed impossible to put forward a single drafting approach.

In Stage 2 (analysing the proposal), UK drafters came to realise that they were called upon to disengage the UK legal system from EU legislation without, however, knowing what the concrete scope of the exercise would be. In the absence of a final and detailed agreement, or even a sketchy one, drafters only knew that only the first scenario of this chapter could be excluded, namely a complete and absolute disengagement from the EU. In other words, they were instructed clearly that the UK government intended to continue trading with the EU, and therefore intended to maintain a degree of cooperation with the EU even post-Brexit. This exclusion left UK drafters with two possible scenarios, namely a continuing collaboration of some description after Brexit or even continued participation of the UK in specific policies at a financial cost and without decision-making powers.

In Stage 3 (designing the law), to provide for these unusually vague, ever-changing, and unremittingly provisional (subject to agreement from the EU) instructions, UK drafters designed the UK's legislative strategy with great flexibility and technical ingenuity. The design involved three steps: first, start the Brexit process by declaring the UK's intention to withdraw from the EU; second, introduce the main principles and framework for Brexit by means of an umbrella text; and third, deal with the concrete pre-Brexit legislative texts that need to be repealed or amended per field of substantive law.

In Stage 4 (composing the law), the three design steps were expressed in legislative instruments. The UK's intention to exit the EU was provided in the European Union (Notification of Withdrawal) Act 2017. The Act is a hymn

---

[8] For a measured analysis of the political side of Brexit, see H Clarke, M Goodwin and P Whiteley, *Brexit: Why Britain Decided to Leave the EU* (Cambridge University Press, Cambridge, 2017).

to effectiveness, clarity and easified language. In fact, the Act showcases like no other the level of legislative quality that can be achieved when the desired regulatory result is clear, and the legislative effort is focused on the unhindered delivery of the main regulatory message. In a succinct and clear introductory text the Act states that it confers 'power on the Prime Minister to notify, under Article 50(2) of the Treaty on European Union, the United Kingdom's intention to withdraw from the EU'. And in an equally technically perfect single section, headed 'Power to notify withdrawal from the EU', the section repeats the main regulatory message '(1) The Prime Minister may notify, under Article 50(2) of the Treaty on European Union, the United Kingdom's intention to withdraw from the EU.' For all users, even the lay users of group1, there is no doubt as to what the government is legislating for. And the main regulatory message is conferred in a most effective manner, using its placement in the first section of the Act, its repetition for depth of impression, its unequivocally staccato tone and easified legislative expression. The group 3 learned users are also informed by means of subsection 2 that '(2) This section has effect despite any provision made by or under the European Communities Act 1972 or any other enactment', thus averting the possible implied repeal of subsection 2 by the older yet specific European Communities Act 1972. In the Explanatory Notes of the Act, the drafters refer to the Supreme Court judgement on *R (on the application of Miller and Dos Santos) v Secretary of State for Exiting the European Union* [2017] UKSC 5, where the Supreme Court held that, in view of the European Communities Act 1972, the Prime Minister could only give notice of withdrawal to the European Union after an Act of Parliament.[9] This justifies both the necessity of the Act itself, and the cautious reference to the European Communities Act 1972 in subsection 2. The European Union (Notification of Withdrawal Act) 2017 came into force following Royal Assent on 16 March 2017, and completed the first legislative step towards Brexit by placing the UK in an exit route.

The next design step was the introduction of an umbrella Act to introduce the main principles of the legal framework after the date of accession.[10] This was composed as The European Union (Withdrawal) Act 2018, known as the Withdrawal Act, supplemented by The European Union (Withdrawal) Act 2018 (Consequential Amendments) Regulations 2018 and The European

---

[9] For an analysis of the case and the constitutional issues that it showcases, see P Eeckhout, 'The Emperor has No Clothes: Brexit and the UK Constitution' in B Martill and U Staiger, above n 1, 165; also see T Poole, 'Devotion to Legalism: On the Brexit Case' (2017) *Modern Law Review* 696.

[10] On the constitutional effects of Brexit, see A Young, 'The Constitutional Implications of Brexit' (2017) *European Public Law* 757; also see G Anthony, 'Brexit and the Common Law Constitution' (2018) *European Public Law* 673.

Union (Withdrawal) Act 2018 (Commencement and Transitional Provisions) Regulations 2018. The Withdrawal Act attempts to reduce the change in the UK statute book as a result of exit to the absolutely necessary.[11] The Withdrawal Act has a dual task, as expressly stated in its introductory text. One, to repeal the European Communities Act 1972 (the ECA 1972). The repeal of the accession Act renders EU law irrelevant in the UK after exit. The principles of supremacy, of direct applicability, and of direct effect no longer apply to the UK. This ends the legal value of EU law in the UK after exit and is expressly confirmed in section 5 of the Withdrawal Act that kills the principle of supremacy and the Charter of Fundamental Rights upon exit from the EU.[12] Moreover, the repeal could impliedly repeal the bulk of transposition instruments. As the UK normally transposes by means of delegated legislation enabled by the ECA Act 192, the repeal of the Act could (unless otherwise specified in the Act) also repeal, albeit impliedly, all the transposition instruments that derived from the Act. Furthermore, the repeal pulls the rug from under any invocation of EU law in the UK courts, as the principle of direct effect no longer applies in the UK. This is a most radical and extensive repeal ever experienced in UK law. The effect of this radical shake up of the statute book could have been catastrophic both from the point of view of predictability of the law and from the point of view of legal certainty. Thankfully, the repeal is counterbalanced by the second task of the Withdrawal Act, which is to replace what is repealed at the same moment that the repeal kicks in. Thus, in an equally radical and extensive savings provision, section 2 of the Withdrawal Act saves from repeal all EU-derived domestic legislation.[13] So, despite the repeal of the ECA Act

---

[11] For an analysis of the Withdrawal Act, see M Elliott and S Tierney, 'Political Pragmatism and Constitutional Principle: The European Union (Withdrawal) Act 2018' (2019) *Public Law* 37; also see P Craig, 'The European Union (Withdrawal) Act 2018' (2019) 82 *Modern Law Review* 319.

[12] See C Barnard, 'So Long, Farewell, Auf Wiedersehen, Adieu: Brexit and the Charter of Fundamental Rights' (2019) *The Modern Law Review*, 350; also see N Bamforth, M Campbell, P Craig, S Fredman and A Young, 'The EU Charter after Brexit', https://mail.brexitlawni.org/library/resources/eu-charter-brexit/ accessed 15 December 2023; also see A Lang, V Miller and J Simson Caird, 'EU (Withdrawal) Bill: The Charter, general principles of EU law, and 'Francovich' damages', House of Commons Briefing Paper, Number 8140, 17 November 2017; Joint Committee on Human Rights, 'Legislative Scrutiny: The EU (Withdrawal) Bill: A Right by Right Analysis' HL 70, HC 774 (26 January 2018); and C Mccorkindale, 'Brexit and Human Rights' (2018) *Edinburgh Law Review* 126.

[13] The devolution provisions of the Withdrawal Act are outside the scope of this analysis but see R Rawlings, 'Brexit and the Territorial Constitution: Devolution, Reregulation and Inter-governmental Relations' (Constitution Society, 2017); also see P Bowers, 'The European Union (Withdrawal) Bill: Devolution', House of Commons Briefing Paper 8154, 24 November 2017.

1972 and the severing of any effect of EU law on the UK statute book directly, the legislation produced in the UK on the basis of the ECA Act 1972 does continue to have effect as before. This includes both primary and delegated legislation that can be considered to be deriving from EU law. Thus, it would be fair to state that the generic approach of UK drafters is to erase EU law from the statute book, and copy and paste it as domestic law into the same statute book. Their default position is that EU law is repealed and transformed into domestic law, unless expressly repealed. Their task to minimise any disruption in the law post accession[14] is clearly achieved.

To succeed with this task, UK drafters defined the new term of EU-derived domestic law rather broadly. Section 2 of the Withdrawal Act defines as EU-derived domestic law any enactment passed (via primary legislation) or made under (delegated legislation) or even simply operating under section 2(2)(a) and (b) of the ECA Act 1972. The breadth of the definition can be fully appreciated in combination with the equally broad section to which it refers. Section 2(2)(a) and (b) of the ECA Act 1972 is the all-encompassing enabling clause empowering Ministers to make delegated legislation for the purposes of implementing EU legislation and of providing for any issues arising from EU law. As a result of this widely drafted umbrella provision, the Withdrawal Act introduces the default position after exit: EU law ceases to have effect in the UK at the moment after exit, and at exactly the same moment in time it is transformed to UK law. The provisions remain the same (unless expressly provided otherwise). It is simply the legitimacy source that is moved from EU supremacy to UK sovereignty.

The transformation of EU law into UK law is undertaken by means of a number of provisions in the Withdrawal Act. Section 3 incorporates direct EU legislation operative immediately before exit day into UK law. It is worth noting that direct EU legislation includes 'any EU regulation, EU decision or EU tertiary legislation', thus allowing the possibility of including CJEU judgements in its scope of application. This is further confirmed by paragraph 24 of the Explanatory Notes of the Withdrawal Act. However, interestingly, section 6(4) clarifies that the Supreme Court is not bound by the case law of the CJEU, not even case law that is retained. This seems to indicate that lower court judging in the first instance are bound by the case law of the CJEU as it stood before exit, but courts judging in the second or last instance are not.[15] The application of this oxymoron in practice seems rather difficult to envisage,

---

[14] See Legislating for the United Kingdom's Withdrawal from the European Union, Cm 9446 (2017) at [1.13].

[15] For a thorough analysis of this point, and the interesting proposal for a special international court dealing with disputes arising from Brexit, see J Odermatt, 'How to Resolve Disputes Arising from Brexit' (2018) *International Organizations Law Review*

although the minimal resort of UK litigants to the Supreme Court, compared to continental cassation courts, may reflect the intent to allow the CJEU to continue to exercise influence in most cases before the UK courts post-exit, apart from selected cases of wide public interest that may end up before the Supreme Court.

Section 4 of the Withdrawal Act extends the life of rights deriving from the Treaties or international agreements in a clear, precise and unconditional manner without relevant express provisions. These rights continue to apply after exit, unless they are subsequently repealed or amended. Repeal or amendment is possible by means of delegated legislation that can easily respond to the details of any final agreement between the EU and the UK on exit. The Explanatory Notes of the Withdrawal Act provide this indicative and non-exclusive table of rights along with the TFEU articles that constitutes their legal source (Table 8.1).

The replacement of EU law with, by and large, the same UK enactments creates a new body of law in the UK, termed as 'retained EU law'. Most of EU-derived law constitutes retained EU law, unless expressly provided otherwise.[16] Retained EU law encompasses some domestic primary but mostly secondary UK legislation enacted to implement EU obligations; and most of the directly applicable and therefore not expressly transposed EU Regulations, EU tertiary legislation and decisions.

The third design step, after the start of the exit process and the introduction of the main framework of the statute book after exit, is to concretise the generic provisions by painstakingly combing the statute book as applied in practice, and identifying the specific enactments that must be expressly transferred into UK legislative instruments. The estimated number of EU instruments that must be catalogued and drafted into the UK statute book is impossible to count but there are reports that there are 12,000 EU Regulations alone,[17] and 19,000

295; also see N Fennelly, 'Brexit: Legal Consequences for the EU' (2018) *ERA Forum* 493.

16 See P Craig, 'European Union (Withdrawal) Bill: Legal Status of EU Retained Law', 26 February 2018, *UK Constitutional Law Blog*, https:// ukconstitutionallaw.org accessed 15 December 2023; also see Sir S Laws, 'Giving 'Deemed' Domestic Law Status to Retained EU Law', 28 February 2018, *UK Constitutional Law Blog*, https://ukconstitutionallaw.org accessed 15 December 2023; and P Craig, 'European Union (Withdrawal) Bill: Legal Status and Effect of Retained Law', 8 March 2018, *UK Constitutional Law Blog*, https://ukconstitutionallaw.org accessed 15 December 2023.

17 See I Morgan and R Spitz, 'Brexit: A Catalyst for Change in Legislative Drafting' (2019) *The Loophole*, https://www.calc.ngo/sites/default/files/loophole/Loophole%20-%202019-03%20%282019-10-07%29-1.pdf, 93, 96.

Table 8.1 *Table of rights*

Article 18	Non-discrimination on ground of nationality
Article 20 (except Article 20(2)(c))	Citizenship rights
Article 21(1)	Rights of movement and residence deriving from EU citizenship
Article 28	Establishes customs union, prohibition of customs duties, common external tariff
Article 30	Prohibition on customs duties
Article 34	Prohibition on quantitative restrictions on imports
Article 35	Prohibition on quantitative restrictions on exports
Article 36	Exception to quantitative restrictions
Article 37(1) and (2)	Prohibition on discrimination regarding the conditions under which goods are procured
Article 45(1), (2) and (3)	Free movement of workers
Article 49	Freedom of establishment
Article 56	Freedom to provide services
Article 57	Services
Article 63	Free movement of capital
Article 101(1)	Competition
Article 102	Abuse of a dominant position
Article 106(1) and (2)	Public undertakings
Article 107(1)	State aid
Article 108(3)	Commission consideration of plans regarding state aid
Article 110	Internal taxation
Article 112	Non-discrimination in indirect taxes
Article 157	Equal pay
Protocol 5 – Articles 13, 20(2), 23(1) and (4), 26, 27 (second and third sub-paragraphs), 28(4)	EIB
Protocol 7 – Article 21	Privileges and immunities of the EIB

Source: The author.

EU instruments in total.[18] Apart from this task, any amendments to retained direct EU legislation must also be concretised and expressly provided. Around 500 'Exit Statutory Instruments' are ready to come to effect on exit day and

[18] See D Jason, 'British Bill Sets Up More Brexit Strife; Government publishes draft legislation that would allow Parliament to keep, change or drop', 13 July 2017, *Wall Street Journal*, New York.

they are reported to make in the region of 100,000 amendments to both the home-grown retained EU law and the domesticated EU instruments.[19]

The second policy option for exit to the EU seems to be geometrically disproportionate to the drafting exercise that it requires. Exit from the EU with the parallel maintenance of close cooperation with the organisation seems to be a rational and pragmatic policy decision for exit. But in order to put it in effect, what is really required is a drafting folly. The design offered by UK drafters seems to be equally measured as the policy decision that informs it. Whether this will work in practice remains to be seen. What does not require a crystal ball, however, is the conviction that drafting for exit does not stop on exit day. Prepared as the Office may be, the true verification of this drafting process lies in its application in practice. This is where any gaps or clashes will crop up, and it is at this point that prompt corrective drafting is required. Section 8 of the Withdrawal Act already foresees the need for drafting interventions for provisions that have no practical application after the UK has left the EU; provisions on functions that are currently being carried out in the EU on the UK's behalf, for example by an EU agency; provisions on reciprocal arrangements or rights between the UK and other EU Member States that are no longer in place or are no longer appropriate; any other arrangements or rights, including through EU treaties, that are no longer in place or no longer appropriate; and EU references that are no longer appropriate. The probability of the need for corrective drafting is enhanced by the great diversity between the drafting styles of the EU and the UK: conceptualisation, structure, language, and interpretation are so different that transplanting EU legislative instruments in the UK statute book as they stand is really looking for trouble. But the extreme time pressures of Brexit and the eternal misleading effect of ready drafts, here E instruments, that steer the drafter into editing the text rather than re-conceptualising it are sirens that can mesmerise drafters whose task is to domesticate EU instruments within the shortest of times. But, in a way, this is exactly what the dual strategy of an umbrella provision supplemented by concrete specific ones can address: there is always a fall-back position. And, although legislation by implication is a rather unsatisfactory and risky business, it is the best that can be offered in cases of legal earthquakes such as exit from the EU.

19 See I Morgan and R Spitz, above n 17, 93, 96.

C. DRAFTING FOR EXIT AND CONTINUING PARTICIPATION TO POLICIES AS A THIRD COUNTRY

The third policy scenario selects membership à la carte. Although the term is not a prevalent one, but it is used here to reflect the duality of the relationship with the EU: in some policies full participation with complete transposition and budgetary contribution, albeit without participation in decision-making, and in other policies no participation whatsoever. There is little doubt that the policy decision to go down that route is one of compromise and of mutual interest between the EU and the country in question.

Before proceeding with the analysis of the drafting task involved in this option, it is necessary to draw the difference between this and the previous option, namely exit with the maintenance of a degree of cooperation. Both options aim to achieve close cooperation with the EU without the bindingness of membership. Both options require a bilateral agreement to set out the full eccentricities of this special relationship. The difference between the two lies in the breadth of that relationship. In the previous option, the third country does not accept the full range of Single Market and Customs Union policies, and chooses to focus on specific aspects of the core of EU policies by means of bespoke bilateral free trade and customs agreements. Examples include the Swiss tariff-free trade, and access to services, but not to the free movement of people; or the Ukrainian access to goods and services, but not to the free movement of people; or the Canadian tariff-free trade for industrial goods and some agricultural produce, but not for services. In this option, which forges the closest relationship with the EU outside membership,[20] the third country accepts the core of the Single Market, thus participating in the whole of the main policies of the EU. For example, the Norway model involves participation in the EU Single Market, albeit not the Customs Union, thus offering full access to the Single Market for goods and services and continued abidance by the EU's four freedoms. Moreover, the influence of the CJEU continues,

---

[20] For an analysis of the closeness offered by the EEA agreement, see T Blanchet, R Piipponen and M Westman-Clement, *The Agreement on the European Economic Area* (Oxford University Press, Oxford, 1994); T Blanchet, R Piipponen and J Delors, *The Agreement on the European Economic Area (EEA): A Guide to the Free Movement of Goods and Competition Rules* (Clarendon Press, London, 1994); C Baudenbacher, *The Fundamental Principles of EEA Law: EEA* (Springer, the Hague, 2017); P-C Müller-Graff and E Selvig, *EEA–EU Relations* (Spitz Verlag, Berlin, 1999); S Norberg, *EEA Law – A Commentary on the EEA Agreement* (Springer, Berlin, 1994).

albeit indirectly, via the acceptance of the competence of the EFTA court that respects the case law of the CJEU.[21]

This creates a rather schizophrenic drafting task. The drafting instructions here are to replicate drafting for membership in the core EU policies, and drafting in detachment from EU law in some other policies. The question here is, how can a drafter draw the line between the two sets of EU provisions, especially in view of the fact that the core policies introduce overarching principles that apply and extend beyond the artificial barriers of the core policies. For example, it is difficult to decide whether the EU measures on biodiversity and nature protection are purely environmental measures that could be ignored by the third country or whether they are relevant to what can be traded within the EU, thus constituting measures for implementation by countries adopting the Swiss, Ukrainian, and Canadian models. And so one of the main challenges for national drafters in this option is to clearly understand which aspects of EU law affect the areas replicating EU membership, and which are outside the parameters of cooperation with the EU. The Annex to the EEA Agreement is of some help but a degree of discretion is inevitable.[22] Another aspect requiring clarification for national drafters is the legal effect of incomplete or incorrect implementation of relevant EU instruments. Questions arising here relate to the jurisdiction of the CJEU, and especially the possible effects of an EFTA judgement against the State. This needs to be balanced in combination with any punitive clauses in the cooperation agreement, as a means of gauging the proportionality of the risk of non-implementation when the interests of the State so require.

Once the classification of the EU instrument has been made as relevant to the third country or not in Stage 1 and 2 of the national drafting process (understanding the proposal and analysing the proposal), national drafters proceed with Stage 2. Let us take the drafting process forward, focusing on relevant EU instruments that require full implementation and non-relevant EU instruments where implementation is not necessary by the terms of the bilateral agreement between the country in question and the EU.

In cases where the EU instrument falls within the scope of the cooperation agreement, national drafters focus on the task of complete and timely implementation. The drafting process and techniques applicable in this case are not dissimilar to those used in the case of transposition during membership. Faithful, complete, and timely transposition is the aim, and effectiveness of

---

[21] For an analysis of a possibility of preliminary ruling in international agreements, see P Koutrakos, 'The Interpretation of Mixed Agreements under the Preliminary Reference Procedure' (2002) 7 *European Foreign Affairs Review* 25.

[22] See EEA Agreement [1994] OJ L1/3.

national legislation is the measure of success. But of course here the possible effects matter more. In the case of membership, the worst case scenario lies with infringement proceedings before the CJEU and perhaps a fine. But the process is so lengthy that Member State have plenty of opportunity to act before any negative effects. Moreover, membership is a protective shield against effects on trade. In contrast to the membership scenario, in the case of a third country, there is a lot at stake, and in fact it can be immediate. Lack of application of EU standards can lead to an immediate stall in trade. And there is no safety net to cushion, mitigate, or avert these effects. The task of national drafters is not just pressing, as proven immediately above, but also rather complex. As EU law in not a generic source of national law, the national implementing measures cannot just copy the EU text. Drafters are required to undertake creative elaboration that results in a national legislative instrument that can fill in the gaps of general principles or other EU legislative texts not falling within the scope of the agreed fields of cooperation. Moreover, as fragmented implementation of EU law deprives the national legal system from indirect harmonisation of drafting styles and terminology, national implementing measures must also address these diversities with ad hoc techniques. Examples include the treatment of recitals in EU instruments, or of definitions deriving from EU legislative texts outside the scope of the agreement between the EU and the third country, or even of interpretation, not least by the CJEU, to relevant provisions of EU instruments both within and outside the scope of the agreement. Finally, and perhaps more importantly, the effectiveness of the national implanting text does not coincide with that of the EU text. It is not even necessary that the one feeds into the other. The effectiveness of the national text is the unhindered cooperation with the EU. It is therefore imperative that compliance with standards is not just full but also obvious enough not to raise doubts and debates.

In the case of non-relevant EU instruments, where implementation is not necessary by the terms of the bilateral agreement between the country in question and the EU, the task is equally eccentric and complex. Although there is no direct express obligation for the third country to implement the EU instrument, its provisions may enhance, supplement, or even impliedly repeal instruments that do fall within the scope of the agreement. Legal debates on the legal basis of the EU instrument and its role in the theoretical application to the third country's law may go a long way in an academic discussion. But in practice even a brief moment of hesitation to trade or to the provision of services can easily amount to millions. Pragmatism, based on the proportionality of risk against possible hefty damages, requires careful monitoring of the whole of EU legislation, and its critical examination for the identification of its possible effect on the policy that the third country does observe. Of course, in this set of circumstances decisions tend to be more policy than drafting related. But drafters continue to carry the task of reminding policy-makers that the law is not neatly classified as relevant or irrelevant, and that the ultimate criterion for its classification as one or the other lies with the selection of the most appropriate decision for the achievement of the desired regulatory results. Once the strategy is designed, drafters can proceed with the composition of the national implementing legislation. Here, they will need to assess what part of the EU instrument needs to be implemented, what form the implementing measure can take, and whether the end result can be achieved by means of an amending national law or a new enactment.

Once again, user testing can assist drafters to verify or falsify their assumptions, by testing whether the national and EU stakeholders receive the regulatory message as intended. User testing results can inform drafters in the pre-legislative scrutiny of the national implementing text. The final external verification is undertaken by Parliament, where debate on the proposed legislative text is undertaken without the delimitations of EU membership that are currently expressed in the parliamentary practices of most Member States as a choice of mostly delegated implementing measures that do not merit parliamentary debate.

CONCLUSIONS

This chapter examined the intricacies of drafting for exit from the EU. In Stage 1 of the drafting process, drafters receive their instructions. In the case of exit from the EU, there are three possible scenarios, namely complete divorce from the EU, departure from the EU core but maintenance of some degree of relationship, or departure combined with participation to core EU policies.

Drafting for exit and complete disengagement from the EU signifies a return to the club of third countries and WTO standards. The drafting task imposed by this rather radical policy option is mammoth. It amounts to the identification of all EU derived or EU compatible laws, their repeal, and their replacement with new enactments where appropriate. This could be drafted via an umbrella provision repealing EU derived law combined with transitional provisions until new enactments are passed.

Departure from the EU core but maintenance of some degree of relationship could be designed and composed in three steps. One, legislate for withdrawal from the EU by empowering the government to express intent to invoke Article 50. Two, introduce a negative umbrella provision killing off EU derived law after exit or a positive umbrella provision extending the life of EU derived law after exit. And three, introduce detailed lists of pre-exit enactments that fall within the scope of the umbrella provision. The case study of Brexit showcases the techniques required here. First, start the Brexit process by declaring the UK's intention to withdraw from the EU. Second, introduce the main principles and framework for Brexit by means of a positive umbrella enactment. And third, deal with the concrete pre-Brexit legislative texts that need to be repealed or amended per field of substantive law.

Drafting for exit and continuing participation to policies as a third country signifies membership à la carte. This classifies EU law into two categories, namely the part that must be implemented faithfully and the part that can be ignored. In the case of EU law that falls within the scope of application of the agreement, the exiting country can replicate its former transposition techniques, with the noted disadvantages of non-participation in the decision-making process, not opportunity for reservation, and no transposition assistance. In the case of EU that falls outside the scope of the cooperation agreement, national drafters have no legal obligation to implement. But they must be alert to identify EU instruments whose provisions enhance, supplement, or even impliedly repeal instruments that do fall within the scope of the agreement. In which case, they must draft accordingly.

9. A transposition-led drafting style for Regulations

The analysis of transposition as a drafting task, its five stages, the scope of each stage and its requirements brought to light a surprisingly long set of calls for the reform of the drafting style of EU Acts. These are detailed in the end of each of the relevant chapters.

The question remains how these recommendations for a new transposition-led drafting style for EU Acts can be applied in practice. For that purpose, the next two chapters will use two EU Acts as representative samples for recent EU Regulations and EU Directives. They are Regulation (EU) 2021/953 on a framework for the issuance, verification and acceptance of interoperable COVID-19 vaccination, test and recovery certificates (EU Digital COVID Certificate) to facilitate free movement during the COVID-19 pandemic;[1] and Directive (EU) 2023/970 of the European Parliament and of the Council of 10 May 2023 to strengthen the application of the principle of equal pay for equal work or work of equal value between men and women through pay transparency and enforcement mechanisms.[2]

The criteria for their selection are as follows. One, they are recent (2021 and 2023 respectively): this ensures currency of observations on bad practices and consequent currency of subsequent recommendations for changes to the drafting style. Two, they are samples of the two main types of EU Acts: Regulations and Directives carry different transposition requirements, and recommendations apply to each of them separately. Three, they are EU Acts with an obvious social element: they are not purely technical and this facilitates both their treatment from a content-naïve drafting expert but also, and of course most importantly, they do carry a message directly relevant to EU citizens. They are therefore fertile for the application of a citizen-centred drafting style such as the one proposed here.

---

1 See https://eur-lex.europa.eu/legal-content/EN/TXT/PDF/?uri=OJ:L:2021:211:FULL accessed 15 December 2023.

2 See https://eur-lex.europa.eu/legal-content/EN/TXT/?toc=OJ%3AL%3A2023%3A132%3ATOC&uri=uriserv%3AOJ.L_.2023.132.01.0021.01.ENG accessed 15 December 2023.

The disadvantage of the selection of very recent EU Acts lies with the unpredictability of their efficacy. Having had no time for implementation, there is no data on the achievement of their desired regulatory results as yet.

REGULATION (EU) 2021/953 ON A FRAMEWORK FOR THE ISSUANCE, VERIFICATION AND ACCEPTANCE OF INTEROPERABLE COVID-19 VACCINATION, TEST AND RECOVERY CERTIFICATES (EU DIGITAL COVID CERTIFICATE) TO FACILITATE FREE MOVEMENT DURING THE COVID-19 PANDEMIC

Before proceeding with the analysis of the quality of each type of drafting provision within this Act, it is important to note that the scope of this analysis is not to assess whether the current drafting rules for EU Acts have been followed. Instead, the scope of this analysis is to dissect this representative sample of EU Regulations, identify their strengths and weaknesses, and repurpose them as a means of rendering them user-centred and therefore fertile for the communication of their regulatory message.

In order to facilitate the reader to apply each textual comment to the text of the Regulation, comments are made on the side of the relevant text. A text applying the recommendations, without amending the legislative expression in general, will follow in order to allow the read to compare the current version of the Regulation with the treated one.

Table 9.1 Comments to the Regulation

The Text of the Regulation	Comments
REGULATION (EU) 2021/953 OF THE EUROPEAN PARLIAMENT AND OF THE COUNCIL of 14 June 2021 on a framework for the issuance, verification and acceptance of interoperable COVID-19 vaccination, test and recovery certificates (EU Digital COVID Certificate) to facilitate free movement during the COVID-19 pandemic **(Text with EEA relevance)**	The title of the Regulation should serve two purposes: to identify the topic of the EU Act and to distinguish the Act from relevant Acts on the same topic. Instead, this is a convoluted, user unfriendly title, which starts with a long reference to institutional bodies, date, and includes objectives. There is no doubt that the legal/constitutional elements of the title are necessary, but one wonders whether they need to be at the very top of the text, confusing the user, or whether a citation Article could be added to the end of the Act for use of learned audiences as follows: **Title: Regulation (EU) 2021/953 on the EU Digital COVID Certificate (issuance, verification, acceptance, certificates).** **Citation Article (at the end of the Regulation): This Act is the REGULATION (EU) 2021/953 OF THE EUROPEAN PARLIAMENT AND OF THE COUNCIL of 14 June 2021 on the EU Digital COVID Certificate (issuance, verification, acceptance, certificates).** There is no table of content in the Act, as published. This deprives the user of a roadmap of provisions, which has proven welcome and helpful in most European national jurisdictions.

THE EUROPEAN PARLIAMENT AND THE COUNCIL OF THE EUROPEAN UNION,

Having regard to the Treaty on the Functioning of the European Union, and in particular Article 21(2) thereof,

Having regard to the proposal from the European Commission,

After transmission of the draft legislative act to the national parliaments,

Having regard to the opinion of the European Economic and Social Committee,

Acting in accordance with the ordinary legislative procedure,

Whereas:

In this Regulation, and this is not uncommon, there are 64 recitals. They usurp the prime time of users' attention and deprive the text of the opportunity to serve the regulatory message within the attention span of the user. Bibliography sets this at anywhere between four seconds and six minutes. Regulators have six minutes within which they have the golden opportunity to be heard by users, especially lay users. It is a real shame that all this valuable time is taken up by recitals. It would be much more sensible to reconsider the scope and utility of recitals and limit them to what is absolutely necessary in order to offer the user context and to showcase the legitimacy of the EU Act.

At the same time as weeding out generic statements of a political character, which have no place in legislation, recitals may be repurposed in an Annex to the EU Act entitled 'Notes' or could be placed within the Statement of the Commission.

(1) Every citizen of the Union has the fundamental right to move and reside freely within the territory of the Member States, subject to the limitations and conditions laid down in the Treaties and by the measures adopted to give effect to them. Directive 2004/38/EC of the European Parliament and of the Council lays down detailed rules as regards the exercise of that right.

1. This is a generic political statement that cannot be in an EU Act.

(2) On 30 January 2020, the Director-General of the World Health Organization (WHO) declared a public health emergency of international concern over the global outbreak of severe acute respiratory syndrome coronavirus 2 (SARS-CoV-2), which causes coronavirus disease 2019 (COVID-19). On 11 March 2020, the WHO made an assessment characterising COVID-19 as a pandemic.

2. This is helpful for context and can be left in the text.

(3) To limit the spread of SARS-CoV-2, the Member States have adopted some measures which have had an impact on the exercise by Union citizens of their right to move and reside freely within the territory of the Member States, such as entry restrictions or requirements for cross-border travellers to undergo quarantine or self-isolation or to be tested for SARS-CoV-2 infection.

3. This is also helpful to establish context and convey the thinking process of the regulators that can persuade users to apply the regulatory requirements.

(4) On 13 October 2020, the Council adopted Recommendation (EU) 2020/1475, which introduced a coordinated approach to the restriction of free movement in response to the COVID-19 pandemic in the following key areas: the application of common criteria and thresholds when deciding whether to introduce restrictions to free movement, a mapping of risk areas of SARS-CoV-2 transmission based on an agreed colour code and a coordinated approach to any appropriate measures which could be applied to persons travelling to or from risk areas, depending on the level of risk of SARS-CoV-2 transmission in those areas. In view of their specific situation, the Recommendation emphasises that travellers with an essential function or need, as listed in point 19 of the Recommendation, and persons living in border regions and travelling across the border on a daily or frequent basis for the purposes of work, business, education, family, medical care or caregiving, whose lives are particularly affected by such restrictions, in particular those who exercise critical functions or who are essential for critical infrastructure, should in general be exempted from travel restrictions linked to the COVID-19 pandemic.

4. This is not relevant to lay users and should be transferred to the proposed Notes Annex at the end of the Regulation.

(5) Using the criteria and thresholds established in Recommendation (EU) 2020/1475, the European Centre for Disease Prevention and Control (ECDC) has been publishing, on a weekly basis, a map of Member States, with data on the notification, testing and test positivity rates of COVID-19, broken down by region, in order to support Member States' decision-making.

5. To be moved to the Notes Annex.

(6) Member States may, in accordance with Union law, limit the fundamental right of free movement on grounds of public health. Any restrictions to the free movement of persons within the Union that are put in place to limit the spread of SARS-CoV-2 should be based on specific and limited public interest grounds, namely the safeguarding of public health as emphasised by Recommendation (EU) 2020/1475. It is necessary for such limitations to be applied in accordance with the general principles of Union law, in particular proportionality and non-discrimination. Any measures taken should therefore be strictly limited in scope and time, in line with the efforts to restore free movement within the Union, and should not extend beyond what is strictly necessary to safeguard public health. Furthermore, such measures should be consistent with measures taken by the Union to ensure the seamless free movement of goods and essential services across the internal market, including the free movement of medical supplies and medical and healthcare personnel through the 'green lane' border crossings referred to in the Commission communication of 23 March 2020 on the implementation of the Green Lanes under the Guidelines for border management measures to protect health and ensure the availability of goods and essential services.

6. To be moved to the Notes Annex or even deleted as it is evident.

(7) Persons who are vaccinated or who have had a recent negative COVID-19 test result and persons who have recovered from COVID-19 in the previous six months seem to have a reduced risk of infecting people with SARS-CoV-2, according to current and still evolving scientific evidence. The free movement of persons who, according to sound scientific evidence, do not pose a significant risk to public health, for example because they are immune to and cannot transmit SARS-CoV-2, should not be restricted, as such restrictions would not be necessary to achieve the objective of safeguarding public health. Where the epidemiological situation allows, such persons should not be subject to additional restrictions to free movement linked to the COVID-19 pandemic, such as travel-related testing for SARS-CoV-2 infection or travel-related quarantine or self-isolation, unless such additional restrictions are, based on the latest available scientific evidence and in line with the precautionary principle, necessary and proportionate for the purpose of safeguarding public health, and non-discriminatory.

7. To remain as relevant to the decision made by the regulators.

(8) Many Member States have launched or plan to launch initiatives to issue COVID-19 vaccination certificates. However, for such vaccination certificates to be used effectively in a cross-border context when Union citizens exercise their right to free movement, they need to be fully interoperable, compatible, secure and verifiable. A common approach is required among Member States on the content, format, principles, technical standards and the level of security of such vaccination certificates.

8. To be deleted as superfluous.

(9) Unilateral measures to limit the spread of SARS-CoV-2 have the potential to cause significant disruption to the exercise of the right to free movement and to hinder the proper functioning of the internal market, including the tourism sector, as national authorities and passenger transport services, such as airlines, trains, coaches and ferries, could be confronted with a wide array of diverging document formats, not only regarding certificate holders' COVID-19 vaccination, but also their test results and recovery.

9. To be deleted as superfluous (making a self-evident statement).

(10) In its resolution of 25 March 2021 on establishing an EU strategy for sustainable tourism, the European Parliament called for a harmonised approach to tourism across the Union by means of implementing common criteria for safe travel, with a Union Health Safety protocol for testing and quarantine requirements, a common vaccination certificate, once there is sufficient scientific evidence that vaccinated persons do not transmit SARS-CoV-2, and the mutual recognition of vaccination procedures.	10. Irrelevant to lay users, to be transferred to the proposed Notes Annex.
(11) In their statement of 25 March 2021, the Members of the European Council called for preparations to start on a common approach to the gradual lifting of restrictions to free movement in order to ensure that efforts are coordinated when the epidemiological situation allows for an easing of existing measures and for the work on COVID-19 interoperable and non-discriminatory digital certificates to be taken forward as a matter of urgency.	11. Irrelevant to lay users, to be transferred to the proposed Notes Annex.
(12) To facilitate the exercise of the right to move and reside freely within the territory of the Member States, a common framework for the issuance, verification and acceptance of interoperable COVID-19 vaccination, test and recovery certificates (EU Digital COVID Certificate) should be established. That common framework should be binding and directly applicable in all Member States. It should facilitate, whenever possible on the basis of scientific evidence, the gradual lifting of restrictions in a coordinated manner by Member States, taking into account the lifting of restrictions within their own territory. Regulation (EU) 2021/954 of the European Parliament and of the Council extends that common framework to third-country nationals who are legally staying or residing in the Schengen area without controls at internal borders and applies as a matter of Schengen acquis, without prejudice to the specific rules on the crossing of internal borders set out in Regulation (EU) 2016/399 of the European Parliament and of the Council Facilitating freedom of movement is one of the key preconditions for starting an economic recovery.	12. This is a description of the content of the Regulation and it should be set apart in a separate Article at the start of the Act. The last sentence here hides the objective of the Regulation, which (enriched with evidence-based, concrete regulatory goals) must be set aside in Article 1 of the Regulation, thus answering the question –Why legislate?

(13) Although this Regulation is without prejudice to Member States' competence to impose restrictions to free movement, in accordance with Union law, to limit the spread of SARS-CoV-2, it should contribute to facilitating the gradual lifting of such restrictions in a coordinated manner whenever possible, in accordance with Recommendation (EU) 2020/1475. Such restrictions could be waived in particular for vaccinated persons, in line with the precautionary principle, to the extent that scientific evidence on the effects of COVID-19 vaccination becomes increasingly available and more consistently conclusive with regard to the breaking of the transmission chain.

13. This can be deleted as it makes an obvious statement.

(14) This Regulation is intended to facilitate the application of the principles of proportionality and non-discrimination with regard to restrictions to free movement during the COVID-19 pandemic, while pursuing a high level of public health protection. It should not be understood as facilitating or encouraging the adoption of restrictions to free movement, or restrictions to other fundamental rights, in response to the COVID-19 pandemic, given their detrimental effects on Union citizens and businesses. Any verification of the certificates making up the EU Digital COVID Certificate should not lead to further restrictions to the freedom of movement within the Union or to restrictions on travel within the Schengen area. The exemptions to the restrictions of free movement in response to the COVID-19 pandemic referred to in Recommendation (EU) 2020/1475 should continue to apply and the specific situation of cross-border communities, which have been particularly affected by such restrictions, should be taken into account. At the same time, the EU Digital COVID Certificate framework is intended to ensure that interoperable certificates are also available to travellers with an essential function or need.

14. This is irrelevant to the lay user and could be placed in the Notes Annex.

(15) The introduction of a common approach for the issuance, verification and acceptance of interoperable COVID-19 certificates relies upon mutual trust. The use of counterfeit COVID-19 certificates poses a significant risk to public health. Authorities in one Member State need assurance that the information included in a certificate issued in another Member State is trustworthy, that the certificate has not been forged, that the certificate belongs to the person presenting it, and that anyone verifying the certificate has access only to the minimum amount of information necessary.

15. This is self-evident and altogether unnecessary

(16) On 1 February 2021, Europol issued an Early Warning Notification on the illicit sales of counterfeit COVID-19 test certificates indicating a negative result. Given the availability and ease of access to technological means, such as high-resolution printers and graphics editor software, fraudsters are able to produce high-quality counterfeit COVID-19 certificates. Cases of illicit sales of counterfeit COVID-19 test certificates have been reported, which involve organised forgery rings and opportunistic individuals selling counterfeit COVID-19 certificates on and offline.

16. Perhaps for the Notes Annex but it needs more empirical evidence to showcase the extent of the problem.

(17) It is important to make available sufficient resources to implement this Regulation and to prevent, detect, investigate and prosecute fraud and illicit practices regarding the issuance and use of the certificates making up the EU Digital COVID Certificate.

17. Irrelevant to the lay user. Also self-evident.

(18) To ensure the interoperability of and equal access to the certificates making up the EU Digital COVID Certificate for all Union citizens, including for vulnerable persons, such as persons with disabilities, and for persons with limited access to digital technologies, Member States should issue such certificates in a digital or paper-based format, or both. The prospective holders should be entitled to receive the certificates in the format of their choice. This would allow them to request to receive a paper copy of the certificate, or to receive it in a digital format to be stored and displayed on a mobile device, or both. The certificates should contain an interoperable, digitally readable barcode giving access only to the data relevant to the certificates. Member States should ensure the authenticity, validity and integrity of the certificates through the use of electronic seals. To ensure a high level of trust in the authenticity, validity and integrity of certificates, Member States should, where possible, prioritise the use of advanced electronic seals as defined in point (26) of Article 3 of Regulation (EU) No 910/2014 of the European Parliament and of the Council. The information on the certificate should be shown in human-readable format, printed or displayed as plain text. The layout of the certificates should be easy to understand and ensure simplicity and user-friendliness. To avoid obstacles to free movement, the certificates should be issued free of charge, and Union citizens and their family members should have a right to have certificates issued to them. To prevent abuse or fraud, it should be possible to charge appropriate fees for the issuance of a new certificate in cases of repeated loss. Member States should issue the certificates making up the EU Digital COVID Certificate automatically or upon request, ensuring that they can be obtained easily and swiftly. Member States should also provide, where needed, the necessary support to allow for equal access by all Union citizens. A separate certificate should be issued for each vaccination, test result or recovery and should not contain data from previous certificates except where otherwise provided for in this Regulation.

18. This is self-evident and therefore unnecessary. The Act itself provides so.

(19) Authentic certificates making up the EU Digital COVID Certificate should be individually identifiable by means of a unique certificate identifier, taking into account that holders might be issued more than one certificate during the COVID-19 pandemic. The unique certificate identifier is composed of an alphanumeric string and Member States should ensure that it does not contain any data linking it to other documents or identifiers, such as to passport or identity card numbers, in order to prevent directly identifying the holder. The unique certificate identifier should be used only for its intended purposes, which include requests for the issuance of a new certificate if a certificate is no longer available to the holder and the revocation of certificates. In addition, the use of a unique certificate identifier avoids the need to process other personal data that would otherwise be necessary to identify individual certificates. For medical and public health reasons and in the event of fraudulently issued or obtained certificates, Member States should be able to establish and exchange with other Member States for the purpose of this Regulation certificate revocation lists in limited cases, in particular in order to revoke certificates that have been issued erroneously, as a result of fraud or following the suspension of a COVID-19 vaccine batch found to be defective. Certificate revocation lists should not contain any personal data other than unique certificate identifiers. Holders of revoked certificates should be promptly informed about the revocation of their certificates and the reasons for the revocation.

19. This details the requirements of the Certificate and is provided in the Act. It is unnecessary here, and it carries risk of confusion as it is a paraphrasis of the text of the Act.

(20) The issuance of certificates pursuant to this Regulation should not lead to discrimination on the basis of the possession of a specific category of certificate.

20. Self-evident and unnecessary.

(21) Universal, timely and affordable access to COVID-19 vaccines and tests for SARS-CoV-2 infection, which form the basis for the issuance of the certificates making up the EU Digital COVID Certificate, is crucial in the fight against the COVID-19 pandemic and essential to restore freedom of movement within the Union. To facilitate the exercise of the right to free movement, Member States are encouraged to ensure affordable and widely available testing possibilities, taking into account that not the entire population would have had the opportunity to be vaccinated before the date of application of this Regulation.

21. This is a substantive provision, which is simply paraphrased here and should be deleted.

(22) The security, authenticity, validity and integrity of the certificates making up the EU Digital COVID Certificate and their compliance with Union data protection law are key to their acceptance in all Member States. It is therefore necessary to establish a trust framework laying out the rules on and infrastructure for the reliable and secure issuance and verification of COVID-19 certificates. The infrastructure should be developed, with a strong preference for the use of open-source technology, to function on different major operating systems, while ensuring that it is protected from cybersecurity threats. The trust framework should ensure that the verification of COVID-19 certificates can be carried out offline and without the issuer or any other third party being informed about the verification. The trust framework should be based on a public-key infrastructure with a trust chain from Member States' health authorities or other trusted authorities to the individual entities issuing the COVID-19 certificates. The trust framework should allow for the detection of fraud, in particular forgery. The eHealth Network's Outline Interoperability of Health Certificates Trust Framework of 12 March 2021 adopted pursuant to Article 14 of Directive 2011/24/EU of the European Parliament and of the Council should form the basis for the trust framework for the EU Digital COVID Certificate.

22. This is a combination of a political statement, and a substantive provision paraphrased from within the Act. It must be deleted.

(23) Pursuant to this Regulation, the certificates making up the EU Digital COVID Certificate should be issued to the persons referred to in Article 3 of Directive 2004/38/EC, namely Union citizens and their family members, irrespective of their nationality, by the Member State where the vaccination was administered or the test carried out, or where the recovered person is located. Where reference is made to issuance by Member States, this should be understood as also covering issuance by designated bodies on behalf of Member States, including when COVID-19 certificates are issued in overseas countries and territories or the Faroe Islands on behalf of a Member State. Where relevant or appropriate, the certificates should be issued to another person on behalf of the vaccinated, tested or recovered person, for example to the legal guardian on behalf of legally incapacitated persons or to parents on behalf of their children. The certificates should not be subject to legalisation or any other similar formalities.

23. This is a substantive provision that must be provided for within the Act. It is paraphrased here and must be deleted.

(24) In accordance with Recommendation (EU) 2020/1475, Member States should pay particular attention to persons living in border regions and travelling across the border on a daily or frequent basis for the purposes of work, business, education, family, medical care or caregiving.

24. This is a political statement, which carries no consequence. It must be further elaborated and provided for within the Act.

(25) It should be possible for the certificates making up the EU Digital COVID Certificate to be issued to nationals or residents of Andorra, Monaco, San Marino and the Vatican or Holy See.

25. This is a substantive provision and must be placed in the text. As it is, its bindingness is doubtful or at least debatable.

(26) Agreements on free movement of persons concluded by the Union and the Member States, of the one part, and certain third countries, of the other part, provide for the possibility to restrict free movement on grounds of public health in a non-discriminatory manner. Where such an agreement does not contain a mechanism of incorporation of Union legal acts, COVID-19 certificates issued to beneficiaries of such agreements should be accepted under the conditions laid down in this Regulation. Such acceptance should be conditional on an implementing act to be adopted by the Commission establishing that such a third country issues COVID-19 certificates in accordance with this Regulation and has provided formal assurances that it will accept COVID-19 certificates issued by the Member States.

26. This is a substantive provision adding a category of possible users of the Certificate and must be within the Act. But not here.

(27) Regulation (EU) 2021/954 applies to third-country nationals who do not fall within the scope of this Regulation and who stay or reside legally in the territory of a Member State to which that Regulation applies and who are entitled to travel to other Member States in accordance with Union law.

27. Substantive provision that must be within the body of the Act.

(28) The trust framework to be established for the purpose of this Regulation should seek to ensure consistency with global initiatives, in particular involving the WHO and the International Civil Aviation Organisation. Such consistency should include, where possible, interoperability between technological systems established at global level or by third countries with which the Union has close links and the systems established for the purpose of this Regulation to facilitate the exercise of the right to free movement within the Union, including through the participation in a public key infrastructure or the bilateral exchange of public keys. To facilitate the exercise of the right to free movement by Union citizens and their family members vaccinated or tested in third countries or in the overseas countries or territories referred to in Article 355(2) of the Treaty on the Functioning of the European Union (TFEU) and listed in Annex II thereto or the Faroe Islands, this Regulation should provide for the acceptance of COVID-19 certificates issued by third countries or by overseas countries or territories or the Faroe Islands to Union citizens and their family members where the Commission finds that those COVID-19 certificates are issued in accordance with standards that are to be considered as equivalent to those established pursuant to this Regulation.

28. This is a wish list, and therefore a political statement. It needs elaboration and expression in a substantive provision within the body of the Regulation.

(29) For the purpose of facilitating free movement, and to ensure that restrictions to free movement currently in place during the COVID-19 pandemic can be lifted in a coordinated manner based on the latest scientific evidence and guidance made available by the Health Security Committee established by Article 17 of Decision No 1082/2013/EU of the European Parliament and of the Council, ECDC and the European Medicines Agency (EMA), an interoperable vaccination certificate should be established. Such a vaccination certificate should serve to confirm that the holder has received a COVID-19 vaccine in a Member State and should contribute to the gradual lifting of restrictions to free movement. The vaccination certificate should contain only the information necessary to clearly identify the holder as well as the COVID-19 vaccine administered, the number of doses, and the date and place of vaccination. Member States should issue vaccination certificates to persons who have received COVID-19 vaccines that have been granted a marketing authorisation pursuant to Regulation (EC) No 726/2004 of the European Parliament and of the Council, those who have received COVID-19 vaccines that have been granted a marketing authorisation by the competent authority of a Member State pursuant to Directive 2001/83/EC of the European Parliament and of the Council, and those who have received COVID-19 vaccines the distribution of which has been temporarily authorised pursuant to Article 5(2) of that Directive.

29. This is repetitive.

(30) Persons who have been vaccinated before the date of application of this Regulation, including as part of a clinical trial, should also have the right to obtain a vaccination certificate in accordance with this Regulation given that the EU Digital COVID Certificate provides the mutually accepted framework to facilitate the exercise of the right to free movement. Where Union citizens or their family members are not in possession of a vaccination certificate that complies with the requirements of this Regulation, in particular because they have been vaccinated before the date of application of this Regulation, they should be given every reasonable opportunity to prove by other means that they should benefit from the waiving of relevant restrictions to free movement afforded by a Member State to holders of vaccination certificates issued pursuant to this Regulation. This should not be understood as affecting the obligation of Member States to issue vaccination certificates that comply with the requirements of this Regulation nor the right of Union citizens or their family members to receive, from Member States, such vaccination certificates. At the same time, Member States should remain free to issue proof of vaccination in other formats for other purposes, in particular for medical purposes.

30. This includes a substantive provision that should be within the body of the Regulation under persons entitled to a Certificate.

(31) Member States may also issue upon request vaccination certificates to persons who have been vaccinated in a third country and who provide all necessary information, including reliable proof to that effect. This is of particular importance to allow the persons concerned to make use of an interoperable and accepted vaccination certificate when exercising their right to free movement within the Union. This should apply in particular to Union citizens and their family members vaccinated in a third country for whom the health system of a Member State allows for the issuance of an EU Digital COVID Certificate and provided that the Member State has been provided with reliable proof of vaccination. A Member State should not be required to issue a vaccination certificate where the COVID-19 vaccine concerned is not authorised for use on its territory. There is no requirement for Member States to issue vaccination certificates at consular posts.

31. This is a substantive provision suitable for the body of the Regulation under persons entitled to a Certificate.

(32) On 12 March 2021, the eHealth Network updated its Guidelines on Verifiable Vaccination Certificates – Basic Interoperability Elements. Those guidelines, in particular the preferred code standards, should form the basis for the technical specifications to be adopted for the purpose of this Regulation.

32. This is suitable for the Notes Annex.

(33) Before the date of application of this Regulation several Member States already exempted vaccinated persons from certain restrictions to free movement within the Union. Where Member States accept proof of vaccination in order to waive restrictions to free movement put in place, in accordance with Union law to limit the spread of SARS-CoV-2, such as a requirement to undergo quarantine or self-isolation or to be tested for SARS-CoV-2 infection, they should be required to accept, under the same conditions, vaccination certificates issued by other Member States in accordance with this Regulation. Such acceptance should take place under the same conditions, meaning that, for example, where a Member State considers a single dose of a vaccine administered to be sufficient, it should do so also for holders of a vaccination certificate indicating a single dose of the same vaccine. Where Member States lift restrictions to free movement on the basis of proof of vaccination, they should not subject vaccinated persons to additional restrictions to free movement linked to the COVID-19 pandemic, such as travel-related testing for SARS-CoV-2 infection or travel-related quarantine or self-isolation, unless such additional restrictions are, based on the latest available scientific evidence, necessary and proportionate for the purpose of safeguarding public health, and non-discriminatory.

33. This is a substantive provision appropriate for the body of the Regulation under persons entitled to a Certificate.

(34) Regulation (EC) No 726/2004 puts in place harmonised procedures, involving all Member States, for the authorisation and surveillance of medicinal products at Union level, ensuring that only high-quality medicinal products are placed on the market and administered to persons throughout the Union. As a result, the marketing authorisations granted by the Union pursuant to that Regulation, including the underlying evaluation of the medicinal product concerned in terms of quality, safety and efficacy, are valid in all Member States. In addition, efficacy follow-up and supervision procedures of medicinal products authorised pursuant to that Regulation are carried out centrally for all Member States. The assessment and approval of vaccines via the centralised procedure follow shared standards and are done in a consistent way on behalf of all Member States. Participation of Member States in the review and endorsement of the assessment is ensured through various committees and groups. The assessment also benefits from the expertise of the European medicines regulatory network. The authorisation via the centralised procedure provides the confidence that all Member States can rely on the data on efficacy and safety and on the consistency of the batches being used for vaccination. The obligation to accept, under the same conditions, vaccination certificates issued by other Member States should therefore cover COVID-19 vaccines that have been granted a marketing authorisation pursuant to Regulation (EC) No 726/2004. In order to support the work of WHO and to strive for better global interoperability, Member States are in particular encouraged to accept vaccination certificates issued for other COVID-19 vaccines that have completed the WHO emergency use listing procedure.

34. This is relevant to learned users and can go to the Notes Annex.

(35) Harmonised procedures under Regulation (EC) No 726/2004 should not prevent Member States from deciding to accept vaccination certificates issued for other COVID-19 vaccines that have been granted a marketing authorisation by the competent authority of a Member State pursuant to Directive 2001/83/EC, vaccines the distribution of which has been temporarily authorised pursuant to Article 5(2) of that Directive, and vaccines that have completed the WHO emergency use listing procedure. Where such a COVID-19 vaccine is subsequently granted a marketing authorisation pursuant to Regulation (EC) No 726/2004, the obligation to accept vaccination certificates under the same conditions would also cover vaccination certificates issued by a Member State for that COVID-19 vaccine, regardless of whether the vaccination certificates were issued before or after the authorisation via the centralised procedure.

35. For the Notes Annex.

(36) It is necessary to prevent direct or indirect discrimination against persons who are not vaccinated, for example because of medical reasons, because they are not part of the target group for which the COVID -19 vaccine is currently administered or allowed, such as children, or because they have not yet had the opportunity or chose not to be vaccinated. Therefore, possession of a vaccination certificate, or the possession of a vaccination certificate indicating a COVID-19 vaccine, should not be a pre-condition for the exercise of the right to free movement or for the use of cross-border passenger transport services such as airlines, trains, coaches or ferries or any other means of transport. In addition, this Regulation cannot be interpreted as establishing a right or obligation to be vaccinated.

36. This is a political statement that cannot form part of an EU Act.

(37) Many Member States have been requiring persons travelling to their territory to undergo a test for SARS-CoV-2 infection before or after arrival. At the beginning of the COVID-19 pandemic, Member States typically relied on reverse transcription polymerase chain reaction (RT-PCR), which is a nucleic acid amplification (NAAT) test for COVID-19 diagnostics considered by the WHO and the ECDC to be the most reliable methodology for the testing of cases and contacts. As the pandemic has progressed, a new generation of faster and cheaper tests has become available on the Union market, the so-called rapid antigen tests, which detect the presence of viral proteins (antigens) to detect an ongoing SARS-CoV-2 infection. Commission Recommendation (EU) 2020/1743 sets out guidance for Member States regarding the use of such rapid antigen tests.

37. This is irrelevant to this Regulation. If considered relevant, then it is suitable for the Notes Annex.

(38) The Council Recommendation of 21 January 2021 sets out a common framework for the use and validation of rapid antigen tests and the mutual recognition of COVID-19 test results in the Union and provides for the development of a common list of COVID-19 rapid antigen tests. On the basis of that Recommendation, the Health Security Committee agreed, on 18 February 2021, on a common list of COVID-19 rapid antigen tests, a selection of rapid antigen tests for which Member States will mutually recognise their results and a common standardised set of data to be included in COVID-19 test certificates.

38. Suitable for the Notes Annex.

(39) Despite those common efforts, Union citizens and their family members exercising their right to free movement still face problems when trying to have the test result obtained in one Member State accepted in another. Those problems are often linked to the language in which the test result is issued, or to a lack of trust in the authenticity of the document shown. In that context, the cost of tests also needs to be taken into account. Such problems are aggravated for persons who cannot be vaccinated yet, in particular children, for whom test results may be the only way to travel where restrictions are in place.

39. This can only be used as factors leading to the decision to proceed with the Certificate and can be used as a basis for data showcasing the effectiveness of the Regulation (for example, decrease of rejections of lawful certificates by 20 per cent over a period of three years) or as an objective of the Regulation that is directed to EU citizens themselves and answer the question, what does this EU Act offer me (added value)?

(40) To improve the level of acceptance of results of tests carried out in another Member State when presenting such results for the purpose of exercising the right to free movement, an interoperable test certificate should be established, containing the information necessary to clearly identify the holder as well as the type, date and result of the test for SARS-CoV-2 infection. To ensure the reliability of the test result, only the results of NAAT tests and rapid antigen tests featured in the list established on the basis of the Council Recommendation of 21 January 2021 should be eligible for a test certificate issued on the basis of this Regulation. The common standardised set of data to be included in test certificates agreed by the Health Security Committee on the basis of the Council Recommendation of 21 January 2021, in particular the preferred code standards, should form the basis for the technical specifications to be adopted for the purpose of this Regulation.

40. This is a political statement, which has no place in the body of the Act unless expressed in a legal provision providing the requirements of the tests leading to a Certificate.

(41) The use of rapid antigen tests would serve to facilitate the issuance of test certificates on an affordable basis. Universal, timely and affordable access to COVID-19 vaccines and tests for SARS-CoV-2 infection, which form the basis for the issuance of the certificates making up the EU Digital COVID Certificate, is crucial in the fight against the COVID-19 pandemic. Among other things, easy access to inexpensive rapid antigen tests meeting quality criteria can contribute to lower costs, in particular for persons who cross borders on a daily or other frequent basis for work or education, to visit close relatives, to seek medical care, or to take care of loved ones, for other travellers with an essential function or need, for economically disadvantaged persons and for students. On 11 May 2021, the Health Security Committee adopted an updated list of rapid antigen tests, increasing the number of rapid antigen tests recognised as meeting quality criteria to 83. Before the date of application of this Regulation, several Member States already provided large-scale testing possibilities to their populations. To support the testing capacity of Member States, the Commission has mobilised EUR 100 million to purchase over 20 million rapid antigen tests. EUR 35 million were also mobilised through an agreement with Red Cross to increase testing capacity in Member States through mobile testing capacities.

41. As per 40. The Regulation could include an objective to lower the cost of cross-border travel, especially to those doing so frequently.

(42) COVID-19 test certificates indicating a negative result issued by Member States in accordance with this Regulation should be accepted, under the same conditions, by Member States requiring proof of a test for SARS-CoV-2 infection in order to waive the restrictions to free movement put in place to limit the spread of SARS-CoV-2. Where the epidemiological situation allows, holders of test certificates indicating a negative result should not be subject to additional restrictions to free movement linked to the COVID-19 pandemic, such as additional travel-related testing for SARS-CoV-2 infection upon arrival or travel-related quarantine or self-isolation, unless such additional restrictions are, based on the latest available scientific evidence, necessary and proportionate for the purpose of safeguarding public health, and non-discriminatory.

42. This is a substantive provision that details the binding effect of the Certificate and is already within the body of the Act. To be deleted as a risky paraphrasis.

(43) According to existing scientific evidence, it is possible for persons who have recovered from COVID-19 to continue to test positive for SARS-CoV-2 for a certain period after the onset of symptoms. Where such persons are required to undergo a test prior to exercising their right to free movement, they could therefore be effectively prevented from travelling despite no longer being infectious. For the purpose of facilitating free movement, and to ensure that restrictions to free movement currently in place during the COVID-19 pandemic can be lifted in a coordinated manner based on the latest scientific evidence available, an interoperable certificate of recovery should be established, containing the information necessary to clearly identify the person concerned and the date of a previous positive test result for SARS-CoV-2 infection. A certificate of recovery should be issued at the earliest 11 days after the date on which the person was first subject to a NAAT test which produced a positive result and should be valid for not more than 180 days. According to the ECDC, recent evidence shows that despite shedding of viable SARS-CoV-2 between ten and 20 days from the onset of symptoms, convincing epidemiological studies have failed to show onward SARS-CoV-2 transmission after ten days. The Commission should be empowered to change that period on the basis of guidance from the Health Security Committee or from ECDC, which is closely studying the evidence base for the duration of acquired immunity after recovery.

43. This is a political statement that is not necessary. It hides a substantive provision on the usage of the Certificate by those recently recovered but this should be within the body of the Regulation.

(44) Before the date of application of this Regulation, several Member States already exempted recovered persons from certain restrictions to free movement within the Union. Where Member States accept proof of recovery in order to waive restrictions to free movement put in place, in accordance with Union law, to limit the spread of SARS-CoV-2, such as a requirement to undergo quarantine or self-isolation or to be tested for SARS-CoV-2 infection, they should be required to accept, under the same conditions, certificates of recovery from COVID-19 issued by other Member States in accordance with this Regulation. On 15 March 2021, the eHealth Network, in cooperation with Health Security Committee, issued guidelines on COVID-19 citizen recovery interoperable certificates - minimum dataset. Where Member States lift restrictions to free movement on the basis of a certificate of recovery, they should not subject the recovered persons to additional restrictions to free movement linked to the COVID-19 pandemic, such as travel-related testing for SARS-CoV-2 infection or travel-related quarantine or self-isolation, unless such additional restrictions are, based on the latest available scientific evidence, necessary and proportionate for the purpose of safeguarding public health, and non-discriminatory.

44. This is a substantive provision that must be in the body of the Act, not in recitals.

(45) To be able to obtain a common position quickly, the Commission should be able to ask the Health Security Committee, the ECDC or EMA to issue guidance on the available scientific evidence on the effects of medical events documented in the certificates established in accordance with this Regulation, including the effectiveness and duration of the immunity conferred by COVID-19 vaccines, whether vaccines prevent asymptomatic infection and SARS-CoV-2 transmission, the situation of people having recovered from COVID-19, and the impacts of the new SARS-CoV-2 variants on people who have been vaccinated or already infected.

45. This is irrelevant here. Is there something that prevents the Commission from asking the HSC, the ECDC or EMA to issue guidance? If not, then this is unnecessary. If yes, then power to the Commission to do so must be foreseen within the body of the Act.

(46) In order to ensure uniform conditions for the implementation of the trust framework established by this Regulation, implementing powers should be conferred on the Commission. Those powers should be exercised in accordance with Regulation (EU) No 182/2011 of the European Parliament and of the Council.

46. This can remain in recitals and foreseen within the Regulation as it introduces the legitimacy of implementing texts by the Commission.

(47) The Commission should adopt immediately applicable implementing acts where, in duly justified cases relating, in particular to the need to ensure a timely implementation of the trust framework, imperative grounds of urgency so require or when new scientific evidence becomes available.

47. This is not appropriate for an EU Act: Acts speak to the users, not to the regulators themselves. If the action from the Commission is mandatory, then the relevant duty must be introduced with a substantive provision within the Regulation.

(48) Regulation (EU) 2016/679 of the European Parliament and of the Council applies to the processing of personal data carried out when implementing this Regulation. This Regulation establishes the legal ground for the processing of personal data within the meaning of point (c) of Article 6(1) and point (g) of Article 9(2) of Regulation (EU) 2016/679, necessary for the issuance and verification of the interoperable certificates provided for in this Regulation. It does not regulate the processing of personal data related to the documentation of a vaccination, a test or a recovery event for other purposes, such as for the purposes of pharmacovigilance or for the maintenance of individual personal health records. Member States may process personal data for other purposes, if the legal basis for the processing of such data for other purposes, including the related retention periods, is provided for in national law, which must comply with Union data protection law and the principles of effectiveness, necessity and proportionality, and should contain provisions clearly identifying the scope and extent of the processing, the specific purpose involved, the categories of entity that can verify the certificate as well as the relevant safeguards to prevent discrimination and abuse, taking into account the risks to the rights and freedoms of data subjects. Where the certificate is used for non-medical purposes, personal data accessed during the verification process are not to be retained, as provided for in this Regulation.

48. Irrelevant for this Regulation but can be mentioned in the Notes Annex.

(49) Where a Member State has adopted or adopts, on the basis of national law, a system of COVID-19 certificates for domestic purposes, it should ensure for the period of application of this Regulation that certificates making up the EU Digital COVID Certificate can also be used and are also accepted for domestic purposes, in order to avoid that persons travelling to another Member State and using the EU Digital COVID Certificate are obliged to obtain an additional national COVID-19 certificate.	49. This is self-evident so unnecessary. If needed, it must be added within the body of the text under the obligations of Member States.
(50) In line with the principle of data minimisation, COVID-19 certificates should contain only the personal data strictly necessary for the purpose of facilitating the exercise of the right to free movement within the Union during the COVID-19 pandemic. The specific categories of personal data and data fields to be included in the COVID-19 certificates should be set out in this Regulation.	50. This is a substantive provision that must be in the body of the Regulation without paraphrasis here.
(51) For the purposes of this Regulation, personal data on individual certificates do not need to be transmitted or exchanged across borders. In line with the public-key infrastructure approach, only the public keys of the issuers need to be transferred or accessed across borders, which will be ensured by an interoperability gateway set up and maintained by the Commission. In particular, the presence of the certificate combined with the public key of the issuer should allow for the verification of the authenticity, validity and integrity of the certificate. To prevent and detect fraud, Member States should be able to exchange lists of revoked certificates. In line with the principle of data protection by default, verification techniques not requiring transmission of personal data on individual certificates should be employed.	51. This is a wish list, not a legal provision.
(52) The retention of personal data obtained from the certificate by the Member State of destination or transit or by the cross-border passenger transport services operators required by national law to implement certain public health measures during the COVID-19 pandemic should be prohibited. This Regulation does not provide a legal basis for setting up or maintaining a centralised database at Union level containing personal data.	52. This is a political statement, the prohibition must be in the body of the Act without paraphrasis here.

(53) In accordance with Regulation (EU) 2016/679, the data controllers and processors of personal data are to take appropriate technical and organisational measures to ensure a level of security appropriate to the risk of the processing.

53. This is a wish, not a statement that has place in the Regulation. It must be expressed in a legal statement of concrete obligations within the body of the Regulation.

(54) The authorities or other designated bodies responsible for issuing the certificates making up the EU Digital COVID Certificate, as controllers within the meaning of Regulation (EU) 2016/679, are accountable for how they process personal data falling within the scope of this Regulation. This includes ensuring a level of security appropriate to the risks, including by establishing a process for regularly testing, assessing and evaluating the effectiveness of technical and organisational measures for ensuring the security of the processing. The powers of the supervisory authorities established under Regulation (EU) 2016/679 apply in full, in order to protect natural persons in relation to the processing of their personal data.

54. This is self-evident on the basis of data protection legislation. If further elaboration is deemed necessary, then it should be within the body of the Regulation or, to the extent that it refers to Regulation (EU) 2026/679 to the Notes Annex.

(55) To ensure coordination, the Commission and the other Member States should be informed when a Member State requires holders of certificates to undergo, after entry into its territory, quarantine or self-isolation or to be tested for SARS-CoV-2 infection, or if it imposes other restrictions on holders of such certificates.

55. The obligation for information must be introduced in the body of the Regulation without paraphrasis here.

(56) Clear, comprehensive and timely communication to the public, including holders, on the purpose, issuance and acceptance of each type of the certificates making up the EU Digital COVID Certificate is crucial to ensure predictability for travel and legal certainty. The Commission should support the efforts of Member States in this regard, for example by making available the information provided by Member States on the 'Re-open EU' web platform.

56. This is not part of a Regulation, which is a text binding on its users. If an obligation to the Commission is imposed, it should be expressed concretely (what does 'support the efforts' mean really and how is it measured?) within the body of the Regulation without paraphrasis here.

(57) A phasing-in period should be provided for, to give Member States which are unable to issue certificates in the format that complies with this Regulation from its date of application the possibility to continue issuing COVID-19 certificates which are not yet in compliance with this Regulation. During the phasing-in period, such COVID-19 certificates and COVID-19 certificates issued before the date of application of this Regulation should be accepted by Member States provided that they contain the necessary data.

57. These are legal provisions that must be within the body of the Act without paraphrasis here.

(58) In accordance with Recommendation (EU) 2020/1475, any restrictions to the free movement of persons within the Union put in place to limit the spread of SARS-CoV-2 should be lifted as soon as the epidemiological situation allows. This also applies to requirements to present documents other than those required by Union law, in particular Directive 2004/38/EC, such as the certificates covered by this Regulation. This Regulation should apply for 12 months from its date of application. By four months after the date of application of this Regulation, the Commission should submit a report to the European Parliament and to the Council. At the latest three months before the end of the period of application of this Regulation, taking into account the evolution of the epidemiological situation with regard to the COVID-19 pandemic, the Commission should submit a second report to the European Parliament and the Council, on the lessons learned from the application of this Regulation, including on its impact on the facilitation of free movement and on data protection.

58. This is a set of legal requirements, which should be in the body of the Act without paraphrasis here.

(59) In order to take into account the scientific progress in containing the COVID-19 pandemic, or to ensure interoperability with international standards, the power to adopt acts in accordance with Article 290 TFEU should be delegated to the Commission to amend this Regulation by modifying or removing the data fields to be included in the EU Digital COVID Certificate regarding the identity of the holder, information about the COVID-19 vaccine, the test for SARS-CoV-2 infection, past SARS-CoV-2 infection and the certificate metadata, by adding data fields regarding information about the COVID-19 vaccine, the test for SARS-CoV-2 infection, past SARS-CoV-2 infection and certificate metadata and by amending the number of days after which a certificate of recovery is to be issued. In order to take into account guidance received, the power to adopt acts in accordance with Article 290 TFEU should be delegated to the Commission to amend the provisions of this Regulation with regard to the certificate of recovery by providing for its issuance on the basis of a positive rapid antigen test, antibody test, including serological testing for antibodies against SARS-CoV-2, or any other scientifically reliable method. Such delegated acts should include the necessary data fields on the categories of data laid down by this Regulation to be included in the certificate of recovery. They should also contain specific provisions on the maximum validity period, which may depend on the type of the test carried out. It is of particular importance that the Commission carry out appropriate consultations during its preparatory work, including at expert level, and that those consultations be conducted in accordance with the principles laid down in the Interinstitutional Agreement of 13 April 2016 on Better Law-Making. In particular, to ensure equal participation in the preparation of delegated acts, the European Parliament and the Council receive all documents at the same time as Member States' experts, and their experts systematically have access to meetings of Commission expert groups dealing with the preparation of delegated acts.

59. This paraphrases legal provisions and is therefore, apart from risky, repetitive and unnecessary. The duty of the Commission to apply the Interinstitutional Agreement is self-evident and has no place in legislation.

(60) In accordance with Regulation (EU) 2018/1725 of the European Parliament and of the Council, the Commission is to consult the European Data Protection Supervisor when preparing delegated acts or implementing acts that impact on the protection of individuals' rights and freedoms with regard to the processing of personal data. The Commission may also consult the European Data Protection Board where such acts are of particular importance for the protection of rights and freedoms of individuals with regard to the processing of personal data.

60. This is irrelevant here, and self-evident on the basis of existing legislation.

(61) Since the objective of this Regulation, namely to facilitate the exercise of the right to free movement within the Union during the COVID-19 pandemic by establishing a framework for the issuance, verification and acceptance of interoperable COVID-19 certificates on a person's COVID-19 vaccination, test result or recovery, cannot be sufficiently achieved by the Member States but can rather, by reason of the scale and effects of the action, be better achieved at Union level, the Union may adopt measures, in accordance with the principle of subsidiarity as set out in Article 5 of the Treaty on European Union. In accordance with the principle of proportionality, as set out in that Article, this Regulation does not go beyond what is necessary in order to achieve that objective.

61. This is not the objective of the Regulation. The objective refers to a policy goal, and that is the recovery of the economy post-Covid.
What is introduced here as an objective is the subject matter of the Regulation, which is the means by which the objective is to be attained.
The objective and the subject matter must be in separate articles at the start of the Regulation as a means of explaining to the users the added value of the initiative, the objective of the regulatory effort, the means by which it is pursued, and the evidence-based measurements of effectiveness in pre- and post-legislative scrutiny.
These new articles are crucial in establishing participation of the users to the regulatory effort and achieving legislative effectiveness and regulatory efficacy.

(62) This Regulation respects the fundamental rights and observes the principles recognised in particular by the Charter of Fundamental Rights of the European Union (the 'Charter'), including the right to respect for private and family life, the right to the protection of personal data, the right to equality before the law and non-discrimination, the freedom of movement and the right to an effective remedy. Member States are to comply with the Charter when implementing this Regulation.

62. This is self-evident. But creates a legitimate question: does this Regulation only respect what is expressly included here out of the acquis? Whatever is not mentioned here is not respected? This is a classical drafting error known as over-precision.

(63) Given the urgency of the situation related to the COVID-19 pandemic, this Regulation should enter into force on the day of its publication in the *Official Journal of the European Union*.

63. Suitable for the Notes Annex.

(64) The European Data Protection Supervisor and the European Data Protection Board were consulted in accordance with Article 42 of Regulation (EU) 2018/1725 and delivered a joint opinion on 31 March 2021.

64. Suitable for the Notes Annex.

HAVE ADOPTED THIS REGULATION:

Excellent enacting clause, clear, precise, brief. What is missing here is an objectives provision, laying our clearly and measurably the regulatory results pursued by the Regulation. They should be talking to the main users, namely EU citizens, detailing what the benevolent aims of the regulatory initiative are, how their success will be measured, and within what period of time. An objectives provision, properly drafted, can persuade the user that this is a worthwhile pursuit in which they must participate. It is a crucial tool to ensure participation, and therefore legislative effectiveness. But it is also an equally crucial message for the direct communication of the EU with EU citizens to share the policy goals, to instil trust to the objective and the means by which these are to be achieved, and to, in the long run, instil loyalty for sustainable integration and longevity.

Article 1
Subject matter
This Regulation lays down a framework for the issuance, verification and acceptance of interoperable COVID-19 vaccination, test and recovery certificates (EU Digital COVID Certificate) for the purpose of facilitating the holders' exercise of their right to free movement during the COVID-19 pandemic. This Regulation shall also contribute to facilitating the gradual lifting of restrictions to free movement put in place by the Member States, in accordance with Union law, to limit the spread of SARS-CoV-2, in a coordinated manner.
It provides for the legal ground to process the personal data necessary to issue such certificates and to process the information necessary to verify and confirm the authenticity and validity of such certificates in full compliance with Regulation (EU) 2016/679.

The subject matter coveys the main points of the Regulation. It is there to offer the user an opportunity to quickly read what the Act is about, to identify if it is relevant to them, and to invite them to continue reading the Articles if this is the case.
Although ideally it should be user-centred, namely speaking the main points of the Regulation from the focal point of the citizen, it is successful in conveying the points here.

Article 2
Definitions
For the purposes of this Regulation, the following definitions apply:

(1) 'holder' means a person to whom an interoperable certificate containing information about that person's COVID-19 vaccination, test result or recovery has been issued in accordance with this Regulation;

(2) 'EU Digital COVID Certificate' means interoperable certificates containing information about the vaccination, test result or recovery of the holder issued in the context of the COVID-19 pandemic;

(3) 'COVID-19 vaccine' means an immunological medicinal product indicated for active immunisation to prevent COVID-19 caused by SARS-CoV-2;

There is no reason to have definitions at the start of the Regulation, taking up more of the limited users' attention span. Those of the lay users who have survived the recitals will now be lost in definitions, thus derailing from the main regulatory message. Those learned users who need definitions are trained and resilient enough to look for them in a Definitions Annex immediately after the body of the text.
And so, Article 2 can just be a hanging provision for the definitions annex. Leaving the placement of definitions aside, the drafting of definitions in EU Regulations is flawed. Definitions provide a tool to either extend or delimit the semantic field of the concept that is being defined.

(4) 'NAAT test' means a molecular nucleic acid amplification test, such as reverse transcription polymerase chain reaction (RT-PCR), loop-mediated isothermal amplification (LAMP) and transcription-mediated amplification (TMA) techniques, used to detect the presence of the SARS-CoV-2 ribonucleic acid (RNA);

(5) 'rapid antigen test' means a test that relies on detection of viral proteins (antigens) using a lateral flow immunoassay that gives results in less than 30 minutes;

They do not allow for a departure from the common meaning of the concept. So a holder (definition 1) is a device or person that keeps something in place. It is not 'a person to whom an interoperable certificate containing information about that person's COVID-19 vaccination, test result or recovery has been issued in accordance with this Regulation'. The definition is used erroneously. Instead, the text should have used the precise term 'certificate holder' for which no definition is needed. The result of the use of the same generic term defined differently in EU texts creates ambiguity on the meaning of the term across EU legislation.

(6) 'antibody test' means a laboratory-based test aiming to detect if a person has developed antibodies against SARS-CoV-2, thus indicating that the holder has been exposed to SARS-CoV-2 and has developed antibodies, regardless of whether that person was symptomatic;

(7) 'interoperability' means the capability of verifying systems in a Member State to use data encoded by another Member State;

(8) 'barcode' means a method of storing and representing data in a visual, machine-readable format;

(9) 'electronic seal' means electronic seal as defined in point (25) of Article 3 of Regulation (EU) No 910/2014;

(10) 'unique certificate identifier' means a unique identifier given, in accordance with a common structure, to each certificate issued in accordance with this Regulation;

(11) 'trust framework' means the rules, policies, specifications, protocols, data formats and digital infrastructure regulating and allowing for the reliable and secure issuance and verification of certificates to ensure their trustworthiness by confirming their authenticity, validity and integrity, through the use of electronic seals.

Moreover, definitions do not define terms that do not need it, namely terms that carry an ordinary meaning that is neither expended nor delimited. A rapid antigen test is known already and there is no need to define it. This applies to definitions 3, 4, 5, 6 and 8. Finally, definitions cannot introduce a legal provision. Which is what definition 2 is doing here.

One last drafting point. Definitions should be introduced as follows: '*In this* Regulation the following definition apply' rather than the current '*For the purposes of this Regulation'*. The current expression invites interpretation of definitions on a teleological basis, which creates grounds for individuality and possibly judicial activism. Both of which negate the reason for having definitions anyway.

Article 3

EU Digital COVID Certificate

1. The EU Digital COVID Certificate framework shall allow for the issuance, cross-border verification and acceptance of any of the following certificates:
   (a) a certificate confirming that the holder has received a COVID-19 vaccine in the Member State issuing the certificate (vaccination certificate);
   (b) a certificate confirming that the holder has been subject to a NAAT test or a rapid antigen test listed in the common and updated list of COVID-19 rapid antigen tests established on the basis of the Council Recommendation of 21 January 2021 carried out by health professionals or by skilled testing personnel in the Member State issuing the certificate and indicating the type of test, the date on which it was carried out and the result of the test (test certificate);
   (c) a certificate confirming that, following a positive result of a NAAT test carried out by health professionals or by skilled testing personnel the holder has recovered from a SARS-CoV-2 infection (certificate of recovery).

The Commission shall publish the list of COVID-19 rapid antigen tests established on the basis of the Council Recommendation of 21 January 2021, including any updates.

The main body of the Regulation consists of 14 Articles. For the analysis of the legislative style of the EU under the focal point of user friendliness, the main comment to be made concerns the structure of the Regulation, namely the sequence of Articles. In application of the layered structure, the Regulation could be restructured as follows:

Part 1 (for lay users)

- Article new with the main regulatory message for EU citizens introducing the new rights offered by the Regulation.
- Article 3 EU Digital Covid certificate
- Article 10 Data Protection

2. Member States, or designated bodies acting on behalf of Member States, shall issue the certificates referred to in paragraph 1 of this Article in a digital or paper-based format, or both. The prospective holders shall be entitled to receive the certificates in the format of their choice. Those certificates shall be user-friendly and shall contain an interoperable barcode allowing for the verification of their authenticity, validity and integrity. The barcode shall comply with the technical specifications established pursuant to Article 9. The information contained in the certificates shall also be shown in human-readable form and shall be provided in at least the official language or languages of the issuing Member State and English.
3. A separate certificate shall be issued for each vaccination, test result or recovery. Such a certificate shall not contain data from previous certificates except where otherwise provided for in this Regulation.
4. The certificates referred to in paragraph 1 shall be issued free of charge. The holder shall be entitled to request the issuance of a new certificate if the personal data contained in the original certificate are not or are no longer accurate or up to date, including with regard to the vaccination, test result or recovery of the holder, or if the original certificate is no longer available to the holder. Appropriate fees may be charged for the issuance of a new certificate in cases of repeated loss.
5. The certificates referred to in paragraph 1 shall include the following text:

'This certificate is not a travel document. The scientific evidence on COVID-19 vaccination, testing and recovery continues to evolve, including with regard to new virus variants of concern. Before travelling, please check the applicable public health measures and related restrictions applicable at the point of destination.'

Member States shall provide the holder with clear, comprehensive and timely information on the issuance and purpose of vaccination certificates, test certificates, or certificates of recovery for the purposes of this Regulation.

6. Possession of the certificates referred to in paragraph 1 shall not be a precondition for exercising the right to free movement.

Part 2 (for Member States) listing their duties and powers: Articles 4, 5, 6, 7, 11, 15.
Part 3 (legal): Articles 3, 8, 9, 12, 13, 14, 16, 17 including a review clause. Article 3 details the main regulatory messages but they are not addressed to EU citizens.

7. The issuance of certificates pursuant to paragraph 1 of this Article shall not lead to discrimination on the basis of the possession of a specific category of certificate as referred to in Article 5, 6 or 7.
8. Issuance of the certificates referred to in paragraph 1 shall not affect the validity of any other proof of vaccination, test result or recovery issued before 1 July 2021 or for other purposes, in particular for medical purposes.
9. Cross-border passenger transport service operators required by national law to implement certain public health measures during the COVID-19 pandemic shall ensure that the verification of the certificates referred in paragraph 1 is integrated into the operation of cross-border transport infrastructure such as airports, ports and railway and bus stations, where appropriate.
10. The Commission may adopt implementing acts establishing that COVID-19 certificates issued by a third country with which the Union and the Member States have concluded an agreement on the free movement of persons allowing the contracting parties to restrict such free movement on grounds of public health in a non-discriminatory manner and which does not contain a mechanism of incorporation of Union legal acts are equivalent to those issued in accordance with this Regulation. Where the Commission adopts such implementing acts, the certificates concerned shall be accepted under the conditions referred to in Article 5(5), Article 6(5) and Article 7(8).

Before adopting such implementing acts, the Commission shall assess whether such a third country issues certificates equivalent to those issued in accordance with this Regulation and has provided formal assurances that it will accept certificates issued by the Member States.
The implementing acts referred to in the first subparagraph of this paragraph shall be adopted in accordance with the examination procedure referred to in Article 14(2).

11. Where necessary, the Commission shall ask the Health Security Committee, the ECDC or EMA to issue guidance on the available scientific evidence on the effects of medical events documented in the certificates referred to in paragraph 1, in particular with regard to new SARS-CoV-2 variants of concern.

Article 4

Trust framework for the EU Digital COVID Certificate

1. The Commission and the Member States shall set up and maintain a trust framework for the EU Digital COVID Certificate.
2. The trust framework shall be based on a public key infrastructure and allow for the reliable and secure issuance and verification of the authenticity, validity and integrity of the certificates referred to in Article 3(1). The trust framework shall allow for the detection of fraud, in particular forgery. In addition, it may support the bilateral exchange of certificate revocation lists containing the unique certificate identifiers of revoked certificates. Such certificate revocation lists shall not contain any other personal data. The verification of the certificates referred to in Article 3(1) and, where applicable, certificate revocation lists shall not give rise to the issuer being notified of the verification.
3. The trust framework shall seek to ensure interoperability with technological systems established at international level.

Article 4 relates to the maintenance of a trust framework. It is a provision addressed mainly to Member States and should be in Part 2 of the Regulation. But instead of a list of political wishes, it should detail the obligations of Member States and of the Commission that can achieve the trust framework. As it stands, it is merely wishful thinking, which is unacceptable in a Regulation, which is considered to require no further elaboration at the national level. One wonders whether such a vague provision points to a Directive rather than a Regulation.

Article 5

Vaccination certificate

1. Each Member State shall, automatically or upon request by the persons concerned, issue the vaccination certificates referred to in point (a) of Article 3(1) to persons to whom a COVID-19 vaccine has been administered. Those persons shall be informed of their right to a vaccination certificate.
2. The vaccination certificate shall contain the following categories of personal data:
   (a) the identity of the holder;
   (b) information about the COVID-19 vaccine and the number of doses administered to the holder;
   (c) certificate metadata, such as the certificate issuer or a unique certificate identifier.

Articles 5–7 belong in Part 2 of the text as they are addressed to Member States. They could have been better introduced as a list of obligations for Member States. This chunk of this and other Articles (5, 6, 7 etc) are authorisations to the Commission to adopt delegated acts. They must be gathered together in a final provision entitled Duties (the Commission must...) or Powers (the Commission may...) so that the Commission can easily identify what duties or powers they have and monitor if they have been exercised.

The personal data shall be included in the vaccination certificate in accordance with the specific data fields set out in point 1 of the Annex.

The Commission is empowered to adopt delegated acts in accordance with Article 12 to amend point 1 of the Annex by modifying or removing data fields, or by adding data fields falling under the categories of personal data referred to in points (b) and (c) of the first subparagraph of this paragraph, where such an amendment is necessary to verify and confirm the authenticity, validity and integrity of the vaccination certificate, in the case of scientific progress in containing the COVID-19 pandemic, or to ensure interoperability with international standards.

3. The vaccination certificate shall be issued in a secure and interoperable format in accordance with Article 3(2) after the administration of each dose and shall clearly indicate whether or not the vaccination course has been completed.
4. Where, in the case of newly emerging scientific evidence or to ensure interoperability with international standards and technological systems, imperative grounds of urgency so require, the procedure provided for in Article 13 shall apply to delegated acts adopted pursuant to this Article.
5. Where Member States accept proof of vaccination in order to waive restrictions to free movement put in place, in accordance with Union law, to limit the spread of SARS-CoV-2, they shall also accept, under the same conditions, vaccination certificates issued by other Member States in accordance with this Regulation for a COVID-19 vaccine that has been granted a marketing authorisation pursuant to Regulation (EC) No 726/2004.

Member States may also accept, for the same purpose, vaccination certificates issued by other Member States in accordance with this Regulation for a COVID-19 vaccine that has been granted a marketing authorisation by the competent authority of a Member State pursuant to Directive 2001/83/EC, a COVID-19 vaccine the distribution of which has been temporarily authorised pursuant to Article 5(2) of that Directive, or a COVID-19 vaccine that has completed the WHO emergency use listing procedure.

Where Member States accept vaccination certificates for a COVID-19 vaccine referred to in the second subparagraph, they shall also accept, under the same conditions, vaccination certificates issued by other Member States in accordance with this Regulation for the same COVID-19 vaccine.

Article 6
Test certificate

1. Each Member State shall, automatically or upon request by the persons concerned, issue the test certificates referred to in point (b) of Article 3(1) to persons tested for SARS-CoV-2 infection. Those persons shall be informed of their right to a test certificate.
2. The test certificate shall contain the following categories of personal data:
   (a) the identity of the holder;
   (b) information about the NAAT test or rapid antigen test to which the holder was subject;
   (c) certificate metadata, such as the certificate issuer or a unique certificate identifier.

The personal data shall be included in the test certificate in accordance with the specific data fields set out in point 2 of the Annex.
The Commission is empowered to adopt delegated acts in accordance with Article 12 to amend point 2 of the Annex by modifying or removing data fields, or by adding data fields falling under the categories of personal data referred to in points (b) and (c) of the first subparagraph of this paragraph, where such an amendment is necessary to verify and confirm the authenticity, validity and integrity of the test certificate, in the case of scientific progress in containing the COVID-19 pandemic, or to ensure interoperability with international standards.

3. The test certificate shall be issued in a secure and interoperable format in accordance with Article 3(2).

Authorisation to adopt delegated acts: to be transferred to a dedicated Article at the end.

4. Where, in the case of newly emerging scientific evidence or to ensure interoperability with international standards and technological systems, imperative grounds of urgency so require, the procedure provided for in Article 13 shall apply to delegated acts adopted pursuant to this Article.
5. Where Member States require proof of a test for SARS-CoV-2 infection in order to waive the restrictions to free movement put in place, in accordance with Union law and taking into account the specific situation of cross-border communities, to limit the spread of SARS-CoV-2, they shall also accept, under the same conditions, test certificates indicating a negative result issued by other Member States in accordance with this Regulation.

Article 7 **Certificate of recovery**	Authorisation to adopt delegated acts: to be transferred to a dedicated Article at the end.
1. Each Member State shall issue, upon request, the certificates of recovery referred to in point (c) of Article 3(1).	Article 7(6) should be transferred to Article 16.

Certificates of recovery shall be issued at the earliest 11 days after the date on which a person was first subject to a NAAT test which produced a positive result.
The Commission is empowered to adopt delegated acts in accordance with Article 12 to amend the number of days after which a certificate of recovery is to be issued, on the basis of guidance received from the Health Security Committee in accordance with Article 3(11) or on scientific evidence reviewed by ECDC.

2. The certificate of recovery shall contain the following categories of personal data:
   (a) the identity of the holder;
   (b) information about past SARS-CoV-2 infection of the holder following a positive test result;
   (c) certificate metadata, such as the certificate issuer or a unique certificate identifier.

The personal data shall be included in the certificate of recovery in accordance with the specific data fields set out in point 3 of the Annex.

The Commission is empowered to adopt delegated acts in accordance with Article 12 to amend point 3 of the Annex by modifying or removing data fields, or by adding data fields falling under categories of personal data referred to in points (b) and (c) of the first subparagraph of this paragraph, where such an amendment is necessary to verify and confirm the authenticity, validity and integrity of the certificate of recovery, in the case of scientific progress in containing the COVID-19 pandemic, or to ensure interoperability with international standards.

3. The certificate of recovery shall be issued in a secure and interoperable format in accordance with Article 3(2).
4. On the basis of guidance received pursuant to Article 3(11), the Commission is empowered to adopt delegated acts in accordance with Article 12 to amend paragraph 1 of this Article and point (c) of Article 3(1) to allow for the issuance of the certificate of recovery on the basis of a positive rapid antigen test, antibody test, including a serological test for antibodies against SARS-CoV-2, or any other scientifically validated method. Such delegated acts shall also amend point 3 of the Annex by adding, modifying or removing the data fields falling under the categories of personal data referred to in points (b) and (c) of paragraph 2 of this Article.
5. Following the adoption of the delegated acts referred to in paragraph 4 the Commission shall publish the list of antibody tests on the basis of which a certificate of recovery may be issued, which is to be established by the Health Security Committee, including any updates.
6. In the report provided for in Article 16(1), the Commission shall assess the appropriateness and feasibility, in light of the available scientific evidence, of adopting the delegated acts referred to in paragraph 4 of this Article. Before submitting that report, the Commission shall seek regular guidance pursuant to Article 3(11) on the available scientific evidence and level of standardisation regarding the possible issuance of certificates of recovery based on antibody tests, including serological testing for antibodies against SARS-CoV-2, taking into account the availability and accessibility of such tests.

7. Where, in the case of newly emerging scientific evidence or to ensure interoperability with international standards and technological systems, imperative grounds of urgency so require, the procedure provided for in Article 13 shall apply to delegated acts adopted pursuant to this Article.
8. Where Member States accept proof of recovery from SARS-CoV-2 infection in order to waive restrictions to free movement put in place, in accordance with Union law, to limit the spread of SARS-CoV-2, they shall accept, under the same conditions, certificates of recovery issued by other Member States in accordance with this Regulation.

Article 8

COVID-19 certificates and other documentation issued by a third country

This belongs to Part 3 as it tackles a legal point.

1. Where a vaccination certificate has been issued in a third country for a COVID-19 vaccine that corresponds to one of the COVID-19 vaccines referred to Article 5(5) and the authorities of a Member State have been provided with all the necessary information, including reliable proof of vaccination, those authorities may, upon request, issue a vaccination certificate as referred to in point (a) of Article 3(1) to the person concerned. A Member State shall not be required to issue a vaccination certificate for a COVID-19 vaccine that is not authorised for use on its territory.

Authorisation to adopt implementing acts: to be transferred to a dedicated Article at the end.

2. The Commission may adopt an implementing act establishing that COVID-19 certificates issued by a third country in accordance with standards and technological systems that are interoperable with the trust framework for the EU Digital COVID Certificate and that allow for the verification of the authenticity, validity and integrity of the certificate, and which contain the data set out in the Annex, are to be considered as equivalent to certificates issued by Member States in accordance with this Regulation, for the purpose of facilitating the holders' exercise of their right to free movement within the Union.

Before adopting such an implementing act, the Commission shall assess whether COVID-19 certificates issued by the third country fulfil the conditions set out in the first subparagraph.
The implementing act referred to in the first subparagraph of this paragraph shall be adopted in accordance with the examination procedure referred to in Article 14(2).
The Commission shall make the list of implementing acts adopted pursuant to this paragraph publicly available.

3. The acceptance by the Member States of the certificates referred to in this Article shall be subject to Article 5(5), Article 6(5) and Article 7(8).
4. Where Member States accept vaccination certificates issued by a third country for a COVID-19 vaccine as referred to in the second subparagraph of Article 5(5), they shall also accept, under the same conditions, vaccination certificates issued by other Member States in accordance with this Regulation for the same COVID-19 vaccine.
5. This Article shall apply to COVID-19 certificates and other documentation issued by the overseas countries and territories referred to in Article 355(2) TFEU and listed in Annex II thereto, and by the Faroe Islands. It shall not apply to COVID-19 certificates and other documentation issued in the overseas countries and territories referred to in Article 355(2) TFEU and listed in Annex II thereto, or in the Faroe Islands on behalf of a Member State.

Article 9 **Technical specifications**	This belongs to Part 3. The title is wrong, these are not the technical specifications of the Certificate, it is simply a duty of the Commission to adopt implementing acts to identify the specifications.
1. In order to ensure uniform conditions for the implementation of the trust framework established by this Regulation, the Commission shall adopt implementing acts containing the technical specifications and rules for the purpose of: (a) securely issuing and verifying the certificates referred to Article 3(1); (b) ensuring the security of personal data, taking into account the nature of the data; (c) populating the certificates referred to Article 3(1), including the coding system and any other relevant elements; (d) laying down the common structure of the unique certificate identifier; (e) issuing a valid, secure and interoperable barcode; (f) seeking to ensure interoperability with international standards and technological systems; (g) allocating responsibilities among controllers and as regards processors, in accordance with Chapter IV of Regulation (EU) 2016/679. (h) ensuring accessibility for persons with disabilities to the human-readable information contained in the digital certificate and in the paper-based certificate in accordance with the accessibility requirements under Union law. 2. Those implementing acts shall be adopted in accordance with the examination procedure referred to in Article 14(2). 3. On duly justified imperative grounds of urgency, in particular to ensure a timely implementation of the trust framework, the Commission shall adopt immediately applicable implementing acts in accordance with the procedure referred to in Article 14(3). Implementing acts adopted pursuant to this paragraph shall remain in force for the period of the application of this Regulation.	Authorisation to adopt implementing acts: to be transferred to a dedicated Article at the end.
Article 10 **Protection of personal data**	This is a provision that is relevant to lay users who must be reassured of the protection of their personal data. It belongs to Part 1.

1. Regulation (EU) 2016/679 shall apply to the processing of personal data carried out when implementing this Regulation.
2. For the purpose of this Regulation, the personal data contained in the certificates issued pursuant to this Regulation shall be processed only for the purpose of accessing and verifying the information included in the certificate in order to facilitate the exercise of the right of free movement within the Union during the COVID-19 pandemic. After the end of period of the application of this Regulation, no further processing shall occur.
3. The personal data included in the certificates referred to in Article 3(1) shall be processed by the competent authorities of the Member State of destination or transit, or by the cross-border passenger transport services operators required by national law to implement certain public health measures during the COVID-19 pandemic, only to verify and confirm the holder's vaccination, test result or recovery. To that end, the personal data shall be limited to what is strictly necessary. The personal data accessed pursuant to this paragraph shall not be retained.
4. The personal data processed for the purpose of issuing the certificates referred to in Article 3(1), including the issuance of a new certificate, shall not be retained by the issuer longer than is strictly necessary for its purpose and in no case longer than the period for which the certificates may be used to exercise the right to free movement.
5. Any certificate revocation lists exchanged between Member States pursuant to Article 4(2) shall not be retained after the end of period of the application of this Regulation.
6. The authorities or other designated bodies responsible for issuing the certificates referred to in Article 3(1) shall be considered to be controllers as defined in point (7) of Article 4 of Regulation (EU) 2016/679.
7. The natural or legal person, public authority, agency or other body that has administered a COVID-19 vaccine or carried out the test for which a certificate is to be issued shall transmit to the authorities or other designated bodies responsible for issuing the certificates the personal data necessary to complete the data fields set out in the Annex.

8. Where a controller as referred to in paragraph 6 uses a processor for the purposes referred to in Article 28(3) of Regulation (EU) 2016/679, no transfer of personal data by the processor to a third country shall take place.

Article 11
Restrictions to free movement and information exchange

This is addressed to Member States and belongs to Part 2.

1. Without prejudice to Member States' competence to impose restrictions on grounds of public health, where Member States accept vaccination certificates, test certificates indicating a negative result or certificates of recovery, they shall refrain from imposing additional restrictions to free movement, such as additional travel-related testing for SARS-CoV-2 infection or travel-related quarantine or self-isolation, unless they are necessary and proportionate for the purpose of safeguarding public health in response to the COVID-19 pandemic, also taking into account available scientific evidence, including epidemiological data published by the ECDC on the basis of Recommendation (EU) 2020/1475.
2. Where a Member State requires, in accordance with Union law, holders of the certificates referred to in Article 3(1) to undergo, after entry into its territory, quarantine or self-isolation or to be tested for SARS-CoV-2 infection, or if it imposes other restrictions on the holders of such certificates because, for example, the epidemiological situation in a Member State or in a region within a Member State worsens quickly, in particular as a result of a SARS-CoV-2 variant of concern or interest, it shall inform the Commission and the other Member States accordingly, if possible 48 hours in advance of the introduction of such new restrictions. To that end, the Member State shall provide the following information:

   (a) the reasons for such restrictions;

   (b) the scope of such restrictions, specifying which certificate holders are subject to or exempt from such restrictions;

   (c) the date and duration of such restrictions.

3. Member States shall inform the Commission and the other Member States of the issuance and the conditions of acceptance of the certificates referred to in Article 3(1), including the COVID-19 vaccines they accept pursuant to the second subparagraph of Article 5(5).
4. Member States shall provide the public with clear, comprehensive and timely information with regard to paragraphs 2 and 3. As a general rule, Member States shall make that information publicly available 24 hours before new restrictions come into effect, taking into account that some flexibility is required for epidemiological emergencies. In addition, the information provided by the Member States may be made publicly available by the Commission in a centralised manner.

Article 12

Exercise of the delegation

Authorisation to adopt delegated acts: to be transferred to a dedicated Article at the end.

1. The power to adopt delegated acts is conferred on the Commission subject to the conditions laid down in this Article.
2. The power to adopt delegated acts referred to in Article 5(2), Article 6(2) and Article 7(1) and (2) shall be conferred on the Commission for a period of 12 months from 1 July 2021.
3. The delegation of power referred to in Article 5(2), Article 6(2) and Article 7(1) and (2) may be revoked at any time by the European Parliament or by the Council. A decision to revoke shall put an end to the delegation of the power specified in that decision. It shall take effect the day following the publication of the decision in the *Official Journal of the European Union* or at a later date specified therein. It shall not affect the validity of any delegated acts already in force.
4. Before adopting a delegated act, the Commission shall consult experts designated by each Member State in accordance with the principles laid down in the Interinstitutional Agreement of 13 April 2016 on Better Law-Making.
5. As soon as it adopts a delegated act, the Commission shall notify it simultaneously to the European Parliament and to the Council.

6. A delegated act adopted pursuant to Article 5(2), Article 6(2) or Article 7(1) or (2) shall enter into force only if no objection has been expressed either by the European Parliament or by the Council within a period of two months of notification of that act to the European Parliament and the Council or if, before the expiry of that period, the European Parliament and the Council have both informed the Commission that they will not object. That period shall be extended by two months at the initiative of the European Parliament or of the Council.

Article 13
Urgency procedure

1. Delegated acts adopted under this Article shall enter into force without delay and shall apply as long as no objection is expressed in accordance with paragraph 2. The notification of a delegated act to the European Parliament and to the Council shall state the reasons for the use of the urgency procedure.
2. Either the European Parliament or the Council may object to a delegated act in accordance with the procedure referred to in Article 11(6). In such a case, the Commission shall repeal the act immediately following the notification of the decision to object by the European Parliament or by the Council.

As this is about delegated acts, it should be placed under the proposed dedicated Article at the end.

Article 14
Committee procedure

1. The Commission shall be assisted by a committee. That committee shall be a committee within the meaning of Regulation (EU) No 182/2011.
2. Where reference is made to this paragraph, Article 5 of Regulation (EU) No 182/2011 shall apply.
3. Where reference is made to this paragraph, Article 8 of Regulation (EU) No 182/2011, in conjunction with Article 5 thereof, shall apply.

This is vague about what the Commission will be assisted with. If it is about delegated acts, then it should be below the authorisation.

Article 15

Phasing-in period

1. COVID-19 certificates issued by a Member State before 1 July 2021 shall be accepted by the other Member States until 12 August 2021 in accordance with Article 5(5), Article 6(5) and Article 7(8), where they contain the data set out in the Annex.
2. Where a Member State is not able to issue the certificates referred to in Article 3(1) in a format that complies with this Regulation from 1 July 2021, it shall inform the Commission and the other Member States accordingly. Where they contain the data set out in the Annex, the COVID-19 certificates issued by such a Member State in a format that does not comply with this Regulation shall be accepted by the other Member States in accordance with Article 5(5), Article 6(5) and Article 7(8) until 12 August 2021.

This refers to Member States, it should be phrased as an obligation to accept certificates issued before 1 July 2021 and should be in Part 2.

Article 16

Commission reports

This is well placed.

1. By 31 October 2021, the Commission shall submit a report to the European Parliament and to the Council. The report shall include an overview of:
   (a) the number of certificates issued pursuant to this Regulation;
   (b) guidance requested pursuant to Article 3(11) on the available scientific evidence and level of standardisation regarding the possible issuance of certificates of recovery based on antibody tests, including serological testing for antibodies against SARS-CoV-2, taking into account the availability and accessibility of such tests; and
   (c) the information received pursuant to Article 11.
2. By 31 March 2022, the Commission shall submit a report to the European Parliament and to the Council on the application of this Regulation.

The report shall contain, in particular, an assessment of the impact of this Regulation on the facilitation of free movement, including on travel and tourism and the acceptance of the different types of vaccine, fundamental rights and non-discrimination, as well as on the protection of personal data during the COVID-19 pandemic. The report may be accompanied by legislative proposals, in particular to extend the period of application of this Regulation, taking into account the evolution of the epidemiological situation with regard to the COVID-19 pandemic.

Article 17

Entry into force

This is well placed but should include a review clause.

This Regulation shall enter into force on the day of its publication in the *Official Journal of the European Union*.

It shall apply from 1 July 2021 to 30 June 2022.

This Regulation shall be binding in its entirety and directly applicable in all Member States.

Done at Brussels, 14 June 2021.

For the European Parliament

The President

D. M. SASSOLI

For the Council

The President

A. COSTA

Table 9.2 Table of contents

Recitals	
Article 1 (new)	Objectives
Article 2 (original 1)	Subject matter
Article 3 (original 2)	Definitions
Part A: To EU citizens	
Article 4 (original 3)	EU Digital Covid Certificate: Your rights
Article 5 (original 10)	Protection of personal data
Part B: To Member States	
Article 6 (original 4	Trust framework for the EU Digital COVID Certificate
Article 7 (original 5)	Vaccination certificate
Article 8 (original 6)	Test certificate
Article 9 (original 7)	Certificate of recovery
Article 10 (original 11)	Restrictions to free movement and information exchange
Article 11 (original 15)	Phasing-in period
Part C: To EU institutions	
Article 12 (original 3)	EU Digital COVID Certificate: Process
Article 13 (original 8)	COVID-19 certificates and other documentation issued by a third country
Article 14 (original 9)	Technical specifications
Article 15 (original 12)	Exercise of the delegation
Article 16 (original 13)	Urgency procedure
Article 17 (original 14)	Committee procedure
Article 18 (original 16)	Commission reports
Article 19 (new)	Citation
Article 20 (original 17)	Entry into force and review clause
Annex 1	DEFINITIONS
Annex 2	CERTIFICATE DATASETS
Annex 3	NOTES AND COMMISSION STATEMENT

Source: The author.

Having commented on the text of the Regulation, let's see it clean, with all the changes transposed to its text:

Regulation (EU) 2021/953 on the EU Digital COVID Certificate (issuance, verification, acceptance, certificates)

THE EUROPEAN PARLIAMENT AND THE COUNCIL OF THE EUROPEAN UNION

Having regard to the following:

(1) On 30 January 2020, the Director-General of the World Health Organization (WHO) declared a public health emergency of international concern over the global outbreak of severe acute respiratory syndrome coronavirus 2 (SARS-CoV-2), which causes coronavirus disease 2019 (COVID-19). On 11 March 2020, the WHO made an assessment characterising COVID-19 as a pandemic.

(2) On 13 October 2020, the Council adopted Recommendation (EU) 2020/1475 (4), which introduced a coordinated approach to the restriction of free movement in response to the COVID-19 pandemic in the following key areas: the application of common criteria and thresholds when deciding whether to introduce restrictions to free movement, a mapping of risk areas of SARS-CoV-2 transmission based on an agreed colour code and a coordinated approach to any appropriate measures which could be applied to persons travelling to or from risk areas, depending on the level of risk of SARS-CoV-2 transmission in those areas. In view of their specific situation, the Recommendation emphasises that travellers with an essential function or need, as listed in point 19 of the Recommendation, and persons living in border regions and travelling across the border on a daily or frequent basis for the purposes of work, business, education, family, medical care or caregiving, whose lives are particularly affected by such restrictions, in particular those who exercise critical functions or who are essential for critical infrastructure, should in general be exempted from travel restrictions linked to the COVID-19 pandemic.

(3) Persons who are vaccinated or who have had a recent negative COVID-19 test result and persons who have recovered from COVID-19 in the previous six months seem to have a reduced risk of infecting people with SARS-CoV-2, according to current and still evolving scientific evidence. The free movement of persons who, according to sound scientific evidence, do not pose a significant risk to public health, for example because they are immune to and cannot transmit SARS-CoV-2, should not be restricted, as such restrictions would not be necessary to achieve the objective of safeguarding public health. Where the epidemiological situation allows, such persons should not be subject to additional restrictions to free movement linked to the COVID-19 pandemic, such as travel-related testing for SARS-CoV-2 infection or travel-related quarantine or self-isolation, unless such additional restrictions are, based on

the latest available scientific evidence and in line with the precautionary principle, necessary and proportionate for the purpose of safeguarding public health, and non-discriminatory.

(4) In order to ensure uniform conditions for the implementation of the trust framework established by this Regulation, implementing powers should be conferred on the Commission. Those powers should be exercised in accordance with Regulation (EU) No 182/2011 of the European Parliament and of the Council (14).

HAVE ADOPTED THIS REGULATION:

Article 1: Objectives

The objectives of this Regulation are:

(a) to protect the livelihood of EU citizens after the COVID pandemic by starting an economic recovery (evidence based measurable criteria of efficacy to be added, for example, amounting to growth of GDP by 3 per cent within the EU within a period of three years and decrease of inflation within the EU by 2 per cent over the same period of time);

(b) to reduce the administrative costs of certification for cross-border travel, especially in particular for persons who cross borders on a daily or other frequent basis for work or education, to visit close relatives, to seek medical care, or to take care of loved ones, for other travellers with an essential function or need, for economically disadvantaged persons and for students; and

(c) to reduce the number of rejected lawful certificates often caused by language or mistrust in the authenticity of foreign documents by 20 per cent over a period of three years.

Article 2: Subject matter

To achieve these objectives, this Regulation facilitates the exercise of the right to move and reside freely within the territory of the Member States, by introducing a common framework for the issuance, verification and acceptance of interoperable COVID-19 vaccination, test and recovery certificates (EU Digital COVID Certificate).

The common framework is binding and directly applicable in all Member States.

It facilitates, whenever possible on the basis of scientific evidence, the gradual lifting of restrictions in a coordinated manner by Member States, taking into account the lifting of restrictions within their own territory.

Regulation (EU) 2021/954 of the European Parliament and of the Council (5) extends that common framework to third-country nationals who are legally staying or residing in the Schengen area without controls at internal borders and applies as a matter of Schengen acquis, without prejudice to the specific rules on the crossing of internal borders set out in Regulation (EU) 2016/399 of the European Parliament and of the Council (6).

Article 3: Definitions

Definitions for this Regulation are in Annex A.

Part A: To EU citizens

Article 4 – EU Digital Covid Certificate: Your rights

This Regulation introduces the certificates required to allow you to move freely within the EU without endangering the life and health of you and others due to Covid-19.

Article 5 – Data Protection

1. The Regulation protects fully your data.
2. Regulation (EU) 2016/679 applies to the processing of personal data carried out when implementing this Regulation.
3 In this Regulation, the personal data contained in the certificates issued pursuant to this Regulation can be processed only for the purpose of accessing and verifying the information included in the certificate in order to facilitate the exercise of the right of free movement within the Union during the COVID-19 pandemic. After the end of period of the application of this Regulation, no further processing can occur.
4. The personal data included in the certificates referred to in Article 3(1) must be processed by the competent authorities of the Member State of destination or transit, or by the cross-border passenger transport services operators required by national law to implement certain public health measures during the COVID-19 pandemic, only to verify and confirm the holder's vaccination, test result or recovery. To that end, the personal data must be limited to what is strictly necessary. The personal data accessed pursuant to this paragraph can not be retained.
5. The personal data processed for the purpose of issuing the certificates referred to in Article 3(1), including the issuance of a new certificate, must not be retained by the issuer longer than is strictly necessary for its

purpose and in no case longer than the period for which the certificates may be used to exercise the right to free movement.

6. Any certificate revocation lists exchanged between Member States pursuant to Article 4(2) must not be retained after the end of period of the application of this Regulation.
7. The authorities or other designated bodies responsible for issuing the certificates referred to in Article 3(1) are controllers, as defined in point (7) of Article 4 of Regulation (EU) 2016/679.
8. The natural or legal person, public authority, agency or other body that has administered a COVID-19 vaccine or carried out the test for which a certificate is to be issued must transmit to the authorities or other designated bodies responsible for issuing the certificates the personal data necessary to complete the data fields set out in the Annex.
9. Where a controller as referred to in paragraph 6 uses a processor for the purposes referred to in Article 28(3) of Regulation (EU) 2016/679, no transfer of personal data by the processor to a third country can take place.

Part B: To Member States

Article 6 – Trust framework for the EU Digital COVID Certificate

1. The Commission and the Member States shall set up and maintain a trust framework for the EU Digital COVID Certificate.
2. The trust framework shall be based on a public key infrastructure and allow for the reliable and secure issuance and verification of the authenticity, validity and integrity of the certificates referred to in Article 3(1). The trust framework shall allow for the detection of fraud, in particular forgery. In addition, it may support the bilateral exchange of certificate revocation lists containing the unique certificate identifiers of revoked certificates. Such certificate revocation lists shall not contain any other personal data. The verification of the certificates referred to in Article 3(1) and, where applicable, certificate revocation lists shall not give rise to the issuer being notified of the verification.
3. The trust framework shall seek to ensure interoperability with technological systems established at international level.

Article 7 – Vaccination certificate

1. Each Member State shall, automatically or upon request by the persons concerned, issue the vaccination certificates referred to in point (a) of Article 3(1) to persons to whom a COVID-19 vaccine has been admin-

istered. Those persons shall be informed of their right to a vaccination certificate.

2. The vaccination certificate shall contain the following categories of personal data:
   (a) the identity of the holder;
   (b) information about the COVID-19 vaccine and the number of doses administered to the holder;
   (c) certificate metadata, such as the certificate issuer or a unique certificate identifier.

   The personal data shall be included in the vaccination certificate in accordance with the specific data fields set out in point 1 of the Annex.

   The Commission is empowered to adopt delegated acts in accordance with Article … to amend point 1 of the Annex by modifying or removing data fields, or by adding data fields falling under the categories of personal data referred to in points (b) and (c) of the first subparagraph of this paragraph, where such an amendment is necessary to verify and confirm the authenticity, validity and integrity of the vaccination certificate, in the case of scientific progress in containing the COVID-19 pandemic, or to ensure interoperability with international standards.
3. The vaccination certificate shall be issued in a secure and interoperable format in accordance with Article … after the administration of each dose and shall clearly indicate whether or not the vaccination course has been completed.
4. Where, in the case of newly emerging scientific evidence or to ensure interoperability with international standards and technological systems, imperative grounds of urgency so require, the procedure provided for in Article … shall apply to delegated acts adopted pursuant to this Article.
5. Where Member States accept proof of vaccination in order to waive restrictions to free movement put in place, in accordance with Union law, to limit the spread of SARS-CoV-2, they shall also accept, under the same conditions, vaccination certificates issued by other Member States in accordance with this Regulation for a COVID-19 vaccine that has been granted a marketing authorisation pursuant to Regulation (EC) No 726/2004.

   Member States may also accept, for the same purpose, vaccination certificates issued by other Member States in accordance with this Regulation for a COVID-19 vaccine that has been granted a marketing authorisation by the competent authority of a Member State pursuant to Directive 2001/83/EC, a COVID-19 vaccine the distribution of which has been temporarily authorised pursuant to Article 5(2) of that Directive, or a COVID-19 vaccine that has completed the WHO emergency use listing procedure.

Where Member States accept vaccination certificates for a COVID-19 vaccine referred to in the second subparagraph, they shall also accept, under the same conditions, vaccination certificates issued by other Member States in accordance with this Regulation for the same COVID-19 vaccine.

Article 8 – Test certificate

1. Each Member State shall, automatically or upon request by the persons concerned, issue the test certificates referred to in point (b) of Article 3(1) to persons tested for SARS-CoV-2 infection. Those persons shall be informed of their right to a test certificate.
2. The test certificate shall contain the following categories of personal data:
   (a) the identity of the holder;
   (b) information about the NAAT test or rapid antigen test to which the holder was subject;
   (c) certificate metadata, such as the certificate issuer or a unique certificate identifier.

   The personal data shall be included in the test certificate in accordance with the specific data fields set out in point 2 of the Annex.

   The Commission is empowered to adopt delegated acts in accordance with Article 12 to amend point 2 of the Annex by modifying or removing data fields, or by adding data fields falling under the categories of personal data referred to in points (b) and (c) of the first subparagraph of this paragraph, where such an amendment is necessary to verify and confirm the authenticity, validity and integrity of the test certificate, in the case of scientific progress in containing the COVID-19 pandemic, or to ensure interoperability with international standards.
3. The test certificate shall be issued in a secure and interoperable format in accordance with Article 3(2).
4. Where, in the case of newly emerging scientific evidence or to ensure interoperability with international standards and technological systems, imperative grounds of urgency so require, the procedure provided for in Article 13 shall apply to delegated acts adopted pursuant to this Article.
5. Where Member States require proof of a test for SARS-CoV-2 infection in order to waive the restrictions to free movement put in place, in accordance with Union law and taking into account the specific situation of cross-border communities, to limit the spread of SARS-CoV-2, they shall also accept, under the same conditions, test certificates indicating

a negative result issued by other Member States in accordance with this Regulation.

Article 9 – Certificate of recovery

1. Each Member State shall issue, upon request, the certificates of recovery referred to in point (c) of Article ....

   Certificates of recovery shall be issued at the earliest 11 days after the date on which a person was first subject to a NAAT test which produced a positive result.

   The Commission is empowered to adopt delegated acts in accordance with Article 12 to amend the number of days after which a certificate of recovery is to be issued, on the basis of guidance received from the Health Security Committee in accordance with Article 3(11) or on scientific evidence reviewed by ECDC.
2. The certificate of recovery shall contain the following categories of personal data:
   (a) the identity of the holder;
   (b) information about past SARS-CoV-2 infection of the holder following a positive test result;
   (c) certificate metadata, such as the certificate issuer or a unique certificate identifier.

   The personal data shall be included in the certificate of recovery in accordance with the specific data fields set out in point ... of the Annex.

   The Commission is empowered to adopt delegated acts in accordance with Article ... to amend point ... of the Annex by modifying or removing data fields, or by adding data fields falling under categories of personal data referred to in points (b) and (c) of the first subparagraph of this paragraph, where such an amendment is necessary to verify and confirm the authenticity, validity and integrity of the certificate of recovery, in the case of scientific progress in containing the COVID-19 pandemic, or to ensure interoperability with international standards.
3. The certificate of recovery shall be issued in a secure and interoperable format in accordance with Article ....
4. On the basis of guidance received pursuant to Article ..., the Commission is empowered to adopt delegated acts in accordance with Article ... to amend paragraph 1 of this Article and point (c) of Article ... to allow for the issuance of the certificate of recovery on the basis of a positive rapid antigen test, antibody test, including a serological test for antibodies against SARS-CoV-2, or any other scientifically validated method. Such

delegated acts shall also amend point 3 of the Annex by adding, modifying or removing the data fields falling under the categories of personal data referred to in points (b) and (c) of paragraph 2 of this Article.

5. Following the adoption of the delegated acts referred to in paragraph 4 the Commission shall publish the list of antibody tests on the basis of which a certificate of recovery may be issued, which is to be established by the Health Security Committee, including any updates.
6. In the report provided for in Article …, the Commission shall assess the appropriateness and feasibility, in light of the available scientific evidence, of adopting the delegated acts referred to in paragraph 4 of this Article. Before submitting that report, the Commission shall seek regular guidance pursuant to Article … on the available scientific evidence and level of standardisation regarding the possible issuance of certificates of recovery based on antibody tests, including serological testing for antibodies against SARS-CoV-2, taking into account the availability and accessibility of such tests.
7. Where, in the case of newly emerging scientific evidence or to ensure interoperability with international standards and technological systems, imperative grounds of urgency so require, the procedure provided for in Article … shall apply to delegated acts adopted pursuant to this Article.
8. Where Member States accept proof of recovery from SARS-CoV-2 infection in order to waive restrictions to free movement put in place, in accordance with Union law, to limit the spread of SARS-CoV-2, they shall accept, under the same conditions, certificates of recovery issued by other Member States in accordance with this Regulation.

Article 10 – Restrictions to free movement and information exchange

1. Without prejudice to Member States' competence to impose restrictions on grounds of public health, where Member States accept vaccination certificates, test certificates indicating a negative result or certificates of recovery, they shall refrain from imposing additional restrictions to free movement, such as additional travel-related testing for SARS-CoV-2 infection or travel-related quarantine or self-isolation, unless they are necessary and proportionate for the purpose of safeguarding public health in response to the COVID-19 pandemic, also taking into account available scientific evidence, including epidemiological data published by the ECDC on the basis of Recommendation (EU) 2020/1475.
2. Where a Member State requires, in accordance with Union law, holders of the certificates referred to in Article … to undergo, after entry into its territory, quarantine or self-isolation or to be tested for SARS-CoV-2 infection, or if it imposes other restrictions on the holders of such certif-

icates because, for example, the epidemiological situation in a Member State or in a region within a Member State worsens quickly, in particular as a result of a SARS-CoV-2 variant of concern or interest, it shall inform the Commission and the other Member States accordingly, if possible 48 hours in advance of the introduction of such new restrictions. To that end, the Member State shall provide the following information:
   (a) the reasons for such restrictions;
   (b) the scope of such restrictions, specifying which certificate holders are subject to or exempt from such restrictions;
   (c) the date and duration of such restrictions.
3. Member States shall inform the Commission and the other Member States of the issuance and the conditions of acceptance of the certificates referred to in Article …, including the COVID-19 vaccines they accept pursuant to the second subparagraph of Article ….
4. Member States shall provide the public with clear, comprehensive and timely information with regard to paragraphs 2 and 3. As a general rule, Member States shall make that information publicly available 24 hours before new restrictions come into effect, taking into account that some flexibility is required for epidemiological emergencies. In addition, the information provided by the Member States may be made publicly available by the Commission in a centralised manner.

Article 11 – Phasing-in Period

1. COVID-19 certificates issued by a Member State before 1 July 2021 shall be accepted by the other Member States until 12 August 2021 in accordance with Article …, where they contain the data set out in the Annex.
2. Where a Member State is not able to issue the certificates referred to in Article … in a format that complies with this Regulation from 1 July 2021, it shall inform the Commission and the other Member States accordingly. Where they contain the data set out in the Annex, the COVID-19 certificates issued by such a Member State in a format that does not comply with this Regulation shall be accepted by the other Member States in accordance with …until 12 August 2021.

Part C: To EU institutions

Article 12 – Exercise of the Delegation

1. The power to adopt delegated acts is conferred on the Commission subject to the conditions laid down in this Article.

2. The power to adopt delegated acts referred to in Article …shall be conferred on the Commission for a period of 12 months from 1 July 2021.
3. The delegation of power referred to in Article …may be revoked at any time by the European Parliament or by the Council. A decision to revoke shall put an end to the delegation of the power specified in that decision. It shall take effect the day following the publication of the decision in the Official Journal of the European Union or at a later date specified therein. It shall not affect the validity of any delegated acts already in force.
4. Before adopting a delegated act, the Commission shall consult experts designated by each Member State in accordance with the principles laid down in the Interinstitutional Agreement of 13 April 2016 on Better Law-Making.
5. As soon as it adopts a delegated act, the Commission shall notify it simultaneously to the European Parliament and to the Council.
6. A delegated act adopted pursuant to Article …shall enter into force only if no objection has been expressed either by the European Parliament or by the Council within a period of two months of notification of that act to the European Parliament and the Council or if, before the expiry of that period, the European Parliament and the Council have both informed the Commission that they will not object. That period shall be extended by two months at the initiative of the European Parliament or of the Council.

Article 13 – COVID-19 Certificates and Other Documentation Issued by a Third Country

1. Where a vaccination certificate has been issued in a third country for a COVID-19 vaccine that corresponds to one of the COVID-19 vaccines referred to Article … and the authorities of a Member State have been provided with all the necessary information, including reliable proof of vaccination, those authorities may, upon request, issue a vaccination certificate as referred to … to the person concerned. A Member State shall not be required to issue a vaccination certificate for a COVID-19 vaccine that is not authorised for use on its territory.
2. The Commission may adopt an implementing act establishing that COVID-19 certificates issued by a third country in accordance with standards and technological systems that are interoperable with the trust framework for the EU Digital COVID Certificate and that allow for the verification of the authenticity, validity and integrity of the certificate, and which contain the data set out in the Annex, are to be considered as equivalent to certificates issued by Member States in accordance with this Regulation, for the purpose of facilitating the holders' exercise of their right to free movement within the Union.

Before adopting such an implementing act, the Commission shall assess whether COVID-19 certificates issued by the third country fulfil the conditions set out in the first subparagraph.

The implementing act referred to in the first subparagraph of this paragraph shall be adopted in accordance with the examination procedure referred to in Article ....

The Commission shall make the list of implementing acts adopted pursuant to this paragraph publicly available.

3. The acceptance by the Member States of the certificates referred to in this Article shall be subject to ....
4. Where Member States accept vaccination certificates issued by a third country for a COVID-19 vaccine as referred to in the second subparagraph of Article ..., they shall also accept, under the same conditions, vaccination certificates issued by other Member States in accordance with this Regulation for the same COVID-19 vaccine.
5. This Article shall apply to COVID-19 certificates and other documentation issued by the overseas countries and territories referred to in Article 355(2) TFEU and listed in Annex II thereto, and by the Faroe Islands. It shall not apply to COVID-19 certificates and other documentation issued in the overseas countries and territories referred to in Article 355(2) TFEU and listed in Annex II thereto, or in the Faroe Islands on behalf of a Member State.

Article 14 – Technical specifications

1. In order to ensure uniform conditions for the implementation of the trust framework established by this Regulation, the Commission shall adopt implementing acts containing the technical specifications and rules for the purpose of:
   (a) securely issuing and verifying the certificates referred to Article ...;
   (b) ensuring the security of personal data, taking into account the nature of the data;
   (c) populating the certificates referred to Article ..., including the coding system and any other relevant elements;
   (d) laying down the common structure of the unique certificate identifier;
   (e) issuing a valid, secure and interoperable barcode;
   (f) seeking to ensure interoperability with international standards and technological systems;

(g) allocating responsibilities among controllers and as regards processors, in accordance with Chapter IV of Regulation (EU) 2016/679.

(h) ensuring accessibility for persons with disabilities to the human-readable information contained in the digital certificate and in the paper-based certificate in accordance with the accessibility requirements under Union law.

2. Those implementing acts shall be adopted in accordance with the examination procedure referred to in Article ….
3. On duly justified imperative grounds of urgency, in particular to ensure a timely implementation of the trust framework, the Commission shall adopt immediately applicable implementing acts in accordance with the procedure referred to in Article 14(3). Implementing acts adopted pursuant to this paragraph shall remain in force for the period of the application of this Regulation.

Article 15 – Exercise of the Delegation

1. The power to adopt delegated acts is conferred on the Commission subject to the conditions laid down in this Article.
2. The power to adopt delegated acts referred to in Article … shall be conferred on the Commission for a period of 12 months from 1 July 2021.
3. The delegation of power referred to in Article … may be revoked at any time by the European Parliament or by the Council. A decision to revoke shall put an end to the delegation of the power specified in that decision. It shall take effect the day following the publication of the decision in the Official Journal of the European Union or at a later date specified therein. It shall not affect the validity of any delegated acts already in force.
4. Before adopting a delegated act, the Commission shall consult experts designated by each Member State in accordance with the principles laid down in the Interinstitutional Agreement of 13 April 2016 on Better Law-Making.
5. As soon as it adopts a delegated act, the Commission shall notify it simultaneously to the European Parliament and to the Council.
6. A delegated act adopted pursuant to Article … shall enter into force only if no objection has been expressed either by the European Parliament or by the Council within a period of two months of notification of that act to the European Parliament and the Council or if, before the expiry of that period, the European Parliament and the Council have both informed the Commission that they will not object. That period shall be extended by two months at the initiative of the European Parliament or of the Council.

Article 16 – Urgency Procedure

1. Delegated acts adopted under this Article shall enter into force without delay and shall apply as long as no objection is expressed in accordance with paragraph 2. The notification of a delegated act to the European Parliament and to the Council shall state the reasons for the use of the urgency procedure.
2. Either the European Parliament or the Council may object to a delegated act in accordance with the procedure referred to in Article .... In such a case, the Commission shall repeal the act immediately following the notification of the decision to object by the European Parliament or by the Council.

Article 17 – Committee Procedure

1. The Commission shall be assisted by a committee. That committee shall be a committee within the meaning of Regulation (EU) No 182/2011.
2. Where reference is made to this paragraph, Article 5 of Regulation (EU) No 182/2011 shall apply.
3. Where reference is made to this paragraph, Article 8 of Regulation (EU) No 182/2011, in conjunction with Article 5 thereof, shall apply.

Article 18 – Commission Reports

1. By 31 October 2021, the Commission shall submit a report to the European Parliament and to the Council. The report shall include an overview of:
   (a) the number of certificates issued pursuant to this Regulation;
   (b) guidance requested pursuant to Article ... on the available scientific evidence and level of standardisation regarding the possible issuance of certificate of recovery based on antibody tests, including serological testing for antibodies against SARS-CoV-2, taking into account the availability and accessibility of such tests; and
   (c) the information received pursuant to Article ...
2. By 31 March 2022, the Commission shall submit a report to the European Parliament and to the Council on the application of this Regulation.

   The report shall contain, in particular, an assessment of the impact of this Regulation on the facilitation of free movement, including on travel and tourism and the acceptance of the different types of vaccine, fundamental rights and non-discrimination, as well as on the protection of personal data during the COVID-19 pandemic.

   The report may be accompanied by legislative proposals, in particular to extend the period of application of this Regulation, taking into account the evolution of the epidemiological situation with regard to the COVID-19 pandemic.

Article 19 – Citation

This Act is REGULATION (EU) 2021/953 OF THE EUROPEAN PARLIAMENT AND OF THE COUNCIL of 14 June 2021 on the EU Digital COVID Certificate (issuance, verification, acceptance, certificates).

Article 20 – Entry into Force and Review Clause

Annex 1 – DEFINITIONS

In this Regulation, the following definitions apply:

(1) 'interoperability' means the capability of verifying systems in a Member State to use data encoded by another Member State;
(2) 'electronic seal' means electronic seal as defined in point (25) of Article 3 of Regulation (EU) No 910/2014;
(3) 'unique certificate identifier' means a unique identifier given, in accordance with a common structure, to each certificate issued in accordance with this Regulation;
(4) 'trust framework' means the rules, policies, specifications, protocols, data formats and digital infrastructure regulating and allowing for the reliable and secure issuance and verification of certificates to ensure their trustworthiness by confirming their authenticity, validity and integrity, through the use of electronic seals.

Annex 2 – CERTIFICATE DATASETS

Annex 3 – NOTES AND COMMISSION STATEMENT

CONCLUSIONS

The analysis of the existing representative sample of EU Regulations has showcased the possibilities open to the regulators for a new drafting style for Regulations. It is not a matter of language or stylistic expression. It is much more than that, yet much easier than that.

What is proposed is a change of drafting philosophy, where the users lead on drafting dilemmas, rather than tradition or esoteric legalese. This supports the following changes in the drafting style of Regulations:

1. Shorter title pinpointing the topic of the Regulation, leaving the legal requirement for a full name to a citation article at the end of the text.
2. Introduction of a table of contents to be used as a roadmap for users.
3. Radical culling of recitals by maintaining only those needed for context for EU citizens, and transferring the rest to the Notes Annex addressed to learned users.
4. Introduction of a new article 1 on objectives, with clear measurable regulatory goals and evidence led criteria for effectiveness.
5. Culling of definitions and correct use of them solely to extend or delimit the ordinary meaning of the defined term.
6. Use of the article on subject matter to list the main points of the Act, thus narrating briefly to the citizen what follows.
7. Division of the Regulation into three Parts, addressed to EU citizens, to Member States, and to EU Institutions respectively, each containing regulatory messages relevant to each group and speaking to them in the appropriate easified language.
8. Collection of all authorisation for implementing and delegated acts in a list within one Article towards the end of the Regulation.
9. Introduction of a citation article as penultimum to the Regulation stating that "This Regulation is…" and including the full current title of the Regulation.
10. Introduction of review clauses in the article on entry into force.
11. Introduction of an Annex on Definitions.
12. Introduction of an Annex for Notes and Statement of the Commission, offering space for the pollical context of the Regulation, for references to relevant EU Acts, and miscellaneous topics.

The list is short. But radical in its conception.

Does it apply to Directives? Let us try it. And actually let us up the game. In this chapter the redrafted Regulation kept the whole content of each Article as it stood: this was just a light redraft. In the next chapter, let us redraft the Directive by transferring to each of the three Parts of the redrafted Directive not whole articles but paragraphs: this promises to be a heavier redraft. But of course the text of the Act will remain intact.

10. A transposition-led drafting style for Directives

Directive (EU) 2023/970 of the European Parliament and of the Council of 10 May 2023 to strengthen the application of the principle of equal pay for equal work or work of equal value between men and women through pay transparency and enforcement mechanisms[1] constitutes a representative sample of a recent Directive with an obvious social element. It tackles the issue of equal pay across genders and in that respect it is mainly addressed to EU citizens.

Identifying all the main key audiences of the Directive is quite straightforward. Chapter 4 identified the three user groups for EU Acts and analysed their characteristics.

Group 1 includes lay users of EU legislation, EU citizens, who may or may not have any topical or legal sophistication and reach out to the text to find answers to their everyday questions.

In this Directive, for example, Group 1 users are all EU citizens who want to find out how the principle of equal pay across genders can defend their employment rights. Possible questions can be, What protection is offered? What are my rights? What can I expect from my employer and what can I ask for? Who is covered by that protection: men, women, transgender, gender fluid, other categories of LGDPQI+? Where can I get justice if my rights are not respected?

This set of questions leads to the prioritised regulatory messages that the EU must offer to Group 1 users. And this guides as to the titles (and content) of Part 1 articles. What rights are offered? Who enjoys those rights? What if things go wrong? These are all questions detailing the added value of EU legislation and the EU as an organisation. If they are conveyed directly to EU citizens, they associate the rights and protection with the EU, rather than the intermediary Member State that implements the EU Act.

Group 2 users are Member States, mainly through the national authorities that must or may undertake the necessary steps to achieve the regulatory goals of the Directive. From their perspective the question is what must be done

1 See https://eur-lex.europa.eu/legal-content/EN/TXT/?toc=OJ%3AL%3A2023%3A132%3ATOC&uri=uriserv%3AOJ.L_.2023.132.01.0021.01.ENG accessed 15 December 2023.

and by which time? And what options and discretion do I have to increase the protection offered to EU citizens by means of the Directive?

If the EU switches to a user-centred drafting style, then Part 2 would include articles answering those questions. It may be beneficial to introduce the duties and powers of Member States in two separate lists. Duties can be listed together in one article, with a deadline attached to them. This can facilitate Member States in identifying the transposition task ahead, to ensure that all tasks are completed within the set deadline (internal verification of transposition legislation), and to inform the Commission that the list is ticked, and how. This is not a novel concept, transposition tables and checklists are old and tested tools for the scrutiny of transposition legislation. What is proposed is a focused and dry list of tasks that promotes an *a priori* mutual understanding of what needs to be done and by when. It can focus the mind of national authorities on a complete plan for the transposition task, it can reduce time and resources spent in identifying this plan by national drafters, and it can reduce the time and resources needed by the Commission to verify quality of transposition. A list, albeit long, is much more fit for purpose than pages long texts relevant or irrelevant to the transposition task. Moreover, a focused list of Member States' duties can indirectly instigate greater precision in the drafting of the EU Directive, and similarly in the planning and drafting of the national implementing measures.

A second article, or clusters of articles, in Part 2 can collect all powers for Member States. If minimum duties are set, are there options for national authorities to go beyond their duties and offer further protection? Here Member States can be offered transposition alternatives. Not in the form of a drafting guidance but in the form of possibilities that the EU suggests as possible ways forward. Often, currently, these can be found in Transposition Guidance. There is scope to include them in the body of the Directive as a means of making them binding in an exhaustive manner, thus preventing gold plating. And as a means of completing the regulatory package with satisfactory options for regulatory action at the national level, thus offering further control on the machinery used for joint regulatory efficacy. This can be a good place to acknowledge national diversities and proceed further with integration, where agreement for uniformity cannot be reached. The routes for additional regulatory action can be used to prepare the ground for further integration later on, when Member States will have implemented their chosen route from the ones suggested, thus reducing the regulatory position on the topic to two or more trends deriving from the suggestion in the Directive.

Group 3 of EU Directives tends to be EU institutions and relates to the mechanics of transposition. Powers and duties are already covered in Part 2. What remains here is monitoring and reporting, deadline for implementation, entry into force, and review clause. Along with an article on citation, as detailed in Chapter 9.

For Directives the recommendations on Regulations and their analysis in the previous chapter stands fully. In this chapter, focus will be placed in the layered structure of the Directive. This was hinted for Regulations as well, but it is precisely in Directives where the biggest possible impact can be had by a reform of structure and format.

As was the case in the previous chapter, the wording of the Directive will only be touched minimally. This is to focus the readers' mind on the drafting reforms proposed here rather than in a holistic reform of the EU's legislative expression. Not that this is not needed, especially for Group 1 in Part 1. But it can wait, for now.

Let us comment on the text of the Directive.

Table 10.1 Comments on the Directive

DIRECTIVE (EU) 2023/970 OF THE EUROPEAN PARLIAMENT AND OF THE COUNCIL of 10 May 2023 to strengthen the application of the principle of equal pay for equal work or work of equal value between men and women through pay transparency and enforcement mechanisms (Text with EEA relevance)	Comments The title is too long and user unfriendly. It is better to rid the title of legal content and maintain only the information needed by users to identify the topic and distinguish the Directive from Acts with similar topics.
	A table of contents can serve as a roadmap for users in navigating through the text. It is already available in the html version of the Directive on Eur Lex, and so it can be easily made available in the others versions of the text and in the OJ.
THE EUROPEAN PARLIAMENT AND THE COUNCIL OF THE EUROPEAN UNION,	
Having regard to the Treaty on the Functioning of the European Union, and in particular Article 157(3) thereof, Having regard to the proposal from the European Commission, After transmission of the draft legislative act to the national parliaments, Having regard to the opinion of the European Economic and Social Committee, Acting in accordance with the ordinary legislative procedure,	These are constitutional steps required for the legality of the Directive but they are not relevant to EU citizens. Plus, they take up part of the valuable time offered for the transmission of the real regulatory messages. They can form part of a Notes Annex.

Whereas:

'Whereas' is ambiguous, as it indicates antithesis. 'Considering that' seems accurate.

(1) Article 11 of the United Nations Convention of 18 December 1979 on the Elimination of All Forms of Discrimination against Women, which all Member States have ratified, provides that States Parties are to take all appropriate measures to ensure, inter alia, the right to equal remuneration, including benefits, and to equal treatment in respect of work of equal value, as well as equality of treatment in the evaluation of the quality of work.

(1) This is too generic and irrelevant for the user who only needs to identify the rationale behind the regulatory initiative that led to the Directive.

(2) Article 2 and Article 3(3) of the Treaty on European Union enshrine the right to equality between women and men as one of the essential values of the Union.

(2)–(5) Recitals 2–5 can be reduced to a single entry reassuring that equal pay across sexes is protected in EU law. The detailed list of provisions can form part of the Notes Annex.

(3) Articles 8 and 10 of the Treaty on the Functioning of the European Union (TFEU) require the Union to aim to eliminate inequalities, to promote equality between men and women and to combat discrimination based on sex in all its policies and activities.

(4) Article 157(1) TFEU obliges each Member State to ensure that the principle of equal pay for male and female workers for equal work or work of equal value is applied. Article 157(3) TFEU provides for the adoption by the Union of measures to ensure the application of the principle of equal opportunities and equal treatment of men and women in matters of employment and occupation, including the principle of equal pay for equal work or work of equal value (the 'principle of equal pay').

(5) The Court of Justice of the European Union (the 'Court of Justice') has held that the scope of the principle of equal treatment of men and women cannot be confined to discrimination based on the fact that a person is of one or other sex. In view of its purpose and the nature of the rights which it seeks to safeguard, that principle also applies to discrimination arising from gender reassignment.	
(6) In some Member States, it is currently possible for persons to legally register as having a third, often a neutral, gender. This Directive does not affect relevant national rules giving effect to such recognition as regards matters of employment and pay.	(6) This is an important regulatory message and must be provided for within the text.
(7) Article 21 of the Charter of Fundamental Rights of the European Union (the 'Charter') prohibits any discrimination, inter alia, on the grounds of sex. Article 23 of the Charter provides that equality between women and men must be ensured in all areas, including employment, work and pay.	(7)–(8) Recitals 7–8 can be transferred to the Notes Annex.
(8) Article 23 of the Universal Declaration of Human Rights states, inter alia, that everyone, without any discrimination, has the right to equal pay for equal work, to free choice of employment, to just and favourable conditions of work and to just remuneration ensuring an existence worthy of human dignity.	For the Notes Annex.
(9) The European Pillar of Social Rights, jointly proclaimed by the European Parliament, the Council, and the Commission, incorporates among its principles equality of treatment and opportunities between women and men, and the right to equal pay for work of equal value.	

(10) Directive 2006/54/EC of the European Parliament and of the Council provides that for the same work or for work to which equal value is attributed, direct and indirect discrimination on grounds of sex with regard to all aspects and conditions of remuneration is to be eliminated. In particular, where a job classification system is used for determining pay, it is to be based on the same gender-neutral criteria and should be drawn up so as to exclude any discrimination on grounds of sex.

(11) The 2020 evaluation of the relevant provisions of Directive 2006/54/EC found that the application of the principle of equal pay is hindered by a lack of transparency in pay systems, a lack of legal certainty on the concept of work of equal value, and by procedural obstacles faced by victims of discrimination. Workers lack the necessary information to make a successful equal pay claim and, in particular, information about the pay levels for categories of workers who perform the same work or work of equal value. The report found that increased transparency would allow revealing gender bias and discrimination in the pay structures of an undertaking or organisation. It would also enable workers, employers and the social partners to take appropriate action to ensure the application of the right to equal pay for equal work and work of equal value (the 'right to equal pay').

(11) This is the crux of the rationale for regulatory action. It constitutes the justification for it and sets the parameters of legislative effectiveness and regulatory efficacy for the Directive and the regulatory initiative respectively.

(12) Following a thorough evaluation of the existing framework on equal pay for equal work or work of equal value and a wide-ranging and inclusive consultation process, the Communication of the Commission of 5 March 2020 on 'A Union of Equality: Gender Equality Strategy 2020–2025' announced that the Commission would propose binding measures on pay transparency.

(12) For the Notes Annex.

(13) The economic and social consequences of the COVID-19 pandemic have had a disproportionately negative impact on women and gender equality, and job losses have often been concentrated in low-paid, female-dominated sectors. The COVID-19 pandemic has highlighted the continued, structural undervaluation of work predominantly carried out by women and has demonstrated the high socio-economic value of women's work in front-line services, such as health care, cleaning, childcare, social care and residential care for older people and other adult dependents, which stands in strong contrast to its low visibility and recognition.

(13) For the Notes Annex.

(14) The effects of the COVID-19 pandemic will therefore further widen gender inequalities and the gender pay gap unless the recovery response is gender sensitive. Those consequences have made it even more pressing to tackle the issue of equal pay for equal work or work of equal value. Strengthening the implementation of the principle of equal pay through further measures is particularly important to ensure that the progress which has been made in addressing disparities in pay is not compromised.

(14) That can stay.

(15) The Union gender pay gap persists: it stood at 13 per cent in 2020, with significant variations across Member States, and has decreased only minimally over the last ten years. The gender pay gap is caused by various factors, such as gender stereotypes, the perpetuation of the 'glass ceiling' and the 'sticky floor', horizontal segregation, including the overrepresentation of women in low-paid service jobs, and unequal sharing of care responsibilities. In addition, the gender pay gap is partly caused by direct and indirect gender-based pay discrimination. All those elements constitute structural obstacles that form complex challenges to achieving good quality jobs and equal pay for equal work or work of equal value and have long-term consequences such as a pension gap and the feminisation of poverty.

(15) This offers data that can be used in the objective article of the Directive: for example, to reduce the pay gap by 10 per cent over a period of three years.

(16) A general lack of transparency about pay levels within organisations maintains a situation where gender-based pay discrimination and bias can go undetected or, where suspected, are difficult to prove. Binding measures are therefore needed to improve pay transparency, encourage organisations to review their pay structures to ensure equal pay for women and men performing the same work or work of equal value, and to enable victims of discrimination to exercise their right to equal pay. Such binding measures need to be complemented by provisions clarifying existing legal concepts, such as the concepts of pay and work of equal value, and measures improving enforcement mechanisms and access to justice.

(16) This is self-evident and therefore unnecessary, although in a much-reduced form it could be added to the Notes Annex.

(17) The application of the principle of equal pay should be enhanced by eliminating direct and indirect pay discrimination. This does not preclude employers from paying workers performing the same work or work of equal value differently on the basis of objective, gender-neutral and bias-free criteria, such as performance and competence.

(17) This is self-evident and therefore unnecessary.

(18) This Directive should apply to all workers, including part-time workers, workers on a fixed-term contract and persons with a contract of employment or employment relationship with a temporary agency, as well as workers in management positions, who have an employment contract or employment relationship as defined by law, collective agreements and/or practice in force in each Member State, taking into account the case-law of the Court of Justice. Provided that they fulfil relevant criteria, domestic workers, on-demand workers, intermittent workers, voucher based-workers, platform workers, workers in sheltered employment, trainees and apprentices fall within the scope of this Directive. The determination of the existence of an employment relationship should be guided by the facts relating to the actual performance of the work and not by the parties' description of the relationship.

(18) This is a substantive provision that should be provided in the body of the Directive, without risky paraphrasis here.

(19) An important element of eliminating pay discrimination is pay transparency prior to employment. This Directive should therefore also apply to applicants for employment.

(19) The field of application of the Directive should be provided in the Directive without paraphrasis here.

(20) In order to remove obstacles for victims of gender-based pay discrimination to exercise their right to equal pay, and to guide employers in ensuring respect of that right, the core concepts related to equal pay for equal work or work of equal value, such as pay and work of equal value, should be clarified in accordance with the case-law of the Court of Justice. This should facilitate the application of those concepts, especially for micro, small and medium-sized enterprises.

(20) This is self-evident and therefore unnecessary.

(21) The principle of equal pay should be observed with regard to wages, salaries or any other consideration, whether in cash or in kind, which workers receive directly or indirectly, in respect of their employment from their employer. In accordance with the case-law of the Court of Justice, the concept of pay should comprise not only salary, but also complementary or variable components of the pay. Under complementary or variable components, any benefits in addition to the ordinary basic or minimum wage or salary, which the worker receives directly or indirectly, whether in cash or in kind, should be taken into account. Such complementary or variable components may include, but are not limited to, bonuses, overtime compensation, travel facilities, housing and food allowances, compensation for attending training, payments in the case of dismissal, statutory sick pay, statutory required compensation and occupational pensions. The concept of pay should include all elements of remuneration due under law, collective agreements and/or practice in each Member State.

(21) This constitutes the field of application of the Directive and should be provided in the Directive without risky paraphrasis here.

(22) In order to ensure a uniform presentation of the information required by this Directive, pay levels should be expressed as gross annual pay and the corresponding gross hourly pay. It should be possible to base the calculation of pay levels on the actual pay specified in regard to the worker, regardless of whether it is set annually, monthly, hourly or otherwise.

(22) This is a substantive provision to be included in the Directive, without paraphrasis here.

(23) Member States should not be obliged to set up new bodies for the purpose of this Directive. It should be possible for them to confer tasks deriving from it upon established bodies, including the social partners, in accordance with national law and/or practice, provided that the Member States comply with the obligations set out in this Directive.

(23) This is an option for Member States to be provided in the Powers article of the Directive.

(24) In order to protect workers and to address their fear of victimisation in the application of the principle of equal pay, they should be able to be represented by a representative. This could be trade unions or other workers' representatives. If there are no workers' representatives, workers should be able to be represented by a representative of their choice. Member States should have a possibility to take into account their national circumstances and different roles concerning workers' representation.

(24) This is a substantive provision for the Directive without paraphrasis here.

(25) Article 10 TFEU provides that, in defining and implementing its policies and activities, the Union is to aim to combat discrimination based on sex, racial or ethnic origin, religion or belief, disability, age or sexual orientation. Article 4 of Directive 2006/54/EC provides that there is to be no direct or indirect discrimination on grounds of sex in relation to pay. Gender-based pay discrimination where a victim's sex plays a crucial role can take many different forms in practice. It may involve an intersection of various axes of discrimination or inequality where the worker is a member of one or several groups protected against discrimination on the basis of sex, on the one hand, and racial or ethnic origin, religion or belief, disability, age or sexual orientation, as protected under Council Directive 2000/43/EC or 2000/78/EC, on the other.

Women with disabilities, women of diverse racial and ethnic origin including Roma women, and young or elderly women are among groups which may face intersectional discrimination. This Directive should therefore clarify that, in the context of gender-based pay discrimination, it should be possible to take such a combination into account, thus removing any doubt that may exist in this regard under the existing legal framework and enabling national courts, equality bodies and other competent authorities to take due account of any situation of disadvantage arising from intersectional discrimination, in particular for substantive and procedural purposes, including to recognise the existence of discrimination, to decide on the appropriate comparator, to assess the proportionality, and to determine, where relevant, the level of compensation awarded or penalties imposed.

(25) For the Notes Annex.

An intersectional approach is important for understanding and addressing the gender pay gap. This clarification should not change the scope of employers' obligations in regard to the pay transparency measures under this Directive. In particular, employers should not be required to gather data related to protected grounds other than sex.

(26) In order to respect the right to equal pay, employers must have pay structures in place ensuring that there are no gender-based pay differences between workers performing the same work or work of equal value that are not justified on the basis of objective, gender-neutral criteria. Such pay structures should allow for the comparison of the value of different jobs within the same organisational structure. It should be possible to base such pay structures on existing Union guidelines related to gender-neutral job evaluation and classification systems, or on indicators or gender-neutral models.

In accordance with the case law of the Court of Justice, the value of work should be assessed and compared on the basis of objective criteria, including educational, professional and training requirements, skills, effort, responsibility and working conditions, irrespective of differences in working patterns. To facilitate the application of the concept of work of equal value, especially for micro, small and medium-sized enterprises, the objective criteria to be used should include four factors: skills, effort, responsibility and working conditions. Those factors have been identified by the existing Union guidelines as being essential and sufficient for evaluating the tasks performed in an organisation regardless of to which economic sector the organisation belongs.

(26) This is self-evident and therefore unnecessary unless the drafter wants to provide for it in the Directive.

As not all factors are equally relevant for a specific position, each of the four factors should be weighed by the employer depending on the relevance of those criteria for the specific job or position concerned. Additional criteria may also be taken into account, where they are relevant and justified. Where appropriate, the Commission should be able to update existing Union guidelines, in consultation with the European Institute for Gender Equality (EIGE).

(27) National systems for wage-setting vary and can be based on collective agreements and/or elements decided by the employer. This Directive does not affect the various national systems for wage setting.

(27) For the Notes Annex.

(28) The identification of a valid comparator is an important parameter in determining whether work may be considered of equal value. It enables workers to show that they were treated less favourably than a comparator of a different sex performing equal work or work of equal value. Building on the developments brought by the definition of direct and indirect discrimination in Directive 2006/54/EC, in situations where no real-life comparator exists, the use of a hypothetical comparator should be allowed, to enable workers to show that they have not been treated in the same way as a hypothetical comparator of another sex would have been treated.

This would lift an important obstacle for potential victims of gender-based pay discrimination, especially in highly gender-segregated employment markets where a requirement of finding a comparator of the opposite sex makes it almost impossible to bring an equal pay claim.

(28) This is self-evident but can be included in the Notes Annex.

In addition, workers should not be prevented from using other facts from which an alleged discrimination can be presumed, such as statistics or other available information. This would allow gender-based pay inequalities to be more effectively addressed in gender-segregated sectors and professions, especially in female-dominated ones such as the care sector.

(29) The Court of Justice has clarified that in order to assess whether workers are in a comparable situation, the comparison is not necessarily limited to situations in which men and women work for the same employer. Workers may be in a comparable situation even when they do not work for the same employer whenever the pay conditions can be attributed to a single source establishing those conditions and where those conditions are equal and comparable.

This may be the case when the relevant pay conditions are regulated by statutory provisions or agreements relating to pay applicable to several employers, or when such conditions are laid down centrally for more than one organisation or business within a holding company or conglomerate.

Furthermore, the Court of Justice has clarified that the comparison is not limited to workers employed at the same time as the claimant. Additionally, when performing the actual assessment, it should be recognised that a difference in pay may be explained by factors unrelated to sex.

(29) For the Notes Annex.

(30) Member States should ensure that training and specific tools and methodologies are made available to support and guide employers in the assessment of what constitutes work of equal value. This should facilitate the application of that concept, especially for micro, small and medium-sized enterprises. Taking into account national law, collective agreements and/or practice, Member States should be able to entrust the development of specific tools and methodologies to the social partners or develop them in cooperation with, or after consulting, the social partners.	(30) This is a duty for Member States to be provided in the Directive, without paraphrasis here.
(31) Job classification and evaluation systems can, if not used in a gender-neutral manner, in particular when they assume traditional gender stereotypes, result in gender-based pay discrimination. In such cases, they contribute to and perpetuate the pay gap by evaluating male and female dominated jobs differently in situations where the work performed is of equal value. Where gender-neutral job evaluation and classification systems are used, however, they are effective in establishing a transparent pay system and are instrumental in ensuring that direct or indirect discrimination on grounds of sex is excluded. They detect indirect pay discrimination related to the undervaluation of jobs typically done by women. They do so by measuring and comparing jobs the content of which is different but of equal value and so support the principle of equal pay.	(31) Substantive provision.

(32) The lack of information on the envisaged pay range of a position creates an information asymmetry which limits the bargaining power of applicants for employment. Ensuring transparency should enable prospective workers to make an informed decision about the expected salary without limiting in any way the employer's or worker's bargaining power to negotiate a salary even outside the indicated range. Transparency would also ensure an explicit, non-gender-biased basis for pay setting and would disrupt the undervaluation of pay compared to skills and experience. Transparency would also address intersectional discrimination where non-transparent pay settings allow for discriminatory practices on several discrimination grounds.

Applicants for employment should receive information about the initial pay or its range in a manner such as to ensure an informed and transparent negotiation on pay, such as in a published job vacancy notice, prior to the job interview, or otherwise prior to the conclusion of any employment contract. The information should be provided by the employer or in a different manner, for instance by the social partners.

(32) To stay.

(33) In order to disrupt the perpetuation of the gender pay gap affecting individual workers over time, employers should ensure that job vacancy notices and job titles are gender neutral and that recruitment processes are led in a non-discriminatory manner, so as not to undermine the right to equal pay. Employers should not be allowed to enquire or proactively try to obtain information about the current pay or prior pay history of an applicant for employment.

(33) Duty to be provided in the Directive, without paraphrasis here.

(34) Pay transparency measures should protect workers' right to equal pay while limiting, to the extent possible, costs and administrative burden for employers, paying specific attention to micro, small and medium-sized enterprises. Where appropriate, measures should be tailored to the size of employers, taking into account employers' headcount. The number of workers employed by employers to be applied as a criterion whether an employer is subject to pay reporting as referred to in this Directive is set taking into account Commission Recommendation 2003/361/EC on micro, small and medium-sized enterprises.	(34) Substantive provision paraphrased here.
(35) Employers should make accessible to workers the criteria that are used to determine pay levels and pay progression. Pay progression refers to the process of how a worker moves to a higher pay level. Criteria related to pay progression can include, inter alia, individual performance, skills development and seniority. When implementing this obligation, Member States should pay particular attention to avoiding excessive administrative burden for micro and small enterprises. Member States should also be able to provide, as a mitigating measure, ready-made templates to support micro and small enterprises in complying with the obligation. Member States should be able to exempt employers which are micro or small enterprises from the obligation related to pay progression, for instance by allowing them to make the pay progression criteria available upon request by workers.	(35) Substantive provision paraphrased here.

(36) All workers should have the right to obtain information, upon their request, on their individual pay level and on the average pay levels, broken down by sex, for the category of workers performing the same work as them or work of equal value to theirs. They should also have the possibility to receive the information through workers' representatives or through an equality body. Employers should inform workers of that right on an annual basis, as well as of the steps to be undertaken in order to exercise the right. Employers may also, on their own initiative, opt to provide such information without workers needing to request it.

(36) Substantive provision paraphrased here.

(37) This Directive should ensure that persons with disabilities have adequate access to the information provided pursuant to it to applicants for employment and workers. Such information should be provided to those persons taking into account their particular disabilities, in a format and appropriate form of assistance and support to ensure their access to and comprehension of the information. This could include the provision of information in an understandable way which they can perceive, in fonts of adequate size, using sufficient contrast or other format appropriate to the type of their disability. Where relevant, Directive (EU) 2016/2102 of the European Parliament and of the Council applies.

(37) This is a task on the Directive. No need to have it here, drafter, just make it so!

(38) Employers with at least 100 workers should regularly report on pay, as provided for by this Directive. That information should be published by the Member States' monitoring bodies in a suitable and transparent manner. Employers may publish those reports on their website or make them publicly available in another manner, for instance by including the information in their management report, where applicable in the management report drawn up under Directive 2013/34/EU of the European Parliament and of the Council. Employers that are subject to the requirements of that Directive may choose to report on pay alongside other worker-related matters in their management report. To maximise the coverage of pay transparency of workers, Member States may increase the frequency of reporting or make regular reporting on pay mandatory for employers with fewer than 100 workers.	(38) Substantive provision paraphrased here.
(39) Pay reporting should allow employers to evaluate and monitor their pay structures and policies, allowing them to proactively comply with the principle of equal pay. Reporting and joint pay assessments contribute to an increased awareness of gender bias in pay structures and of pay discrimination and contribute to addressing such bias and discrimination in an effective and systemic way, thereby benefitting all workers employed by the same employer.	(39) Substantive provision paraphrased here.

At the same time, the sex-disaggregated data should assist competent public authorities, workers' representatives and other stakeholders in monitoring the gender pay gap across sectors (horizontal segregation) and functions (vertical segregation). Employers may wish to accompany the published data by an explanation of any gender pay differences or gaps. Where differences in average pay for the same work or work of equal value between female and male workers are not justified on the basis of objective, gender-neutral criteria, the employer should take measures to remove the inequalities.

(40) To reduce the burden on employers, Member States could gather and interlink the necessary data through their national administrations allowing for a computation of the pay gap between female and male workers per employer. Such data gathering may require interlinking data from several public administrations, such as tax inspectorates and social security offices, and would be possible if administrative data matching employers' data, at company or organisational level, to workers' data, at individual level, including benefits in cash and in kind, are available.

Member States could gather that information not only for employers that are covered by the pay reporting obligation under this Directive, but also for employers that are not covered by the obligation and that report voluntarily. The publication of the required information by Member States should replace the obligation of pay reporting on those employers covered by the administrative data provided that the result intended by the reporting obligation is achieved.

(40) Transposition guidance, to be provided for in the Directive.

(41) In order to make the information on the gender pay gap at organisational level widely available, Member States should entrust the monitoring body designated pursuant to this Directive to compile the data on the pay gap received from employers without putting an additional burden on the latter. The monitoring body should make those data public, including by publishing them on an easily accessible website, allowing comparison of the data of individual employers, sectors and regions of the Member State concerned.	(41) Substantive provision paraphrased here.
(42) Member States may acknowledge employers that are not subject to the reporting obligations set out in this Directive, which voluntarily report on their pay, for instance by means of a pay transparency label, with a view to promoting good practices in relation to the rights and obligations laid down in this Directive.	(42) Substantive provision paraphrased here.
(43) Joint pay assessments should trigger the review and revision of pay structures in organisations with at least 100 workers that show pay inequalities. The joint pay assessment should be carried out if employers and the workers' representatives concerned do not agree that the difference in average pay level between female and male workers of at least 5 per cent in a given category of workers can be justified on the basis of objective, gender-neutral criteria, if such a justification is not provided by the employer, or if the employer has not remedied such a difference in pay level within six months of the date of submission of the pay reporting.	(43) Substantive provision paraphrased here.

The joint pay assessment should be carried out by employers in cooperation with workers' representatives. If there are no workers' representatives, they should be designated by workers for the purpose of the joint pay assessment. Joint pay assessments should lead, within a reasonable period of time, to the elimination of gender-based pay discrimination through the adoption of remedial measures.

(44) Any processing or publication of information under this Directive should comply with Regulation (EU) 2016/679 of the European Parliament and of the Council. Specific safeguards should be added to prevent the direct or indirect disclosure of information of an identifiable worker. Workers should not be prevented from voluntarily disclosing their pay for the purpose of the enforcement of the principle of equal pay.

(44) Irrelevant here.

(45) It is important that the social partners discuss and pay particular attention to matters of equal pay in collective bargaining. The various features of national social dialogue and collective bargaining systems across the Union and the autonomy and contractual freedom of the social partners, as well as their capacity as representatives of workers and employers should be respected.

Therefore, Member States, in accordance with their national system and practices, should take appropriate measures to encourage the social partners to pay due attention to equal pay matters, which may include discussions at the appropriate level of collective bargaining, measures to stimulate and remove undue restrictions on the exercise of the right to collective bargaining related to the matters concerned and the development of gender-neutral job evaluation and classification systems.

(45) Substantive provision paraphrased here.

(46) All workers should have the necessary procedures at their disposal to facilitate the exercise of their right of access to justice. National legislation providing for the use of conciliation, or making the intervention of an equality body compulsory or subject to incentives or penalties should not prevent parties from exercising their right of access to the courts.	(46) Ok, then, provide the procedures. Unnecessary.
(47) Involving equality bodies, in addition to other stakeholders, is instrumental in effectively applying the principle of equal pay. The powers and mandates of the national equality bodies should therefore be adequate to fully cover gender-based pay discrimination, including any pay transparency or any other rights and obligations laid down in this Directive. In order to overcome the procedural and cost-related obstacles faced by workers who seek to exercise their right to equal pay, equality bodies, as well as associations, organisations and workers' representatives or other legal entities with an interest in ensuring equality between men and women should be able to represent individuals. They should be able to assist workers by acting on their behalf or in support of them, which would allow workers who have suffered discrimination to effectively institute a claim regarding the alleged infringement of their rights and the principle of equal pay.	(47) Irrelevant for the Directive.
(48) Bringing claims on behalf or in support of several workers is a way to facilitate proceedings that would not otherwise have been brought because of procedural and financial barriers or a fear of victimisation. It is also facilitative when workers are facing discrimination on multiple grounds which can be difficult to disentangle.	(48) Irrelevant.

Collective claims have the potential to uncover systemic discrimination and create visibility of the right to equal pay and of gender equality in society as a whole. The possibility of collective redress could motivate pro-active compliance with pay transparency measures, creating peer pressure, increasing employers' awareness and willingness to act preventively, and addressing the systemic nature of pay discrimination.

Member States may decide to set qualification criteria for representatives of workers in court proceedings relating to equal pay claims, in order to ensure that such representatives are adequately qualified.

(49) Member States should ensure the allocation of sufficient resources to equality bodies for the effective and adequate performance of their tasks related to pay discrimination based on sex. Where the tasks are allocated to more than one body, Member States should ensure that they are adequately coordinated. This includes, for instance, allocating amounts recovered as fines to the equality bodies for the purpose of effectively carrying out their functions in regard to the enforcement of the right to equal pay, including bringing pay discrimination claims or assisting and supporting victims in bringing such claims.

(49) Substantive provision paraphrased here.

(50) Compensation should cover in full the loss and damage sustained as a result of gender-based pay discrimination in accordance with the case-law of the Court of Justice. It should include full recovery of back pay and related bonuses or payments in kind, as well as compensation for lost opportunities, such as access to certain benefits depending on pay level, and for non-material damage, such as distress because of the undervaluation of work performed. Where appropriate, the compensation can take into account damage caused by pay discrimination based on sex that intersects with other protected grounds of discrimination. Member States should not fix a prior upper limit for such compensation.	(50) Substantive provision paraphrased here.
(51) In addition to compensation, other remedies should be provided for. Competent authorities or national courts should, for instance, be able to require an employer to take structural or organisational measures to comply with its obligations regarding equal pay. Such measures may include, for instance, an obligation to review the pay setting mechanism based on a gender-neutral evaluation and classification; to set up an action plan to eliminate the discrepancies discovered and to reduce any unjustified gaps in pay; to provide information and raise workers' awareness of their right to equal pay; and to establish a mandatory training for human resources staff on equal pay and gender-neutral job evaluation and classification.	(51) Substantive provision paraphrased here.

(52) In accordance with the case law of the Court of Justice, Directive 2006/54/EC establishes provisions to ensure that the burden of proof shifts to the respondent when there is a prima facie case of discrimination. Nevertheless, it is not always easy for victims and courts to know how to establish even that presumption. In case C-109/88, the Court of Justice held that when a system of pay is totally lacking in transparency, the burden of proof should be shifted to the respondent, irrespective of the worker showing a prima facie case of pay discrimination.

Accordingly, the burden of proof should be shifted to the respondent where an employer does not comply with the pay transparency obligations set out in this Directive, for instance by refusing to provide information requested by the workers or not reporting on the gender pay gap, where relevant, save where the employer proves that such an infringement was manifestly unintentional and of a minor character.

(52) For the Notes Annex.

(53) In accordance with the case law of the Court of Justice, national rules on limitation periods relating to the bringing of claims regarding alleged infringements of the rights provided for in this Directive should be such that they do not render virtually impossible or excessively difficult the exercise of those rights. Limitation periods create specific obstacles for victims of gender-based pay discrimination. For that purpose, common minimum standards should be established.

(53) For the Notes Annex.

Those standards should determine when the limitation period begins to run, the duration thereof and the circumstances under which it is suspended or interrupted, and should provide that the limitation period for bringing claims is at least three years. Limitation periods should not begin to run before the claimant is aware, or can reasonably be expected to be aware, of the infringement. Member States should be able to decide that the limitation period does not begin to run while the infringement is ongoing or before the end of the employment contract or employment relationship.

(54) Litigation costs create a serious disincentive for victims of gender-based pay discrimination to bring claims regarding alleged infringements of their right to equal pay, leading to the insufficient protection of workers and the insufficient enforcement of the right to equal pay. In order to remove that significant procedural obstacle to justice, Member States should ensure that national courts can assess whether an unsuccessful claimant had reasonable grounds for bringing the claim and, if so, whether that claimant should not be required to pay the costs of the proceedings. This should in particular apply where a successful respondent has not complied with the pay transparency obligations set out in this Directive.

(54) Substantive provision paraphrased here.

(55) Member States should provide for effective, proportionate and dissuasive penalties in the event of infringements of national provisions adopted pursuant to this Directive or national provisions that are already in force on the date of entry into force of this Directive and that relate to the right to equal pay. Such penalties should include fines which could be based on the employer's gross annual turnover or on the employer's total payroll. Any other aggravating or mitigating factors that may apply in the circumstances of the case, for instance, where pay discrimination based on sex is combined with other protected grounds of discrimination should be taken into account. It is for the Member States to determine the infringements of the rights and obligations relating to equal pay for equal work or work of equal value for which fines are the most appropriate penalty.	(55) Substantive provision paraphrased here.
(56) Member States should establish specific penalties for repeated infringements of any right or obligation relating to equal pay between men and women for the same work or work of equal value, to reflect the severity of the infringement and to further deter such infringements. Such penalties could include different types of financial disincentives such as the revocation of public benefits or the exclusion, for a certain period of time, from any further award of financial inducements or from any public tender procedure.	(56) Substantive provision paraphrased here.
(57) Obligations on employers stemming from this Directive are part of the applicable obligations in the fields of environmental, social and labour law compliance with which Member States have to ensure under Directives 2014/23/EU, 2014/24/EU and 2014/25/EU of the European Parliament and of the Council in regard to participation in public procurement procedures.	(57) Substantive provision paraphrased here.

In order to comply with those obligations on employers as far as the right to equal pay is concerned, Member States should in particular ensure that economic operators, in the performance of a public contract or concession, have pay setting mechanisms that do not lead to a gender pay gap between workers in any category of workers performing equal work or work of equal value that cannot be justified on the basis of gender-neutral criteria. In addition, Member States should consider requiring contracting authorities to introduce, as appropriate, penalties and termination conditions ensuring compliance with the principle of equal pay in the performance of public contracts and concessions. Contracting authorities should also be able to take into account non-compliance with the principle of equal pay by the bidder or one of the bidder's subcontractors when considering the application of exclusion grounds or when taking a decision not to award a contract to the tenderer submitting the most economically advantageous tender.	
(58) The effective implementation of the right to equal pay requires adequate administrative and court protection against any adverse treatment as a reaction to an attempt by workers to exercise that right, to any complaint to the employer or to any administrative procedure or court proceedings aiming to enforce compliance with that right. According to the case-law of the Court of Justice the category of employees who are entitled to the protection should be interpreted broadly and include all employees who may be subject to retaliatory measures taken by an employer in response to a complaint of discrimination on grounds of sex.	(58) For the Notes Annex.

The protection is not limited solely to employees who have lodged complaints or their representatives, or to those who comply with certain formal requirements governing the recognition of a certain status, such as that of a witness.

(59) In order to improve the enforcement of the principle of equal pay, this Directive should strengthen the existing enforcement tools and procedures in regard to the rights and obligations laid down in this Directive and the equal pay provisions set out in Directive 2006/54/EC.

(59) Well, drafter, make it so! No need to wish it here.

(60) This Directive lays down minimum requirements, thus respecting the Member States' prerogative to introduce and maintain provisions that are more favourable to workers. Rights acquired under the existing legal framework should continue to apply, unless provisions that are more favourable to workers are introduced by this Directive. The implementation of this Directive cannot be used to reduce existing rights set out in existing Union or national law in this field, nor can it constitute valid grounds for reducing the rights of workers in regard to the principle of equal pay.

(60) Excellent point.

(61) In order to ensure proper monitoring of the implementation of the right to equal pay, Member States should set up or designate a dedicated monitoring body. That body, which should be able to be part of an existing body pursuing similar objectives, should have specific tasks in relation to the implementation of the pay transparency measures provided for in this Directive and gather certain data to monitor pay inequalities and the impact of the pay transparency measures. Member States should be able to designate more than one body, provided that the monitoring and analysis functions set out in this Directive are ensured by a central body.

(61) Substantive provision paraphrased here.

(62) Compiling wage statistics broken down by sex and providing the Commission (Eurostat) with accurate and complete statistics is essential for analysing and monitoring changes in the gender pay gap at Union level. Council Regulation (EC) No 530/1999 requires Member States to compile four-yearly structural earnings statistics at micro level, which provide harmonised data for the calculation of the gender pay gap. Annual high-quality statistics could increase transparency and enhance monitoring and awareness of gender pay inequality. The availability and comparability of such data is instrumental for assessing developments both at national level and throughout the Union. Relevant statistics transmitted to the Commission (Eurostat) should be collected for statistical purposes within the meaning of Regulation (EC) No 223/2009 of the European Parliament and of the Council.	(62) Irrelevant here, perhaps for the Notes Annex.
(63) Since the objectives of this Directive, namely a better and more effective application of the principle of equal pay through the establishment of common minimum requirements which should apply to all undertakings and organisations across the Union, cannot be sufficiently achieved by the Member States but can rather, by reason of their scale and effects, be better achieved at Union level, the Union may adopt measures, in accordance with the principle of subsidiarity as set out in Article 5 of the Treaty on European Union. In accordance with the principle of proportionality as set out in that Article, this Directive, which limits itself to setting minimum standards, does not go beyond what is necessary in order to achieve those objectives.	(63) Excellent point on necessity and subsidiarity.

(64) The role of the social partners is of key importance in designing the way pay transparency measures are implemented in Member States, especially in those with high collective bargaining coverage. Member States should therefore have the possibility to entrust the social partners with the implementation of all or part of this Directive, provided that Member States take all the necessary steps to ensure that the results sought by this Directive are guaranteed at all times.	(64) Wish list not relevant within the Directive.
(65) In implementing this Directive, Member States should avoid imposing administrative, financial and legal constraints in a way which would hold back the creation and development of micro, small or medium-sized enterprises. Member States should therefore assess the impact of their transposition measures on micro, small and medium-sized enterprises in order to ensure that those enterprises are not disproportionately affected, giving specific attention to microenterprises, to alleviate the administrative burden, and to publish the results of such assessments.	(65) This is an existing obligation, so it not necessary to repeat it here.
(66) The European Data Protection Supervisor was consulted in accordance with Article 42 of Regulation (EU) 2018/1725 of the European Parliament and of the Council and delivered an opinion on 27 April 2021,	(66) For the Notes Annex or perhaps under 'whereas'.
HAVE ADOPTED THIS DIRECTIVE:	Excellent enacting clause
CHAPTER I GENERAL PROVISIONS	The Directive fails to introduce its regulatory objectives with measurable criteria for legislative effectiveness.

Article 1 **Subject matter** This Directive lays down minimum requirements to strengthen the application of the principle of equal pay for equal work or work of equal value between men and women (the 'principle of equal pay') enshrined in Article 157 TFEU and the prohibition of discrimination laid down in Article 4 of Directive 2006/54/EC, in particular through pay transparency and reinforced enforcement mechanisms.	The Article is vague: it fails to state what rights are introduced and what measures are imposed on Member States for the achievement of the objectives of the Directive.
Article 2 **Scope** 1. This Directive applies to employers in public and private sectors. 2. This Directive applies to all workers who have an employment contract or employment relationship as defined by law, collective agreements and/or practice in force in each Member State with consideration to the case law of the Court of Justice. 3. For the purposes of Article 5, this Directive applies to applicants for employment.	Although this is expressed as an application provision, which is a solid choice for a legal text, a user-centred text would include it in the first substantive Article for to Group 1 in the form of : If you are…., you now have the right to….
Article 3 **Definitions** 1. For the purposes of this Directive, the following definitions apply:	To be placed in a Definitions Annex with a hanging provision within the Directive. In this Directive, not for the purposes
(a) 'pay' means the ordinary basic or minimum wage or salary and any other consideration, whether in cash or in kind, which a worker receives directly or indirectly (complementary or variable components) in respect of his or her employment from his or her employer;	(a) This is not a useful definition as it does not extend or delimit the term.
(b) 'pay level' means gross annual pay and the corresponding gross hourly pay;	(b) This is a wrong definition: what is defined is not pay level, which can only be the amount of remuneration offered for employment.

(c) 'gender pay gap' means the difference in average pay levels between female and male workers of an employer expressed as a percentage of the average pay level of male workers;	(c) Self-evident, unnecessary.
(d) 'median pay level' means the pay level at which half of the workers of an employer earn more and half of them earn less;	(d) Self-evident, unnecessary.
(e) 'median gender pay gap' means the difference between the median pay level of female and median pay level of male workers of an employer expressed as a percentage of the median pay level of male workers;	(e) Unnecessary.
(f) 'quartile pay band' means each of four equal groups of workers into which they are divided according to their pay levels, from the lowest to the highest;	
(g) 'work of equal value' means work that is determined to be of equal value in accordance with the non-discriminatory and objective gender-neutral criteria referred to in Article 4(4);	(g) This is a cyclical definition.
(h) 'category of workers' means workers performing the same work or work of equal value grouped in a non-arbitrary manner based on the non-discriminatory and objective gender-neutral criteria referred to in Article 4(4), by the workers' employer and, where applicable, in cooperation with the workers' representatives in accordance with national law and/or practice.	(h) This is an erroneous definition because it departs fully from the ordinary meaning of the term.
(i) 'direct discrimination' means the situation in which one person is treated less favourably on grounds of sex than another person is, has been or would be treated in a comparable situation;	(i) Unnecessary.

(j) 'indirect discrimination' means the situation in which an apparently neutral provision, criterion or practice would put persons of one sex at a particular disadvantage compared with persons of the other sex, unless that provision, criterion or practice is objectively justified on the basis of a legitimate aim, and the means of achieving that aim are appropriate and necessary;	
(k) 'labour inspectorate' means the body or bodies responsible, in accordance with national law and/or practice, for control and inspection functions in the labour market, save that, where provided for in national law, the social partners may carry out those functions;	
(l) 'equality body' means the body or bodies designated pursuant to Article 20 of Directive 2006/54/EC;	
(m) 'workers' representatives' means the workers' representatives in accordance with national law and/or practice.	(m) Unnecessary.
2. For the purposes of this Directive, discrimination includes:	In this Directive (for the purposes invites teleological interpretation) 2 is not a definition, it is substantive provision that must be included in the body of the Act.
(a) harassment and sexual harassment, within the meaning of Article 2(2), point (a), of Directive 2006/54/EC, as well as any less favourable treatment based on a person's rejection of, or submission to, such conduct, when such harassment or treatment relates to or results from the exercise of the rights provided for in this Directive;	
(b) any instruction to discriminate against persons on grounds of sex;	
(c) any less favourable treatment related to pregnancy or maternity leave within the meaning of Council Directive 92/85/EEC (24);y	

(d) any less favourable treatment, within the meaning of Directive (EU) 2019/1158 of the European Parliament and of the Council (25),z based on sex, including with regard to paternity leave, parental leave or carers' leave;	
(e) intersectional discrimination, which is discrimination based on a combination of sex and any other ground or grounds of discrimination protected under Directive 2000/43/EC or 2000/78/EC.	
3. Paragraph 2, point (e), shall not entail additional obligations on employers to gather data as referred to in this Directive with regard to protected grounds of discrimination other than sex.	3. This is not a definition.

Article 4

Equal work and work of equal value

1. Member States shall take the necessary measures to ensure that employers have pay structures ensuring equal pay for equal work or work of equal value.	Part B
2. Member States shall, in consultation with equality bodies, take the necessary measures to ensure that analytical tools or methodologies are made available and are easily accessible to support and guide the assessment and comparison of the value of work in accordance with the criteria set out in this Article. Those tools or methodologies shall allow employers and/or the social partners to easily establish and use gender-neutral job evaluation and classification systems that exclude any pay discrimination on grounds of sex.	Part B
3. Where appropriate, the Commission may update Union-wide guidelines related to gender-neutral job evaluation and classification systems, in consultation with the European Institute for Gender Equality (EIGE).	Part C

4. Pay structures shall be such as to enable the assessment of whether workers are in a comparable situation in regard to the value of work on the basis of objective, gender-neutral criteria agreed with workers' representatives where such representatives exist. Those criteria shall not be based directly or indirectly on workers' sex. They shall include skills, effort, responsibility and working conditions, and, if appropriate, any other factors which are relevant to the specific job or position. They shall be applied in an objective gender-neutral manner, excluding any direct or indirect discrimination based on sex. In particular, relevant soft skills shall not be undervalued. — Part C

CHAPTER II — Part A

PAY TRANSPARENCY

Article 5

Pay transparency prior to employment

1. Applicants for employment shall have the right to receive, from the prospective employer, information about:
   (a) the initial pay or its range, based on objective, gender-neutral criteria, to be attributed for the position concerned; and
   (b) where applicable, the relevant provisions of the collective agreement applied by the employer in relation to the position.

   Such information shall be provided in a manner such as to ensure an informed and transparent negotiation on pay, such as in a published job vacancy notice, prior to the job interview or otherwise.
2. An employer shall not ask applicants about their pay history during their current or previous employment relationships.

3. Employers shall ensure that job vacancy notices and job titles are gender-neutral and that recruitment processes are led in a non-discriminatory manner, in order not to undermine the right to equal pay for equal work or work of equal value (the 'right to equal pay').

Article 6

Transparency of pay setting and pay progression policy

1. Employers shall make easily accessible to their workers the criteria that are used to determine workers' pay, pay levels and pay progression. Those criteria shall be objective and gender neutral. Part A
2. Member States may exempt employers with fewer than 50 workers from the obligation related to the pay progression set out in paragraph 1. Part B

Article 7

Right to information

1. Workers shall have the right to request and receive in writing, in accordance with paragraphs 2 and 4, information on their individual pay level and the average pay levels, broken down by sex, for categories of workers performing the same work as them or work of equal value to theirs. Part A
2. Workers shall have the possibility to request and receive the information referred to in paragraph 1 through their workers' representatives, in accordance with national law and/or practice. They shall also have the possibility to request and receive the information through an equality body. Part A

If the information received is inaccurate or incomplete, workers shall have the right to request, personally or through their workers' representatives, additional and reasonable clarifications and details regarding any of the data provided and receive a substantiated reply.	
3. Employers shall inform all workers, on an annual basis, of their right to receive the information referred to in paragraph 1 and of the steps that the worker is to undertake to exercise that right.	Part A
4. Employers shall provide the information referred to in paragraph 1 within a reasonable period of time but in any event within two months from the date on which the request is made.	Part A
5. Workers shall not be prevented from disclosing their pay for the purpose of the enforcement of the principle of equal pay. In particular, Member States shall put in place measures to prohibit contractual terms that restrict workers from disclosing information about their pay.	Part A
6. Employers may require workers who have obtained information pursuant to this Article, other than information concerning their own pay or pay level, not to use that information for any purpose other than to exercise their right to equal pay.	Part A
Article 8	
Accessibility of information	
Employers shall provide any information shared with workers or applicants for employment pursuant to Articles 5, 6 and 7 in a format which is accessible to persons with disabilities and which takes into account their particular needs.	Part A
Article 9	
Reporting on pay gap between female and male workers	

Part B

1. Member States shall ensure that employers provide the following information concerning their organisation, in accordance with this Article:
   (a) the gender pay gap;
   (b) the gender pay gap in complementary or variable components;
   (c) the median gender pay gap;
   (d) the median gender pay gap in complementary or variable components;
   (e) the proportion of female and male workers receiving complementary or variable components;
   (f) the proportion of female and male workers in each quartile pay band;
   (g) the gender pay gap between workers by categories of workers broken down by ordinary basic wage or salary and complementary or variable components.
2. Employers with 250 workers or more shall, by 7 June 2027 and every year thereafter, provide the information set out in paragraph 1 relating to the previous calendar year.
3. Employers with 150 to 249 workers shall, by 7 June 2027 and every three years thereafter, provide the information set out in paragraph 1 relating to the previous calendar year.
4. Employers with 100 to 149 workers shall, by 7 June 2031 and every three years thereafter, provide the information set out in paragraph 1 relating to the previous calendar year.
5. Member States shall not prevent employers with fewer than 100 workers from providing the information set out in paragraph 1 on a voluntary basis. Member States may, as a matter of national law, require employers with fewer than 100 workers to provide information on pay.

6. The accuracy of the information shall be confirmed by the employer's management, after consulting workers' representatives. Workers' representatives shall have access to the methodologies applied by the employer.	Part A
7. The information referred to in paragraph 1, points (a) to (g), of this Article shall be communicated to the authority in charge of compiling and publishing such data pursuant to Article 29(3), point (c). The employer may publish the information referred to in paragraph 1, points (a) to (f), of this Article on its website or make it publicly available in another manner.	
8. Member States may compile the information set out in paragraph 1, points (a) to (f), of this Article themselves, on the basis of administrative data such as data provided by employers to the tax or social security authorities. The information shall be made public pursuant to Article 29(3), point (c).	Part B
9. Employers shall provide the information referred to in paragraph 1, point (g), to all their workers and to the workers' representatives of their workers. Employers shall provide the information to the labour inspectorate and the equality body upon request. The information from the previous four years, if available, shall also be provided upon request.	Part A

10. Workers, workers' representatives, labour inspectorates and equality bodies shall have the right to ask employers for additional clarifications and details regarding any of the data provided, including explanations concerning any gender pay differences. Employers shall respond to such requests within a reasonable time by providing a substantiated reply. Where gender pay differences are not justified on the basis of objective, gender-neutral criteria, employers shall remedy the situation within a reasonable period of time in close cooperation with workers' representatives, the labour inspectorate and/or the equality body.

Article 10

Joint pay assessment

1. Member States shall take appropriate measures to ensure that employers who are subject to pay reporting pursuant to Article 9 conduct, in cooperation with their workers' representatives, a joint pay assessment where all the following conditions are met: Part B

   (a) the pay reporting demonstrates a difference in the average pay level between female and male workers of at least 5 per cent in any category of workers;

   (b) the employer has not justified such a difference in the average pay level on the basis of objective, gender-neutral criteria;

   (c) the employer has not remedied such an unjustified difference in the average pay level within six months of the date of submission of the pay reporting.

2. The joint pay assessment shall be carried out in order to identify, remedy and prevent differences in pay between female and male workers which are not justified on the basis of objective, gender-neutral criteria, and shall include the following: Part B

(a) an analysis of the proportion of female and male workers in each category of workers;

(b) information on average female and male workers' pay levels and complementary or variable components for each category of workers;

(c) any differences in average pay levels between female and male workers in each category of workers;

(d) the reasons for such differences in average pay levels, on the basis of objective, gender-neutral criteria, if any, as established jointly by the workers' representatives and the employer;

(e) the proportion of female and male workers who benefited from any improvement in pay following their return from maternity or paternity leave, parental leave or carers' leave, if such improvement occurred in the relevant category of workers during the period in which the leave was taken;

(f) measures to address differences in pay if they are not justified on the basis of objective, gender-neutral criteria;

(g) an evaluation of the effectiveness of measures from previous joint pay assessments.

3. Employers shall make the joint pay assessment available to workers and workers' representatives and shall communicate it to the monitoring body pursuant to Article 29(3), point (d). They shall make it available to the labour inspectorate and the equality body upon request.	Part A

4. When implementing the measures arising from the joint pay assessment, the employer shall remedy the unjustified differences in pay within a reasonable period of time, in close cooperation, in accordance with national law and/or practice, with the workers' representatives. The labour inspectorate and/or the equality body may be asked to participate in the process. The implementation of the measures shall include an analysis of the existing gender-neutral job evaluation and classification systems or the establishment of such systems, to ensure that any direct or indirect pay discrimination on the grounds of sex is excluded. — Part A

Article 11 — Part B

Support for employers with fewer than 250 workers

Member States shall provide support, in the form of technical assistance and training, to employers with fewer than 250 workers and to the workers' representatives concerned, to facilitate their compliance with the obligations laid down in this Directive.

Article 12

Data protection

1. To the extent that any information provided pursuant to measures taken under Articles 7, 9, and 10 involves the processing of personal data, it shall be provided in accordance with Regulation (EU) 2016/679. — Part A
2. Any personal data processed pursuant to Articles 7, 9 or 10 of this Directive shall not be used for any purpose other than for the application of the principle of equal pay.

3. Member States may decide that, where the disclosure of information pursuant to Articles 7, 9 and 10 would lead to the disclosure, either directly or indirectly, of the pay of an identifiable worker, only the workers' representatives, the labour inspectorate or the equality body shall have access to that information. The workers' representatives or the equality body shall advise workers regarding a possible claim under this Directive without disclosing actual pay levels of individual workers performing the same work or work of equal value. For the purposes of monitoring pursuant to Article 29, the information shall be made available without restriction.	Part B
Article 13 **Social dialogue** Without prejudice to the autonomy of the social partners and in accordance with national law and practice, Member States shall take adequate measures to ensure the effective involvement of the social partners, by means of discussing the rights and obligations laid down in this Directive, where applicable upon their request. Member States shall, without prejudice to the autonomy of the social partners and taking into account the diversity of national practices, take adequate measures to promote the role of the social partners and encourage the exercise of the right to collective bargaining on measures to tackle pay discrimination and its adverse impact on the valuation of jobs predominantly carried out by workers of one sex.	Part B
CHAPTER III REMEDIES AND ENFORCEMENT	
Article 14 **Defence of rights**	Part B

Member States shall ensure that, after possible recourse to conciliation, court proceedings for the enforcement of rights and obligations relating to the principle of equal pay are available to all workers who consider themselves wronged by a failure to apply the principle of equal pay. Such proceedings shall be easily accessible to workers and to persons who act on their behalf, even after the end of the employment relationship in which the discrimination is alleged to have occurred.

Article 15 — Part B

Procedures on behalf or in support of workers

Member States shall ensure that associations, organisations, equality bodies and workers' representatives or other legal entities which have, in accordance with criteria laid down in national law, a legitimate interest in ensuring equality between men and women, may engage in any administrative procedure or court proceedings regarding an alleged infringement of the rights or obligations relating to the principle of equal pay. They may act on behalf of, or in support of, a worker who is an alleged victim of an infringement of any right or obligation relating to the principle of equal pay, with that person's approval.

Article 16

Right to compensation

1. Member States shall ensure that any worker who has sustained damage as a result of an infringement of any right or obligation relating to the principle of equal pay has the right to claim and to obtain full compensation or reparation, as determined by the Member State, for that damage. — Part B
2. The compensation or reparation referred to in paragraph 1 shall constitute real and effective compensation or reparation, as determined by the Member State, for the loss and damage sustained, in a dissuasive and proportionate manner. — Part A

3. The compensation or reparation shall place the worker who has sustained damage in the position in which that person would have been if he or she had not been discriminated against based on sex or if there had been no infringement of any of the rights or obligations relating to the principle of equal pay. Member States shall ensure that the compensation or reparation includes full recovery of back pay and related bonuses or payments in kind, compensation for lost opportunities, non-material damage, any damage caused by other relevant factors which may include intersectional discrimination, as well as interest on arrears.	Part C
4. The compensation or reparation shall not be restricted by the fixing of a prior upper limit.	Part C

Article 17

Other remedies

1. Member States shall ensure that, in the case of an infringement of rights or obligations related to the principle of equal pay, competent authorities or national courts may, in accordance with national law, at the request of the claimant and at the expense of the respondent, issue:
   (a) an order to stop the infringement;
   (b) an order to take measures to ensure that the rights or obligations related to the principle of equal pay are applied.
2. Where a respondent does not comply with any order issued pursuant to paragraph 1, Member States shall ensure that their competent authorities or national courts are able, where appropriate, to issue a recurring penalty payment order, with a view to ensuring compliance.

Article 18

Shift of burden of proof

Part A

1. Member States shall take the appropriate measures, in accordance with their national judicial systems, to ensure that, when workers who consider themselves wronged because the principle of equal pay has not been applied to them establish before a competent authority or national court facts from which it may be presumed that there has been direct or indirect discrimination, it shall be for the respondent to prove that there has been no direct or indirect discrimination in relation to pay.
2. Member States shall ensure that, in administrative procedures or court proceedings regarding alleged direct or indirect discrimination in relation to pay, where an employer has not implemented the pay transparency obligations set out in Articles 5, 6, 7, 9 and 10, it is for the employer to prove that there has been no such discrimination.

   The first subparagraph of this paragraph shall not apply where the employer proves that the infringement of the obligations set out in Articles 5, 6, 7, 9 and 10 was manifestly unintentional and of a minor character.
3. This Directive shall not prevent Member States from introducing evidential rules which are more favourable to a worker who institutes an administrative procedure or court proceedings regarding an alleged infringement of any of the rights or obligations relating to the principle of equal pay.
4. Member States need not apply paragraph 1 to procedures and proceedings in which it is for the competent authority or the national court to investigate the facts of the case.
5. This Article shall not apply to criminal proceedings, unless national law provides otherwise.

Article 19

Proof of equal work or work of equal value

1. When assessing whether female and male workers are carrying out the same work or work of equal value, the assessment of whether workers are in a comparable situation shall not be limited to situations in which female and male workers work for the same employer, but shall be extended to a single source establishing the pay conditions. A single source shall exist where it stipulates the elements of pay relevant for the comparison of workers. Part C
2. The assessment of whether workers are in a comparable situation shall not be limited to workers who are employed at the same time as the worker concerned.
3. Where no real comparator can be established, any other evidence may be used to prove alleged pay discrimination, including statistics or a comparison of how a worker would be treated in a comparable situation.

Article 20 Part A

Access to evidence

1. Member States shall ensure that in proceedings concerning an equal pay claim, competent authorities or national courts are able to order the respondent to disclose any relevant evidence which lies in the respondent's control, in accordance with national law and practice. Part B
2. Member States shall ensure that competent authorities or national courts have the power to order the disclosure of evidence containing confidential information where they consider it relevant to the equal pay claim. Member States shall ensure that, when ordering the disclosure of such information, competent authorities or national courts have at their disposal effective measures to protect such information, in accordance with national procedural rules.

3. This Article shall not prevent Member States from maintaining or introducing rules which are more favourable to claimants.

Article 21

Limitation periods

1. Member States shall ensure that national rules applicable to limitation periods for bringing equal pay claims determine when such periods begin to run, the duration thereof and the circumstances under which they may be suspended or interrupted. The limitation periods shall not begin to run before the claimant is aware, or can reasonably be expected to be aware, of an infringement. Member States may decide that limitation periods do not begin to run while the infringement is ongoing or before the end of the employment contract or employment relationship. Such limitation periods shall be no shorter than three years. Part B
2. Member States shall ensure that a limitation period is suspended or, depending on national law, interrupted, as soon as a claimant undertakes action by bringing a complaint to the attention of the employer or by instituting proceedings before a court, directly or through the workers' representatives, the labour inspectorate or the equality body.
3. This Article does not apply to rules on the expiry of claims. Part C

Article 22 **Legal costs** Member States shall ensure that, where a respondent is successful in proceedings relating to a pay discrimination claim, national courts can assess, in accordance with national law, whether the unsuccessful claimant had reasonable grounds for bringing the claim and, if so, whether it is appropriate not to require that claimant to pay the costs of the proceedings.	Part B
Article 23 **Penalties**	
1. Member States shall lay down the rules on effective, proportionate and dissuasive penalties applicable to infringements of the rights and obligations relating to the principle of equal pay. Member States shall take all measures necessary to ensure that those rules are implemented and shall, without delay, notify the Commission of those rules and of those measures and of any subsequent amendment affecting them.	Part B
2. Member States shall ensure that the penalties referred to in paragraph 1 guarantee a real deterrent effect with regard to infringements of the rights and obligations relating to the principle of equal pay. Those penalties shall include fines, the setting of which shall be based on national law.	
3. The penalties referred to in paragraph 1 shall take into account any relevant aggravating or mitigating factor applicable to the circumstances of the infringement, which may include intersectional discrimination.	
4. Member States shall ensure that specific penalties apply in the case of repeated infringements of the rights and obligations relating to the principle of equal pay.	
5. Member States shall take all measures necessary to ensure that the penalties provided for pursuant to this Article are effectively applied in practice.	

Article 24

Equal pay in public contracts and concessions

1. The appropriate measures that Member States take in accordance with Article 30(3) of Directive 2014/23/EU, Article 18(2) of Directive 2014/24/EU and Article 36(2) of Directive 2014/25/EU shall include measures to ensure that, in the performance of public contracts or concessions, economic operators comply with their obligations relating to the principle of equal pay. Part C

2. Member States shall consider requiring contracting authorities to introduce, as appropriate, penalties and termination conditions ensuring compliance with the principle of equal pay in the performance of public contracts and concessions. Part B

   Where Member States' authorities act in accordance with Article 38(7), point (a), of Directive 2014/23/EU, Article 57(4), point (a), of Directive 2014/24/EU, or Article 80(1) of Directive 2014/25/EU in conjunction with Article 57(4), point (a), of Directive 2014/24/EU, contracting authorities may exclude or may be required by Member States to exclude any economic operator from participation in a public procurement procedure where they can demonstrate by any appropriate means an infringement of the obligations referred to in paragraph 1 of this Article, related either to a failure to comply with pay transparency obligations or a pay gap of more than 5 per cent in any category of workers which is not justified by the employer on the basis of objective, gender-neutral criteria. This shall be without prejudice to any other rights or obligations set out in Directive 2014/23/EU, 2014/24/EU or 2014/25/EU.

Article 25 **Victimisation and protection against less favourable treatment** 1. Workers and their workers' representatives shall not be treated less favourably on the ground that they have exercised their rights relating to equal pay or have supported another person in the protection of that person's rights.	Part A
2. Member States shall introduce in their national legal systems such measures as are necessary to protect workers, including workers who are workers' representatives, against dismissal or other adverse treatment by an employer as a reaction to a complaint within the employer's organisation or to any administrative procedure or court proceedings for the purpose of the enforcement of any rights or obligations relating to the principle of equal pay.	Part B
Article 26 **Relationship with Directive 2006/54/EC** Chapter III of this Directive shall apply to proceedings concerning any right or obligation relating to the principle of equal pay set out in Article 4 of Directive 2006/54/EC.	Part C
CHAPTER IV HORIZONTAL PROVISIONS *Article 27* **Level of protection**	
1. Member States may introduce or maintain provisions that are more favourable to workers than those laid down in this Directive.	Part B
2. The implementation of this Directive shall under no circumstances constitute grounds for reducing the level of protection in the fields covered by this Directive.	Part C

Article 28

Equality bodies

1. Without prejudice to the competence of labour inspectorates or other bodies that enforce the rights of workers, including the social partners, the equality bodies shall be competent with regard to matters falling within the scope of this Directive.	Part C
2. Member States shall, in accordance with national law and practice, take active measures to ensure close cooperation and coordination among the labour inspectorates, the equality bodies and, where applicable, the social partners with regard to the principle of equal pay.	Part B
3. Member States shall provide their equality bodies with the adequate resources necessary for effectively carrying out their functions with regard to the respect for the right to equal pay.	Part B

Article 29

Monitoring and awareness raising

1. Member States shall ensure the consistent and coordinated monitoring of and support for the application of the principle of equal pay and the enforcement of all available remedies.	Part B
2. Each Member State shall designate a body for the monitoring and support of the implementation of national measures implementing this Directive (monitoring body) and shall make the necessary arrangements for the proper functioning thereof. The monitoring body may be part of an existing body or structure at national level. Member States may designate more than one body for the purpose of awareness-raising and data collection, provided that the monitoring and analysis functions provided for in paragraph 3, points (b), (c) and (e), are ensured by a central body.	

3. Member States shall ensure that the tasks of the monitoring body include the following:
   (a) raising awareness among public and private undertakings and organisations, the social partners and the public to promote the principle of equal pay and the right to pay transparency, including by addressing intersectional discrimination in relation to equal pay for equal work or work of equal value;
   (b) analysing the causes of the gender pay gap and devising tools to help assess pay inequalities, making use, in particular, of the analytical work and tools of the EIGE;
   (c) collecting data received from employers pursuant to Article 9(7), and promptly publishing the data referred to in Article 9(1), points (a) to (f), in an easily accessible and user-friendly manner that allows comparison between employers, sectors and regions of the Member State concerned, and ensuring that the data from the previous four years is accessible if available;
   (d) collecting the joint pay assessment reports pursuant to Article 10(3);
   (e) aggregating data on the number and types of pay discrimination complaints brought before the competent authorities, including equality bodies, and claims brought before the national courts.
4. By 7 June 2028 and every two years thereafter, Member States shall, in a single submission, provide the Commission with the data referred to in paragraph 3, points (c), (d), and (e).

Article 30 **Collective bargaining and action** This Directive shall not affect in any way the right to negotiate, conclude and enforce collective agreements or to take collective action in accordance with national law or practice.	Part C
Article 31 **Statistics** Member States shall, on an annual basis, provide the Commission (Eurostat) with up-to-date national data for the calculation of the gender pay gap in unadjusted form. Those statistics shall be broken down by sex, economic sector, working time (full-time/part-time), economic control (public/private ownership) and age and shall be calculated on an annual basis. The data referred to in the first paragraph shall be transmitted from 31 January 2028 for reference year 2026.	This data can form the measurable criteria for effectiveness to be introduced in an article on objectives.
Article 32 **Dissemination of information** Member States shall take active measures to ensure that the provisions which they adopt pursuant to this Directive, together with the relevant provisions already in force, are brought by all appropriate means to the attention of the persons concerned throughout their territory.	Part B
Article 33 **Implementation** Member States may entrust the social partners with the implementation of this Directive in accordance with national law and/or practice with regard to the role of the social partners, provided that Member States take all the necessary steps to ensure that the results sought by this Directive are guaranteed at all times. The implementation tasks entrusted to the social partners may include: (a) the development of analytical tools or methodologies as referred to in Article 4(2);	Part B

(b) financial penalties equivalent to fines, provided that they are effective, proportionate and dissuasive.

Article 34

Transposition

1. Member States shall bring into force the laws, regulations and administrative provisions necessary to comply with this Directive by 7 June 2026. They shall immediately inform the Commission thereof. When informing the Commission, Member States shall also provide it with a summary of the results of an assessment regarding the impact of their transposition measures on workers and employers with fewer than 250 workers and a reference to where such assessment is published.	Part B
2. When Member States adopt the measures referred to in paragraph 1 they shall contain a reference to this Directive or shall be accompanied by such a reference on the occasion of their official publication. The methods of making such reference shall be laid down by Member States.	

Article 35

Reporting and review

1. By 7 June 2031, Member States shall inform the Commission about the implementation of this Directive and its impact in practice.	Part B
2. By 7 June 2033, the Commission shall submit a report to the European Parliament and to the Council on the implementation of this Directive. The report shall examine, inter alia, the employer thresholds provided for in Articles 9 and 10, as well as the 5 % trigger for the joint pay assessment provided for in Article 10(1). The Commission shall, if appropriate, propose any legislative amendments that it considers to be necessary on the basis of that report.	Part C

Article 36 **Entry into force** This Directive shall enter into force on the twentieth day following that of its publication in the Official Journal of the European Union.	Review clause required to enhance ex post scrutiny.
Article 37 **Addressees** This Directive is addressed to the Member States. Done at Strasbourg, 10 May 2023. For the European Parliament The President R. METSOLA For the Council The President J. ROSWALL	The addresses are also E citizens and legal/technical users.

Having commented on the text of the Directive, let's see it clean, with all the changes transposed to its text:

DIRECTIVE (EU) 2023/970 on equal pay for equal work or work of equal value between men and women (Pay transparency and enforcement mechanisms)

THE EUROPEAN PARLIAMENT AND THE COUNCIL OF THE EUROPEAN UNION

Considering that:

(1) Equality between men and women is a right for EU citizens protected under:
   a. Article 2 and Article 3(3) of the Treaty on European Union on the right to equality,
   b. Articles 8 and 10 of the Treaty on the Functioning of the European Union (TFEU) on the elimination of inequality,
   c. Article 157(1) TFEU on equal pay for male and female workers for equal work or work of equal value is applied,
   d. Article 157(3) TFEU on measures of application of the principle of equal opportunities and equal treatment of men and women in matters of employment and occupation, including the principle of equal pay for equal work or work of equal value (the 'principle of equal pay'), and

e. The established case law of the Court of Justice of the European Union on the extension of the principle of equal treatment of men and women beyond sex discrimination, and the application of the principle to discrimination arising from gender reassignment.

Table 10.2 Table of Contents

Recitals	
PART A: To EU citizens	
Article 1	Objective of the Directive: What the EU aims to achieve for you
Article 2	Subject matter: How will the EU reach the objective
Article 3	Definitions in Annex A
Article 4	Your new rights
Article 5	The source of your rights: Who legislates
PART B: To Member States	
Article 6	Duties
Article 7	Powers
PART C: Legal and technical provisions	
Article 8	Discrimination
Article 9	Union-wide guidelines on gender neutral evaluation and classification systems
Article 10	Level of compensation and reparation
Article 11	Proof of equal work or work of equal value
Article 12	Equal pay in public contracts and concessions
Article 13	Relationship with Directive 2006/54/EU
Article 14	Level of protection
Article 15	Monitoring and awareness raising
Article 16	Collective bargaining and action
Article 17	Implementation
Article 18	Reporting and review
Article 19	Citation
Article 20	Entry into force and review clause
Article 21	Addressees
ANNEX 1	**DEFINITIONS**
ANNEX 2	**NOTES**

Source: The author.

(2) In some Member States, it is currently possible for persons to legally register as having a third, often a neutral, gender. This Directive does not

affect relevant national rules giving effect to such recognition as regards matters of employment and pay.

(3) The 2020 evaluation of the relevant provisions of Directive 2006/54/EC found that the application of the principle of equal pay is hindered by a lack of transparency in pay systems, a lack of legal certainty on the concept of work of equal value, and by procedural obstacles faced by victims of discrimination. Workers lack the necessary information to make a successful equal pay claim and, in particular, information about the pay levels for categories of workers who perform the same work or work of equal value. The report found that increased transparency would allow revealing gender bias and discrimination in the pay structures of an undertaking or organisation. It would also enable workers, employers and the social partners to take appropriate action to ensure the application of the right to equal pay for equal work and work of equal value (the 'right to equal pay').

(4) The effects of the COVID-19 pandemic will further widen gender inequalities and the gender pay gap unless the recovery response is gender sensitive. Those consequences have made it even more pressing to tackle the issue of equal pay for equal work or work of equal value. Strengthening the implementation of the principle of equal pay through further measures is particularly important to ensure that the progress which has been made in addressing disparities in pay is not compromised.

(5) The Union gender pay gap persists: it stood at 13 per cent in 2020, with significant variations across Member States, and has decreased only minimally over the last ten years. The gender pay gap is caused by various factors, such as gender stereotypes, the perpetuation of the 'glass ceiling' and the 'sticky floor', horizontal segregation, including the overrepresentation of women in low-paid service jobs, and unequal sharing of care responsibilities. In addition, the gender pay gap is partly caused by direct and indirect gender-based pay discrimination. All those elements constitute structural obstacles that form complex challenges to achieving good quality jobs and equal pay for equal work or work of equal value and have long-term consequences such as a pension gap and the feminisation of poverty.

(6) The lack of information on the envisaged pay range of a position creates an information asymmetry which limits the bargaining power of applicants for employment. Ensuring transparency should enable prospective workers to make an informed decision about the expected salary without limiting in any way the employer's or worker's bargaining power to negotiate a salary even outside the indicated range. Transparency would also ensure an explicit, non-gender-biased basis for pay setting and

would disrupt the undervaluation of pay compared to skills and experience. Transparency would also address intersectional discrimination where non-transparent pay settings allow for discriminatory practices on several discrimination grounds. Applicants for employment should receive information about the initial pay or its range in a manner such as to ensure an informed and transparent negotiation on pay, such as in a published job vacancy notice, prior to the job interview, or otherwise prior to the conclusion of any employment contract. The information should be provided by the employer or in a different manner, for instance by the social partners.

(7) Since the objectives of this Directive, namely a better and more effective application of the principle of equal pay through the establishment of common minimum requirements which should apply to all undertakings and organisations across the Union, cannot be sufficiently achieved by the Member States but can rather, by reason of their scale and effects, be better achieved at Union level, the Union may adopt measures, in accordance with the principle of subsidiarity as set out in Article 5 of the Treaty on European Union. In accordance with the principle of proportionality as set out in that Article, this Directive, which limits itself to setting minimum standards, does not go beyond what is necessary in order to achieve those objectives.

(8) This Directive lays down minimum requirements, thus respecting the Member States' prerogative to introduce and maintain provisions that are more favourable to workers. Rights acquired under the existing legal framework should continue to apply, unless provisions that are more favourable to workers are introduced by this Directive. The implementation of this Directive cannot be used to reduce existing rights set out in existing Union or national law in this field, nor can it constitute valid grounds for reducing the rights of workers in regard to the principle of equal pay.

HAVE ADOPTED THIS DIRECTIVE:

Part A: To EU citizens

Article 1 – Objective of the Directive: What the EU Aims to Achieve for you

The objective of this Directive is to reduce the pay gap between men and women within the EU by 10 per cent over a period of three years by strengthening the application of the principle of equal pay for equal work or work of equal value to all EU citizens, irrespective of their sex.

Article 2 – Subject Matter: How will the EU Achieve the Objective

This Directive requires Member States to strengthen pay transparency and reinforce enforcement mechanisms.

Article 3 – Definitions

Definitions are in Annex 1.

Article 4 – Your new rights

If you are an applicant or a worker with an employment contract or employment relationship in the Member State of employment, irrespective of your sex, you have the following rights:

(a) The right to equal pay for equal work or work of equal value;
(b) The right to pay transparency prior to employment, including the right to receive from your prospective employer, information about:
  a. the initial pay or its range, based on objective, gender-neutral criteria, to be attributed for the position concerned; and
  b. where applicable, the relevant provisions of the collective agreement applied by the employer in relation to the position. Such information shall be provided in a manner such as to ensure an informed and transparent negotiation on pay, such as in a published job vacancy notice, prior to the job interview or otherwise;
(c) The right not to be asked about your pay history during your current or previous employment relationships;
(d) The right to expect job vacancy notices and job titles that are gender-neutral and that recruitment processes are led in a non-discriminatory manner;
(e) The right to transparency of pay setting and pay progression policy via easy accessibility to the criteria used to determine workers' pay, pay levels and pay progression, and via criteria that are objective and gender neutral.
(f) The right to information, namely:
  a. the right to request and receive,
    i. in writing,
    ii. within a reasonable period of time not exceeding two months from the date of your request, and

iii. in a format which is accessible to persons with disabilities and which takes into account their particular needs,

information on your individual pay level and the average pay levels, broken down by sex, for categories of workers performing the same work as them or work of equal value to theirs;

b. the possibility to request and receive the information referred to in i. through your workers' representatives, in accordance with national law or practice or through an equality body;
c. in the event that the information received is inaccurate or incomplete, you have the right to request, personally or through your workers' representatives, additional and reasonable clarifications and details regarding any of the data provided and receive a substantiated reply;

(g) The right to be reminded by your employers, on an annual basis, of your right to receive the information referred to in i and of the steps that you must undertake to exercise that right;

(h) The right to disclose your pay for the purpose of the enforcement of the principle of equal pay; but your employer may require you not to use information other than on your own pay or pay level for any purpose other than to exercise your right to equal pay.

(i) The right (individual, through your workers' representatives, labour inspectorates and equality bodies) to ask employers for additional clarifications and details regarding any of the data provided, including explanations concerning any gender pay differences. Employers shall respond to such requests within a reasonable time by providing a substantiated reply. Where gender pay differences are not justified on the basis of objective, gender-neutral criteria, employers shall remedy the situation within a reasonable period of time in close cooperation with workers' representatives, the labour inspectorate or the equality body.

(j) The right for you, your representatives, and the monitoring body to be informed of the joint pay assessment, which must also be available to the labour inspectorate and the equality body upon request.

(k) In the implementation of the measures arising from the joint pay assessment, the right to remedy of the unjustified differences in pay within a reasonable period of time, in close cooperation, in accordance with your national law or practice, with your representatives. The labour inspectorate and the equality body may be asked to participate in the process. The implementation of the measures shall include an analysis of the existing gender-neutral job evaluation and classification systems or the establishment of such systems, to ensure that any direct or indirect pay discrimination on the grounds of sex is excluded.

(l) The right to the protection of your personal data:
   a. To the extent that any information provided pursuant to measures taken under this Directive, and 10 involves the processing of personal data, it shall be provided in accordance with Regulation (EU) 2016/679.
   b. Any personal data processed pursuant to this Directive shall not be used for any purpose other than for the application of the principle of equal pay.

(m) The right to full, real, and effective compensation or reparation for any damage as a result of an infringement of any right or obligation relating to the principle of equal pay, in a dissuasive and proportionate manner.

(n) The right to access to evidence in compensation or reparation proceedings.

(o) The right to be protected from victimisation and less favourable treatment: you and your workers' representatives shall not be treated less favourably on the ground that you have exercised your rights relating to equal pay or have supported another person in the protection of that person's rights.

Article 5 – The Source of Your Rights: Who Legislates

(1) The Directive introduces your rights, and you can rely on it before your national courts.

(2) The complete legislation for the protection of your rights is laid down by Member States, which must comply with Article 6 below.

PART B: To the Member States

Article 6 – Duties

By the end of the transposition period you must:

(1) Take the necessary measures to ensure that employers have pay structures ensuring equal pay for equal work or work of equal value;

(2) In consultation with equality bodies, take the necessary measures to ensure that analytical tools or methodologies are made available and are easily accessible to support and guide the assessment and comparison of the value of work in accordance with the criteria set out in this Article;

(3) Put in place measures to prohibit contractual terms that restrict workers from disclosing information about their pay;

(4) Report on pay gap between female and male workers by ensuring that ensure that employers provide the following information concerning their organisation:
   a. the gender pay gap;
   b. the gender pay gap in complementary or variable components;
   c. the median gender pay gap;
   d. the median gender pay gap in complementary or variable components;
   e. the proportion of female and male workers receiving complementary or variable components;
   f. the proportion of female and male workers in each quartile pay band;
   g. the gender pay gap between workers by categories of workers broken down by ordinary basic wage or salary and complementary or variable components.
   h. Employers with 250 workers or more shall, by 7 June 2027 and every year thereafter, provide this information relating to the previous calendar year.
   i. Employers with 150 to 249 workers shall, by 7 June 2027 and every three years thereafter, provide this information relating to the previous calendar year.
   j. Employers with 100 to 149 workers shall, by 7 June 2031 and every three years thereafter, provide this information relating to the previous calendar year.
   k. Employers with fewer than 100 workers may provide this information on a voluntary basis, and must do so if provided by national law.
   l. The information shall be communicated to the authority in charge of compiling and publishing such data, published by the employer on its website or made publicly available in another manner, and provided by the employer to all their workers and to the workers' representatives of their workers, to the labour inspectorate and the equality body upon request. The information from the previous four years, if available, shall also be provided upon request.

(5) Take appropriate measures to ensure that employers who are subject to pay reporting conduct, in cooperation with their workers' representatives, a joint pay assessment where all the following conditions are met:
   a. the pay reporting demonstrates a difference in the average pay level between female and male workers of at least 5 per cent in any category of workers;
   b. the employer has not justified such a difference in the average pay level on the basis of objective, gender-neutral criteria;
   c. the employer has not remedied such an unjustified difference in the average pay level within six months of the date of submission of the pay reporting.

d. The joint pay assessment shall be carried out in order to identify, remedy and prevent differences in pay between female and male workers which are not justified on the basis of objective, gender-neutral criteria, and shall include the following:
   i. an analysis of the proportion of female and male workers in each category of workers;
   ii. information on average female and male workers' pay levels and complementary or variable components for each category of workers;
   iii. any differences in average pay levels between female and male workers in each category of workers;
   iv. the reasons for such differences in average pay levels, on the basis of objective, gender-neutral criteria, if any, as established jointly by the workers' representatives and the employer;
   v. the proportion of female and male workers who benefited from any improvement in pay following their return from maternity or paternity leave, parental leave or carers' leave, if such improvement occurred in the relevant category of workers during the period in which the leave was taken;
   vi. measures to address differences in pay if they are not justified on the basis of objective, gender-neutral criteria;
   vii. an evaluation of the effectiveness of measures from previous joint pay assessments.

(6) Provide support, in the form of technical assistance and training, to employers with fewer than 250 workers and to the workers' representatives concerned, to facilitate their compliance with the obligations laid down in this Directive.

(7) Without prejudice to the autonomy of the social partners and in accordance with national law and practice, take adequate measures to ensure the effective involvement of the social partners, by means of discussing the rights and obligations laid down in this Directive, where applicable upon their request.

(8) Without prejudice to the autonomy of the social partners and taking into account the diversity of national practices, take adequate measures to promote the role of the social partners and encourage the exercise of the right to collective bargaining on measures to tackle pay discrimination and its adverse impact on the valuation of jobs predominantly carried out by workers of one sex.

(9) Ensure that, after possible recourse to conciliation, court proceedings for the enforcement of rights and obligations relating to the principle of equal pay are available to all workers who consider themselves wronged by a failure to apply the principle of equal pay. Such proceedings shall be

easily accessible to workers and to persons who act on their behalf, even after the end of the employment relationship in which the discrimination is alleged to have occurred.

(10) Ensure that associations, organisations, equality bodies and workers' representatives or other legal entities which have, in accordance with criteria laid down in national law, a legitimate interest in ensuring equality between men and women, may engage in any administrative procedure or court proceedings regarding an alleged infringement of the rights or obligations relating to the principle of equal pay. They may act on behalf of, or in support of, a worker who is an alleged victim of an infringement of any right or obligation relating to the principle of equal pay, with that person's approval.

(11) Ensure that, in the case of an infringement of rights or obligations related to the principle of equal pay, competent authorities or national courts may, in accordance with national law, at the request of the claimant and at the expense of the respondent, issue:

a. an order to stop the infringement;
b. an order to take measures to ensure that the rights or obligations related to the principle of equal pay are applied.

(12) Where a respondent does not comply with any order issued pursuant to k, ensure that their competent authorities or national courts are able, where appropriate, to issue a recurring penalty payment order, with a view to ensuring compliance.

(13) Take the appropriate measures, in accordance with their national judicial systems, to ensure that, when workers who consider themselves wronged because the principle of equal pay has not been applied to them establish before a competent authority or national court facts from which it may be presumed that there has been direct or indirect discrimination, it shall be for the respondent to prove that there has been no direct or indirect discrimination in relation to pay.

(14) In administrative procedures or court proceedings regarding alleged direct or indirect discrimination in relation to pay, where an employer has not implemented the pay transparency obligations set out in this Directive, ensure that it is for the employer to prove that there has been no such discrimination.

a. This shall not apply where the employer proves that the infringement of the obligations was manifestly unintentional and of a minor character.
b. This shall not apply to criminal proceedings, unless national law provides otherwise.

(15) Ensure that in proceedings concerning an equal pay claim, competent authorities or national courts are able to order the respondent to disclose

any relevant evidence which lies in the respondent's control, in accordance with national law and practice.

(16) Ensure that competent authorities or national courts have the power to order the disclosure of evidence containing confidential information where they consider it relevant to the equal pay claim.

(17) Ensure that, when ordering the disclosure of such information, competent authorities or national courts have at their disposal effective measures to protect such information, in accordance with national procedural rules.

(18) Ensure that national rules applicable to limitation periods for bringing equal pay claims determine when such periods begin to run, the duration thereof and the circumstances under which they may be suspended or interrupted. The limitation periods shall not begin to run before the claimant is aware, or can reasonably be expected to be aware, of an infringement. Member States may decide that limitation periods do not begin to run while the infringement is ongoing or before the end of the employment contract or employment relationship. Such limitation periods shall be no shorter than three years.

   a. This does not apply to rules on the expiry of claims.

(19) Ensure that a limitation period is suspended or, depending on national law, interrupted, as soon as a claimant undertakes action by bringing a complaint to the attention of the employer or by instituting proceedings before a court, directly or through the workers' representatives, the labour inspectorate or the equality body.

   a. This does not apply to rules on the expiry of claims.

(20) Ensure that, where a respondent is successful in proceedings relating to a pay discrimination claim, national courts can assess, in accordance with national law, whether the unsuccessful claimant had reasonable grounds for bringing the claim and, if so, whether it is appropriate not to require that claimant to pay the costs of the proceedings.

(21) Lay down the rules on effective, proportionate and dissuasive penalties applicable to infringements of the rights and obligations relating to the principle of equal pay. Member States shall take all measures necessary to ensure that those rules are implemented and shall, without delay, notify the Commission of those rules and of those measures and of any subsequent amendment affecting them.

(22) Ensure that the penalties referred to in paragraph 1 guarantee a real deterrent effect with regard to infringements of the rights and obligations relating to the principle of equal pay. Those penalties shall include fines, the setting of which shall be based on national law. The penalties shall take into account any relevant aggravating or mitigating factor

applicable to the circumstances of the infringement, which may include intersectional discrimination.

(23) Ensure that specific penalties apply in the case of repeated infringements of the rights and obligations relating to the principle of equal pay.

(24) Take all measures necessary to ensure that the penalties provided for pursuant to this Article are effectively applied in practice.

(25) Introduce in the national legal systems such measures as are necessary to protect workers, including workers who are workers' representatives, against dismissal or other adverse treatment by an employer as a reaction to a complaint within the employer's organisation or to any administrative procedure or court proceedings for the purpose of the enforcement of any rights or obligations relating to the principle of equal pay.

(26) Without prejudice to the competence of labour inspectorates or other bodies that enforce the rights of workers, including the social partners, ensure that the equality bodies shall be competent with regard to matters falling within the scope of this Directive.

(27) In accordance with national law and practice, take active measures to ensure close cooperation and coordination among the labour inspectorates, the equality bodies and, where applicable, the social partners with regard to the principle of equal pay.

(28) Provide equality bodies with the adequate resources necessary for effectively carrying out their functions with regard to the respect for the right to equal pay.

(29) Ensure the consistent and coordinated monitoring of and support for the application of the principle of equal pay and the enforcement of all available remedies.

(30) Designate a body for the monitoring and support of the implementation of national measures implementing this Directive (monitoring body) and shall make the necessary arrangements for the proper functioning thereof. The monitoring body may be part of an existing body or structure at national level. Member States may designate more than one body for the purpose of awareness-raising and data collection, provided that the monitoring and analysis functions provided for in [renumbered from originl text] ee (b), (c), and (e) below are ensured by a central body.

(31) Ensure that the tasks of the monitoring body include the following:

a. raising awareness among public and private undertakings and organisations, the social partners and the public to promote the principle of equal pay and the right to pay transparency, including by addressing intersectional discrimination in relation to equal pay for equal work or work of equal value;

b. analysing the causes of the gender pay gap and devising tools to help assess pay inequalities, making use, in particular, of the analytical work and tools of the EIGE;
c. collecting data received from employers, and promptly publishing the data, in an easily accessible and user-friendly manner that allows comparison between employers, sectors and regions of the Member State concerned, and ensuring that the data from the previous four years is accessible if available;
d. collecting the joint pay assessment reports;
e. aggregating data on the number and types of pay discrimination complaints brought before the competent authorities, including equality bodies, and claims brought before the national courts.

(32) On an annual basis, provide the Commission (Eurostat) with up-to-date national data for the calculation of the gender pay gap in unadjusted form. Those statistics shall be broken down by sex, economic sector, working time (full-time/part-time), economic control (public/private ownership) and age and shall be calculated on an annual basis.
   a. The data shall be transmitted from 31 January 2028 for reference year 2026.

(33) Take active measures to ensure that the provisions which they adopt pursuant to this Directive, together with the relevant provisions already in force, are brought by all appropriate means to the attention of the persons concerned throughout their territory.

(34) Bring into force the laws, regulations and administrative provisions necessary to comply with this Directive by 7 June 2026. They shall immediately inform the Commission thereof.

(35) When informing the Commission, provide it with a summary of the results of an assessment regarding the impact of their transposition measures on workers and employers with fewer than 250 workers and a reference to where such assessment is published.

(36) When adopting the measures referred to in ii, include a reference to this Directive or attach such a reference on the occasion of their official publication. The methods of making such reference shall be laid down by Member States.

(37) By 7 June 2031, inform the Commission about the implementation of this Directive and its impact in practice.

Article 7 – Powers

(1) Notwithstanding the right to transparency of pay setting and pay progression policy, Member States may exempt employers with fewer than 50 workers from the obligation related to pay progression.
(2) When reporting on the pay gap Member States may, as a matter of national law, require employers with fewer than 100 workers to provide information on pay.
(3) Member States may decide that, where the disclosure of information pursuant to Articles 7, 9 and 10 would lead to the disclosure, either directly or indirectly, of the pay of an identifiable worker, only the workers' representatives, the labour inspectorate or the equality body shall have access to that information. The workers' representatives or the equality body shall advise workers regarding a possible claim under this Directive without disclosing actual pay levels of individual workers performing the same work or work of equal value. For the purposes of monitoring, the information shall be made available without restriction.
(4) Despite the Directive, Member States may introduce evidential rules which are more favourable to a worker who institutes an administrative procedure or court proceedings regarding an alleged infringement of any of the rights or obligations relating to the principle of equal pay.
(5) Member States need not apply paragraph 5 (n) to procedures and proceedings in which it is for the competent authority or the national court to investigate the facts of the case.
(6) Member States shall consider requiring contracting authorities to introduce, as appropriate, penalties and termination conditions ensuring compliance with the principle of equal pay in the performance of public contracts and concessions. Where Member States' authorities act in accordance with Article 38(7), point (a), of Directive 2014/23/EU, Article 57(4), point (a), of Directive 2014/24/EU, or Article 80(1) of Directive 2014/25/EU in conjunction with Article 57(4), point (a), of Directive 2014/24/EU, contracting authorities may exclude or may be required by Member States to exclude any economic operator from participation in a public procurement procedure where they can demonstrate by any appropriate means an infringement of the obligations referred to in paragraph 1 of this Article, related either to a failure to comply with pay transparency obligations or a pay gap of more than 5 per cent in any category of workers which is not justified by the employer on the basis of objective, gender-neutral criteria. This shall be without prejudice to any other rights or obligations set out in Directive 2014/23/EU, 2014/24/EU or 2014/25/EU.

(7) On the level of protection, Member States may introduce or maintain provisions that are more favourable to workers than those laid down in this Directive.
(8) The duties on access to evidence shall not prevent Member States from maintaining or introducing rules which are more favourable to claimants.

PART C – LEGAL AND TECHNICAL PROVISIONS

Article 8 – Interpretation of discrimination

(1) In this Directive, discrimination includes:
   (a) harassment and sexual harassment, within the meaning of Article 2(2), point (a), of Directive 2006/54/EC, as well as any less favourable treatment based on a person's rejection of, or submission to, such conduct, when such harassment or treatment relates to or results from the exercise of the rights provided for in this Directive;
   (b) any instruction to discriminate against persons on grounds of sex;
   (c) any less favourable treatment related to pregnancy or maternity leave within the meaning of Council Directive 92/85/EEC (24);
   (d) any less favourable treatment, within the meaning of Directive (EU) 2019/1158 of the European Parliament and of the Council (25), based on sex, including with regard to paternity leave, parental leave or carers' leave;
   (e) intersectional discrimination, which is discrimination based on a combination of sex and any other ground or grounds of discrimination protected under Directive 2000/43/EC or 2000/78/EC.

(2) Paragraph 1, point (e), shall not entail additional obligations on employers to gather data as referred to in this Directive with regard to protected grounds of discrimination other than sex.

Article 9 – Union-wide Guidelines on Gender-neutral Evaluation and Classification Systems

Where appropriate, the Commission may update Union-wide guidelines related to gender-neutral job evaluation and classification systems, in consultation with the European Institute for Gender Equality (EIGE).

Article 10 – Level of Compensation and Reparation

(1) The compensation or reparation awarded for damage as a result of an infringement of any right or obligation relating to the principle of equal pay shall place the worker who has sustained damage in the position in which that person would have been if he or she had not been discriminated against based on sex or if there had been no infringement of any of the rights or obligations relating to the principle of equal pay. Member States shall ensure that the compensation or reparation includes full recovery of back pay and related bonuses or payments in kind, compensation for lost opportunities, non-material damage, any damage caused by other relevant factors which may include intersectional discrimination, as well as interest on arrears.

(2) The compensation or reparation shall not be restricted by the fixing of a prior upper limit.

Article 11 – Proof of Equal Work or Work of Equal Value

(1) When assessing whether female and male workers are carrying out the same work or work of equal value, the assessment of whether workers are in a comparable situation shall not be limited to situations in which female and male workers work for the same employer, but shall be extended to a single source establishing the pay conditions. A single source shall exist where it stipulates the elements of pay relevant for the comparison of workers.

(2) The assessment of whether workers are in a comparable situation shall not be limited to workers who are employed at the same time as the worker concerned.

(3) Where no real comparator can be established, any other evidence may be used to prove alleged pay discrimination, including statistics or a comparison of how a worker would be treated in a comparable situation.

Article 12 – Equal Pay in Public Contracts and Concessions

The appropriate measures that Member States take in accordance with Article 30(3) of Directive 2014/23/EU, Article 18(2) of Directive 2014/24/EU and Article 36(2) of Directive 2014/25/EU shall include measures to ensure that, in the performance of public contracts or concessions, economic operators comply with their obligations relating to the principle of equal pay.

Article 13 - Relationship with Directive 2006/54/EC

This Directive shall apply to proceedings concerning any right or obligation relating to the principle of equal pay set out in Article 4 of Directive 2006/54/EC.

Article 14 – Level of Protection

The implementation of this Directive shall under no circumstances constitute grounds for reducing the level of protection in the fields covered by this Directive.

Article 15 – Monitoring and Awareness Raising

By 7 June 2028 and every two years thereafter, Member States shall, in a single submission, provide the Commission with the data on the pay gap, the joint pay assessment reports, and aggregating data on the number and types of pay discrimination complaints brought before the competent authorities, including equality bodies, and claims brought before the national courts.

Article 16 – Collective Bargaining and Action

This Directive shall not affect in any way the right to negotiate, conclude and enforce collective agreements or to take collective action in accordance with national law or practice

Article 17 – Implementation

Member States may entrust the social partners with the implementation of this Directive in accordance with national law and/or practice with regard to the role of the social partners, provided that Member States take all the necessary steps to ensure that the results sought by this Directive are guaranteed at all times. The implementation tasks entrusted to the social partners may include:

(a) the development of analytical tools or methodologies as referred to in Article 4(2);
(b) financial penalties equivalent to fines, provided that they are effective, proportionate and dissuasive.

Article 18 – Reporting and review

By 7 June 2033, the Commission shall submit a report to the European Parliament and to the Council on the implementation of this Directive. The report shall examine, inter alia, the employer thresholds, as well as the 5 per cent trigger for the joint pay assessment. The Commission shall, if appropriate, propose any legislative amendments that it considers to be necessary on the basis of that report.

Article 19 – Citation

This Directive is DIRECTIVE (EU) 2023/970 OF THE EUROPEAN PARLIAMENT AND OF THE COUNCIL of 10 May 2023 to strengthen the application of the principle of equal pay for equal work or work of equal value between men and women through pay transparency and enforcement mechanisms (Text with EEA relevance).

Article 20 – Entry into Force and Review Clause

(1) This Directive shall enter into force on the twentieth day following that of its publication in the Official Journal of the European Union.
(2) This Directive shall expire after 10 May 2028, unless it is extended following ex post evaluation.

Article 21 – Addressees

(1) Part A of this Directive is addressed to EU citizens.
(2) Part B of the Directive is addressed to the Member States.
(3) Part C of this Directive is addressed to Member States and EU institutions.
(4) Nevertheless, the Directive is binding on its entirety.

Done at Strasbourg, 10 May 2023.
For the European Parliament
The President
R. METSOLA
For the Council
The President
J. ROSWALL

ANNEX 1 – DEFINITIONS

In this Directive, the following definitions apply:

(1) indirect discrimination' means the situation in which an apparently neutral provision, criterion or practice would put persons of one sex at a particular disadvantage compared with persons of the other sex, unless that provision, criterion or practice is objectively justified on the basis of a legitimate aim, and the means of achieving that aim are appropriate and necessary;
(2) labour inspectorate' means the body or bodies responsible, in accordance with national law and/or practice, for control and inspection functions in the labour market, save that, where provided for in national law, the social partners may carry out those functions;
(3) 'equality body' means the body or bodies designated pursuant to Article 20 of Directive 2006/54/EC;

ANNEX 2 – NOTES

...

CONCLUSIONS

The superficial attempt to redraft the Directive focusing on matters of structure and user-friendliness, rather than formatting and content, has produced breathtaking, and unexpected, results.

The application of the layered approach to the Directive has confirmed that the approach can work very well. It is feasible to distinguish between regulatory messages for EU citizens, for Member States, and for the learned users including EU institutions. Thus, any doubts on feasibility have been laid to rest. Equally, any concerns on the pragmatism of dividing the regulatory messages expressed via the provisions of the Directive into three have been hushed. Of course, the Directive must be read as a whole but the layered approach makes it more focused, and therefore more inviting to the users. These findings are not surprising, at least not to this author.

What is surprising is the extent of the utility of the layered approach.

In Part A, which is addressed to EU citizens, the application of the layered approach has facilitated a direct communication from the EU to its citizens. This has transformed a legalistic, user unfriendly, and therefore user detached Act into an authentic presentation of each and every right that the Directive awards EU workers, who can now understand what the EU offers them. In combination with Article 5 detailing in lay terms the direct effect of Article 4, EU workers are in no doubt that these rights are offered to them by the EU, and that, even without national implementation, they can rely on them before their national courts. This offers citizens a full picture as to the positive benefit that they receive via this Directive from the EU.

Moreover, Article 5 explains that the teeth of the protection of these new rights lay with their Member States. This hushes populist voices and blocks national politicians from claiming the glory of the introduction of the new workers' rights.

Finally, and rather unexpectedly, the list of rights in Article 4 has shone light on to their number and importance. Instead of burying them within legal provisions, the rights are there to be seen. There to be marvelled at for their number, depth, extend, and completeness.

Equally unexpectedly, their listing in a single Article at the start of the Directive, they instigate drafting in a manner that enhances direct effect. Which not only enhances their strength to the benefit of the workers, but also their effectiveness in the legislation and ultimately their contribution to efficacy of regulation.

Efficacy and effectiveness are further enhanced by the new Article 1 on objectives, which explains to the users what is being pursued, and facilitates transparency and accountability by introducing measurable criteria of effectiveness. Although this seems hard to achieve, the Directive already provides for the collection of data on equal pay. If the exercise of the chapter extended to an additional revision of the content of the Articles, then the objectives would have been enriched with measurements signalling progress in the statistical data that reporting will be collecting.

Part B proves equally startling. In dividing the obligations and discretion of Member States, it sets a clear and exhaustive list of duties in Article 6 and powers in Article 7 respectively. It therefore allows clarity, precision, and unambiguity in the measures required or permitted to Member States for the purposes of transposition. In that way, it facilitates concrete and content-based scrutiny of transposition by checking national measures against the concrete lists of Article 6 and, to a lesser extent, 7. In turn this invites a content-based, substantive scrutiny by the Commission, detaching it from the current formalistic table of equivalence between EU Acts and national measures.

But, unexpectedly, the exercise has brough to light the fact that the Directive imposes no less than 37 obligations on Member States. In an era where reduction of administrative burdens is promoted, 437 obligations from a single Directive is a shocking reality. It validates the complaints of Member States on the enormity of the transposition task. And it explains, to a great degree, why Member States simply copy out Directives. With their valuable parliamentary time already stretched to its limits, adding such a heavy regulatory package with a single Directive leaves Member States little option but to copy out and hope for the best. Of course, this is not a practice conducive to regulatory efficacy. It is therefore necessary for the EU legislators to take stock of these findings, assess the regulatory requirements of each EU Act, and find the balance between regulatory efficacy at EU level and regulatory feasibility at the Member State level. Breaking down Article 6 on Duties into smaller Articles has been tempting but it would deprive the EU legislator and the national drafters from the benefit of these revelations.

Moreover, the article on powers introduced a clear list of regulatory options for Member States. If copy out is ever reduced, this list of powers can (and should) invite national regulatory discussions that can greatly increase the effectiveness of national implementing measures. Although powers are obligatory and ensure a level of harmonisation amongst Member States, powers allow for flexibility addressing national eccentricities in national law and practice. This flexibility can serve the fine-tuning of the regulatory package towards an ideal national regulatory design that serves each Member States best.

Part C allowed for the inclusion in the Directive of provisions that go beyond Parts A and B. Since these are addressed to learned users of all categories, they can continue to be expressed in the structure and language currently used in EU Acts. After all, learned users are both resistant and trained enough to keep their attention until the end of the Act and deal with the finer issues of legality and technicality.

What shines through Part C is:

a. the citation Article 19, which allows for the Directive to carry a user-friendly short title at the start, whilst including all necessary legal details there;
b. the review clause in Article 20, which imposes evaluation ex post after a period of five years on the basis of the effectiveness criteria of Article 1, thus applying the principles of Better Regulation and Better Legislation; and
c. the reformed Article 21 on addressees, which includes EU citizens, Member States, and learned users, thus reflecting the true audiences of the Directive.

The exercise in this chapter completed the application of the lessons learnt for EU drafting in Chapters 2–6 on transposition. It showed that a reform in the drafting style of EU Acts can achieve its regulatory objective for better legislation on a technical level and without the need for grand Treaty reforms or changes in the governance structures of the EU.

But how exactly can a change in legislative style be pursued?

11. How do I get there? A methodology for the reform of EU legislation: Better Regulation applied

It is evident from the analysis of the last two chapters that in order to achieve better, transposition enhancing, and citizen-focused legislation, the EU must reform the drafting style of EU Acts. This chapter aims to answer how, how we can get from the current state of EU legislation to the goal of effectiveness, at the EU and national levels. This chapter introduces a methodology for a better legislation strategy for the EU and its Member States. This is not just a technical chapter. It sets out a roadmap for the proposed better legislation strategy. And, in doing so, it explores the feasibility of such a strategy. If a better legislation strategy is not feasible, then the proposals of the previous chapters for better EU and transposing legislation are simply academic. So, it would be fair to state that it is this chapter that solidifies both the rationale behind this book but also, and certainly much more importantly, the applicability of the recommendations that derive from our analysis.

Is a strategy for better EU legislation necessary? There is nothing to suggest that individual recommendations for reform cannot be taken up without a concerted holistic strategy. However pro-actively individual recommendations are undertaken and applied, a fragmented approach to better legislation can only produce fragmented results. As Better Regulation was needed in the form of a holistic and inter-institutional strategy, similarly better legislation would ideally require a holistic strategy, across policies, across units, across institutions, and across Member States. It is therefore suggested that an overarching strategy for better legislation is agreed and introduced, if better legislation as a tool for sustainable integration is to reap tangible and measurable results. Legislation is not a collection of individual legislative texts. Like regulation, it is a collective strategic effort across the EU whose demands, and consequent, results spread over the institutions and the Member States.

Within EU institutions the successful passing of an EU legislative text is viewed as a cause for celebration. From a political perspective, it is. After all, every new piece of EU legislation is another step towards integration, another step towards the realisation of the EU vision. From a legislative perspective, however, every new EU legislative text in its current, inherently flawed and incomplete format as *droit diplomatique*, adds to the complexity of EU law and pushes the EU's boat further into the troubled waters of bad legislation. This is accentuated by the fragmented view of legislating in the EU. Although assessing the EU's legislative policy holistically and introducing an overarching strategy for EU law-making is present in the post-2014 narrative of the Commission's Better Regulation, institutions and Member States continue to focus on each legislative text as it happens to come along. The aim of this chapter is to connect individual legislative dossiers into a collective legislative approach, and to suggest a methodology for better legislation overarching policies and institutions.

But where can one look for such a methodology? It is suggested that Better Regulation itself can, and must, be used as a tested, evidence-based methodology for a new better EU legislation strategy.[1]

A. THE PROBLEM

The EU is at the forefront of regulatory innovation.[2] EU Regulation is widely viewed as a desirable model for innovative responses to the popular need for structured, methodologically sound, flexible, and easily applicable regulatory response to challenges of competitiveness. Effectiveness, of regulation and legislation, is at the forefront of the regulatory philosophy of the EU. Doing less more efficiently is the goal.[3]

However, despite the wide acceptance of the wisdom of the EU's regulatory framework, EU legislation, which is a main regulatory tool, remains sub-standard. One can attribute this legislative ineffectiveness to a number of objective factors. First, and the most frequently quoted within EU circles, is the inevitable futility of attempting to accommodate within a single text a multitude of national legal systems, legal and spoken languages, and legislative

---

1 For a first take on using BR methodology here, see H Xanthaki, 'Using Better Regulation as a Methodology for Achieving Better EU Legislation – A First Approach' in H de Waele and E Mastenbroek (eds), *Perspectives on Better Regulation in the EU, ZEI Discussion Paper C 256/2019*, 7; also see H Xanthaki, 'The "one in, one out" Principle: A Real Better Lawmaking Tool?', Policy Department for Citizens' Rights and Constitutional Affairs, European Parliament, IP/C/JURI/IC/2023-044.

2 See OECD Regulatory Policy Outlook 2018: https://www.oecd.org/governance/oecd-regulatory-policyoutlook-2018-9789264303072-en.htm accessed 15 December 2023; also see A Bürgin, 'The Implications of the Better Regulation Agenda for the European Parliament's Inter- and Intra-institutional Power Relations' (2019) 41 *Journal of European Integration* 187.

3 See C Radaelli, 'Halfway Through the Better Regulation Strategy of the Juncker Commission: What Does the Evidence Say?' (2018) 56 *Journal of Common Market Studies*, 85, 90.

styles;[4] and to host them all under a harmonised umbrella of ever-changing aspirations of integration. There is little doubt that the hurdles presented to such an effort are, to an extent, insurmountable, even after 60 years of legal integration. Second, and well established in bibliography, is the lack of an agreed definition of effectiveness, even within the EU institutions that seek to achieve it. Effectiveness has been defined with reference to regulatory concepts but not yet with reference to the legislative product. Most Better Regulation documents discuss effectiveness as a regulatory goal but fail to translate it to a defined concept with reference to legislation. Without an agreed definition of legislative effectiveness as a goalpost for EU regulation and legislation, it is rather impossible to draft a roadmap to achieve it. Third, is the relative exclusion of legislation from the Better Regulation agenda. In the EU's past, numerous initiatives have been introduced to perfect EU legislation: from the Sutherland criteria to Inter-institutional Agreements and the Joint Handbook. But they tend to focus on esoteric stylistic rules for the drafting of EU legislative texts, without any principled focus on effectiveness, on the use of legislation as a form of communication with the end users, on the identification of end-users, or the pitch of language that renders legislation accessible by them. After all, 'the Commission seems to prioritise smaller steps rather than giant leaps'.[5] Better/Smart/Better Regulation explores regulation, and post-legislative scrutiny, but not legislation as a process and a product.[6]

---

[4] EU drafters try to accommodate the national systems and terminology in the EU legislative texts, but only if this does not create diversity of interpretations, especially since all the versions of the same text must mean the same in all languages. In drafting EU legislation, the 'supremacy' rule is followed. In Union texts it is often necessary to avoid using a term of national law which does not exactly cover a given notion, or which corresponds to a more general notion (see point 5 of the Joint Practical Guide). In such a case a new, a more appropriate term will be used in its place, even if it is less elegant: see 'Manual of Precedents for Acts established within the Council of the European Union, 107.

[5] See A Alemanno, 'How Much Better is Better Regulation? Assessing the Impact of the Better Regulation Package on the European Union - A Research Agenda' (2015) 3 *European Journal of Risk Regulation* 344, 345.

[6] See A Renda, 'From Impact Assessment to the Policy Cycle: Drawing Lessons from the EU'S Better-Regulation Agenda' (2016) The School of Public Policy Publications 9.33, 1, 29.

B. THE EXCLUSION OF LEGISLATION FROM BETTER/SMART/BETTER REGULATION[7]

As early as 1995 and 1996 the Commission's Better Law-making Reports identified the regulatory aims of the EU's legislative policy: legislative quality, consistency, openness in the drafting process, carefully planned and coordinated legislative process, and thorough monitoring and evaluation of the legislation.[8] The Commission also identified the crucial role of legislative quality in the national implementing measures as a factor of quality of EU regulation both in Member States[9] and in accession countries, or pre- and post-accession.[10] Less,[11] and clear and simple legislation helps businesses and citizens to comply

---

[7] For a fuller analysis, see H Xanthaki, 'The Problem of Quality in EU legislation: What on Earth is Really Wrong?' 38 (2001) *Common Market Law Review* 651–76; H Xanthaki, 'Implementation of EU legislation' Oral Evidence, Public Hearing at the Legal Affairs Committee of the European Parliament 'Better Regulation' Hearing, Brussels, 21 June 2011; also see H Xanthaki, 'Improving the Quality of EU Legislation: Limits and Opportunities?' in S Garben and I Govaere (eds), The Better Regulation Agenda: A Critical Assessment (Hart, Oxford, 2018) pp.28-47; H Xanthaki, 'Quality of Legislation: Focus on Smart EU and post-Smart Transposition' 2 (2015) TPLeg 329-342; and H Xanthaki, 'EU Legislative quality post-Lisbon: the challenges of Smart Regulation' (2014) 35 *Statute Law Review* 66–80.

[8] See Better Law-making 1995: Report of the Commission to the European Council [of Madrid] on the application of the principles of subsidiarity and proportionality, on simplification and codification, CSE (95) 580, Bulletin, 11-1995, point 1.9.2; also Better Law-making 1996: report of the Commission to the European Council [of Dublin] on the application of the principles of subsidiarity and proportionality, on simplification and consolidation, CSE (96) 7.

[9] See Communication from the Commission to the Council and the European Parliament, 'Simpler Legislation for the Internal Market (SLIM): A Pilot Project', COM (96) 204 fin.; also Resolution of the EP of 10 April 1997 on the communication from the Commission to the Council and the EP, 'Simpler Legislation for the Internal Market (SLIM): A Pilot Project', COM (96) 204 fin. (A4-0108/97, OJ No. C 132/213 of 28 April 1997); also see Commission's approach to simplification COM (97) 618 final, p. 2; Informal Meeting of Internal Ministers on 13–14 February 1998, Bulletin EU 11-1997, point 1.1.1.; 'Better Law-making Report 1998: A Shared Responsibility', Bulletin EU 5-1998, point 1.8.3. and COM (1998) 715 final.

[10] See Annual Report 2007 on monitoring the application of Community law COM (2008) 777 (18 November 2008); 'A Europe of results—Applying Community Law' COM (2007) 502 (5 September 2007); Annual Report 2006 on monitoring the application of Community law; COM (2007) 398 (17 July 2007) + Annex SEC (2007) 976; Annual report 2005 on monitoring the application of Community law COM (2006) 416 (24 July 2006); Better monitoring the application of Community law Commission communication – COM (2002) 725.

[11] See Commission Communication to the European Council, 'Legislate Less to Act Better: The Facts', COM (1998) 495.

with the law without excessive burdens, facilitates enforcement, and addresses complaints for excessive red tape often leading to cases for damages.[12] Ease of transposition and application is enhanced.[13]

This flurry of activity culminated with a set of detailed, form-focused, technical drafting tools, such as the 2011 Inter-institutional Style Guide, the 2015 Joint Practical Guide of the European Parliament, the Council and the Commission for persons involved in the drafting of European Union legislation, and the 2019 Joint Handbook for the Presentation and Drafting of Acts subject to the Ordinary Legislative Procedure. Useful as these are for the institutional drafters, they do accentuate the perception that legislation is a technical effort, relevant to institutional technocrats and detached from both regulation and the end-users of regulation and legislation. A critical engagement with the philosophy of legislation, the principles of legislative drafting and the evolving use of legislation as a regulatory tool communicating with citizens as participants to the regulatory process seems to have ended some time back in 2003.[14] And the EU, whilst leading on regulatory reform, has been left behind in the many advances of legislative practices led by drafters in its own Member States, and especially the UK, the Netherlands, Italy, and Sweden.

Even the highly innovative Smart Regulation Agenda excludes legislation as a product.[15] The October 2010 Commission Communication on Smart Regulation constitutes the formal passing from the old Better Regulation Agenda to the new Smart Regulation Agenda. Although Smart Regulation has since been re-labelled as Better Regulation, it is worth analysing as it formulated the basis of the EU's current and continuing approach to regulation, policy and legislation. In Smart Regulation the Commission identified three key messages in the agenda. First, Smart Regulation is about the whole

---

[12] See 1998 Commission Staff Working Paper 'Making Single Market Rules More Effective, Quality in Implementation and Enforcement', SEC (1998) 903, 25 May 1998, 3–5.

[13] See 1998 Regulatory Policy Guidelines of the Commission and the 2002 General principles and minimum standards for consultation of interested parties by the Commission; also see Communication from the Commission to the European Parliament and the Council, 'Making Simple Market Rules More Effective', COM (1998) 296 final; and Towards a Reinforced Culture of Consultation and Dialogue—General Principles and Minimum Standards for Consultation of Interested Parties by the Commission, Commission communication—COM (2002) 704.

[14] See e.g., the Commission's Communication, 'Questions and Answers on the Better Regulation', Brussels, 29 April 2021, where no mention of legislative intervention is amongst the improvements planned for Better Regulation, QANDA/21/1902.

[15] See European Commission, 'Smart Regulation in the European Union' Commission communication, COM (2010) 543, 8 October 2010, http://eur-lex.europa.eu/LexUriServ/LexUriServ.do?uri=CELEX:52010DC0543:EN:NOT accessed 15 December 2023.

policy cycle and thus touches upon the design of a piece of legislation, its implementation, enforcement, evaluation, and revision.[16] Second, Smart Regulation remains a shared responsibility between the EU institutions and the Member States. Third, the views of users of regulation have a key role to play in Smart Regulation, as consultation is an element of democracy.[17] In the recent Communication 'Better Regulation: taking stock and sustaining our commitment' the Commission confirmed that Better Regulation, including its previous form of Smart Regulation, 'has improved the way policy is made' but confessed that there is 'room for further improvement', which 'will depend on a stronger shared effort by all those involved in designing and implementing policy solutions'.[18] This express reference to policy in the exclusion of legislation is also found in 'Completing the better regulation agenda – better solutions for better results' and in 'Delivering better results for a stronger Union'.[19]

There is no doubt that Better Regulation is a revolutionary concept, which has already delivered tangible policy results.[20] After all, the OECD consistently ranks the EU amongst the first in stakeholder engagement, impact assessment policy, and evaluation.[21] Better Regulation introduces impact assessments for every appropriate new regulatory proposal,[22] improved roadmaps, the introduction of the independent Regulatory Scrutiny Board to replace the Impact Assessment Board,[23] systematic ex post evaluations from

---

16 On closing the policy cycle see C Radaelli, 'Halfway Through the Better Regulation Strategy of the Juncker Commission: What Does the Evidence Say?' (2018) 56 *Journal of Common Market Studies* 85.

17 See http://ec.europa.eu/governance/better_regulation/smart_regulation/consultation_en.htm accessed 15 December 2023.

18 See https://ec.europa.eu/info/sites/info/files/better-regulation-taking-stock_en_0.pdf accessed 15 December 2023, p.5.

19 See 'Completing the better regulation agenda – better solutions for better results', COM(2017) 651 final; and 'Delivering better results for a stronger Union', COM(2016) 615 final.

20 See contra, A Alemanno, 'How Much Better is Better Regulation: Assessing the Impact of the Better Regulation Package on the European Union - a Research Agenda' (2015) 6 *European Journal of Risk Regulation* 344, 355.

21 See http:// www .oecd .org/ governance/ oecd -regulatory -policy -outlook -2018 -9789264303072-en.htm accessed 15 December 2023. Also see OECD (2019), Better Regulation Practices across the European Union, OECD Publishing, Paris, https:// doi.org/ 10.1787/ 9789264311732-en. And for the most recent OECD (2022), Better Regulation Practices across the European Union 2022, OECD Publishing, Paris, https:// doi.org/10.1787/6e4b095d-en.

22 See SWD(2017)350: Better Regulation Guidelines, Box 1; https://ec.europa.eu/ info/sites/info/files/better-regulation-guidelines.pdf accessed 15 December 2023.

23 See https://ec.europa.eu/info/law/law-making-process/regulatory-scrutiny-board_en accessed 15 December 2023.

the end-users' perspective,[24] strengthened role of the High Level Group, and enhanced public consultations.[25] Better Regulation follows Stefanou's identification of the drafting process as a part of the legislative process, which is a part of the policy process:[26] this places legislation in the broader concept of regulation, and establishes a firm connection between legislation and regulation. Better Regulation confirms that EU regulation is a shared responsibility of the institutions and Member States and confesses that further cooperation is needed between the EU and national co-legislators, in order to achieve effective regulation. And it affirms the need for in-depth consultation and citizen participation as a means of enhancing legitimacy.[27]

Focus is placed on the simplification of EU law via the reduction of administrative burdens; evaluation of law effectiveness and efficiency ex ante via fitness checks on key areas (environment, etc.),[28] and via strategic general policy evaluations; selection of the 'the best possible' legislation through Impact Assessment,[29] improvement of implementation record via post-legislative scrutiny, SOLVIT,[30] and EU Pilot; and achieving clearer

---

24 See paras 22 and 23 of the 'Inter-institutional Agreement on Better Law-Making'; also see 'Special report 16/2018 of the European Court of Auditors: Ex-post review of EU legislation: a well-established system, but incomplete', paras 52–56, 85–87 and Recommendation No.1, https://www.eca.europa.eu/Lists/ECADocuments/SR18_16/SR_BETTER_REGULATION_EN.pdf; 'Council Conclusions of 29/30 November 2018' st14137/18 approved by COREPER on 14 November 2018, http://data.consilium.europa.eu/doc/document/ST-14137-2018-INIT/en/pdf accessed 15 December 2023.

25 See 'Common Position Paper of the Five European Independent Advisory Boards for Cutting Red Tape and Better Regulation', Adviescollege Toetsing Regeldruk (ACTAL), The Netherlands; Nationaler Normenkontrollrat (NKR), Germany; Regelrådet, Sweden; Regulatory Impact Assessment Board (RIAB), Czech Republic; Regulatory Policy Committee (RPC), UK http://www.regel-radet.se/wp-content/uploads/2012/09/2012-Reaction-on-consultation-Smart-Regulation.pdf accessed 15 December 2023.

26 See C Stefanou, 'Drafters, Drafting and the Policy Process' in C Stefanou and H Xanthaki, *Drafting Legislation: A Modern Approach* (Ashgate Aldershot 2008), 321–333.

27 See A Alemanno, 'Better Regulation: Holding Martin Selmayr Accountable', https://papers.ssrn.com/sol3/papers.cfm?abstract_id=3251856.

28 For examples of fitness checks, see also http://ec.europa.eu/dgs/secretariat_general/evaluation/docs/fitness_check_en.pdf; also http://ec.europa.eu/environment/water/blueprint/fitness_en.htm; and http://ec.europa.eu/transport/air/fitness_check_en.htm accessed 15 December 2023.

29 On impact assessments, see also http://ec.europa.eu/governance/impact/key_docs/key_docs_en.htm; http://ec.europa.eu/governance/impact/key_docs/docs/meg_guidelines.pdf; and http://ec.europa.eu/governance/impact/iab/members_en.htm accessed 15 December 2023.

30 See http://ec.europa.eu/solvit/site/about/index_en.htm accessed 15 December 2023.

and accessible legislation via simple language, codification, recasting, and e-access.

The list seems endless, and the possible benefits rather attractive. However, one wonders how these noble aims are going to be achieved, especially with reference to legislation rather than regulation. Simplification of EU law is indeed a worthy goal. But it cannot be taken to mean simply a reduction of administrative burdens. In fact, the Smart Regulation agenda neglects to address a number of crucial aspects of simplification without which reduction of administrative burdens cannot be achieved. What about simplicity of the chosen policies? If a policy choice is complex in itself, then the reduction of red tape will not suffice to make it accessible to the citizens. What about simplicity in the selected regulatory means? Is the inherently user-unfriendly legislation not a most complex regulatory tool? And thus, reducing administrative burdens via legislation carries inherent complexity, which may well endanger the end result. What about the chosen drafting style as a means of simplifying the expression of a simple policy when a simpler regulatory tool is considered ineffective? A complex legislative style would diminish the actual effect of any simplification effort irrespective of what the percentage of administrative burdens in the simple policy chosen may be: if the users cannot understand the language of the law, how can they benefit from the opportunities created by a policy of reduced red tape? What about straightforward enforcement methods? And could one rely on a reduction of administrative burdens within the EU text, if the national implementing measures are complex and seize on any opportunity for discretion in the EU text in order to add further burdens? And finally, could EU law be considered simple when the methods of pre- and post-legislative scrutiny utilised are inherently complex and therefore inaccessible for the users?

Similarly, evaluation of law effectiveness and efficiency ex ante is a solid initiative. In theory. But can it be achieved simply via fitness checks and general policy evaluations? In a legislative environment where the definition of effectiveness has not been provided conclusively, the goal that the regulatory team is supposed to be trying to achieve becomes a moving target, a vague and ambiguous goalpost, which carries a different meaning for the different actors in the regulatory process, much more so between EU and national levels. But even where the concept of effectiveness appears clear, what are the specific criteria of effectiveness by way of successful regulation that must be used in reference to a specific piece of legislation? The application of the generic elements of the semantic field of the concept of effectiveness in the specific context of a piece of legislation as applied in the specific legal system that serves a specific society in a specific time is not an easy task and should not really be ignored or left to chance. There is a dire need to ensure that the criteria for effectiveness of any piece of legislation are agreed upon by policy-makers, law experts, and legislative drafters and that they are clearly expressed in the legislation itself via perhaps their inclusion in a purpose clause or an objectives article. These can then be carried through to post-legislative scrutiny and then utilised to confirm effectiveness, thus allowing the text to continue its legislative life.

But how will ineffectiveness be addressed? What if the effectiveness criteria are not met by the piece of legislation at the pre-set time of post-legislative monitoring: will the legislation die an automatic death via perhaps a sunset clause, will it continue to plague the Official Journal as it stands, at least until an enlightened decision-maker decides to address the problem, or will it lead to an automatic exercise of fine-tuning via perhaps an amending piece of legislation?

Moreover, Better/Smart/Better Regulation fails to identify the way in which, if at all, evaluation will take place at the Member State level. Here, other considerations should also come into play. Will national scrutiny be compulsory or could the Member States be offered discretion on the basis of national sovereignty in the legislative process? Moreover, Smart Regulation fails to address the extent of any national scrutiny process, namely, whether it must relate strictly to the national implementing measures or whether it can refer to the original EU text. This is rather crucial, especially in reference to national legislation, which departs from the policy and law of the EU by means of either a direct or indirect breach or even legitimately by means of an acceptable exercise of discretion as would be the case with the implementation of a Directive. And what if the national scrutiny exercise identifies a flaw in the EU policy? Can that be reported back to the EU and will this result in any action at the EU level?

The improvement of the implementation record is a third worthy point of reference for Better/Smart/Better Regulation. But once again, one has to distinguish between the aim and the proposed methods for its achievement. Can implementation be improved solely via post-legislative scrutiny, availability of SOLVIT, and the EU Pilot on clarification and assistance with the application of EU legislation? What about clear guidance on the definition of complete transposition for new, older, and aspiring Member States? What about clear guidance on the definition of quality in legislation for the purposes of EU drafting and also EU transposition? What about the establishment of national drafting offices with trained specialist drafters vetting (if not drafting) implementation measures on the possible example of the UK model for drafting national primary legislation [Office of Parliamentary Counsel]? What about extending the scrutiny of implementation beyond substantive transposition to technical quality of transposition?

And finally, who would disagree with the selection of the 'the best possible' legislation? But is this really achievable simply via Impact Assessments, clearer and accessible legislation, simple language, codification, recasting, and e-access? What about opening the debate for a holistic approach to effectiveness in the sense of the use of legislation as a tool for regulation? What about setting a hierarchy of drafting virtues that can serve as guidance for drafters in their inevitable subjective drafting dilemmas? What about training drafters to achieve these goals? What about considering a central drafting office with trained drafters within EU institutions, including the Commission, the Council, and the Parliament? What about training national drafters to contribute to the effort?

The move to regulatory quality as the main focus of the EU's better governance campaign is by no means a negative development in the field. Indeed, legislative quality is an intrinsic part of regulatory quality: without regulatory quality, one cannot perceive the notion of legislative quality. As legislative drafting can only aspire to effectiveness, namely, to the production of a legislative text that, with the cooperation and synergy of all other actors in the policy process, can achieve the regulatory aims, one cannot possibly expect it possible to produce quality legislation, when the regulatory aims are erroneous or illegal, when the choice of legislation as a regulatory tool is inappropriate, or indeed when the implementation of the legislation has not been thought through. Better Regulation addresses all of these issues.[31] But, at the same time, one cannot possibly perceive regulatory quality without, in cases where legislation is the appropriate regulatory tool, legislative quality. Whilst focusing on regulation, the EU seems to have forgotten about legislation, somehow trying to simply wish away the continuing problems of legislative quality.[32] The same focus away from legislation is present in the 2020 Agenda for Europe.[33]

The question is why this is the case. It is difficult to unlock the conscious or unconscious choice of the Commission to focus on regulation and leave legislation aside. There is little doubt that the start of the process towards better regulation would be the policy. This lies at the root of regulation. Policy conception and formulation was not yet mapped, as it constituted an esoteric procedural affair of the institutions, whose cryptic nature remained almost justified within past environments of trust to bureaucracies and States. Even past discussions on the democratic deficit of the EU focused on the powers of the European Parliament, rather than the internal processes of the institutions.

---

[31] See G Listorti, E Basyte Ferrari, S Acs, G Munda, E Rosenbaum, P Paruolo and P Smits, *The Debate on the EU Better Regulation Agenda: A Literature Review* (2019, Publications Office of the European Union, Luxembourg).

[32] See C-H Montin, 'Smart Regulation in the European Union', http://montin.com/documents/smartregulation.pdf.

[33] See http://ec.europa.eu/europe2020/index_en.htm accessed 15 December 2023.

Turning to transparency and participation in policy conception and formulation came very recently, as Juncker's response to the need to regain trust and legitimacy amongst stakeholders and citizens.

So, one could support the wisdom of the EU's start with regulation. But, ultimately, a detachment from legislative quality and a focus on regulatory quality instead, can also be perfectly justified, if one takes a closer look at the purpose clause of Smart and Better Regulation: removing barriers for businesses, and rendering them competitive against non-EU enterprises. Their focus on the reduction of administrative burdens and competitiveness and their identification as crucial factors in the economic stealth of EU businesses justifies and supports the EU's choice to focus on regulation. Businesses require a better regulatory environment in which they can flourish and produce for the EU's economy. The quality of legislation is not as relevant to them as it is for EU citizens, since most businesses have the luxury of using legal experts to 'interpret' EU legislation for them. In view of this, Smart and Better Regulation have achieved their initial goal and have opened the way to the 2020 competitiveness Agenda.

However, recently, the goalpost has been moved.[34] The imbalance[35] between enterprises and citizens in the Smart Regulation, the Better Regulation, and the 2020 Agenda for Europe is beginning to tip over, with clear mention of EU citizens in most Better Regulation documents after 2014. Since then, the Commission is quoted to introduce Better Regulation as an effort for 'opening up policy and law-making and listening more to the people it affects'.[36] This demonstrates the priority now placed on EU citizens as users and a subsequent move towards law-making rather than pure regulation: 'bringing the EU closer to its citizens'[37] and completing Better Regulation 'for the benefit of EU citizens'.[38] In the updated objectives of Better Regulation, the Commission

---

[34] See C Radaelli, 'Whither Better Regulation for the Lisbon Agenda?' (2007) 14 *Journal of European Public Policy* 190, 207.

[35] See A Alemanno, 'Better Regulation: Holding the European Commission Accountable?', IDEAS Working Paper Series from RePEc (2018).

[36] See https://ec.europa.eu/info/law/law-making-process/planning-and-proposing-law/better-regulation-why-and-how_en accessed 15 December 2023.

[37] See Political Guidelines for the next European Commission, by Candidate for the President of the European Commission Jean-Claude Juncker, Strasbourg, 15 July 2014.

[38] See Communication from the Commission to the European Parliament, the Council, the European Economic and Social Committee and the Committee of the Regions, 'Completing the Better Regulation Agenda: Better solutions for better results', SWD(2017) 675 final, https://ec.europa.eu/info/sites/info/files/completing-the-better-regulation-agenda-better-solutions-for-better-results_en.pdf accessed 15 December 2023; also see Communication from the Commission to the European Parliament, the European Council and the Council 'Better Regulation: Delivering better results for

includes the reduction of regulatory burdens, but introduces them as a tool that benefits not just businesses but also citizens and public administration. Additional objectives are open and transparent decision-making, EU actions based on evidence[39] and impact, and policy- and law-making process where citizens and stakeholders can contribute. It is rather notable that citizens are included in each and every one of the four objectives of Better Regulation, and that law-making is clearly included and expressly set apart from policy.[40] In the 2017 Better Regulation Stock-taking, the necessity of Better Regulation is not competitiveness but 'the desire for better European governance'[41] and 'for anchoring sustainable development in the Union's policymaking'.[42] And the rationale for better regulation in this 'post-fact' world of disinformation, social media echo chambers and outright propaganda calls for better regulation and legislation to reverse legitimacy, democracy, and support of EU citizens to the EU vision. Despite early criticisms that the Better Regulation Agenda would plateau,[43] the Commission took it one step further. In the 2017 Better Regulation update, the Commission confirmed their focus on its ten political priorities[44] 'for the benefit of the Union's citizens; to support growth and jobs, to make the internal market work better, to tackle security threats, to protect consumers and workers and to improve public health and the environment'.[45] In the 2019 Better Regulation restocking exercise[46] the Commission confessed

---

a stronger Union', COM/2016/0615 final, https://eur-lex.europa.eu/legal-content/EN/TXT/?uri=CELEX%3A52016DC0615 accessed 15 December 2023.

[39] Thus enhancing accountability: see C Radaelli and A Meuwese, 'Hard Questions, Hard Solutions: Proceduralisation through Impact Assessment in the EU' (2010) 33 *West European Politics* 136.

[40] See https://ec.europa.eu/info/law/law-making-process/planning-and-proposing-law/better-regulation-why-and-how_en accessed 15 December 2023.

[41] See 'Commission Work Programme 2015 – A New Start', COM(2014) 910 final.

[42] See 'European Governance – A White Paper', COM(2001) 428, https://eur-lex.europa.eu/legal-content/EN/TXT/?uri=celex:52001DC0428 accessed 15 December 2023.

[43] See R E Lofstedt, 'The "Plateauing" of the European Better Regulation Agenda: An Analysis of Activities Carried out by the Barroso Commission' (2007) 10 *Journal of Risk Research* 423, 447.

[44] See https://ec.europa.eu/commission/index_en accessed 15 December 2023.

[45] See European Commission, 'Communication from the Commission to the European Parliament, the Council, the European Economic and Social Committee and the Committee of the Regions, Completing the Better Regulation Agenda: Better solutions for better results', COM/2017/0651 final, 24.10.2017, https://eur-lex.europa.eu/legal-content/EN/TXT/?uri=CELEX%3A52017DC0651 accessed 15 December 2023, 1.

[46] See European Commission, 'Communication from the Commission to the European Parliament, the Council, the European Economic and Special Committee and

that the application of Better Regulation can be further improved by, amongst others, improving EU legislation.

These documents show a clear change to the focus of the EU, and to the reasoning behind it. As the world changes and bureaucracies need to justify their actions and entice citizen trust and participation, legislation as a tool of direct communication with the citizens becomes a new area of focus. Citizens, as end users, acquire prime importance. And legislation becomes an as yet unexploited tool to communicate the necessity and rationale of legislative intervention to their lives, and to persuade them of the wisdom of legislative action.[47] Achieving this can lead not just to their participation in the regulatory efforts of the bureaucracy in this specific legislative demand, but also, and much more importantly, to their ascribing to the holistic regulatory goals of the bureaucracy and to its general political vision. But, in order to achieve this goal, legislation must speak to the citizens as end-users. And this requires a radical change in the way in which legislation is drafted, structured and published.

C. THE QUESTION AND ITS METHODOLOGICAL VALIDITY

The question is how can the goal of better EU legislation be achieved? In other words, what can be a solid methodology for achieving better legislation? Selecting the methodology for the achievement of better EU legislation is not just an academic pursuit. A solid methodology is conducive to solid results. The question is, which methodological sequence can be applied here. One thing is for sure: the re-balanced goal of better EU legislation to the service of enterprises and EU citizens[48] cannot be fully serviced by the current processes. These have proved inadequate.

In pursuing a methodology for better legislation, one can draw wisdom from the Better Regulation Agenda. If one views better legislation as a regulatory goal for the EU, a methodology can be drawn using the Commission's Better Regulation Guidelines (SWD(2017)) as supplemented by the 2017 Better Regulation toolbox. In other words, if one views the achievement of effec-

---

the Committee of the Regions, Better regulation: taking stock and sustaining our commitment', COM(2019)178 final, 15.4.2019, 13.

[47] On the need for better legislation within the Better Regulation Agenda, see R Rácz, 'The Better Regulation Agenda of the European Union' (2009) 7 *European Integration Studies* 85, 104.

[48] See European Commission, 'Communication from the Commission to the European Parliament, the European Council and the Council, Better Regulation: Delivering better results for a stronger Union, COM (2016) 615 final, 14.9.2016, 1.

tive legislation for enterprises and EU citizens as a policy goal for the EU, achieving better legislation is nothing more (or less) than a new policy goal. To achieve this policy goal, the EU must regulate its legislative framework in order to render it fertile for better legislation. In the EU there is already a tried, tested, and acclaimed regulatory method, namely the Better Regulation method. It would make enormous sense therefore to draw a new roadmap for better legislation using the methodology of Better Regulation. This would not be a dramatic innovation for the EU, as a strategy for better legislation already exists informally amongst those dealing with legislation in the institutions.[49] The added value of a methodology would be the agreement to a formal roadmap leading to the desired regulatory result by means of agreed tools. In addition, as is the case with any regulatory strategy, an agreed methodology would coordinate and focus the work of all those involved personally and institutionally in legislation to the appropriate means, and would introduce tangible and measurable criteria assessing the efficacy of the new regulation on better EU legislation.

But is it valid to apply Better Regulation to EU legislation? The first question arising here is whether law-making falls within the scope of the Better Regulation Agenda. So, the question is not whether one can apply Better Regulation to individual legislative texts. This is outside our concern here. The question is whether law-making as a strategy is within the field of application of Better Regulation? The Better Regulation Toolbox clarifies that its tools 'cover the relevant aspects of all new initiatives and existing policy interventions'; and the guidelines '... apply to DGs and services involved in the preparation, implementation, application or evaluation of EU interventions and associated stakeholder consultations' (Introductory text; Tool 1.1). Since what is involved here is a new initiative for a policy intervention to achieve better EU legislation, the latter is indeed covered by the Better Regulation Toolbox. Moreover, the Better Regulation guidelines can apply to all law-making persons and institutions that will prepare, implement, apply, and evaluate the new initiative for better legislation. In other words, the Better Regulation Agenda seems to be rather robustly and expressly capable of applying to the proposed new better legislation initiative. And all persons and institutions involved in EU law-making would be bound by the Better Regulation guidelines. Interestingly, as Member States are stakeholders in

---

49 See F Peraldi-Leneuf, 'La formation à la légistique au sein de la Commission européenne - Entretien avec M. Thomas Van Cangh, Policy Officer, Secretariat-General, Unit C.2 Impact Assessment, European Commission' in K Gilberg and C Groulier, *Former a la legistique: Les nouveaux territoires de la pédagogie juridique* (LexisNexis, Paris, 2018), 115, 117.

better legislation, they and their authorities would also be bound by the Better Regulation guidelines.

Before proceeding to the next point, it is worth clarifying that the classification of the proposed better legislation initiative as an initiative in the sense of the Toolbox, as a strategy or as a policy is really irrelevant here. At the end of the day, whatever term is selected, aims to convey a collective joint reform that leads to better legislation. Both 'initiative' and 'strategy' are acceptable terms for that propose. 'Strategy' is the term selected here, solely because it reflects a thoroughly thought out, collective, joint movement. In contrast, the term 'initiative' conveys a smaller scale move, which would be inadequate for the achievement of better legislation. The term 'policy' is to be avoided within the context of the EU, as policies are exclusively (to an extent) introduced in the constituting Treaties. So, unless there is an agreement to reform the Treaties and add a better legislation policy within their text, the term may not be the best option.

Having established that a new strategy for better EU legislation, which can involve all institutions and the Member States, is within the scope of the Better Regulation Agenda, one final question comes to the fore. Can Better Regulation apply to itself, or at least one of its parts? Legislation is a tool for regulation. Therefore, law-making is part of regulation. Can the Better Regulation methodology apply to law-making as one of its constituting parts? One cannot see why not. Since any new initiative can apply the Better Regulation methodology, an initiative for better legislation would certainly benefit from the solidity of Better Regulation.

With this sorted, let us now begin the application of the Better Regulation methodology to EU law-making as a means of achieving better EU legislation.

D. APPLYING BR METHODOLOGY: PASSING THE DECIDE TEST (G 11/12)

Having established the applicability of Better Regulation to a new legislative strategy, let us begin the application by placing the new strategy under the DECIDE test. This ensures that the proposed new EU legislative strategy can be legitimately and effectively pursued by the EU.

The first element of the DECIDE test invites the identification of the key characteristics and type of the proposed initiative. The proposed new EU legislative strategy could qualify as a 'major' initiative for a holistic and principled new strategy for the EU's legislative approach. This classification guides us to the required process, which is political validation from the lead Commissioner, Vice-President and First Vice-President following an entry created in DECIDE and a roadmap agreed with the Secretariat-General. In other words, this new initiative could be initiated by The Quality of Legislation Directorate. It would require political support within the leadership team of the Commission, but one would expect this to be present, if one takes into account the widespread inter-institutional support of regulatory innovations so far.[50] Nonetheless, having delved into the post-2014 documents of the Commission on Better Regulation, one could argue that the start of the new policy has been de facto achieved. The express identification of an EU citizen focused, better legislation as part of the Better Regulation Agenda has now been repeated enough to have already been established as a strategic goal for the EU's regulatory reforms. One wonders, therefore, if a formal pursuit of the DECIDE test would be superfluous. There is a solid argument for the subjection of Better Legislation on to Better Regulation. In fact, there really is no need to start delaying what has already started with joint decisions and permissions to proceed with what has already take place. However, the application of DECIDE, focusing especially on the detailed drafting of the new strategy, would be beneficial, as it would give detailed form and evidence-based vision to Better Legislation. Even if a formal DECIDE is not pursued, the methodological steps of DECIDE can support the new strategy robustly and transparently, and therefore democratically and legitimately.

The second element of the DECIDE test invites the identification of the scope and the objectives of the proposed initiative. There seems to be no struggle in doing so. The scope of a new legislative strategy would be to achieve better EU legislation: since legislation is a tool for regulation, competitiveness and beneficial citizenship can be nurtured by a new less-complex and more user-friendly legislative net that would invite implementation and effectiveness within the EU, and investment and competitiveness from outside the EU. Better Regulation means 'designing EU policies and laws so that they achieve their objectives at minimum cost' (G4): a new legislative strategy would support effectiveness and cost efficiency. Moreover, one could argue that better EU legislation favours not only companies and competitiveness but also EU citizens, thus balancing the financial with a social EU profile. Good legislation would enhance the respect of subsidiarity and proportionality (G4); would provide the means to mainstream sustainable development into the Union's policies (G5); and would contribute to re-establishing direct commu-

---

[50] See OECD, *Better Regulation Practices across the European Union* (2019, OECD Publishing, Paris), https:// doi .org/ 10 .1787/ 9789264311732 -en, 19; also see 'European Parliament resolution of 12 April 2016 on Regulatory Fitness and Performance Programme (REFIT): State of Play and Outlook', http://www.europarl.europa.eu/sides/getDoc.do?type=TA&language=EN&reference=P8-TA-2016-0104; and 'Better regulation to strengthen competitiveness: Council conclusions 26 May 2016; http://www.consilium.europa.eu/en/press/press-releases/2016/05/26-conclusions-better-regulation accessed 15 December 2023.

nication with EU citizens, thus facilitating loyalty to the organisation and its ideal of EU integration.

On the point of subsidiarity, is it the EU that should act for a better EU legislative strategy?[51] The answer can only be affirmative. This is about EU law, designed and produced within the EU. It is the EU and the Commission as the main initiator of EU legislation that must take the initiative. There is no doubt that Member States must learn to share the strategy. After all, Better Regulation views EU legislation as a shared responsibility. But the steering power must come from the EU since results cannot be adequately achieved at the national level (subsidiarity principle).[52]

At this point, it is worth noting that the initiative could be a more holistic one, involving all main EU institutions. In Tool 1 of the Better Regulation Agenda, the European Parliament, Council and Commission reassert their recognition that delivering high-quality legislation is a joint responsibility for legislation meting four criteria. It may be worth considering focusing on such legislation as perhaps a trial and involving all three main institutions.

Of course, one could apply the four conditions to the proposed legislative strategy, thus arguing that, if these are met, the initiative can be a joint one. Let us explore the legality of this option by assessing the strategy against each criterion.

One, this is an area where it has the greatest added-value for European citizens and strengthen the competitiveness and sustainability of the Union's economy. The proposed new legislative strategy fulfils this criterion as the identification of its scope under DECIDE proved that it would be of great benefit to citizens and companies, balancing the EU's financial and social profile.

Two, it must deliver the Union's policy objectives in the simplest, most efficient and effective way possible. This is a rather vague condition. But there is a solid argument to be made that the most efficient and effective legislative step after more than 60 years of legislative integration and continuing legislative fragmentation would be to pause the introduction of even more, fragmented

---

[51] See Communication from the Commission, 'Better Regulation for Better Results, An EU Agenda', COM/2015/0215 final, 19.5.2015, 3.

[52] See Communication from the Commission to the European Parliament, the European Council, the European Economic and Social Committee and the Committee of Regions, 'The principles of subsidiarity and proportionality: Strengthening their role in the EU's policymaking', COM(2018) 490 and COM(2018) 491, https://ec.europa.eu/info/sites/info/files/communication-principles-subsidiarity-proportionality-strengthening-role-policymaking_en.pdf accessed 15 December 2023.

legislative texts.[53] And to now focus on identifying a methodologically sound, principled, and Better Regulation compliant structure for the EU's legislative approach. In the words of Mr Juncker, doing less but more efficiently.[54]

Three, it must avoid over-regulation and unnecessary administrative burdens for citizens, administrations and businesses and particularly SMEs. This a condition easily met by the proposed initiative. The strategy aims to better legislation. Unnecessary regulation and administrative burdens are constitutive elements of the notion of effective law, where necessity and simplicity are *conditia sine qua non*. The condition serves as a good reminder to include these two elements to the philosophy of the legislative strategy proposed here.

Four, it must be designed to facilitate transposition and practical application. The strategy is indeed designed for practical application, this is its whole point. And it does aim to facilitate transposition, as effectiveness of EU law is a joint responsibility with the Member States involving the whole legislative package of EU and national implementing legislation.

It seems therefore that there is scope to investigate the feasibility of a joint initiative of the main institutions towards better legislation in application of the Better Regulation Tools.[55] After all, EU regulation is a joint responsibility of EU institutions.[56]

Finally, Better Regulation invites the identification of the better regulation tools to be applied to the proposed new legislative strategy.[57] These would be evaluation, impact assessment, implementation plan, and public consultation. Let us take them in turn.

---

[53] See 'Mapping the cost of non-Europe 2014-2019', http://www.europarl.europa.eu/thinktank/en/document.html?reference=EPRS_STU(2017)603239 accessed 15 December 2023.

[54] See Scenario 4 of the White Paper 'Doing Less More Efficiently: The EU27 focuses on delivering more and faster in selected policy areas, while doing less elsewhere', https://ec.europa.eu/commission/white-paper-future-europe_en accessed 15 December 2023.

[55] See European Commission, 'Better regulation' toolbox', July 2023, https://commission.europa.eu/system/files/2023-09/BR%20toolbox%20-%20Jul%202023%20-%20FINAL.pdf accessed 15 December 2023.

[56] See European Court of Auditors, 'Law-making in the European Union after almost 20 years of Better Regulation', Review No 2/2020, https://www.eca.europa.eu/lists/ecadocuments/rw20_02/rw_better_regulation_en.pdf accessed 15 December 2023.

[57] See European Commission, 'Better Regulation Guidelines', Brussels, 3.11.2021, SWD(2021)305 final; also see European Commission, 'Better Regulation toolbox', July 2023 edition, https://commission.europa.eu/system/files/2023-09/BR%20toolbox%20-%20Jul%202023%20-%20FINAL.pdf accessed 15 December 2023.

1. Proposed BR Tool 1: Evaluation

Evaluation calls for an assessment on the feasibility and effectiveness of the measures proposed against the goals to be achieved. For the proposed new legislative strategy this is a truly difficult assessment. Not because there is difficulty in reaching a conclusion, but because conclusions can be really hard to bear. The question really is whether an EU of 27 Member States, or more, can really achieve good legislation.

There is little doubt that this is a mammoth task. Not necessarily because of the multiplicity of complexities in a legislature for so many diverse jurisdictions, legal terminologies, languages, and diverse legal traditions. Not even necessarily because compromise lies at the heart of EU law-making. But mainly because the goal pursued is effectiveness of legislation, and this is set against a cultural, legal, social, financial and political environment. By definition, effective legislation serves the particular requirements of a specific executive within the particular environment of the jurisdiction. And thus, effectiveness requirements differ between diverse environments. The EU has not yet reached a level of homogeneity that can allow a single legislative text to serve the same effectiveness in all its Member States to an adequate degree. Despite the levels of standardisation and harmonisation, the peoples and countries of the EU retain their national eccentricities in culture, religion, politics, finances, and law. It is this strength of the EU that prevents it from achieving effectiveness by means of a single legislative text.

This leads to a mismatch between the regulatory goals of the EU and the legislative instruments available to its legislating bodies. Effectiveness could be served if the EU were to legislate solely via Directives, setting common regulatory goals but allowing national implementing measures to introduce diverse mechanisms for their achievement within each Member State. Regulations could prove rather ineffective legislative tools, even when their need for transposition is regained. The result of this proposed switch to Directives as the main legislative tool for regulatory effectiveness could nurture good legislation at the EU and national levels. The downside would be that the EU would have to entrust national drafters to achieve effectiveness of the regulatory package by means of national transposing regulatory [not necessarily legislative] measures. This would require a free-er hand in transposition, and an equally free-er, principled (rather than formalistic) scrutiny of national compliance. This may sound simple but it is not: effective principled scrutiny requires an expert level of understanding of legislative drafting by national and EU officers alike.

It is worth noting that the post-2016 Better Regulation documents upgrade the role of national drafters and Parliaments to one of co-legislators, and stress the importance of their contribution to the legislative efforts of the EU. The understanding of effectiveness as a relative value coloured by national eccentricities and regulatory choices seems to have already created a fertile environment for wider co-legislative choices at the national level. The challenge now seems to be to put the new ethos into effect not only at the EU but also at the national levels. Tuning national co-legislators and the EU in the same concept of regulatory efficacy and legislative effectiveness requires courage, trust, and training especially within the Member States. But it is a worthy goal to the benefit of EU citizens and the EU vision.

2. Proposed BR Tool 2: Impact Assessment

Having completed the evaluation test, an Impact Assessment is to follow. This is where empirical analysis becomes necessary. One is to measure the impact of bad EU regulation and legislation, in order to justify the necessity and proportionality of the new strategy and its measures.

Measuring the cost of bad legislation is by no means a simple task, and inevitably a degree of guesswork is on call. What makes this task even more complex is the lack of basic data on the users of EU legislation. Without knowing who reads EU legislation and who relies on it to make decisions on their activities, one cannot accurately identify who the subjects on the alleged damage by bad EU laws are. Let me explain this point. At the moment, there has been no survey identifying who reads EU law: is it just the local authorities of the Member States, who then use it transpose them into national law, or could it be that companies and perhaps even citizens themselves resort to EU law to learn about new rights and obligations. Knowing who the audience of legislation is can have serious effect on the measurements of the impact of bad EU law.

If the audience of EU law is mainly national authorities, and legal and natural persons read the national implementing measures, then the possible negative effects of EU legislation may already be eliminated by the intervention of national drafters. Measurement of the negative effect of EU legislation would relate to its contribution or loss arising from the competitiveness of EU industries, the attraction of the EU as a foreign investment area, the transposition of EU measures, and any administrative burdens. With reference to transposition, this negative effect would include losses from the cost of transposition of EU law to Member States, the cost of late implementation to the EU and the other Member States, and the cost of non-implementation to the EU and other Member States. Where these costs are measured, note should be taken of the actual cost, namely the cost that is not remedied by national legislation. This may lead to a decision that a new strategy for EU law is not necessary at all, or that the needs of national authorities as the main users of EU legislation can be addressed by means of a consultation with them and a subsequent possible fine-tuning of the current drafting techniques.

If the audience of EU law includes EU citizens, natural and legal persons, the game changes dramatically. If lay users make use of the principles of direct effect and direct applicability and rely on EU instruments for the purposes of claiming their EU rights before the national courts and the national authorities, the alleged negative effect of EU legislation must be measured by reference to them also. Competitiveness of EU industries would be measured as arising from EU legislation only, without remedies from national implementation measures. The attractiveness of the EU as a foreign investment area would relate to the cost of EU laws on the natural and legal persons in third countries that set out to select which geographical area in the world they intend to invest in. The alleged cost arising from the transposition, late implementation or non-implementation of EU measures would include costs to the EU, Member States, companies, and citizens. The negative effect from administrative burdens arising from EU legislation would be measured by reference to the EU, the Member States, and EU citizens natural and legal persons. In all probability, acquiring empirical evidence that direct effect and direct applicability is used by EU citizens would result to a confirmation that a strategy for better EU law is not just justified but long overdue.

The survey of users could, if the question is asked, reveal another possible user anomaly. Since direct effect and direct applicability are justly hailed as conferring power to EU citizens to make use of EU legislation directly and without the need for national implementation, it is worthwhile to learn if EU citizens themselves make use of these tools or whether they leave it to their legal counsellors to do so when the matter reaches national courts. Direct effect and direct applicability are revolutionary tools that bring EU legislation directly to the citizens. If EU citizens do not use them without expert legal advice, it is possible that one of the causes could be the alleged user-unfriendliness of EU legislative texts. Confirmation of user-unfriendliness of EU legislation could explain, to an extent, the current wave of Euroscepticism in quite a few EU Member States: directly effective and directly applicable EU legislation could be a tool of communication of the EU directly to EU citizens, a channel to alert citizens to the added value offered by the EU. Failing to utilise this tool adequately could explain the disturbing prevalence of populist voices that ridicule solidly rooted policy options as dictatorial impositions from a self-absorbed EU bureaucracy. For example, the presentation of EU legislation on crooked cucumbers[58] or even on bendy bananas[59] not as a measure protecting EU crops and farmers from disease-prone varieties but as a dictation of the extent of curve of vegetable produce favoured by EU bureaucrats. Identifying this as a contributing factor to Euroscepticism would upgrade the proposed new EU strategy for better legislation to a strategy contributing to the regain of trust and popularity of the organisation amongst EU citizens, using EU legislation as a direct channel of communication between the EU and its citizens. This is a view shared by a number of legislative studies academics apart from this author but it requires empirical confirmation to get it off the ground. If it is confirmed, then Brexit can be added to the cost of bad EU legislation, strengthening the voice for a new strategy on better EU law even further. It is worth noting that such an approach to EU legislation would not be out of tune with approaches to legislation at the national level. The UK Good Law survey showed beyond doubt that users of legislation in the UK are lay persons by 70 per cent. As a result, UK laws are now drafted in lay language, the regulatory message strengthened by user-friendly explanatory notes, and legislative texts are available online. Similar movements are evident as part of the Better Regulation national agendas in the Netherlands, Germany, Italy, Switzerland, and elsewhere: it seems that there is a pan-European trend for easily accessible legislation that users can use to learn about their rights and obligations directly.

3. Proposed BR Tool 3: Public Consultation

The pre-Impact Assessment survey can produce exciting results that may offer a new impetus for the Europhile movement. Public consultation would be supplementary to the survey and could greatly contribute to a deeper exploration of the inevitably raw results of the survey.

A public consultation could, and should, involve hearing from EU staff on the current process of legislating. They are the ones experienced and interested in EU law-making and transposition monitoring. They are the users of processes, and their voice is valuable and learned.

A public consultation would include drafters and policy officers from the Member States. They are equally users of the system and process of law-making both at the EU and the national levels. They carry experience of approaches to legislation and legislating for transposition and could inform on national implementation hurdles and how these could be overcome.

---

58 Commission Regulation (EEC) No 1677/88 of 15 June 1988 laying down quality standards for cucumbers, OJ L 150, 16/06/1988, 21–25.

59 Commission Regulation (EC) No 2257/94 of 16 September 1994 laying down quality standards for bananas (Text with EEA relevance), *OJ L245*, 20/09/1994, 6–10.

Technical experts at the EU and national levels may have the learned voice but lay users, legal and natural persons citizens of the EU, may have considerable contributions to make, if they are proven to be the end-users of EU legislative texts. Whereas the former may contribute in an open consultation with the identification of weaknesses in the current process and perhaps devices to address the issues, the latter lack the expertise to contribute constructively at this stage. So, involving end-users in the consultation exercise would require a different kind of consultation, perhaps in the form of user testing. Having identified the weaknesses and the preferable solutions, end users can be mobilised to select their preferred text amongst those offered by the consultation experts, thus confirming that the in abstracto solution offered by the experts is indeed achieving accessibility to the end users when applied in practice.

4. Proposed BR Tool 4: Implementation Plan

Having confirmed the necessity of a new strategy and, via consultation, decided on its bare skeleton of problems and preferred solutions, an implementation plan can now be drawn.

Step 1 would consist of the identification and profiling of the users of EU legislation. It is not enough to know who reads EU legislation. It is important to know what it is that users are looking for when reading the text. This will allow EU drafters to determine the main regulatory message sought by users, and adapt their drafting to provide them easily and as a priority.

Step 2 would involve pitching the language of EU legislative texts accordingly. Accessibility includes legislative expression that can be understood by the particular audiences of the legislative text in question. User testing can also assist here by ascertaining that the language used in legislative texts is one that conveys the regulatory message to the users rather than the one that sustains the multiple compromises required to see the text through.

Step 3 could involve revisiting the structure of EU texts and dividing the regulatory messages according to Step 1 conclusions. As there rarely, if ever, is a single audience in legislation, a layered approach to structure can liberate the drafter in pitching diverse messages in various levels of linguistic and legal sophistication that match those of each audience. Understanding who reads EU legislation and for what purpose can lead to the introduction of a text in parts, each addressing lay users, national authorities, and legally trained users. Their language would be different, and their regulatory messages would be allocated by reference to the answers required by each group. For example, a text offering subsidy to oil producers can be structured in three parts: part 1 addressed to oil producers telling them clearly and simply that they are now entitled to a subsidy and that they must fulfil a number of conditions and complete a precise process to get it; part 2 addressed to national authorities detailing the administrative procedure to be followed; part 3 addressed to lawyers and judges dealing with any consequential amendments, any interpretation and definitions, and any appeals. This rather simplified example is a good example of a revised structure.

Step 4 could involve a revisit of the publication of EU legislation. So far, EU legislation is available online free of charge but it is addressed to learned users. Bringing the legislation to lay users would require new techniques, such as hyperlinks to relevant texts, explanatory materials, or variation of colours.

This is all rather radical, so it is anything but simple! But it is not enough. These are suggestions for formalities in drafting techniques that reflect a grander philosophical reform in the EU's legislative strategy. A principled approach to EU legislation would see a promotion of creative drafting to serve effectiveness rather than the current timid formalistic application of models and precedents. Such a liberal approach requires confident drafters, and these are normally professional drafters.

The question is whether, with its current constraints, effectiveness can be achieved at EU level. A feasibility survey would respond to the question. It is not easy for any bureaucracy to reform, and this would be quite a major reform. Can the EU sustain it or is effectiveness only possible at the national level. Effectiveness by definition requires a homogenous setting with similar policy needs and similar policy solutions. EU legislation normally places different policy needs at the EU versus each national level. The EU looks for homogeneity and standardisation in order to achieve further integration. National policy goals are obviously different and may involve competitiveness or social goals. Solutions are by definition different as they aim at different goals. Much more so, since effectiveness at each member state may very well require different approaches. In a Europe of diversity (North versus South, rich versus financial challenged, immigration facing versus immigration deferring etc.), it is difficult to envisage a single legislative solution to achieve EU policy within all 27 Member States.

There are two options here. One, a holistic reform of the EU law-making processes to accommodate the radical reform seemingly necessary for better EU legislation. The Commission, via the post-2016 seems ready to grapple with the necessary reforms, perhaps as a response to the current financial, political, and social challenges, which, by the way, are not solely Europe based. Two, a maintenance of current law-making processes but a reform of drafting techniques to fine-tune EU legislative texts in response to the conclusions of the Better Regulation tools above along with a principled decision to regulate solely or mainly via Directives. These beautiful creatures are flexible enough to accommodate effectiveness at the EU level in the goals and effectiveness at the national level in the options available to Member States in the achievement of the policy goals set. This rather placid solution can produce radical results, if the scrutiny of national implementing measures is no longer formalistic and becomes principled, with a focus to the effectiveness of the proposed national implementing measures.

CONCLUSIONS

The 2017 BR Guidelines and Toolbox already provide principles, guidelines and tools that apply to all EU measures from policy conception to implementation. But Better Regulation has yet to benefit from the self-application of its own principles, guidelines, and tools. Applying Better Regulation to EU law-making provides a valuable methodology for an evidence-based new strategy for better EU legislation to the benefit of the EU, the Member States, and EU citizens.

The completion of a skeletal DECIDE test for a proposed new strategy for the EU's legislative policy detailed a valid step by step methodology for the collection of evidence that can constitute an appropriate basis for effective further action.

There is confidence in hoping that using EU legislation as a tool for direct regulatory communication with EU citizens can offer effectiveness to EU law, can silence populist Eurosceptic voices, and can contribute to a new era of trust and loyalty to the EU ideal. The Commission seems ready to explore the dialogue that was started in the post-2016 Better Regulation documents. The crucial seeds of change are planted: the focus on legislation as part of Better Regulation, the light on EU citizens and the impact of legislation on them, and the use of legislation as a means of direct communication from the EU to its citizens. These benefit from many legislative instruments, in the short term those that award them rights, and, equally importantly, in the long term those that impose them obligations. Sustainable integration, as a goal for the future of Europe, needs participation from EU citizens, and EU legislation can be the tool that entices EU citizens to take part in the formulation and implementation of EU legislation as a tool for successful regulation.

But why would the EU invest in a strategy of reform for better E legislation?

12. Conclusions – legislative reform for sustainability and longevity of the EU

This book set out to inject legislative quality into transposition legislation. In doing so, it revealed the weaknesses of EU Acts and embarked on recommendations for a reform in the drafting style of EU legislation as a means of facilitating transposition and injecting effectiveness to them. The recommendations were applied and tested in two representative sample EU Acts, a Regulation and a Directive, this showcasing the difference that these recommendations can make, and of course proving their feasibility in legislative practice. This led to a call for legislative reform within the EU using the Better Regulation methodology on Better Legislation. Which in turn revealed the great benefit of user-focused effective EU legislation for sustainability and longevity of the EU.

The question is what constitutes good law? In other words, what is the goal for national and EU law-makers? International drafting literature and the EU itself coincide in identifying effectiveness as the criterion for legislative quality. Legislative effectiveness is defined as the capacity of the legislative text to contribute to regulatory efficacy. Effectiveness requires a departure from formalistic rigidity in the assessment of legislative quality. Of course, clarity, precision, and unambiguity contribute to effectiveness. But, at the end of the day, the choice of a specific word is not catastrophic for effectiveness. In contrast, legislative design can be. Since effectiveness is a contributor to regulatory efficacy, the success of a legislative text is assessed by its contribution to the achievement of the desired regulatory results. To achieve those, the text must speak to the users of the legislation and persuade them to undertake the prescribed action. It is only when users act in the way that the law-makers intended, that the law reform is put to effect, and the desired (or at least the envisaged) regulatory goals can be reached. Recognising legislation as a tool for regulation links the policy agenda with the legislative agenda and focuses law-makers to the need to communicate with users effectively in order to promote compliance with the legislation.

The book begun by focusing on law-making for membership, accession and approximation, and exit from the EU. The drafting tasks involved were explored using Thornton's methodology for legislative drafting and its five stages, namely understanding the proposal, analysing the proposal, designing the draft, composing the draft, and evaluating the draft. Although the primary aim of this analysis was to present solid practical guidance on national drafters in their task of implementing EU legislation, the analysis spat out quite a few recommendations for reform of the EU's offering in the area of transposition.

In Thornton's legislative drafting stage 1, understanding the EU legislative text and the parameters of transposition, the application of international literature on drafting instructions identified two inherent weaknesses in current transposition processes: the lack of a clear and open sharing of the desired regulatory results at the EU and national levels, and the unfortunately inherent style of drafting instructions to national drafters in the form of a completed legislative text. Both of these factors are considered crucial hurdles to legislative quality, and this applies also to EU legislation. The lack of a clear expression of the desired regulatory results, both at the EU and national levels, compromises the drafter's ability to express them appropriately, to link them with the legislative text, and to adopt them in post-legislative scrutiny exercises. The provision of the EU text as drafting instructions for transposition blinds national drafters into an editing approach to the EU text rather than in a creative design of the most appropriate design, structure, and language for communication to the national users of the implementing measure.

To facilitate the completion of Stage 1, the EU can consider a revamp of the currently used introductory report and transposition guidelines to also include drafting instructions for national drafters: reference to the EU's regulatory results, apportionment of those to the national level, concrete and measurable effectiveness criteria for the EU text, apportionment of those to the national level, and type of data to be collected for post-legislative scrutiny. Moreover, the use of sunset clauses in EU legislation can be noted as good practice, as it enforces on national drafters the need to monitor and scrutinise the effectiveness of the national implementing text within a set period of time. Encouraging national post-legislative scrutiny exercises that feed into the EU one is one of the main mechanisms for assessing legislative quality both at the national and the EU levels.

In Thornton's legislative drafting stage 2, analysing the proposal, national drafters compile a legislative plan for the implementation of the EU instrument. Their task is again further complicated by the parallel presence of two contexts, namely the EU and the national one. Their analysis, in turn of the EU and the proposed national instrument, focuses on the analysis of the existing law, analysis of the necessity of legislation, analysis of potential danger areas, analysis of the policy options and the preferred legislative solution, and analysis of the practical implications of the legislative proposal. In most of these areas the EU and national analyses may not coincide. A necessary EU instrument may be completely useless at the national level, if the legal system there has already dealt with the underlying issue either legislatively or otherwise. Potential danger areas may also be diverse, with the EU looking. for example. at competences, where the Member State looks at unconstitutionality or illegality. Moreover, policy options and the preferred legislative solution are so closely linked to the regulatory and legislative environment within which they are placed that it is highly possible that regulatory efficacy and legislative effectiveness may be served by diverging options between the EU and the Member State. Of course, there are pre-legislative scrutiny tests that harmonise the questions to be asked, such as Xanthaki's or Mousmouti's effectiveness test. But there is no guarantee whatsoever that the answers in the EU context will coincide with those in the national context.

This leaves national drafters with very little guidance on how to transpose effectively. The detachment of the EU in national drafting choices was a reflection of the EU's respect for national legislative autonomy. But the current recognition of national drafters as co-legislators opens the way for further transposition assistance as a means of achieving effectiveness. In fact, as co-legislators national and EU drafting teams must now be viewed as one merged team where open dialogue, early communication and cross-fertilisation can only further the cause of effectiveness. This could be put to effect with the submission of the MS's legislative plan to the Commission for comments. Of course, the need for such an intervention in national drafting choices can be greatly reduced, if the EU really drafted with transposition in mind. This can be achieved by means of a restructure of transposition guidelines to include a technical, drafting-focused methodology. This methodology can be structured as answers to the seven questions of Xanthaki's effectiveness test including the EU's desired regulatory results, concrete measurable effectiveness criteria, the regulatory deadline, the mischief at the EU level, the link between the EU text and the mischief, language choices in relation to users, and guidance on national terminology. Finally, and perhaps more importantly, it is necessary for the EU to consider a fundamental change of approach towards EU drafting: instead of covering over discrepancies in national positions by means of generic terms and expressions, perhaps a move to a selection of expressions can alert national drafters to the issue and entice them into making a better choice.

In Thornton's legislative stage 3, designing the law, national drafters draw the legislative strategy considered most appropriate for an effective national transposition. This is where most of the reform in law-making is needed. National drafters focus on the choice of the most appropriate legislative mechanism for the achievement of the desired regulatory results, the issues to be included (or excluded) from the draft, the prioritisation of the relevant regulatory message, their packaging in a layered structure, and initial decisions on terminology. For the purposes of transposition, national drafting styles play a pivotal role here, as do the principles of subsidiarity, proportionality, adequacy, synergy, and adaptability. In the elaboration of the design of the national implementing measures, national drafters are led (and delimited) by multitude of criteria. Normative criteria refer to the nature of the transposition measure and the field of law that it tackles: for example, criminal law tends to merit primary legislation as a transposition vehicle, whereas minor issues may ride on an administrative act. Additional criteria refer to the scope of application of the EU legislative text and the avoidance of gold-plating or under-drafting. Then, there is the extent of legislative intervention required for full transposition; the type of the main EU instrument for transposition; and the object of the national implementing measure. Finally, there is the balance between the legitimacy of primary legislation and the expediency of delegated legislation as vehicles for complete and timely transposition. What is important to remember is that all these choices must be made as a means of contributing to legislative effectiveness and regulatory efficacy. And that they are subjective and ad hoc, as are all choices and dilemmas in legislative drafting. Effectiveness does not appear out of thin air, it is achieved via clarity, precision, and unambiguity. In turn, clarity is enhanced by an accurate identification of the groups of legislative users, and the structure of the draft national implementing measure on that basis by means of the layered approach to structure.

A layered implementation measure would include a Part 1 addressed to lay users and introducing the desired regulatory results and their add-on value for EU citizens plus the main regulatory message. Part 2 can be addressed to national authorities that are expected to administer the draft legislation, and would include the secondary regulatory messages, and enforcement mechanisms. Part 3 be addressed to legal experts and would encompass everything that is left out of Parts 1 and 2, such as legal issues, issues of interpretation, deadline, reviews and sunset clauses. Examples of the application of the layered approach to national implementing measures showcase the immense contribution that it can make to the accessibility of the legislation and incitement of trust to EU citizens/users to the European ideal.

Unfortunately, despite the pivotal significance of a tailor-made design for any drafting task, Member States continue to ignore it and simply replicate the EU legislative text. The problem is accentuated further by the complete obliviousness of the potential of design as a tool for better EU legislation in the EU text under transposition. So, a technically challenging structure at the EU level is allowed to risk legislative quality both at the EU and the national levels. In a citizen-focused EU, a user-focused design could emphasise the great value now expressly placed on EU citizens and their following of the EU as an ideal and as an organisation. And so, there is a call for a layered design of EU acts as well. This could involve a Part 1, addressed to EU citizens as lay users, can contain the main regulatory messages, namely, a. why legislate? b. how this benefits citizens and enterprises, and c. what are the awarded rights and imposed obligations? These must be expressed concretely, simply, and accurately. Part 2, addressed to Member States and national authorities, can include the detailed list of regulatory messages. The content, and even language, here would not change from the existing EU legislation. Perhaps it would make sense to divide in separate lists the duties of Member States and their powers: Member States must, as opposed to Member States may. Part 3, addressed to EU and national lawyers and judges, can include everything that is left out of Parts 1 and 2. Recitals can be greatly reduced to the absolutely necessary for context. Or they can join, definitions, legal issues, issues of interpretation, reviews and sunset clauses in Part 3. Although a layered EU Act seems like a very different beast from current Acts, what is really involved is simply the addition of a new Article 1 with the three regulatory messages requested by Group 1 lay users: why, how, and what, in concrete terms; then dividing current content into duties and powers for Member States and authorities; and transferring recitals, definitions, and interpretation from the start of the text, and bundling them to the bottom along with the rest of final provisions.

In Thornton's stage 4 of legislative drafting, the composition, national styles and choices prevail. Despite the focus of traditional legislative studies to the choice of words, expression, and syntax in legislation, these take second place in modern legislative drafting, where emphasis is in the nature of legislation as a tool for regulation and the reflection of this link to the legislative design. Language of course continues to play a role in legislative effectiveness but only as a means of accessibility of each regulatory message to the particular user group to which it speaks. Easification, in the sense of pitching the text to the appropriate level of legal and linguistic sophistication of the intended users, is the main message here.

In Thornton's stage 5 of legislative drafting, verification, drafters confirm that the legislative text expresses accurately and fully the intended regulatory messages. Internal verification already takes place within the drafting teams. But in a co-legislating EU there is plenty of scope for the EU and national drafting teams to come together and verify at least their primary legislative designs with each other. Such meetings are already amongst the most popular tools for drafting guidance in transposition, so why not make the most of them? What is missing from the law-making process of the EU and most Member States is user testing as a means of external verification. Drafters offer the draft text to representatives of user groups and, instead of consulting on its content, ask for an application of the text to a number of hypothetical scenarios. The accuracy of the users' response informs drafters on the accuracy of the regulatory message that these users have received. If the application of the text is inaccurate, then compliance later on will be haphazard. If the application is accurate, then at least drafters confirm that legislative users know what is offered or expected of them from the new legislative text. In which case the text is effective, at least amongst those users that are inclined to comply with legislation.

The application of international standards for legislative drafting in the implementation of EU legislation showcases a number of weaknesses in the current processes and practices. Until now these were attributed to the national drafters. But co-legislating carries with it co-responsibility for the effectiveness of the EU and national texts. In fact, the realisation that EU law applies without any or with very little elaboration from national authorities presents an invitation to EU law-makers to review, reassess, and modernise the legislative practices at the EU level. Although this may seem a dramatic legislative reform, its analysis in this book shows very clearly that in practice it is rather a matter of reshuffling and fine-tuning of existing practices. Perhaps the only colossal reform required is that of the EU's legislative ethos, to depart from the mentality of a *droit diplomatique* that can be mended at the national level on to a solid legislative system that serves its citizens directly. Their recognition as important legislative users, alongside national authorities and legal experts, can alter the emphasis from the currently learned messages to accessible easified declarations of the regulatory results that the legislation aims to achieve and the regulatory messages that this achievement requires. By putting forward the rationale behind the EU's regulatory goals, EU citizens can finally understand what value the EU brings to their lives and livelihoods. This can build a relationship of trust, with shared ideals, and shared goals.

The commentary on the drafting choices in a representative sample of a recent EU Regulation, the application of the proposed changes to its drafting style (without meddling with the content), and the subsequent analysis of the main points of reform and of arising issues led to 12 recommendations. Regulations must be drafted in a different way as follows:

1. Shorter title pinpointing the topic of the Regulation, leaving the legal requirement for a full name to a citation article at the end of the text.
2. Introduction of a table of contents to be used as a roadmap for users.
3. Radical culling of recitals by maintaining only those needed for context for EU citizens, and transferring the rest to the Notes Annex addressed to learned users.
4. Introduction of a new Article 1 on objectives, with clear measurable regulatory goals and evidence led criteria for effectiveness.
5. Culling of definitions and correct use of them solely to extend or delimit the ordinary meaning of the defined term.
6. Use of the article on subject matter to list the main points of the Act, thus narrating briefly to the citizen what follows.
7. Division of the Regulation into three Parts, addressed to EU citizens, to Member States, and to EU institutions respectively, each containing

regulatory messages relevant to each group and speaking to them in the appropriate easified language.

8. Collection of all authorisation for implementing and delegated acts in a list within one Article towards the end of the Regulation.
9. Introduction of a penultimate citation article to the Regulation stating that 'This Regulation is…' and including the full current title of the Regulation.
10. Introduction of review clauses in the article on entry into force.
11. Introduction of an Annex on Definitions.
12. Introduction of an Annex for Notes and Statement of the Commission, offering space for the pollical context of the Regulation, for references to relevant EU Acts, and miscellaneous topics.

The same methodology was applied to a recent Directive. The commentary on the drafting choices in the current text, the application of a new user-focused drafting style for Directives, and consequent lessons learnt led to recommendations.

1. Apply the layered approach: Part A addressed to EU citizens, Part B to Member States, and Part C for legal and technical issues.
2. Simplify the title and introduce the current full title in a citation Article at the end of the Directive.
3. In Part A addressed to EU citizens:
    a. introduce an Article 1 on objectives provision with measurable criteria of effectiveness, explaining what is the regulatory aim of the Directive and how it is beneficial to EU citizens;
    b. introduce and Article 2 on the subject matter explaining the main mechanisms of law reform used to achieve the objectives;
    c. introduce an Article 3 on definitions as a hanging provision for a definitions Annex;
    d. introduce an Article 4 listing all the rights awarded to EU citizens, thus emphasising what the EU offers;
    e. introduce an Article 5 detailing in lay terms the direct effect of Article 4, thus explaining that the Directive awards rights but protection must be afforded by Member States by means of implementation.
4. In Part B addressed to Member States introduce two articles: one with all the duties of Member States arising from the Directive and one with powers. Article 6 listing all duties provides a clear list of transposition requirements that invite content focused scrutiny by the Commission; and can serve as a control mechanism on the burden imposed on Member States for transposition. Article 7 on powers introduces a clear list of regulatory options for Member States, thus inviting for creative and

tailor-made national transposition enhancing effectiveness at the national level.
5. Part C, addressed to learned users of all categories can include everything else.
6. Entry into force must be joined by a review clause.
7. And the Article on addressees must include EU citizens, Member States, and learned users, thus reflecting the complete audiences of the Directive.

The drafting exercises and recommendations on Regulations and Directives lead to a requirement for legislative reform. But how exactly can a change in legislative style be pursued?

Applying the results of the UK's Good Law experiment to EU legislation leads to the identification of three main EU legislative audiences, namely EU citizens, national authorities administering the legislation, and Member States. This realisation can be revolutionary for law-makers. Their intended audience is not just Member States, but mainly EU citizens as a lay audience. This goes against the ethos of EU law-making, where the intended audience has always been Member States and national authorities. The argument has always been that it is the role of national law-makers to convey the EU regulatory message to their national legislative audiences. Unfortunately, drafting practices demonstrate a huge gap in the law-making narrative of the EU. So far, emphasis has been placed on the role of national drafters as EU law-makers, and the joint power and responsibility for the regulatory success of the EU. However, direct applicability of many EU instruments and the prevalence of the copy out transposition technique to the rest of EU instruments leads to a complete lack of legislative intervention by national drafters. Thus, the EU text is now mandated to achieve legislative effectiveness, contribute to regulatory efficacy, and promote sustainability and longevity all on its own. But, EU legislative texts are not designed to achieve this mammoth task in their current form. There are two options here: reform the law-making procedures or reform the law-making practices. The former requires a reform of the constituting treaties at a time where any shake up may endanger the delicate balances between institutions and between the EU and its Member States. The later requires a reform in the process of legislative drafting mainly at the EU level to reflect the now prevalence of the task of the EU text to be effective both at the EU and the national levels.

The rationale is there, the goal is there, what remains to be identified is the methodology for the introduction of an EU initiative for legislative reform. Thankfully, the EU's Better Regulation agenda provides an appropriate methodology. The application of the DECIDE test here suggests that the proposed new EU legislative strategy could qualify as a 'major' initiative. Normally, the process could be initiated by the Quality of Legislation

Directorate, validated from the lead Commissioner, Vice-President and First Vice-President following an entry created in DECIDE and a roadmap agreed with the Secretary-General. But in this case, one can validly argue that new policy has been de facto begun, as demonstrated by the repeated and express identification of an EU-citizen-focused better legislation agenda as part of Better Regulation. The initiative can be a joint, inter-institutional one as it meets the four DECIDE conditions for that purpose: this is an area where it has the greatest added-value for European citizens and strengthen the competitiveness and sustainability of the Union's economy; it delivers the Union's policy objectives in the simplest, most efficient and effective way possible; it avoids over-regulation and unnecessary administrative burdens; and it is designed to facilitate transposition and practical application. Irrespective of its formal start, the DECIDE test requires an identification of scope and objectives. The scope is better EU legislation, which means 'designing EU policies and laws so that they achieve their objectives at minimum cost' (G4). Objectives are enhancement of subsidiarity and proportionality (G4); provision of the means to mainstream sustainable development into the Union's policies (G5); and contribution to re-establishing direct communication with EU citizens, thus facilitating loyalty to the organisation and its ideal of EU integration. Finally, DECIDE offers the better regulation tools for the proposed new legislative strategy, namely evaluation, impact assessment, implementation plan, and public consultation.

Fine, you may say, but why should the EU embark in this journey of legislative reform anyway? The basis for this call lies with Kalypso Nicolaidis's sustainable integration as an alternative to deep and wide integration. The EU as a union and an organisation aims naturally to survive and succeed. So, sustainability and longevity are unavoidably within the mandate of the organisation. Sustainability and longevity are not easy tasks, especially for an organisation that has already survived 60 years and a number of internal and external crises. Adaptability and openness to change can be what might make the difference between success and failure. But, is there adequate reason to propose another shake-up of the EU? There is certainly evidence of a gradually declining support for the EU. This can be attributed to the profile of the organisation, which until recently seemed to place emphasis on financial stability and competitiveness within the international market. But, crucial as the financial side of the Union may be, especially in periods of financial crises, there is a social side and that related directly to the peoples and citizens of the EU. This is where the future lies. The citizen narrative has been increasingly creeping into EU documents, especially within the governance and regulation field, for the last three years or so. And this is not just evidence of the organisation rebalancing itself after the financial crisis. On a par with national regulators, the EU is beginning to realise that even its financial agenda relies on the achievement of the regulatory results set by its regulatory initiatives. For its policy measures to work, in support of its financial and its social agenda, the EU needs to achieve the desired regulatory results. So, any policy demands regulatory efficacy. Since the EU regulates mainly via legislation, legislative effectiveness is now recognised as a crucial actor in the regulatory efficacy of the EU, which in turn feeds into successful policies, which contribute to the prosperity of EU citizens and feeds into sustainability and longevity of the EU. It is all a rather simple chain of factors and actors. The EU has already intervened dramatically and rather successfully in the regulatory link of that chain. But EU law still suffers. And the chain is as weak as its weakest link. Ineffective legislation endangers regulatory success, which in turn endangers sustainability.

At the end of the day, these messages are not new. It is just that, until now, legislative texts have managed to keep them well hidden from their entitled recipients: the citizens of the EU. Is it not time to take them out of their cob-webbed trunk?

Index